Heinemann

ECONOMICS AS and A2

for OCR

BY

Sue Grant *and* **Chris Vidler**

heinemann.co.uk
✓ Free online support
✓ Useful weblinks
✓ 24 hour online ordering

01865 888058

Heinemann

Inspiring generations

Heinemann Educational Publishers
Halley Court, Jordan Hill, Oxford OX2 8EJ
Part of Harcourt Education

Heinemann is the registered trademark of
Harcourt Education Limited

08 07 06 05 04
10 9 8 7 6 5 4 3 2

British Library Cataloguing in Publication Data is
available from the British Library on request.

ISBN 0 435 33084 5

Edited by Caroline Sinclair and Sally Lane
Designed and typeset by Hardlines Ltd, Charlbury, Oxford
Original illustrations © Harcourt Education Limited, 2003
Illustrated by Hardlines Ltd, Charlbury, Oxford

Cover design by Matt Buckley
Printed in the UK by Scotprint, Haddington
Picture research by Sally Cole

Acknowledgements
Text extracts
Section 4.34: Women graduates still suffer the pay gap, by
Lorna Duckworth, *The Independent*: 8/06/02; Sections 4.8,
4.10, 4.14: Crown copyright material is reproduced with the
permission of the Controller of Her Majesty's Stationery
Office and the Queen's Printer for Scotland; Section 5.32:
Q1, Economics Of Development. There's More To Becoming
Rich Than GDP Growth, by Diane Coyle, *The Independent*:
26/09/00, p. 16. Section 5.32: The UK economy. Consumer
boom cannot mask lagging productivity forever, by
Christopher Smallwood, *The Indpendent*: 4/08/03, p. 17.

Section 4.34: Q1, Transport Economics. Motorways in
tunnels will ease congestion, by Ben Webster, *The Times*:
26/11/02, page 14. Section 5.1: Tables of economic
performance of the UK and US, 1999–2000, *National
Institute Economic Review*: Sage publications. Section 5.22:
Table of GNI per capital for selected countries, source,
Section 5.22: Table of infant mortality and life expectancy
for selected countries; Section 5.22: Table of literacy rates
for selected countries, Section 5.22: Table of proportion of
GDP contributed by agricultural sector for selected
countries: ALL Source World Development Indicators Data
Base April 2003, World Bank. Section 5.23: Table of Gini
Co-efficients for Latin America, OCR p. 10, Edexcel p. 20,
Source: UNCTAD 2001. Section 5.23, Table of Gini Co-
efficients for Asia, OCR p. 16, Edexcel p. 26. Section 5.23:
Table of Gini Co-efficients for Sub-Saharan Africa, OCR
p. 21, Edexcel p. 31, Section 5.23: Recipients of FDI, Most
favoured economies for future FDI, by Transnational
Corporations, Edexcel p. 44, OCR p. 44. Section 5.30:
Extract from United Nation's Millennium Declaration, UN.
Section 5.32: Q1, Economics of development. Table 1:
Human development report, 2002. by UNDP, ©2002 United
Nations Development programme. used by permission of
Oxford University press, Inc.

Photos
p.7 Eye Ubiquitous/ Sean Aiden; p.16 Rex Features/ John
Pwell; p.29 PA Photos/EPA; p.29 Eye Ubiquitous/ Dean
Bennet; p.60 Mary Evans Picture Library/Corbis/Corbis/
Bettmann

Tel: 01865 888058 www.heinemann.co.uk

Websites
Up-to-date website links are given throughout the book.
We advise teachers to preview these sites to ensure
accuracy and suitability as legitimate sites can be
appropriated illegally by people wanting to distribute
offensive material. We strongly advise you to purchase
suitable screening software to protect your students.

Alternatively, direct students to access the book's
websites through the address below.

www.heinemann.co.uk/hotlinks.

Then enter the express code **0845P**, and this will take
you to the links you want.

Contents

Introduction – How to use this book   x

AS Economics for OCR

PART 1   **The market system**   1

The market system – an overview   2

1.1   The economic problem   6

1.2   Factors of production   8

1.3   Specialisation   10

1.4   Production possibilities   12

1.5   Demand and supply   14

1.6   Money and markets   16

1.7   Demand   18

1.8   Price elasticity of demand   20

1.9   Other elasticities   22

1.10   Supply   24

1.11   Elasticity of supply   26

1.12   Market equilibrium (i)   28

1.13   Market equilibrium (ii)   30

1.14   Market equilibrium (iii)   32

1.15   Market analysis   34

1.16   Factor markets   36

1.17   Money markets   38

1.18   Costs   40

1.19   Economies of scale   42

1.20   Objectives of firms   44

1.21   Market structures   46

1.22   Activities   48

1.23   Exam practice   50

1.24   Exam guidance   51

PART 2   **Market failure and government intervention**   53

Market failure and government intervention – an overview   54

2.1   Efficiency   58

2.2   Market failure   60

2.3   Negative externalities   62

2.4   Positive externalities   64

2.5   Market dominance   66

2.6   Private and public goods   68

2.7   Merit/demerit goods and imperfect information   70

2.8   Other sources of market failure   72

2.9   Cost benefit analysis   74

2.10   Government intervention: negative externalities and demerit goods   76

2.11   Government regulation: positive externalities and merit goods   78

2.12   Monopoly regulation   80

2.13   Promoting competition   82

2.14   Government failure   84

2.15   Activities   86

2.16   Exam practice   88

2.17   Exam guidance   89

PART 3   **The national and international economy**   91

The national and international economy – an overview   92

3.1   Macroeconomic policy objectives   98

3.2   Output   100

3.3   Economic growth   102

3.4   Unemployment   104

3.5   Inflation   106

3.6   Balance of payments   108

3.7   Activities   110

3.8   Aggregate demand   112

3.9   Aggregate supply   114

3.10   Equilibrium output   116

3.11   Changes in aggregate demand and aggregate supply   118

3.12   The multiplier effect   120

3.13   Activities   122

3.14   Fiscal policy   124

3.15   Monetary policy   126

3.16   Supply-side policies   128

3.17   Policies to reduce unemployment   130

3.18   Policies to control inflation   132

3.19   Policies to promote economic growth   134

3.20   Policies to improve the balance of payments   136

3.21   Activities   138

3.22   Exchange rate changes   140

3.23   Pattern of international trade   142

3.24   The effect of international trade   144

3.25   Protectionism   146

3.26   Arguments for and against protection   148

3.27   Activities   150

3.28   Exam practice   152

3.29   Exam guidance   153

AS further reading   155

A2 Economics for OCR

PART 4   Work and leisure and transport economics   157

Work and leisure and transport economics – an overview   158

WORK AND LEISURE

4.1   Earnings and employment   160

4.2   Work and leisure   164

4.3   Leisure and the national economy   168

4.4   Market structure in leisure markets   173

4.5   Behaviour and efficiency in leisure markets   176

4.6   The demand for labour   179

4.7   The supply of labour   182

4.8   Wage determination and wage differentials   187

4.9   Labour market failure   192

4.10   The role labour organisations   195

4.11   Monopsony employer   198

4.12   Government intervention in labour markets   200

4.13   Labour market flexibility   204

4.14   The distribution of income and wealth   207

4.15   Poverty   214

TRANSPORT ECONOMICS

4.16   Transport, transport trends and the economy   218

4.17   Changes in UK transport   222

4.18   Costs of production   226

4.19   Long-run costs   230

4.20   Total, average and marginal revenue   233

4.21   Perfect competition and the transport industry   236

4.22   Monopoly and the transport industry   240

4.23   Monopolistic competition and the transport industry   243

4.24   Oligopoly and the transport industry   246

4.25   Behaviour in transport markets   250

4.26   Other aspects of oligopolistic behaviour   253

4.27   Competition policy   257

4.28   Promoting competition in transport markets   261

4.29   Government intervention and transport markets   265

4.30   Government transport policies   269

4.31   Cost benefit analysis   273

4.32   Transport congestion   279

4.33   Activities   281

4.34   Exam practice   283

4.35   Exam guidance   286

PART 5   The UK economy and economic development   289

The UK economy and economic development – an overview   290

THE UK ECONOMY

5.1   Measurement and analysis of economic performance   294

5.2   Living standards   298

5.3   Interest rates   303

5.4   Determination of exchange rates   306

5.5   Taxation   309

5.6   Public expenditure   312

5.7   The government's budget position   315

5.8   Direct controls   319

5.9   The multiplier and fiscal policy   322

5.10   Monetarism and the Quantity theory   326

5.11   The credit creation multiplier   329

5.12   International trade (i)   332

5.13   International trade (ii)   335

5.14   The effects of exchange rate changes   337

5.15   Monetary policy   341

5.16   Changes in fiscal, monetary and supply-side policies   344

5.17   Policy conflicts   347

5.18   Phillips curves   350

5.19   The natural rate of unemployment hypothesis   354

5.20   Globalisation   357

5.21   International competitiveness, multinational companies
and foreign direct investment   360

ECONOMIC DEVELOPMENT

5.22   What is development?   364

5.23   Latin America   368

5.24   Asia   373

5.25   Sub-Saharan Africa   377

5.26   Comparative advantage and trade theory   381

5.27   Development theories   383

5.28   Problems of developing economies   387

5.29   Domestically driven policies to promote development   390

5.30   Externally driven policies to promote development   395

5.31   Activities   399

5.32   Exam practice   401

5.33   Exam guidance   404

PART 6   **Economics in the European context**   409

Economics in the European context – an overview   410

6.1   Trading blocs   412

6.2   The new Europe   414

6.3   Transition economies   418

6.4   The single market   422

6.5   Economic and Monetary Union   425

6.6   Monetary policy and the euro   429

6.7   Convergence and integration   433

6.8   Fiscal policies   436

6.9   European unemployment   439

6.10   Regional problems   443

6.11   The Common Agricultural Policy   446

6.12   Environmental, transport and social policies   450

6.13   Competition policy   453

6.14   Exam practice   456

6.15   Exam guidance   458

A2 further reading   460

Glossary   462

Index   470

Introduction – How to use this book

Welcome to AS and A2 economics. This book has been specially written for students taking the OCR course. This means that it:

- follows the OCR specification very closely
- has been written to ensure that all concepts are clearly explained in terms understandable by students taking this subject for the first time
- includes lots of advice written by examiners to help you get the best possible grade.

Finding your way

This book is divided into distinct parts. The first three parts discuss *The market system*, *Market failure and government intervention* and *The national and international economy*, and cover the AS economics units for OCR. The second three parts discuss *Work and leisure and Transport economics*, *The UK economy and Economic development* and *Economics in the European context*, and cover the A2 economics units for OCR. All six parts are designed to meet the requirements of AS and A2 level economics for the OCR specification. Each part has its own introduction to help your understanding of the essential topics from the very start, including some spider diagrams to give you a 'visual' plan of the unit.

At the end of each Part, there are summary activities, exam practice and exam guidance sections to challenge you. Here you can use the information from the part to develop your skills in analysis and to reinforce your understanding of the key issues and terminology. These sections in particular provide a solid foundation for exam preparation.

The A2 part of the book is more complex in style. It contains more challenging material central to the key issues of economics at this level. This material should be read though in conjunction with the AS material as the AS material provides the foundation for understanding at A2. To help you link back from the A2 to the AS sections there are the *Synoptic links* – marginal text that cross-references A2 with AS.

Further reading

Suggestions for 'going for gold' are found in the *Further reading* sections at the end of the AS and A2 parts.

Sample section

The typical layout of each section is illustrated below.

section title

main text

diagrams appear
in the margins

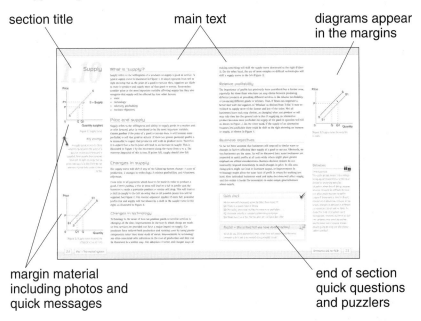

margin material
including photos and
quick messages

end of section
quick questions
and puzzlers

The central body of text is designed to explain the key concept(s) featured
in each section. This always ends with quick questions to test your
understanding.

The margins of each section will contain a different selection of messages
designed to help consolidate your learning and to make the journey from
AS to A2 level a smooth one. These messages relate to further research, give
weblinks and highlight controversial issues, to name but a few. Each has its
own symbol for ease of use, which are explained in more detail below.

Margin messages

The margin messages are the same for both the AS and A2 parts of the book
except for:

 Making connections – This is an AS margin message to help
students make links between economics and life around us.

 Synoptic link – This is used in the A2 text only especially to help
students refer back to concepts and ideas learnt in AS economics.

Shared AS and A2 margin messages

Definitions
These define the key terms and vocabulary used in economics. You must know these and get into the habit of defining the main terms you use in all your exam answers.

Exam hints
Little tips that might make all the difference when it comes to the exam.

Hot potatoes
Some controversial issues you might want to discuss or debate.

Key concepts
These are the ideas that are essential to understanding the section.

Learning tip
Hints that some students will find helpful in developing a good understanding of economics.

Puzzler
Some trickier stuff to get your head around.

Quick check
These are quick questions that are designed to test your understanding of what you have just read.

Research task
These are possible ideas for more in-depth study at AS/A2 and also contain essay questions for A2 students.

Thinking like an economist
Questions and tasks that encourage you to use and apply the tools of economic analysis.

Weblinks
Some useful websites to help consolidate your knowledge.

By the end of this book you will have covered every economics issue needed to pass both the AS and A2 examination for OCR. Don't worry if you don't immediately understand everything you read, but concentrate on getting a feel for what the subject involves. It can be hard going but it is rewarding. Good luck.

PART 1/AS

The market system

The market system – an overview

This Unit is devoted to microeconomics and in order to do well you need to understand how individual markets work, and the strengths and weaknesses of freely operating markets.

Economics is about resource allocation – how societies decide what is going to be produced and who is going to enjoy or consume this production. Many of the world's resources are allocated by the price mechanism and this Unit is designed to help you understand how this works.

This involves understanding what is meant by demand and supply, identifying the factors that can cause both demand and supply to change and using diagrams to analyse the effects of these changes. The understanding of how an individual market might work provides a basis for learning about how a whole series of inter-related markets might work together to allocate resources. Finally, there is an introduction to the theory of the firm, which focuses on how firms might behave

The examination

The examination for this Unit lasts for one hour and consists of a short case study followed by a number of questions, which must all be answered. You have to make sure you have all your knowledge and understanding at your fingertips to use the short time to best advantage. Make sure you leave enough time to answer the higher mark questions, which come at the end of your paper.

Do not make the terrible mistake of thinking that, once this Unit is over, you can forget all about demand and supply. Do not throw away your notes. Do not empty your mind of what you have learned. Your understanding of demand and supply will also be tested when you tackle the examination for the second Unit, and to varying degrees in all three of your A2 examinations.

Exam timing

Most schools and colleges start their teaching programmes with Unit 1 and it is possible for most students to be ready to take their first AS Unit in January of the first year of their course. But beware, some schools and colleges do not give that option to their students. They believe that too many examinations disrupt too much normal teaching. However, if you have the opportunity – take it. It will get you used to the new demands of AS rather than GCSEs. If you get a good grade you will become more confident and even if you do not, you can try again in June.

Exam tactics

If you just study for this Unit, a typical student will take around twelve weeks to reach the required standard. It will take that long to really get used to demand and supply analysis, and its application to different markets, and to understand costs and revenues associated with the theory of the firm. Although you should practise developing your examination techniques from the start, you need a solid grounding in the underpinning theory and concepts before you are fully ready to prepare for the Unit tests. The case study questions will assume that you understand the whole of the Unit. So do not rush into exam preparation. Work through the 3 revision sections only after you have been through the 21 sections making up Part 1: The market system.

Contribution to the final grade

Unit 1 contributes 30 per cent to your final AS mark, and if you carry on for a second year, 15 per cent of your total A level grade A2. As has been already stated, it is worth more than these percentages imply as demand and supply is a cornerstone of economics.

Tackling this Unit

Try to learn as you go along. Do not be tempted to leave everything to the end. Read each section at least three times: once straight through, the second time making sure that all the arguments and concepts are really understood and a final time for reinforcement. Do not do all this at once.

In a very short time you will find that news items in the papers and on TV will make more sense to you. Try to get into the habit of reading the financial sections of newspapers and take advantage of other magazines and periodicals. Two websites, www.bized.net and www.tutor2u.net, provide excellent sites to support your learning. And do not forget your awarding body OCR has a site with useful advice: www.ocr.org.uk.

Learning tip

Build up a file of contemporary economic events. Get used to reading the business sections of newspapers. Look out for articles about controversial topics, especially if they include up-to-date data. Attach a brief commentary to each – always written with a critical eye.

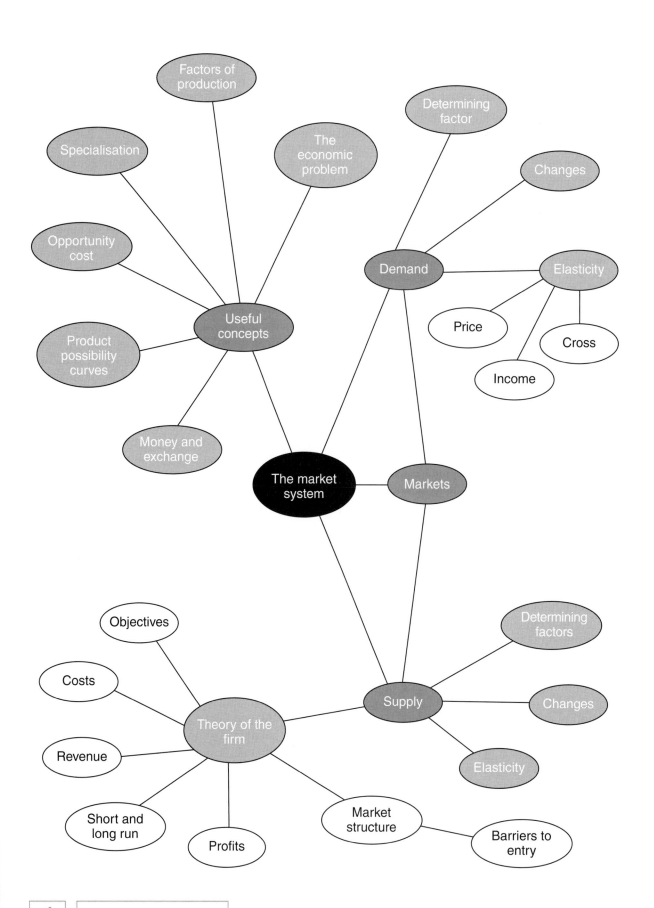

The economic problem 1.1

Introduction

Learning economics will change your life. It will alter the way you see and understand the world. Watching TV, reading newspapers, listening and taking part in conversations will not be the same again. So what is this 'new' subject all about?

So what's the problem?

What is the problem that economics concerns itself with? Economics exists because we live in a world in which resources are finite. There are not endless supplies of energy, minerals, foodstuffs and so on. On the other hand, we live in a world in which the vast majority of people are materialistic in the sense of always wanting more. Two thirds of the world's population do not have enough to eat. Most of us aspire to improving our lifestyles by having more and better and newer and nicer things. In short, people have unlimited wants. Their needs outstrip the means of satisfying them. Put simply, three into two won't go. There is not enough to go round. Some people starve while others enjoy fantastic standards of luxury. This is not a morality tale; rather, it is a description of the world in which we live. Economists use this image to demonstrate the fundamentals of their subject. Economics is about making choices. People have virtually unlimited wants. Resources are finite. Economics is about making more informed choices. It is about understanding that if one choice is made, others have to be forgone. For example, it can be argued that if we want cleaner air, then we need to use cars less. This sacrifice is called an opportunity cost, that is, what has to be given up as the result of a particular choice.

We can't always get what we want. Therefore, all societies need some kind of economic system in order to decide what gets produced, how it is produced and, crucially, who gets what. Unravelling and understanding these sorts of issues is what economics is all about, and learning about the subject gives a better understanding of the forces which have shaped, and will shape, all our lives.

Key concept

Economics exists because in the world we live in we have to make choices. Wants are said to be infinite whereas resources are finite.

Definition

Opportuntity cost: the best alternative forgone

Starting to think like an economist

We all know about economics. We are all consumers and producers. All of us argue, knowingly and unknowingly, about economic issues. People have views about immigration, the destruction of rainforests or restrictions on tobacco advertising. But economics is about more than having views on a range of controversial issues. As it is a social science, economics involves:

- using evidence
- key economic theories and concepts
- specialist technical vocabulary
- choice and politics.

Evidence

Economics is classed as a social science which means that it has much in common with subjects like sociology and psychology. You can't subject people to strict laboratory conditions but at the same time, theories and concepts should be based on the careful collection of evidence. This means that numerical data is very important, as is the development of logical and ordered argument.

Theories and concepts

Economics as we know it today has developed over the last 400 years. Some would argue that its origins are much older, but recent developments are linked with industrialisation and the development of capitalism. Adam Smith, who wrote the Wealth of Nations in 1776, is seen as one of the first economists. He wrote about how specialisation in particular tasks could lead to greater production. As with other disciplines, the subject has constantly evolved and successive generations of economists have argued and debated one another's work. In this way, a body of knowledge and understanding associated with economics has developed. There is broad agreement about parts of this and dispute about others.

Gordon Brown, the Chancellor of the Exchequer, bases his decisions on economic factors

Technical vocabulary

Economics is different from familiar subjects like history and English as only a minority of students study economics before they are sixteen. As with all disciplines, economics has a technical vocabulary all its own. Economists are also very precise in their use of particular terms.

This precise use of particular terms takes some getting used to, but it is important especially in terms of clearly communicating your understanding of the subject and developing economic analysis and argument.

Choice and politics

Finally, economics is about choices. It is often about controversial issues. Economic arguments are often used by politicians to support particular ideas. In fact, economics and argument go hand in hand. Often there are no right or wrong answers. No clear-cut solutions to economic issues. Governments and political parties often disagree about economic issues and this means that economics often appeals to those who enjoy argument and debate, and also take an interest in current affairs and politics.

Quick check ✓
What appeals to you about economics?   What puts you off?

Factors of production

1.2

Introduction

Economists use the same or similar concepts again and again. Most are easy to understand but practice needs to be gained in applying them to a range of different contexts. The ideas of factors of production are a good example of these simple but powerful concepts.

Factors of production

Economics is concerned with a study of how wealth is created. The creation of wealth involves taking resources and transforming them into a product or service which can then be consumed or used in some other way. This process can be illustrated diagrammatically, as is shown in Figure 1 with a simple input/output model.

Although simple, this captures a wide range of issues and concepts important to economists. The use of inputs encompasses environmental economics as it deals with the relationship between economic activity and the world's resources, both renewable and finite. The middle part of the model is concerned with how resources are transformed. Business studies students call this process 'adding value', and it can include complex processes involving the use of highly sophisticated technology, or the more straightforward harvesting and packaging of an agricultural crop. Finally, the output part of the model shows the activity concerned with 'shopping' and enjoying or using outputs in some ways to improve our lives.

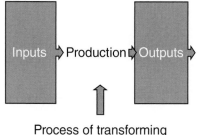

Process of transforming inputs into outputs

Figure 1: Simple input/output model

Types of resources

The simple input/output model outlined above can be expanded to identify and classify different types of resources. Economists call these factors of production and these are illustrated in Figure 2.

1 Land

Land includes all that which is locked up in the earth's surface. It includes not just land in the sense of farmland, building and factory sites, but what are often called 'natural resources', such as minerals, fossil fuels and timber, and what can be grown and harvested. Land includes the products of the seas, the content of our atmosphere and by implication, what has yet to be discovered in space.

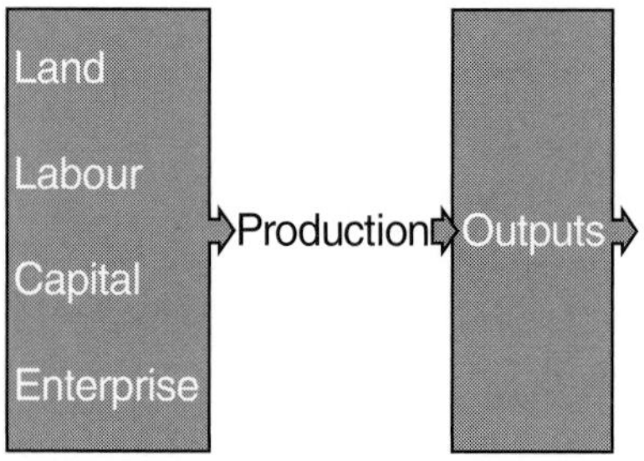

2 Labour

This is a similar 'catch-all' concept, which includes what we as people bring to the production process. This includes personal attributes such as strength and particular aptitudes which we can learn and skills which we are able to develop.

Figure 2: Factors of production

3 Capital

Economists refer to capital as all those assets which are used to produce goods or services. This category, therefore, includes machinery and factories and equipment which is used to transform 'land' into some particular form of output. The term capital is often used in everyday conversation to describe the money that is used to set up and keep a business going. It is also used to describe savings in shares or such like. All these uses are linked directly or indirectly to the actual production process but economists use the term capital in a more restricted sense. It could be said that they are not interested in money as such but the uses to which it can be put, and especially uses which result in economic activity.

4 Enterprise

This is often described as the fourth factor. Economic activity involves the combination of particular quantities of land, labour and capital to produce something. Enterprise is the process of managing and deciding how factors should be combined and to what end. Being enterprising may also involve taking risks and guessing what goods or services are likely to be in demand. It could be argued that the ability and desire to be enterprising is another personal attribute like strength or artistic skills which fall under the heading of labour. Nonetheless, identifying enterprise as a separate factor of production enables economists to emphasise the crucial contribution of deciding how resources are to be used in the success or otherwise of economic activity.

Production

So who decides what is actually produced? There is no simple answer to this. All societies are to varying degrees mixed economies. They consist of privately-owned organisations known as the private sector; national and local governments, confusingly called the public sector; and a range of not-for-profit organisations, often called charities, which make up the voluntary sector. Put very simply, private sector organisations are considered to be primarily concerned with profit-making, the public sector provide public services, and the voluntary sector is primarily concerned with economic activity undertaken for no kind of reward. These are gross over-simplifications, as your further study of economics will show.

Hot potato

Should entrepreneurs earn more than workers?

Quick check

Use the input/output model to demonstrate what happens when beer/crisps are produced.

Specialisation

1.3

Benefits of specialisation

Specialisation is a key economic concept that affects most of our lives. It refers to the extent to which we concentrate on particular jobs or tasks. It is linked to two other concepts, trade and welfare, and knowing how all three have evolved provides a very useful key to understanding how economics has developed. Trade refers to the exchange of goods and services and welfare is a term which is used to indicate how well-off a particular society might be.

Surpluses, trade and specialisation

The development of western and other civilisations is closely linked to the development of trade. Much economic activity in the past could be described as subsistence, whereby small groups within societies attempted to produce through their own labour sufficient food and basic products in order to survive. The survival of many subsistence economies was fragile. Poor harvests could mean that there would not be enough food. Natural disasters could wipe out possessions and shelter. Many people still live like this and famine and natural disaster are still commonplace.

Subsistence economies which became more successful were able to produce more food and goods that were not needed solely for immediate survival. They were able to store unused produce, perhaps to provide a buffer against unforeseen disasters. These surpluses could also be traded with other groups producing surpluses of other products. Trade enabled greater prosperity and higher standards of living. It is likely that early trade would have been by barter by which one group of people with a surplus of, say, fish would swap with another group able to produce more grain than they needed. Expanding trade would have exposed the limitations and inconvenience of barter and there is considerable archaeological evidence of particular tribes using various more portable commodities to simplify the process of trade. Shells and other small precious items were used as early forms of money, and 3000 years ago, coins were being used as we use them today.

The combination of surpluses, money and growing trade provided the foundations for the development of markets, which in turn provided further impetus for the development of economic activities that resulted in economic growth and development.

Research task

Choose an ancient civilisation and find out all you can about how economic activity was organised.

Trade meant that an individual group no longer needed to attempt to produce all its requirements. Other groups might be better at producing particular commodities. Some could specialise in the production of those products they were best or most efficient at producing. Hence, specialisation took place enabling increased trade and the development of larger surpluses. There are additional gains in that those who specialise might become better at what they do, contributing to further increases in output.

Similarly, within tribes and societies different tasks were increasingly delegated to particular individuals and groups. Through this division of labour people were able to improve their skills and increase productivity such that more was produced. In this way past empires and dynasties grew and developed. Those which were most successful were able to use their surpluses to finance buildings, public works, religious celebrations and the like. Anything that would make a society better off without making someone worse off would be described by economists as contributing to the economic welfare of a society – known as welfare for short.

A brief history of time

The interplay between increasing specialisation and the division of labour, trade and growing wealth and the development of society as we know it can be tracked through time. Thus in medieval England there were growing agricultural surpluses, which led to an expanding trade in wool and other products. Greater trade contributed to the early development of towns, helped those who profited by trade and contributed to the early development of banking.

The industrial revolution intensified these changes especially in terms of the organisation of production in factories in which the principle of division of labour was further applied, contributing to even more trade, further economic growth and the creation of more wealth.

Today it is said that we live in a global economy whereby specialisation and the **division of labour** are played out on a worldwide scale. One consequence is the decline of manufacturing in countries like the UK, and increasing inputs from countries whose labour costs are lower. Another is the depletion of non-renewable resources.

Summary

The benefits and costs of specialisation are now becoming increasingly obvious. The growth of trade and the division of labour have allowed some people to enjoy high standards of living that would have been undreamt of even fifty years ago. If you are part of the rich third of the world you can consume products and services to bring both leisure and luxury to your life. However, the bulk of the world's population do not enjoy such benefits, and many are reduced to insecure employment, working for low rates of pay in sweatshop conditions.

Quick check

How is specialisation applied to the production of Nike trainers? Who benefits most?

Definition

Division of labour: the specialisation of labour on particular tasks.

Hot potato

Where would we be without money?

Production possibilities

nother key economic concept useful in developing an understanding of how the economy works is the production possibility curve/frontier (both terms are used). This graphic technique can be used to model how efficient an economy might be and to show the effects of changes in the quantity and quality of resources.

Key concept

Any point within a production possibility curve indicates that some factors of production are not being fully used – i.e. productive inefficiencies occur. Any point on a production possibility curve indicates productive efficiency i.e .no more could be produced. Movements away from the origin indicate economic growth and higher levels of wealth.

Production possibility curves

The efficiency of an economy can be illustrated using production possibility curves. As with other models these are a simplification of how the real world is thought to work. In Figure 1 it is assumed that an economy is capable of producing just two goods: corn and beer. If it were to use all its available factors of production to produce corn it would produce C1. Alternatively, if all resources were devoted to making beer, B would be made. The line between C and B is called a production possibility curve as it shows all the different combinations of beer and corn that could be produced. It also illustrates opportunity cost, i.e. what has to be given up as the result of a particular decision. The movement from a to b on the production possibility curve would indicate an increase in the production of corn. If all resources are being used this can only be achieved by cutting the production of beer from B1 to B2. This is the opportunity cost of increasing the output of corn.

This diagram can be used to represent a variety of changes. Thus, if a new technique were discovered which meant that more beer could be produced with the same amount of resources there would be a movement in the curve from CB1 to CB2.

This new production possibility frontier indicates a higher possible standard of living, and an increase in welfare. This society could now produce both more beer and corn using the same amount of resources.

Point x on the diagram (Figure 1(b)) also illustrates an economy which is not making full use of all its resources. Both more beer and more corn could be produced. This failure to use all resources can be described as unemployment of resources.

(a)

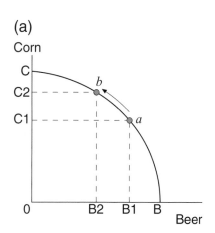

(b)

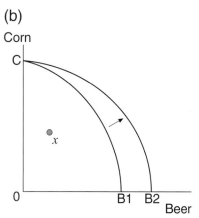

Figure 1: (a) Production possibility frontier; (b) increasing wealth

Capital and consumer goods

Another useful application of production possibility curves helps in understanding the significance of the distinction between capital and consumption goods. Capital goods are those that are used to produce other goods. Machine tools in a factory are an obvious example. Consumption goods, on the other hand, are all those things that we consume and use up. You consume drinks, and maybe crisps. The effects of changing the proportions in an economy in the production of these two categories of goods can be illustrated using production possibility curves. In Figure 2, if a country used all of its factors of production to produce capital goods, P would be produced but the output of consumption goods would be zero. Alternatively if all resources were switched, F consumption goods could be produced but at a cost of zero production of capital goods. The production possibility curve shows the different combinations of capital and consumption goods which could be produced.

This application is a bit more sophisticated because there is a relationship between the output of capital goods and that of consumption goods. Greater investment in capital production will mean greater future production of consumption goods. Conversely, if the production of capital goods falls below a critical level the future production of consumption goods will fall. Thus it is likely that if a country split production 50/50 between consumption and capital goods (point a), in the future its production possibility frontier would move outwards from PF to PF1 showing increased economic growth. Alternatively, if only a very small proportion of resources were devoted to the production of capital goods, a future production possibility frontier will move inwards indicating a fall in productive capacity.

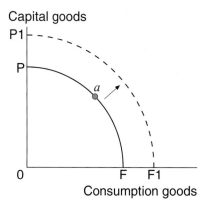

Figure 2: Production possibility curve

Quick check ✓

Use production possibility curves to model the impact of spending more of a nation's resources on fighting Aids rather than more arms.

Puzzler

Why do you think production possibility curves are usually drawn convex to the origin?

Demand and supply

Consumer and producer surpluses

Another two important concepts are:
- Consumer surplus
- Producer surplus

Consumer surplus

This concept uses graphical analysis to illustrate the benefits that customers gain from consuming a particular product or service. In Figure 1, P shows the equilibrium price while the level of sales is given at Q.

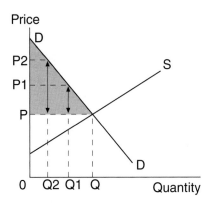

Figure 1: Consumer surplus

The horizontal axis measure the quantity of a particular product demanded and supplied. At the market price of P, customers would demand Q quantity. Some customers, however, would have been prepared to pay more. For instance Q1 quantity could have been sold at a price of P1 and Q2 quantity at a price of P2. With the product actually being sold at a price of P, some customers paid less than they were willing to do. The vertical distances between the market price and top section of the demand curve indicate how much more some customers would have been prepared to pay for the good or service. Taken together the shaded area represents an additional benefit enjoyed by consumers of this product. This is referred to as consumer surplus.

Key concept

Consumer surplus measures the benefits enjoyed by some consumers who are able to buy a good or service for less than they are prepared to pay. Producer surplus measures the benefits enjoyed by some producers who would be prepared to supply a product or service for less than the market price.

Producer surplus

A similar analytical approach can be made to gains made by producers of a good or service. In Figure 2, producers receive a price of P for the sale of Q amount, but they would have been prepared to sell all but the last unit of the good or service for less than the equilibrium price. For a price of P2 they would have supplied Q2 and for a price of P1 they would have offered Q1 for sale.

The shaded area, below the price and above the left section of the supply curve, is said to represent producers' surplus.

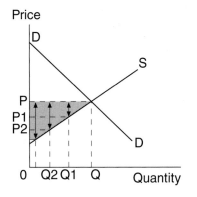

Figure 2: Producer surplus

These diagrams can be combined as shown in Figure 3 with area C showing consumer surplus and P that for producers.

Assessing changing market conditions – reductions in supply

This graphical analysis can be used to model the impact of changes in demand and supply on both consumers and producers. If the supply of a good or service is reduced, the supply curve will shift to the left. This is shown in Figure 4 where comparison of the two levels of consumer surplus shows that cutting supply and higher prices reduces consumer surplus.

Consumer surplus is initially PAB. The rise in price reduces consumer surplus to P1AC.

The converse of this is that increasing supply will benefit consumers.

Assessing the impact on producers

Similar analysis can be used to analyse the effects of changing market conditions on producers. As shown in Figure 5, any rightward shift in the demand curve will result in an increase in producer surplus. The higher demand increases producer surplus from FPG to FP1H.

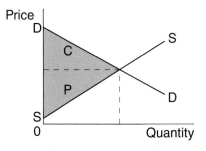

Figure 3: Combined consumer and producer surplus

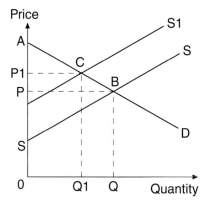

Figure 4: Falling consumer surpluses

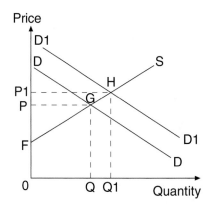

Figure 5: Impact on producer surpluses

Quick check ✓

How might consumer and producer surplus be affected by the following?

* The introduction of broadband access to the Internet
* A reduction in the number of firms in an industry

Money and markets

The growth and development of money and markets have gone hand in hand with the further application of the division of labour and ever greater specialisation.

Money

You have probably heard the old clichés about money making the world go round, and that if we didn't have any we would have to invent it. In a sense they are both true.

History of money – Part 1

Early subsistence economies relied on barter. Put very crudely, if I produced more cows than I needed I would have to hunt around and find someone who had something that I wanted – a pig, perhaps. My efforts to trade would then depend upon my finding someone who had a spare or surplus pig and who also wanted to acquire a cow. Even then, it would be necessary to agree the terms of trade i.e. does one pig = one cow? Or would 2 pigs = 1 cow be fairer? Suffice to say that making a deal would be complicated. Economists use the jargon 'double coincidence of wants' to sum up what is required for barter to work.

It is easy to see that if money of some form were introduced into this transaction, life would run a little more smoothly. Anything that is
- valued
- portable
- storable
- precious

would do, hence the use of shells, bones, small things of value and precious metals like silver and gold.

History of money – part 2

Although we still use small amounts of precious metals in our coinage, most transactions are completed by using pieces of paper, bits of plastic or just electronic impulses. This represents developments which have taken place over the last 800 years and the roles of goldsmiths and silversmiths are often quoted to explain how we have come to accept and use money which has little intrinsic value. Growing wealth in medieval times meant that some people accumulated precious metals and, so the story goes, needed places of safekeeping. Silver and goldsmiths had such facilities and took in baubles and other items, issuing a written receipt in exchange. It was, according to the story, but a short step to these pieces of paper changing hands to settle debts. The key to their acceptability as an early form of paper money was that they represented a claim to something of real value. Another stride in the development of money came when silver and goldsmiths started to act

Figure 1: Bank notes

like modern banks by issuing bits of paper which were used as money even though these were not directly backed by precious metals of the same value. They reasoned that not everyone would want to cash in their bits of paper at the same time and as long as this did not happen, they could profit by printing money. The key to the success of these early banking activities, just as it is today, was the trust that users of promissory notes, as they were called, had in those who had issued them.

Thus the development of money, the growth of trade, and expanding wealth were all tied in together to form the basis of capitalist economies as we know them now.

Research task

Read JK Galbraith's
The Great Crash.

History of money – part 3

Banks now hold fractional deposits to back up their lending. Most transactions are electronic but the same basic principles of trust and confidence still apply as shown by the events surrounding the collapse of the banking system in Argentina in 2002.

Markets

Markets exist wherever those who demand products or services meet those who supply goods or services. Many different kinds of markets exist. The earliest markets moved around the country and were often celebrated as fairs and special events where all kinds of resources were traded. Some were devoted to selling surplus production at harvest time, while others involved selling labour to the highest bidders. Cattle markets retain some of the features of these earlier trading events. Towns and city centres now take on many of the functions of traditional markets and the sellers of products and services use a wide variety of strategies to appeal to consumers. There are many other forms of market, including the following:

- classified advertisements
- flea markets
- the stock market
- black markets
- wholesale markets
- grey markets
- futures markets
- the Internet.
- auctions

This list could easily be extended, but irrespective of the form and frequency of such markets they all involve: buyers, sellers and a means to reach a deal. The rest of this module is devoted to helping you understand how markets work, and the following module will help you judge whether or not markets produce outcomes which are socially acceptable.

Quick check

Why does money have to be valued, portable, storable and precious?

Demand

What is 'demand'?

Demand has a very precise meaning in economics. It refers to how much of a product or service we are prepared and able to buy.

Demand theory is based on a simple generalisation about customer behaviour that most people would regard as 'common sense'. If the price of something rises, consumers are less likely to buy it, whereas falling prices lead to higher demand. This is illustrated in Figure 1.

The quantity demanded of a good or service is measured along the horizontal axis and its price on the vertical. The curve DD slopes downwards from left to right. Thus, if the price is set at P the demand will be at Q. If the price is increased to P1 the demand will fall to Q1, whereas if the price falls to P2 the demand will rise to Q2.

Changes in demand

Many factors are likely to have a potential influence on the demand for a product or service. Economists group these other factors under the following headings:

- Price of other goods and services
- Tastes
- Incomes

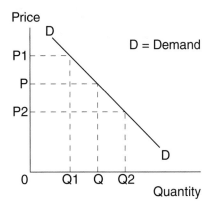

Figure 1: Relationship between demand and price

Key concept

A demand curve shows the likely relationship between the price of a good or service and the quantity sold of that good. It usually slopes downwards from left to right showing that as price falls demand is likely to rise, whereas if price rises demand is likely to fall.

Price of other goods and services

Clearly the decision to buy or not to buy something is not made simply on the basis of its price. Our choice to buy one product is often made by reference to prices of similar products. Goods, such as Ford Fiestas and Renault Clios which could be seen as alternatives for each other, are called substitutes. Whereas products or services which can be brought together, like shampoo and conditioner, are called complements.

Consumer income

Obviously the level of our income will have a powerful effect on our demand. The more we earn the more we can buy and vice versa. To be more precise, economists use the term disposable income to describe the amount of money available for spending.

The demand for some goods like those relating to sport and leisure is known to rise more than proportionally to any increase in disposable income. These are known as superior goods.

Other products are classified as 'inferior' goods, in the sense that as consumer incomes rise, demand falls, and vice versa. Terraced houses in some areas of northern cities can be described in this way. As owners of such houses become better off they are more likely to purchase more expensive substitutes.

Consumers' tastes

This term is used by economists to capture a whole range of other influences on demand. At one level we all like and dislike different things and these personal preferences are likely to affect what we wish to buy. These individual differences are hard for economists to model, but it is easier to identify broad trends and changes in tastes. Advertisers in particular try to change our tastes in order to increase the demand for particular goods or services.

What if key variables change?

The graphical model (Figure 1) used to introduce this section can be used to show the effects of changes in three key variables above. If the price of Renault Clios were to fall and the prices of other similar cars were to stay the same, the demand for Fiestas would fall. This is shown in Figure 2 by a shift in the demand curve to the left. If the opposite were to happen, the curve should shift to the right.

If goods are complements, a rise in the price of one will lead to a fall in demand for the other good.

Rising incomes will lead to an increase in demand for foreign holidays and this is shown also by a shift in the demand curve to the right. If the good is considered inferior then demand will fall as shown by the shift to the left.

Finally changes in tastes can be treated in a similar way. The demand curve for goods which become more fashionable will shift to the right whereas a leftward shift would show that something is no longer fashionable.

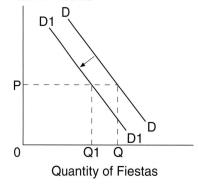

Figure 2: Changes in key variables

Thinking like an economist

Model building is part of the essential tool kit of economists. Demand and supply analysis is one of the most simple and powerful models used by economists. Models are created in order to simplify sets of complex relationships. Just remember the value of any model will be determined by how realistic it is and how it might be used to predict what might happen if changes take place.

Quick check ✓

Which way will the demand curve for Mars Bars move if
(a) The price of Twix is reduced
(b) Child benefit is raised
(c) Eating chocolate is proved to reduce your intelligence
(d) Tesco launch a 'two for the price of one' Mars Bar offer

Puzzler– this is hard!

What do you think economists mean when they talk about the differences between a shift and a movement along a demand curve?

Price elasticity of demand

Elasticity

Elasticity is a key economics concept that comes up time and time again in different contexts. This section on price elasticity of demand is probably the first time you have come across this measure of responsiveness so it pays to give some time to make sure your understanding is secure.

(a)

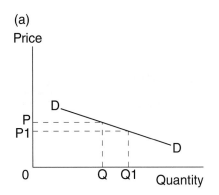

Price elasticity of demand

Basic economics indicates that if the price of a good or service changes the demand will change. An increase in price is likely to result in a fall in demand, whereas a cut in price is likely to lead to an increase in demand. Understanding price elasticity of demand is a way of measuring how much demand changes in response to a change in price. Price elasticity can be analysed in three ways, by diagram, in words and by simple algebra.

Diagrams

The two diagrams in this section (Figure 1) illustrate two very different responses in demand to identical reductions in price.

In the case of Figure 1 (a) a cut of around 10 per cent in house prices leads to a rise in demand of about 50 per cent. In Figure 1 (b) the same price cut causes a much smaller rise in demand – about 5 per cent. In Figure 1 (a) demand is very responsive to changes in price whereas in Figure 1 (b) demand is much less responsive. Given the use of the same axis the slope of the demand curve will indicate the degree of responsiveness to changes in price.

(b)

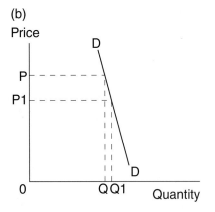

Figure 1: Two responses to identical price reductions

Another aspect shown most effectively by diagrams is to compare the revenue spent before and after the change. Revenue is simply price × quantity. In the first diagram revenue rises and in the second it falls. This has massive implications for businesses selecting an appropriate pricing policy.

Words

Using words to describe the differences between the two preceding diagrams (Figure 1) involves some specialist terminology. If the demand for a good or service is very responsive to changes in price then the demand is said to be relatively elastic, whereas if demand is not very responsive to price change it is described as relatively inelastic.

Calculation

This representation of price elasticity of demand is a much more precise and mathematical way of dealing with the relationship between changes in price and changes in demand. In the diagrams above, the slope or gradient of the demand curve indicates its elasticity. This can be represented by the following equation:

$$Ped = \frac{\text{percentage change in quantity demanded}}{\text{percentage change in price}}$$

Thus a price fall by 10 per cent accompanied by a demand increase of 50 per cent can be inserted into the equation above giving:

$$Ped = \frac{+50}{-10} = -5$$

Alternatively if the price cut of 10 per cent prompted an increase in demand of 5 per cent the same equation would give the following result:

$$Ped = \frac{+5}{-10} = -0.5$$

These answers or values are called coefficients and they give an instant insight into the responsiveness of demand for a product to a change in price. Any value, which is less than −1, e.g. −0.6 or −0.2, indicates that demand for the product is not very responsive to changes in price. To be more precise, any given percentage change in the price of the product will result in a smaller proportional change in quantity demanded.

On the other hand a value, which is larger than −1 e.g. −2.5 or −6, represents a demand which is very responsive to a change in price. The percentage change in quantity demanded for such a product will exceed the percentage change in price. Economists would describe this kind of demand response to be elastic. It may sound fussy but never forget to include the plus or minus sign before the coefficient.

Why elasticities differ

Economists consider that four factors have the greatest impact in determining the price elasticity of demand for a good or service:

- Substitutes – the demand for one brand of crisps will be more **elastic** if there are lots of similar brands on the market
- Disposable income – the higher the consumer's disposable income, the less sensitive the demand to price changes
- Consumer knowledge – if customers do not know what substitutes are available or what they cost, demand is likely to be more elastic
- Time – it may take customers some time to adjust to changes in price; this would make price elasticity of demand more **inelastic** in the short run.

Quick check

When will cutting the price of a good or service raise potential profits?
When can the same objective be achieved by raising prices?
Why do UK governments often raise taxes on tobacco?

Definitions

Elastic demand: when a percentage change in price causes a *greater* percentage change in quantity demanded.
Inelastic demand: when a percentage change in price causes a *smaller* percentage change in quantity demanded.

Key concepts

Price elasticity of demand (Ped)

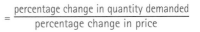

$$= \frac{\text{percentage change in quantity demanded}}{\text{percentage change in price}}$$

Learning tip

Remember: Elasticity =
elastic = stretch = responsiveness

Hot potato

'Charging patients for NHS operations will significantly cut waiting lists' – do you agree?

Other elasticities

Other demand elasticities

At this stage in your studies you need to understand two other ways in which the concept of elasticity is used to help analyse different aspects of markets. They are:

- Income elasticity of demand
- Cross elasticity of demand

Income elasticity of demand

Income elasticity of demand measures the responsiveness of the demand for a product to changes in incomes. It is also represented by a formula or equation. In this case:

$$\text{Income elasticity of demand} = \frac{\text{percentage change in quantity demanded}}{\text{percentage change in income}}$$

Note: Only the bottom of the equation is different.

If the government were to decide to cut income tax rates then all those in work would have higher disposable incomes. Having more to spend might change people's spending patterns, especially if becoming better off makes it possible to afford what might have previously been considered a luxury item. Thus, increasing incomes over the last 30 years have led to an even bigger proportionate increase in the demand for foreign holidays. This could mean that a 10 per cent rise in incomes could lead to a 30 per cent increase in the demand for foreign holidays. Thus:

Income elasticity of demand for foreign holidays would be +30%÷10% = +3.

On the other hand, rising incomes have also been associated with a fall in demand for traditional British seaside holidays. Thus, the same increase in income of 10 per cent might be associated with a 40 per cent fall in demand for some English seaside towns.

The income elasticity in this case would be –40%÷10% = –4. The coefficient for income elasticity of demand would in this case be negative. Economists call goods such as these inferior goods, whereas the more attractive foreign holidays are called superior goods.

Cross elasticity of demand

As indicated in the introductory Unit for demand, it is often helpful to categorise goods as being either substitutes or complements. These can be analysed using the concept of cross elasticity of demand which is used to measure the responsiveness of demand for one good in relation to a change in the price of another.

Hot potato

Why is branding so important in marketing?

Substitutes

Many people might regard peaches and nectarines as being close substitutes for each other. In this case an increase in the price of peaches may lead to an increase in the demand for nectarines. The formula which is used to work out the coefficient of cross elasticity of demand is similar to those used earlier:

Cross elasticity of demand of good x in relation to a change in the price of good y

$$= \frac{\text{percentage change in quantity demanded of good } x}{\text{percentage change in the price of good } y}$$

Thus a 50 per cent increase in the price of peaches might result in a 40 per cent rise in demand for nectarines =+40%+50% = +0.8

The value of the coefficient will always be positive if you are considering two goods which are substitutes for each other.

The size of the coefficient indicates how substitutable the two products are for each other. If there were little brand loyalty and a high degree of customer knowledge, the value of the coefficient would be much larger.

Complements

If two sets of goods are complements, the coefficient of the cross elasticity of demand of one good in respect of a change in the price of another will always be negative. For example, a fall in the mortgage rate is likely to lead to an increase in the demand for homes. In this case, a price cut of one good might lead to an increase in demand for a complement. So a 6.25% cut in the rate of interest from 4% to 3.75% may lead to an 18.75% increase in demand for houses, giving a coefficient of -3.

The relatively large negative figure would indicate that the demand for houses is very sensitive to changes in the mortgage interest rates. If two goods are complements their coefficient for their cross elasticities will always be negative and, as with all the other uses of the concept of elasticity, the smaller the value the less responsive the relationship and vice versa.

Health Warning

At the beginning, all this talk of different elasticities can be confusing. Remember two things: always define the concept you are using and the change in demand always goes on the top half of the equation.

Research task

Investigating cross elasticity of demand

1 Select two clothing brands which you believe to be close substitutes.
2 Devise a suitable questionnaire to collect data to test whether or not you have made a good choice.
3 Select a suitable sampling frame i.e. one which should give you unbiased results and be large enough for you to draw conclusions.
4 Collect your data.
5 Collate your findings.
6 Present them to the rest of your class.

Exam hint

Small value to elasticity co-efficient = weak relationship
Large value = strong relationship
Negative value = inverse relationship

1.10 Supply

Price

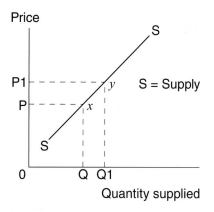

Figure 1: Supply curve

What is 'supply'?

Supply refers to the willingness of a producer to supply a good or service. A typical supply curve is illustrated in Figure 1. It slopes upwards from left to right showing that as the price of a good or service rises, suppliers are likely to want to produce and supply more of that good or service. Economists consider price as the most important variable affecting supply but they also recognise that supply will be affected by four other factors:

- costs
- technology
- relatively profitability
- business objectives.

Price and supply

Supply refers to the willingness and ability to supply goods to a market and, as with demand, price is considered to be the most important variable. *Ceteris paribus* if the price of a good or service rises, it will become more profitable to sell that good or service. If there are greater potential profits it is reasonable to expect that producers will wish to produce more. Therefore it is argued that a rise in price will lead to an increase in supply. This is illustrated in Figure 1 by the movement along the curve from x to y. The converse (opposite) of this is true. If prices fall, supply should also fall.

Changes in supply

The supply curve will shift if any of the following factors change: 1 costs of production; 2 changes in technology; 3 relative profitability, and 4 business objectives.

Costs refer to all payments which have to be made in order to produce a good. *Ceteris paribus*, a rise in costs will lead to a fall in profits and the incentive to make a particular product or service will drop. This will lead to a shift in supply to the left showing that at all possible prices less will be supplied. See Figure 2. The reverse argument applies: if costs fall, potential profits rise and supply will rise shown by a shift in the supply curve to the right, as illustrated in Figure 2.

Changes in technology

Technology in the sense of how we produce goods or provide services is changing all the time. Improvements in the way in which things are made or how services are provided can have a major impact on supply. Car producers have reduced both production and running costs by using plastic components rather than those made of metal. Improvements in technology are often associated with reductions in the cost of production and they can be illustrated in a similar way. The adoption of better and cheaper ways of

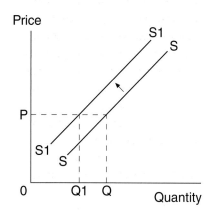

Figure 2: Supply curve showing the effect of a rise in costs

making something will shift the supply curve downward to the right (Figure 3). On the other hand, the use of more complex or difficult technologies will shift a supply curve to the left (Figure 3).

Relative profitability

The importance of profits has previously been considered but a further issue, especially for those firms who have an easy choice between producing different products or providing different services, is the relative profitability of producing different goods or services. Thus, if Tesco can negotiate a better deal with the suppliers of 'Whiskas' as distinct from 'Felix' it may be inclined to supply more of the former and less of the latter. Not all businesses have such easy choices, as changing what you produce or sell may take time but the general rule is that if supplying an alternative product becomes more profitable the supply of the good in question will fall as shown in Figure 2. On the other hand, if the supply of an alternative becomes less profitable there could be shift to the right showing an increase in supply, as shown in Figure 3.

Business objectives

So far we have assumed that businesses will respond in similar ways to changes in factors affecting their supply of a good or service. Obviously, no two businesses are the same. As will be discussed later, some businesses are interested in quick profits at all costs while others might place greater emphasis on ethical considerations. Business decision makers do not necessarily respond immediately to small changes in price. In this case, rising prices might not lead to increased output, or improvements in technology might allow the same level of profit in return for working less hard. How individual businesses work and make decisions will affect supply, and this makes it harder for economists to make simple generalisations about supply.

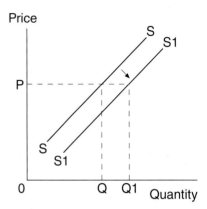

Figure 3: Supply curve showing fall in costs

Definition

Ceteris paribus
This Latin phrase means 'other things being equal'. Economists use this as a device for analysing complex situations when lots of things happen at once. It would be difficult to work out what would happen to coffee supply if there were a frost in Brazil, revolution in Columbia, collapse in tea prices, changes in demand in different countries and so on and so forth. To make this kind of situation more manageable, economists freeze all but the variables they want to analyse and to make sure everyone knows what's going on they use the phrase 'ceteris paribus'.

Quick check ✓

Which way will the supply curve for Mars Bars move if?
(a) There is a severe frost in Ghana
(b) Producing chocolate truffles becomes more profitable
(c) Fairtrade mounts a successful advertising campaign
(d) Tesco launches a 'two for the price of one' Mars Bar offer

Puzzler – this is hard but you have done it before!

What do you think economists mean when they talk about the differences between a shift and a movement along a supply curve?

Elasticity of supply

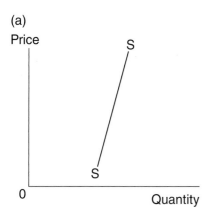

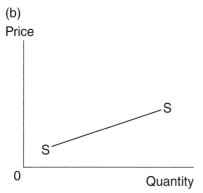

Figure 1: (a) Relatively inelastic supply;
(b) relatively elastic supply

**Thinking like
an economist**

Do not forget to switch tracks
and think of producers making goods
and providing services, whereas
demand analysis focuses on the
behaviour of customers or consumers.

Elasticity of supply

The responsiveness of supply to changes in price is measured using the concept of elasticity of supply. As with other applications of this concept, written, graphical and numerical treatments are used by economists.

Words

If it is easy and quick for a producer to change the output of a good or service in response to changes in price then the supply of that good is described as relatively elastic. Alternatively, if it is difficult and time-consuming to change output in response to price changes then supply is relatively inelastic.

Graphs

Graphical analysis can be quickly used to illustrate supply elasticity. Which of the diagrams on the left (Figure 1) relates to a relatively inelastic supply, a relatively elastic supply, or neither of these?

Calculation

The formula for working out the coefficient is very similar to that relating to price elasticity of demand. It is:

$$\text{Elasticity of supply} = \frac{\text{percentage change in quantity supplied}}{\text{percentage change in price}}$$

Thus, if the price of cars rises by 10 per cent and car producers struggle hard to raise output, increasing supply by only 2 per cent the coefficient would be + 0.2. If, on the other hand, manufacturers have large stocks of unsold cars and can change output quickly in response to a price rise, the coefficient is likely to be larger than 1. It is very unlikely for a negative coefficient to occur, as this would mean that producers expand production in response to a fall in price or cut output in response to a rise in price.

The opposite analysis also applies, as falling prices are associated with a decrease in willingness to produce and supply. Some producers are able to adjust quickly to falling prices while others will find it harder to do.

Factors affecting the elasticity of supply

If prices rise producers are likely to want to respond by increasing production and this could be achieved by undertaking a programme of measures. The elasticity of supply of any product or service is likely to depend up the following factors:

- Availability of stocks, and raw materials: If there are stocks of finished goods, components and other materials it will be relatively easy to expand production and sales. Conversely, expansion could be checked by the unavailability of one small component

- Unused productive capacity: If existing factories and production lines are not being used all the time, supply is likely to be more elastic
- Availability of imports: Many industries are global and companies can switch supplies from contracting markets to those that are growing
- Availability of suitably trained labour: The difficulty and extra costs of attracting skilled workers will limit the responsiveness of producers in meeting increases in demand.

The significance of these factors can be viewed in a different way by using the concept of 'time' i.e. the supply of most products and services is likely to become more elastic over a longer timescale. Changes in elasticity of supply over time are shown in Figure 2, where S1 represents the elasticity of supply in a very short timescale as unused stocks of materials and under-utilised labour is used; S2 for a longer period in which existing productive capacity can be brought into production; and S3 over an even longer period to allow for the acquisition of new plant and machinery along with the training of new workers.

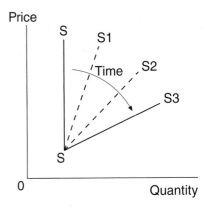

Figure 2: Elasticity of supply changing over time

The significance of technological change

Technological change refers to changes in the way in which goods and services are actually produced. Over the last two decades tremendous advances have been made in communications technology. We all know about the importance of IT in our lives but there have been similar, if less spectacular advances in air and sea transport. These developments have been paralleled by the growth of transnational corporations – many of whom have more economic power than most nations. The cumulative effect of these changes is often referred to as globalisation. It is now possible for production and sales to be organised on a global scale which means that the supply of many products and services has become more and more elastic. As will be shown in latter sections of this book, globalisation is having a major effect on how economies and economists work.

Quick check ✔

What factors are likely to affect the elasticity of supply in the following markets:

(a) wheat production,
(b) electricity generation
(c) T-shirt manufacture?
Which supply is likely to be most responsive to changes in demand/price?

Market equilibrium (i)

Putting demand and supply together

As demand curves and supply curves are drawn against the same axes, it is possible to superimpose one on top of another as illustrated in Figure 1 for the market for new houses.

The demand for new houses slopes downward to the right. It is relatively inelastic, as there are not many close substitutes. This factor is likely to outweigh the significance of housing as taking up a very large portion of most customers' budgets. The supply for new houses is also relatively inelastic, and the supply curve slopes upward to the right, demonstrating that it is not always easy for producers to quickly change output in response to changes in demand and price.

The point a where the supply and demand curves cross shows the price at which demand and supply are equal. In this example the average price of a new house coming onto the market will be £85,000 and 100 houses would be sold each month. This is called the equilibrium price and in a free market this will be established automatically. If the price were for some reason £95,000, demand would equal 90 whereas supply would be 120. The producers of new houses would be attempting to sell more than could be sold. This excess supply of 30 homes would mean that some houses were being built but not sold. Stocks of unwanted houses would build up and sellers would be tempted to cut prices. Falling prices would make new houses more attractive to some consumers, e.g. those on lower incomes would find that they were able to borrow enough money to buy, while some builders may find house building less attractive, and seek alternative building contracts. Demand would rise as supply would fall. According to price theory, this process would stop when the equilibrium price was reached. This pincer movement to the establishment of an equilibrium is shown by the two movements a and b along the demand and supply curves. This process by which markets are brought into equilibrium is called market clearing.

The same logical analysis can be applied to a situation in which new houses were being sold for £75,000 each. In this case demand would be *120* and supply *90*. Excess demand would apply and some prospective house buyers would be forced to go without. New houses coming onto the market would be snapped up quickly, and enterprising estate agents might well attempt to take advantage of shortages of new houses by raising their prices. This process would set a similar pincer movement in operation. Rising prices would put off some potential house buyers but would also make house production more attractive. Demand would fall and supply would rise until equilibrium were reached.

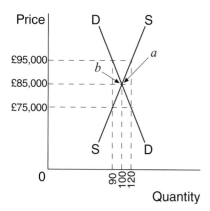

Figure 1: The market for new houses

Key concept

Remember the equilibrium price in any market is that at which demand and supply are equal.

Thinking like an economist

This is the section that will tell you whether or not economics is for you. The concepts are simple but central to micro economics. Markets in different forms are key to how all economics operate. Diagrams are used to model market behaviour. Analysis should be accurate, precise and to the point. This is what economics is all about.

Summary

The key point is that as long as demand curves slope downwards to the right and supply curves slope upwards to the right, and as long as they both cross there will be an equilibrium, and that is the price where demand is equal to supply. In other words, both buyers and sellers can make a deal.

Figure 3 A flea market – another type of market

Quick check

What will happen in a market if price is above the equilibrium?
What will happen in a market if price is below the equilibrium?

Puzzler

Are markets a good idea?

Figure 2 The stock exchange

Market equilibrium (ii)

Markets and changes in demand

If one of the key variables which determine the demand or supply for any product or service changes, the equilibrium will be affected. Using the market analysis introduced in the previous section, we will see how price and/or sales will be affected by a change in any of the variables determining demand or supply.

Changes in demand

Remember Section 1.7. Just in case you do not, demand curves shift if any of the following change:

- the prices of substitutes and complements
- incomes
- consumer tastes.

Decrease in the price of a substitute

Consider the market for seats at the Centre Court for the Wimbledon All-England Open Tennis Championship. The supply is fixed and this would appear as a vertical line as shown by S in Figure 1. Demand is represented by D giving an equilibrium price of P and ticket sales of Q. Those thinking of buying a ticket are likely not only to consider the price of the ticket but also the prices of alternatives. This would include prices of tickets for other courts or for a whole range of other leisure products. If, for example, a test match were being staged in London at the same time and seat prices for that were reduced, it is conceivable that some people may be attracted to cricket rather than tennis and this would cause the demand for Wimbledon tickets to fall as shown by the shift from D to D1 in Figure 1.

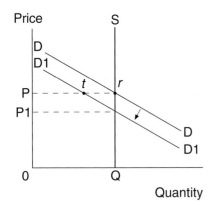

Figure 1: Decrease in demand for seats at Wimbledon

If the price were to remain at P there would be disequilibrium between demand and supply. Supply would exceed demand by *tr*. Excess supply would exist. If the price stayed at P some tickets would be unsold. The managers of Wimbledon may consider cutting prices to the level of P1 in order to make sure all seats were sold. This change in price would be described by economists as being the outcome of 'market forces' at work.

Decrease in the price of a complement

A number of other products or services are likely to be jointly consumed by visitors to Wimbledon. Travel to the courts, the famous strawberries and cream, perhaps having something new to wear could be considered to be complements. Thus, reduced public transport prices to Wimbledon,could result in an increase in demand for Wimbledon tickets (Figure 2).

In this case, demand increases as indicated by the shift to the right from D to D1. If the price remained at P excess demand of *xy* would occur. This would give Wimbledon's managers the opportunity to raise seat prices and a new equilibrium could be established with a higher price at P1. If they didn't take advantage of this opportunity, ticket touts would find themselves able to exploit the situation by selling tickets at inflated prices.

Changes in income

If the country as whole becomes better off, potential ticket sales at Wimbledon are likely to rise. Studies show that the income elasticity of demand for 'products' such as this is highly positive and if incomes in general rise, it is likely that demand for tickets will rise and the effects of this would be similar to those illustrated in Figure 2.

If the product or service under consideration were an inferior good then an increase in income would be associated with a fall in demand – the demand curve shifts to the left leading to a fall in price and sales.

Changes in tastes

The effects of changes in tastes can be modelled in the same way. If a good or service becomes more fashionable, demand shifts to the right resulting in higher prices and sales, whereas if it goes out of fashion, this would lead to falling prices and sales represented by a shift in demand to the left.

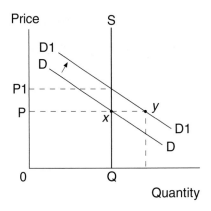

Figure 2: Increase in demand for seats at Wimbledon

Learning tip

Make sure you understand the distinction between shifts and movements in demand curves.

Quick check

What will happen to the price and sales of tennis rackets if:
1 There is a rise in membership fees for tennis clubs
2 Footballers get even higher incomes
3 There is a reduction in income tax
4 Cat gut is shown to be carcinogenic

Puzzler

Why might an understanding of cross elasticity of demand be helpful in forecasting the effects of changes in the price of other goods?

1.14 Market equilibrium (iii)

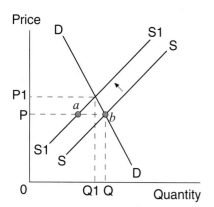

Figure 1: Effects of increased costs faced by organic carrot producers

Markets and changes in supply

Changes in supply are considered in the context of the market for organically grown carrots. In this case supply will change if any of the following happen:

- changes in costs of production
- technological changes
- changes in the objectives of producers.

The market for organic carrots

In this market there will be a considerable number of producers both in this country and abroad. Individually they will have much less influence over the price charged for their product. However, it is reasonable to assume that the supply of organic carrots is likely to slope upwards from left to right, as with S which shows a greater willingness to produce if prices are high and vice versa. The demand curve for organic carrots is likely to be relatively inelastic and this is shown by the steep gradient of D. In this market demand and supply are equal at the price of P, leading to sales of Q.

Increasing costs of production

Organic producers face additional costs in order to assure buyers that their produce is really organic. Thus the Soil Association operate a certification scheme to guarantee the organic origins of products. If they were to increase their registration fees, organic carrot producers would be faced with an increase in costs. This is shown in Figure 1 by the leftward and upward shift in supply to S1.

If the price were to remain at P demand will now exceed supply by *a–b*. Excess demand means that some potential buyers might have to go without; enterprising greengrocers might raise their prices. The price is likely to rise until a new equilibrium is reached. In this case demand will be equal to the reduced supply at P1, and sales will fall to Q1.

Improvements in technology

Alternatively, an improvement could be made in the production process which reduced costs of supply. Potential profits would be higher. Production would be more attractive and the supply curve would shift downwards to the right. If the old price were maintained, disequilibrium would arise in which supply was greater than demand. Prices would fall until a new equilibrium were established showing both a lower price and higher sales. This is illustrated in Figure 2.

Objectives of producers

An increasing number of farmers are turning away from using inorganic fertilisers, herbicides and pesticides, and may prefer to adopt organic techniques for ethical reasons. This trend is likely to lead to an increase in the supply of organic products as shown in Figure 2. The long term effect of these trends is that the supply and sales of organic carrots and other products should increase and prices should fall.

The importance of elasticity

The significance of elasticity of demand is illustrated in Figure 3. In the first graph, demand is highly inelastic, whereas the second shows a highly elastic demand. The same change in supply in both markets will have very different effects.

When demand is inelastic, an increase in supply will have a greater effect on price than on the quantity bought and sold. In contrast, when demand is elastic the main impact is on quantity.

> ### Quick check
>
> How might the price and sales of hot chocolate in the UK be affected by:
> 1. Easier access for African producers to European markets
> 2. A new outbreak of foot and mouth disease in the UK
> 3. More hurricanes in the West Indies
> 4. Lower tea prices

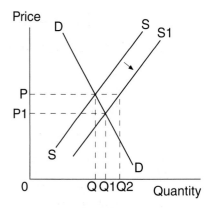

Figure 2: Effects of technological improvements on the organic carrot market

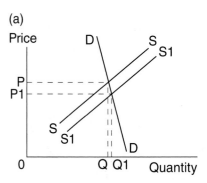

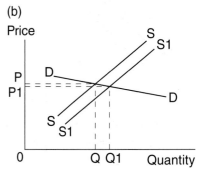

Figure 3: The significance of elasticity of supply

Hot potato

The case for organic food production in the UK is overwhelming. Do you agree?

Market analysis

1.15

Price

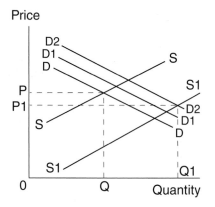

Figure 1: Market for Dell PCs

Research task

Use the tools of economic analysis developed in this Unit to analyse market forces at work in a market of your choice. Use demand and supply analysis to explain trends in prices in this market over the last 5 years. Present your findings as a report to the rest of your class.

The personal computer market

How might an economist analyse the personal computer market? Firstly, demand would be considered. There is nothing special about the demand for PCs that would challenge the generalisation that, other things being equal, lower prices will lead to higher sales and vice versa. Thus, the demand curve for a given PC is likely to be downward-sloping from left to right. Moreover, there are many producers of very similar looking and performing products which should mean that the market is very competitive. This means that the demand for, say Dell PCs, is likely to be relatively elastic as there are a fair number of close substitutes. If these assumptions and observations are accurate, the demand curve for an entry level Dell PC is likely to look something like DD.

Secondly, what can be said about the supply of PCs? Although individual components are very sophisticated, most PCs are relatively simple to make as all that is required is that a particular set of components are linked together and put into a box. Another key supply factor is the very rapid changes in technology. Sometimes it seems that new, faster processors are brought onto the market on a weekly basis. Faster machines with larger and larger memories are being continually developed. In short, PCs can be made relatively easily, in a short period of time but their technical specification changes very quickly. As this is a fast moving market, stocks are likely to be small. The supply curve for an entry level Dell PC is probably fairly elastic as shown in SS.

So can demand and supply analysis help us understand why the price of this kind of PC has fallen so dramatically over the last twelve months? Looking at demand first it is likely that the business demand for this kind of PC has probably slowed reflecting the weaker performance of the US and UK economies, and possible saturation of the market for home users. On the other hand, income elasticities of demand tend to be high and positive, expenditure on advertising is high, and the price of complementary products and services such as access to the Internet continue to fall. It is possible demand continues to grow but at a slower rate. This is also shown in Figure 1 as a series of shifts to the right to D1 and D2.

Such developments would normally lead to rising prices but they ignore changes, which might be happening to supply. Competition between the suppliers of components is intense, and the costs of many PC components have fallen significantly. Some have been over supplied, and those imported from the Far East have become cheaper with the fall in value of their currencies. The effect of this is that there has been an increase in supply shown by the shift from S to S1.

This analysis of a particular market shows that prices have fallen from P to P1 while at the same time sales have increased from Q to Q1.

Price fixing

What happens if attempts are made to fix prices? This can be analysed using market analysis. Manufacturers might try to set prices above the equilibrium level. Governments might want to reduce the prices consumers have to pay for essential items. The possible outcomes of these two kinds of intervention are illustrated in Figure 2. In both cases disequilibrium is likely. Attempts to set a price above equilibrium result in excess supply of *xy*, whereas setting a price below equilibrium will lead to excess demand of *st*.

Summary

Markets bring demand and supply together to determine price and sales. Changes in demand or supply will lead to changes in price and sales. Demand and supply conditions always differ between different markets and it is advisable to always try to consider what might make one set of demand and supply conditions differ from another set.

Quick check ✓

Use demand and supply diagrams to offer a possible explanation for the following:

1 Adopt the role as a promoter of musical events. You have hired a venue with a capacity of 2000. Show the effects of:
   (a) over-pricing tickets
   (b) under-pricing tickets
2 The market for grapes shows widespread fluctuations at different times of the year – prices can vary from 69p a pound to 299p a pound. Why might this be so?

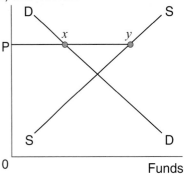

(a) Interest rate

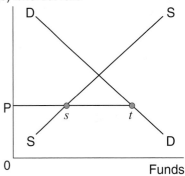

(b) Interest rate

Figure 2: Price fixing resulting in disequilibrium

Exam hint

This may be boring but year after year examiners complain about the poor quality of diagrams. Get into the habit of labelling diagrams, make sure they are a reasonable size, use them to help you write your analysis and check that the outcomes are logical.

Factor markets

The market system includes a whole series of markets for land, labour, capital and enterprise. Collectively these are called factor markets. They play a crucial role in ensuring that customers get the goods and services that they wish to purchase. Although economists consider that there are special features of these markets, demand and supply analysis is used to model the behaviour of aspects pertaining to factor markets.

Demand for factors

Factors of production are in many senses like any other product that is traded in the market place. They have a price. The price, for example of labour, is the wage or salary that has to be paid. Rent is the return earned by the owners of land. Profit is a reward for enterprise and interest or dividends can be seen as the price paid to the owners of money or capital. If a factor of production, other things being equal, is expensive then the demand is likely to be low. If, on the other hand, factors are cheap, demand will be high. Thus the demand for building land will be lower as it becomes more expensive. In other words, the demand for factors is likely to slope downwards from left to right.

Supply of factors

Similar analysis can be applied to the supply of factors. If it is assumed that the owners of factors of production are materialistic (they want to make as good a financial return as possible from the factors which they own) then the supply of land, labour, capital or enterprise can be treated in much the same way as the supply of any commodity. The supply of workers to higher paid jobs is likely to be higher than that to similar jobs paying lower wages. Alternatively, if wages are low then the supply is likely to be low. This means that a supply curve for any factor will slope upwards to the right.

Factor market equilibrium

This is illustrated in Figure 1. Although this looks like any other demand and supply diagram, the axes measure different variables. Thus, if the market for shop workers in Cheltenham is being modelled, wages are represented on the vertical axis and numbers of staff employed on the horizontal. The equilibrium wage rate is given as £6.00 per hour at which the demand for shop workers is matched by the supply. Any change in demand and supply will lead to the establishment of a new equilibrium.

Derived demand

Final goods like cars or houses are demanded for what they are. Factors are demanded not for what they are, but because they are required to produce something else. The nature of the demand for that final product will have a

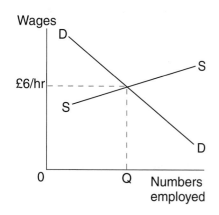

Figure 1: Equilibrium wage for shop workers

direct impact on the demand for the factors required to produce that product. Therefore the demand for pesticide-free land will increase as a result of the increase in demand for organic foodstuffs, while the demand for meat-processing equipment falls because the demand for meat products has fallen. Premier division footballers command enormous salaries because they contribute to the success and earnings of top clubs.

Thus, although the demand curve for a factor of production looks like any other demand curve, its gradient and position will be heavily influenced by the demand for the final product. If the demand for that final product is highly price elastic, then it is likely that the demand for factors to make that product will also tend to be relatively elastic. Similarly, if the demand for the final product is relatively inelastic, factor use is likely to be more stable.

It also follows that if there is a sudden surge in demand for Thai food, there will be a surge in demand, for example, for Thai chefs and they are likely to be paid more than chefs producing different food products.

Factor immobility

The supply of factors is also special in some ways. In the case of labour markets we are considering people and it may not be appropriate to treat ourselves as commodities.

Moreover, people may not work solely for monetary reward. Some jobs are more attractive than others irrespective of wages or salary levels. Some people are loath to leave some parts of the country for others even though wages and salaries might be higher.

The use of others factors of production may be even less flexible because some may be fixed in supply. Thus, in the UK the amount of land for new housing developments tends to be relatively fixed. Land itself is finite. It can't really be moved from one part of the country to another but the use of land can be changed from one purpose to another.

The mobility of labour or any other factor of production can be illustrated by the gradient of the supply curve. In the most extreme case (there is only one David Beckham) the supply curve will be vertical indicating a fixed supply irrespective of the wage or return offered. On the other hand, the supply of Division 3 players is much more elastic. See Figure 2.

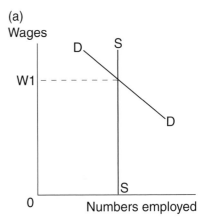

(a)

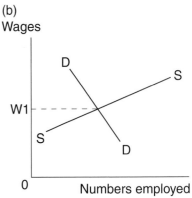

(b)

Figure 2 (a) Supply of a world-class footballer. (b) Supply of Division 3 footballers.

Money markets

Money and other markets

The tools of market analysis which you will now have developed can be applied to a whole range of other markets. Two applications are considered in this section:

- Money markets
- Foreign exchange markets

Money markets

It takes just a few slight changes to adapt the demand and supply model you have been using to analyse money markets i.e. those in which people lend and borrow money. If you decide to take out a loan you will pay interest to the lender. This is usually expressed in percentage terms e.g. 15 per cent, which means that for every £100 you borrow you pay £15 each year. From the point of view of the lender, the interest rate represents what is earned for lending money. The rate of interest can, therefore, be seen as the price of borrowing and gets put on the vertical axis of the demand and supply diagram (Figure 1). The demand for funds is likely to slope down from left to right. If interest rates are low, demand for borrowing is likely to be higher than if interest rates are high. Looked at from the point of view of the bank or supplier of funds, there is greater incentive to supply if interest rates are high, than when they are low. Hence the supply of credit is likely to slope upwards from left to right.

The analysis which follows should almost be automatic. Where the demand and supply curves cross is the equilibrium rate of interest, i.e. the rate at which the supply of funds is equal to the demand. If interest rates were higher, excess supply would drive them down to the equilibrium and if they were lower, excess demand would push rates up.

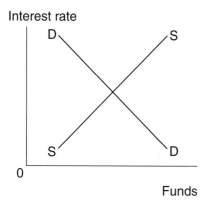

Figure 1: Demand and supply in money markets

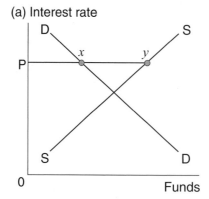 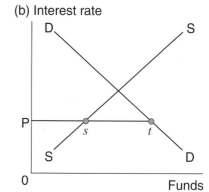

Figure 2: (a) Excess supply (b) Excess demand

Any change in the demand or supply of funds will have a direct impact on the rate of interest. Thus, if the government makes it harder for banks to lend, the supply curve will shift to the left, leading to higher interest rates and lower levels of borrowing. Alternatively, if there were a surge in consumer confidence, the demand curve would shift to the right leading also to higher rates of interest but in this case, higher levels of borrowing.

The foreign exchange market

Another application which you should make great use of as you develop your studies in economics is foreign exchange markets. Although these can be confusing, demand and supply analysis provides a quick and easy way of predicting what is likely to happen to the exchange rate. If we look at the foreign exchange market for £s and euros, we can use the vertical axis to measure the value of £s in terms of euros and the horizontal axis to represent the amount of foreign exchange that changes hands. The demand for £s will come from European firms wanting to buy goods priced in pounds, or European tourists travelling to the UK. The lower the price (exchange rate) the higher the demand and vice versa. Hence, the demand for £s will slope downwards from left to right. £s are supplied by people in the UK wishing to buy European-made goods and services or going to Europe on holiday. They will be more willing to supply if the exchange rate is high and vice versa. Hence the supply of euros slopes upwards from left to right. This is shown in Figure 3.

The equilibrium exchange rate is given at €1.40 as this is where the demand for £s is equal to the supply. If there is a surge in demand in Europe for UK-produced goods, the demand for pounds will increase as shown by the shift to the right to D1 to €1.80. The effect of this will be to force up the exchange rate. If, however, there is a recession in the UK and consumers buy fewer European-produced goods it is likely that they will supply fewer pounds, shifting supply to the left and leading to a higher exchange rate.

Quick check ✓

What will happen to the value of the pound if speculators believe that it is likely to increase in terms of the euro?

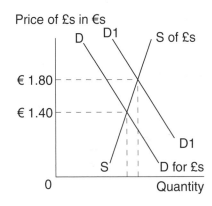

Figure 3: An increased demand for £s

Costs

Costs and revenue of firms

All businesses need to know about the relationship between costs and revenue. In this section various kinds of cost and revenue are defined. This will be related to what businesses set out to do, their objectives, in a following section. This section is devoted to short-run costs.

Costs of production

All payments made by a firm in the production of a good or provision of a service are called costs. They are classified in different ways. Overheads are costs of production which businesses have to pay irrespective of their level of output. For example, rent, business rates, and repayment of loans will remain the same irrespective of how much is sold. These are called fixed costs and they do not change in the short run. Running costs, such as payment of wages, stock purchases and the like which will change as sales change in the short run, are classified as variable costs. The addition of fixed to variable costs gives total costs, which include all the costs faced by a firm in the production of a good or the provision of a service.

The total cost divided by the output of the business gives the short-run average total cost which is usually abbreviated to short-run average cost, or even average cost. This is probably the most useful of these measures as it indicates the cost of producing each item or of providing a service. The average cost is sometimes referred to as the unit cost.

Finally, economists and business people make use of the concept of marginal cost, which is the additional cost of producing an extra unit of output of a particular good or service. In the short run the costs that change as output changes are variable costs. Thus, if a clothing manufacturing company were to produce an extra suit, it would be faced with the costs of additional materials and labour but would not have to pay out any more for design or machine setting costs.

Revenue

Revenue is the term used by economists to describe those flows of money which are received by a firm, as distinct from costs which refer to those payments made by firms. Private sector business revenues will be largely determined by the value of sales of goods and/or services. Average revenue is the amount of money earned for selling each individual good or service. Total revenue refers to the total number of sales multiplied by the selling price of the good, and marginal revenue refers to the change in revenue brought about by changing the number of goods sold.

Key concept

The short run is defined as the amount of time in which it is not possible to change the input of all factors. There is at least one factor fixed in supply. In the long run it is possible to change all four factor inputs, land, labour, capital and enterprise. What is short and what is long run will depend upon the industry and firm in question.

Summary

These two sets of data can be put together and the relationship between costs and revenue provides very important information about how well (or otherwise) a business is doing.

The table below summarises some of these relationships.

Relationship	Explanation	Interpretation
AR = AC	The cost of producing this item is the same as the cost of its production	Normal profit being made on the sale of this item
AR > AC	Revenue exceeds costs	Supernormal profit is being earned
TR > TC	The total amount of revenue is greater than total costs	This business is making supernormal profit
TR < TC	Total costs are greater than total revenue	This business is making a loss
MR > MC	The extra amount of revenue unit gained from selling one extra will exceed the extra costs of production	Producing more will lead to higher profits
MR = MC	The addition to revenue from selling one extra unit is the same as the addition to costs	This level of sales will maximise profits for this business

---

Quick check ✓

What happens in the following situations: AR < AC; TC = TR; or MC > MR?

Economies of scale

1.19

Is bigger better?

The previous section dealt with short-run costs. In the long run it is possible to change inputs of all factors and what actually happens to costs is less predictable. A feature of contemporary economics is the tendency for firms to get bigger and bigger. This can result in both increasing and decreasing average costs. The concept of economies of scale is used to analyse the effects on average costs of businesses getting bigger.

Economies of scale

As firms grow in size there are factors which may reduce costs of production. Thus, it is cheaper for a large company like Tesco to sell milk than it is for a local milkman. These cost reductions which are associated with a firm getting bigger are called economies of scale. These can be divided into internal and external returns to scale.

Internal economies of scale

These relate to reductions in cost associated with the growth of an individual firm, and can occur as a result of:

Technical factors

As firms grow they may be able to afford and sell larger outputs which make it 'economic' to use particular production techniques which are more efficient. For example, a wide-bodied plane such as the Airbus 300 series has lower running costs per passenger mile compared with a smaller plane such as the Boeing 707. The most significant factor leading to this is that larger planes are more fuel-efficient. Similarly, as manufacturing firms grow and produce larger saleable outputs they are more likely to be able to afford more expensive but more efficient computer-driven automated production methods.

Organisational factors

The growth of firms and production of larger outputs enables firms to apply the division of labour and principles of specialisation. Those who work for small firms may have to undertake a range of jobs and will find it hard to develop cost-saving skills and expertise in particular fields. As firms grow they can afford to employ specialists in finance and marketing and the like and this can result in cost savings leading to falling long-run average costs.

Growth and higher revenues can allow firms to invest more heavily in research and development. This is especially important in those industries in which the rate of change is rapid e.g. electronics and pharmaceuticals.

Key concepts

Economies of scale refer to reductions in unit or average costs which arise from firms getting bigger. Diseconomies of scale refer to increases in unit or average cost which are attributable to larger size. Remember scale = size.

Market power

Firms that grow larger can exercise more power in the various market places in which they operate. Expanding output can allow companies to negotiate larger discounts from suppliers. In the UK the major supermarkets are said to be able to compel prospective supplies of foodstuffs to accept ever lower prices while maintaining ever higher standards.

External returns

These relate to changes in long-run costs which are associated with the expansion of a particular industry rather than an individual firm. Long-run costs might fall if an industry expands in a particular area such that suppliers are attracted, leading to a reduction in the transport costs of components. Alternatively, the grouping of related businesses in urban areas such as London generates additional costs of congestion and pollution.

Diseconomies of scale

Before you run away with the idea that big = better, there are factors which may make bigger firms less efficient, higher cost producers. As firms grow they become more complex, more difficult to manage and more impersonal to work for. Size is also often associated with more red tape and bureaucracy. Communications can become slower and less effective. Large businesses might be more distant from their customers, making them less responsive and less effective.

Large, powerful companies can be the targets for dissatisfied customers. Shell, Nike and Esso have been all targeted as they use their size to exploit both workers and consumers.

Evidence of diseconomies comes from those large companies like Marconi who are on the verge of bankruptcy and by the trend of de-merger, whereby large companies are broken up, often in the words of the financial press 'to concentrate on core activities'.

Summary

There is no automatic formula which can be applied to firms as they grow in size. In some industries, e.g. motorcar manufacture, potential economies of scale that benefit firms able to produce on a large scale for a global market are enormous. In others, especially where more traditional methods of production are used, diseconomies of scale may be more significant.

Research task

Pick a large company such as Nike, Starbucks, Esso or IKEA and search the Internet for evidence of worker or customer dissatisfaction.

Hot potato

Airbus Industries is developing a 500–600 seat airliner. Is this good or bad news?

Objectives of firms

Introduction

This Unit considers the importance of objectives in helping understand the behaviour of firms. It relates differing objectives to different types of organisations:

- plcs
- privately owned firms
- public sector
- voluntary sector.

Large Companies (plcs)

In the UK most large firms are 'public limited companies' – plcs. They are allowed to sell shares to the general public, and are legally obliged to publish their accounts in the form of an annual report. These publications are usually freely available to be public and can be used to try to work out the objectives of large, well-known companies. Firms like Vodaphone, Marks and Spencer and British Airways tend to describe their objectives in terms of dividends to shareholders, meeting customer needs and achieving significant market share. Although large companies are usually very conscious of their public image, most place profitability very high on their list of priorities. However, the existence of other objectives may indicate that profits are not the only priority.

Research task

Use the Internet to obtain annual reports or other promotional material and summarise the objectives and performance of three different plcs.

Privately owned companies

These tend to be smaller and their shares cannot be traded on the stock exchange. They have fewer legal obligations and are not compelled to publicise their accounts. It is, therefore, harder to find out and research their aims and objectives. However, in order to survive, privately owned companies must pay their way. They have to pay their workers, their suppliers and others. In order to do this they need to generate revenue. Also, the owners of such companies expect to be compensated for the risks that they are taking by being in business. It is reasonable to deduce, therefore, that making some level of profit is important for this type of firm.

Public sector

In the UK about 42 per cent of national income is spent by national and local government. This includes spending by government departments like 'Trade and Industry', local government, the armed forces, the police and such like. These organisations are not usually regarded as firms, but just as with the private sector, they receive and spend income in different ways.

Public sector organisations or firms are likely to have more complicated objectives than those in the private sector and they are more likely to include reference to service to the community.

Voluntary sector

Organisations as diverse as the Citizens Advice Bureau, the League Against Cruel Sports and Harrow Hill Football Club are all examples of voluntary sector organisations. It is likely that voluntary sector firms emphasise some form of service as their prime objective.

Profit

Most economists would agree that the need or desire to make a profit in some form is common to practically all businesses, even those which exist most obviously to provide some kind of service. For example, the Terrence Higgins Trust provides support to AIDS patients. In order to exist, the Trust has to ensure that it has enough income to fund its services. If its spending exceeds its income, it will be forced either to cut down the help it provides or seek new sources of funding. In this way the Terrence Higgins Trust is as much a business as Virgin Records or Vodaphone. It employs specialists to manage its cash flow. Raising funds is a key objective. Costs have to be carefully controlled. If these business functions were not undertaken the Trust would be less effective in its vital work.

Economists, however, have differing views as to the importance of profit in shaping and determining the behaviour of large privately owned business.

In classical economic theory, the pursuit of profit was seen to be the very engine which drove all business and the economy as a whole. Traditionally, economists have considered that firms seek to earn as large a profit as possible and that this objective overrides all others. This is called 'profit maximisation', and economists have for many years used this generalisation as the basis for arguing that a business which seeks to maximise its profits will choose the output of goods which gives the greatest possible profit.

Some economists consider that the assumption of profit maximisation is too restrictive. It has been argued that large companies may set out to gain enough profit to keep their shareholders happy and then pursue other objectives. This is called profit satisfying. Other economists believe that stakeholder analysis, by which competing expectations about how firms behave are considered, is a more appropriate tool of analysis.

Summary

There is a broad consensus among economists that making a profit is one of the most important objectives facing all firms. Some firms will seek to profit maximise, while others will set other objectives. However, profit is important to all types of businesses irrespective of their size or form of ownership.

Exam hint

Make sure that you can link the objectives of firms to any explanations of why particular businesses act in a particular way.

Hot potato

Why should a firm which seeks to maximise its profits produce the output at which marginal cost equals marginal revenue?

1.21 Market structures

Firms operate in different types of markets and these will have a direct effect on how different businesses behave. You need to know about four different kinds of market structure:

- perfect competition
- monopolistic competition
- oligopoly
- monopoly.

Perfect competition

This is a theoretical structure in which there are a very large number of firms competing with each other. In its extreme form the firms would all be producing the same product and they would have instant and perfect knowledge about what their competitors were up to. It would be easy for new firms to enter the industry and others to leave. Few, if any, industries entirely meet these criteria but the world-wide production of agricultural products like wheat comes close. Important conclusions which follow from these market characteristics are that no one firm can influence the market, individual firms will be forced to maximise profits, and the price of the product or service will be set by the market.

Monopolistic competition

The main characteristic of this type of market is that it consists of a number of different firms producing similar products. As with perfect competition, firms are free to enter and leave the industry. This structure is a bit more realistic compared with perfect competition and it could apply to industries which consist of a number of competing firms such as hairdressers, builders and window cleaners. They would have more influence over their market, but in the long run they would have to seek to maximise profits if they were to stay in business.

Oligopoly

This is the term used to describe competition between the few and is typical of many markets which make up the economy today. Esso, BP, Shell, and Texaco dominate the transport fuels market. It is very hard for other businesses to raise the finance to enter this market. The large companies enjoy significant economies of scale and are able to exert a considerable amount of economic power. They are not, however, totally dominant as shown in the UK by the recent entry of the supermarkets to this industry. However, such large businesses are able to spend enormous sums on advertising. They can buy out competitors and make great profits.

Research task

Try to find the best examples of businesses which meet the criteria for the four different types of market structure.

Monopoly

Finally, in total contrast to perfect competition, a monopoly exists when one firm completely dominates a market. Pure monopolies such as this are not common, but before privatization British Rail was almost the only provider of rail transport in the UK. Local monopolies like those of water utilities exist, and governments sometimes create monopolies like the Bank of England which is the only provider of banknotes in England. It could be argued that your local shop is a monopoly especially when it is the only store open. If a monopoly exists, it follows that there is no direct competition, that firms cannot enter and leave the industry, and that monopolists have tremendous power to push up prices, restrict consumer choice and earn large profits.

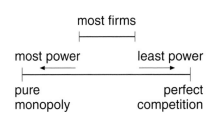

Figure 1: Continuum of competition

The spectrum of competition

Economists recognise that most firms do not fall into extreme categories of being absolute price makers or total price takers. Most firms have some degree of market power which enables them to have some influence on the price for which their good or service sells. A 'continuum' of competition is illustrated in Figure 1.

Most firms are likely to fall in the middle of this continuum, which means that they have some power over their markets but not an absolute power.

Hot potato

Drug companies should not be given monopolies in the production of particular medicines. Do you agree?

Summary

What makes a market competitive or monopolistic? Economists make use of the concept of market entry to help explain why market characteristics differ. This is defined as the ease or otherwise of firms to enter or leave a market. With perfect competition there is said to be complete freedom of entry. In monopoly there are considerable barriers to entry into the market. Oligopoly and monopolistic competition fall between these two extremes. In assessing what market structure the firms in an industry are operating in, economists examine concentration ratios, i.e. the market share of the leading firms.

What you have learned in this section will provide part of the basis for understanding the next module: Market failure and government intervention.

Thinking like an economist

When considering different types of market structure, always be very careful when defining the market you are talking about. The market for cars is very different from that for Rolls Royces. Similarly, there is a big difference in the market for a particular strain of genetically modified soya seed and that for soya seed in general.

Quick check ✓

How might capital requirements, the law, economies of scale, branding and price fixing provide barriers to entry?

Activities

Activity 1

(a) Define demand.
(b) Using a diagram, analyse the impact of a decrease in demand on the market for new cars.

Activity 2

(a) Define the term 'opportunity cost'.
(b) What might have been the opportunity cost of a family going on holiday to Spain.

Activity 3

A firm raises the price of its product from £12 to £18. As a result demand falls from 450 to 300.
(a) Calculate the price elasticity of demand.
(b) Comment on the figure you have calculated.

Activity 4

(a) Explain what is meant by producer surplus.
(b) With the aid of a diagram, explain how higher prices would affect producer surplus.

Activity 5

(a) Distinguish between fixed and variable costs.
(b) Identify three fixed costs of a road haulier.

Activity 6

(a) What does a supply curve indicate?
(b) Explain two influences on price elasticity of supply.

Activity 7

(a) State and describe three characteristics of a monopoly.
(b) To what extent does the UK postal services market match these characteristics?

Activity 8

(a) Explain the advantages of division of labour.

(b) To what extent can a local bakery gain these advantages?

Activity 9

(a) In a free market how is price determined?

(b) Using a demand and supply diagram, analyse the effect on the price of computers of a decrease in production costs.

Activity 10

(a) Distinguish between internal and external economies of scale.

(b) State and explain two possible ways in which the airline industry might benefit from economies of scale.

Jupiter ice cream

Hampton PLC launched a new range of ice cream, called Jupiter, in the spring of 2003. The company carried out market research in the new range, some of which is shown below:

	Jupiter ice cream
PED	−1.5
YED	3.0
XED with respect to changes in the price of Park's ice cream	0.6

To generate interest in the new range, Hampton PLC launched an advertising campaign. It also hoped that the campaign would build up barriers to entry into the industry. The industry operates in an oligopoly market structure.

Expecting high sales, the company shifted some of its resources from production of vanilla ice cream to Jupiter ice cream. The company was aiming in the long run for profit maximisation.

(a) Define 'barriers to entry'. (2)

(b) (i) Use a diagram to illustrate the effect of a successful advertising campaign for Jupiter ice cream. (4)

(ii) Apart from advertising, explain two other influences on demand for ice cream. (4)

(c) (i) Explain how an economist would assess what market structure an industry operates in. (6)

(ii) Describe three characteristics of oligopoly. (6)

(d) (i) Use a production possibility curve diagram to illustrate the effect of a shift in resources. (6)

(ii) Identify three distinct resources. (3)

(e) (i) When are profits maximised? (2)

(ii) Assess how Hampton PLC could use the information in the table. (12)

The examination lasts for one hour. The number of marks allocated is 45. Check through the questions, examine the data and read through the questions again. The amount you should write on each question part is indicated by the space provided in the answer booklet. You can expect to draw at least one diagram and you may have to undertake a calculation.

(a) Define means to give the meaning of. Barriers to entry are obstacles that firms outside the industry face should they try to start operating in the market e.g. patents and economies of scale enjoyed by established firms.

(b) (i) A successful advertising campaign should result in an increase in demand, a rise in price and an extension in supply. Draw a large and clear diagram – at least a third of a page in size. Label the diagram accurately and show the demand curve shifting to the right, price rising and the quantity bought and sold increasing.

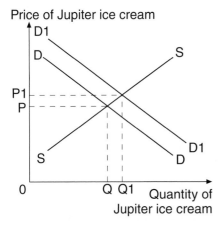

(ii) You need to identify two influences on demand for ice cream and, in each case, explain how changes in these influences would affect demand. For instance, changes in weather conditions and changes in the price of sweets may affect demand for ice cream. A period of hot weather is likely to result in an increased demand for ice cream. In contrast, a fall in the price of sweets may cause a decrease in demand for ice cream as sweets and ice cream are substitutes.

(c) (i) Here you need to refer to the characteristics, behaviour and performance of market structures. Economists assess what market structure an industry is in by examining these three key factors. A main indicator is the market share enjoyed by firms in the industry. This can be measured by market concentration ratios. A high market concentration ratio would indicate that the market is an oligopoly or monopoly. Other indicators include whether there are barriers to entry and exit, the influence individual firms have on price, the number of firms in the industry, the level of profits that firms can earn in the long run, how firms compete and whether productive and allocative efficiency are achieved.

(ii) You should identify three characteristics and briefly describe them. An oligopoly is a market structure where there is high degree of market concentration. This means that the market is dominated by a few large firms. In a oligopoly there are significant barriers to entry and exit meaning that any firms wanting to enter or leave the market will have to overcome obstacles. Another characteristic is that oligopolistic firms often engage in non-price competition. This means that they try to attract customers in ways other than by cutting price, for instance advertising and free gifts.

(d) (i) A shift in resource use is illustrated by a movement inside a production possibility curve or on the curve if the firm is fully using its resources. It is easier to draw the latter. Figure 2 shows the use of some resources being switched from producing vanilla ice cream to producing Jupiter ice cream.

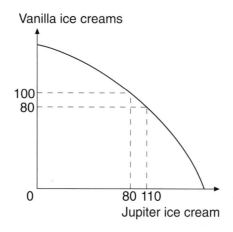

(ii) Other terms for resources are inputs and factors of production. You need to state three e.g. land, labour and capital.

(e) (i) State it is when marginal cost is equal to marginal revenue and when the sale of one more or one less unit would reduce profit.

(ii) This question part is marked on the basis of levels. Level 1 is for basic knowledge, Level 2 for application, Level 3 for analysis and Level 4 for evaluation. To achieve the highest level you need to make judgements, supported by clear analysis. In this case you should discuss the relevance of the firm's product having PED and YED greater than one and XED less than one. When a firm has elastic demand for its product, it can raise revenue by cutting price. What effect this has on profits, however, will also be influenced by what happens to costs when output is raised to cope with the higher demand. A YED of 3.0 indicates that the ice cream is a superior (luxury) good. This is beneficial for the firm as its sales will rise significantly as income rises. The XED figure indicates that Hampton's ice cream and Park's ice cream are substitutes. If Park PLC raises the price of its ice cream, Hampton will benefit. Hampton will, however, have to monitor Park's prices carefully since if Park reduces its price by ten per cent, for instance, demand for Hampton's ice cream will fall by six per cent.

PART 2/AS

Market failure and government intervention

Market failure and government intervention – an overview

Market failure is a generic term that is used to describe market outcomes which might not be economically and socially desirable. If markets were totally unregulated, it is likely that a range of products and services would be provided which some might regard as undesirable, while others would not be produced at all. Essentially, market-based systems rely upon the profit motive to allocate resources. This Unit shows that, under optimum conditions, this allocation of resources is both allocatively and productively efficient. The trouble is that that markets are social constructions; in other words they are created by society and as such they are likely to be imperfect and not match up to the theoretical model of the price mechanism. This Unit will help you understand the interface between theory and reality. Finally, consideration is given to cost benefit analysis and the pros and cons of different forms of market intervention.

There are different ways of categorising market failure and this Unit closely follows the approach adopted by the OCR specification. Probably the most significant potential reason for market failure is when they fail to behave competitively. In other words, once companies have monopoly power they are in a position to dictate what customers get rather than the other way round. Markets also fail when there are third party effects that are not picked up by the price mechanism. The obvious example is when a factory uses clear water for cooling or cleaning and discharges it as dirty and lifeless with an immediate effect on all those who live downstream of the factory. This is called a negative externality. The opposite can occur when there are beneficial third party effects. An efficient health service benefits far more than those who are treated and would be classed as a positive externality.

Other sources of market failure can occur when the participants, the buyers and the sellers, lack crucial information which prevents them from taking informed and rational decisions. We can probably all recognize when we, as consumers, are manipulated by advertising and confused or even ignorant of the relative merits of competing goods.

Finally, markets may work effectively but give rise to outcomes which are not desirable. Widely fluctuating prices may not be acceptable especially as the price that is paid for a particular good or service also represents someone else's income.

As economists and governments generally agree that markets might fail, they also agree that it might be appropriate to try to fix failing markets. Agreement probably ends there, as there is little consensus politically or economically as to the best ways of remedying market failure. Most remedies involve government intervention of some sort. These include government provision, direct controls, the use of taxes and subsidies and efforts to break up monopolies and promote competition.

Because markets do not recognise national boundaries, market failure can be regarded as a global issue requiring global solutions. These can involve international agreement between governments. This is not always easy to achieve.

Remedying market failure is not easy, and government intervention often fails or has unintended consequences. These failing are dealt with in the final section of this Unit on government failure.

Preparing for the examination

The examination for this Unit is very similar to that for Unit 1. You have one hour to answer a number of questions based on a short case study.

Contribution to final grade

Unit 2 contributes 30 per cent to your final AS mark, and if you carry on for a second year, 15 per cent of your total A level grade A2. It pays to get as high a mark as you can as this can ease the pressure in the second year when you might be working really hard to get the grades demanded by universities or potential employers.

Exam tactics

If you just study for this Unit, a typical student will take around twelve weeks to reach the required standard. Although you should practise developing your examination techniques from the start, you need a solid grounding in the underpinning theory and concepts before you are fully ready to prepare for the Unit tests. Do not rush into exam preparation. When you have worked through Sections 1 to 17 of this Unit, you might need to brush up on your understanding of Unit 1. This may involve reading it all again. The spider diagram on page 56 might provide another means of refreshing your understanding. Do the same for Unit 2, trying to get the whole picture of what is involved. Only when you feel that your understanding is secure should you tackle the three revision sections at the end of this Unit (Sections 2.15, 2.16 and 2.17).

Research task

Make sure your file of stories about contemporary economic events includes up-to-the date examples of externalities. Big environmental issues are usually well covered in all newspapers but try digging a little deeper by reading more academic articles. There is lots of stuff on the Internet about monopoly control.

Exam hint

Introductions are useful. When you read them first time you may not understand everything. Do not worry. Work through the Units and then read through the introduction a second time. If it still does not make sense you have a problem and should go and speak to your teacher or lecturer.

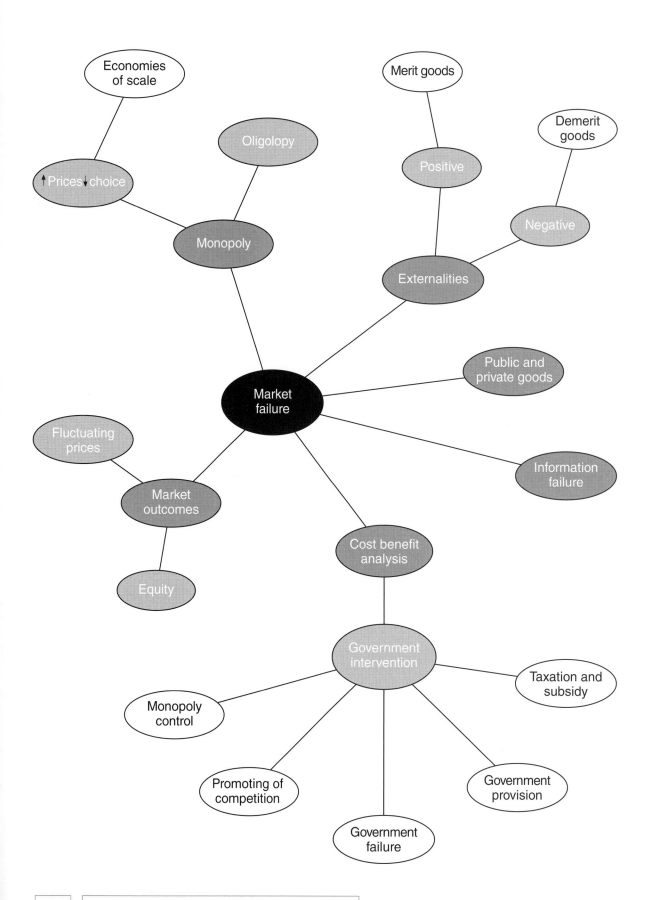

Efficiency

2.1

n order to judge how well competitive markets work, economists use a number of measures of efficiency.

These are:

- Productive
- Allocative
- Pareto.

Key concept

Productive efficiency refers to producing goods and services at the lowest possible cost.

Productive efficiency

This is complicated and will repay careful reading. In the price mechanism it is assumed that just as there are many consumers, there are many producers who will be forced by market pressures to produce outputs at which costs of production are minimised. The reasons for this have been implicit in how competitive markets have been described earlier and can be represented as follows:

Thinking like an economist

How accurately does the free market model describe how our economy actually works? Are consumers sovereign? Are firms compelled to be as efficient as possible?

Assume one firm operating in one industry discovers a new, more efficient way of making what it produces.

↓

Its costs of production will fall.

↓

If no other variables change, this firm will now earn additional profits.

↓

If these profits exceed those regarded as normal, competitors will investigate and copy the new production technique.

↓

Other firms will enter the industry.

↓

Output in the industry will rise.

↓

Rising output (supply) will cause the price of the product to fall.

↓

Falling prices will reduce the revenue earned by the original firm.

↓

Profits in that firm will fall.

↓

Alternatively, if the demand for the industry's product or service falls: Reduced demand leads to a fall in price.

↓

Falling prices will reduce revenues for some firms below what is considered acceptable.

↓

Some firms in the industry will cut output.

↓

The least efficient firms will cease production and effectively leave the industry.

↓

Those firms which remain will receive greater market share/rising demand for their products.

↓

Revenues will rise.

↓

Profits will return to the normal profit level.

In short, the forces of competition are such that any tendency by one firm to be more efficient and to cut costs will be copied by competitors, and any contraction in demand will be accompanied by the disappearance of the least efficient producers. This is a continuing process which should result in ever growing efficiencies in those markets which are truly competitive.

Allocative efficiency

This term is used to show that if the price mechanism were to work in the way that has been described, the consumer would be 'king' or 'queen' of the whole process. It is argued that changes in consumer preferences will eventually determine which of the earth's scarce resources will be used and to what end. Thus if customers want to consume more organic products, they will be prepared to pay more for them than non-organics, retailers will respond by stocking more organics, and these changes will ripple through the price mechanism resulting in some farmers switching to organic methods. At the same time, demand will fall for pesticides and non-organic fertilisers and other products associated with non-organic production methods.

The principle of allocative efficiency relates to the central questions which economics is meant to answer. What gets produced? How is it produced? And who gets what is produced? If the price mechanism is allowed to work freely, it is argued that we actually end up using resources to reflect customer preferences exactly. Changes in these will be reflected by changes in demand and it is argued that competition between firms ensures that customer preferences are satisfied.

Pareto efficiency

A third related measure of efficiency is associated with the Italian social scientist Vilfredo Pareto. He argued that perfect competition should ensure that not only will goods be produced most cheaply in accordance with customer preferences, but also that if all markets were perfectly competitive, it would be impossible to make one member of society better off without making another worse off. This can be illustrated by reference to production possibility curves as introduced in Section 1.4, and shown in Figure 1. In this example, it is assumed that two goods, cars and cattle, can be produced. Any point inside the production possibility curve is inefficient, as it is possible to increase the production of both products without making anyone worse off, simply by moving outwards closer to the curve. This curve shows the highest possible levels of production.

Key concepts

Remember allocative efficiency refers to who gets what. An economy would be allocatively efficient if everybody received exactly those goods and services for which they were prepared to pay the market price.

Quick check

Distinguish between productive and allocative efficiency.

Market failure

2.2

In the first Unit you were introduced to a simple model of how markets work and how they could achieve desirable outcomes. In the previous section, different types of efficiency were presented which could be provided if perfect competition were in operation. This section provides an introduction to what economists have come to call 'market failure'.

Recap on the advantages of the price mechanism

One of the most famous advocates of the price mechanism was Adam Smith. In his book *The Wealth of Nations*, published in 1776, Adam Smith argued that if all members of society pursued what they perceived to be their selfish interest then:

> 'The uniform, constant and uninterrupted effort of every man to better his condition, the principle from which public and national, as well as private opulence is originally derived, is frequently powerful enough to maintain the natural progress of things toward improvement, in spite both of the extravagance of government, and of the greatest errors of administration.'

In other words, society would improve if its individual members were left to their own devices. They would be driven, as if by instinct, to make profits from their activities. Those who were most successful would make the greatest profit. Those who were less successful would fail. Smith argued that an 'invisible hand' linked producers to consumers and to society as a whole. That invisible hand would help ensure that what is actually produced is what people want. In other words, allocative efficiency would be achieved. Competition should also ensure that goods and services are produced at the lowest possible unit cost i.e. it would achieve productive efficiency.

A number of factors might prevent these desirable outcomes. They can be considered under the following headings:

- Externalities
- Monopoly
- Merit and de-merit goods
- Public goods

Externalities

All economic transactions are likely to have 'third party' effects. The benefits and problems associated with producing and consuming particular goods and services are not necessarily confined to the producer and consumer. Thus, improvements to parking facilities might not only benefit motorists and nearby store-owners but also, if congestion is reduced, other transport users and people living in the area. Conversely, a producer who can cut costs by dumping waste products may inflict costs on innocent third

Figure 1: Adam Smith

Research task

Who was Adam Smith? What did he argue? Why is he so important?

Hot potato

Would we all be better off if we relied on the price mechanism to supply education?

parties. The market-based price mechanism focuses on the direct effects on producers and consumers and is likely to ignore external effects. These externalities may be very significant.

Monopolies

Adam Smith identified the dangers of monopoly. He argued that:

'A monopoly granted either to an individual or to a trading company has the same effect as a secret in trade or manufactures. The monopolists, by keeping the market constantly under-stocked, by never fully supplying the effectual demand, sell their commodities much above the natural price, and raise their emoluments, whether they consist in wages or profit, greatly above their natural rate.'

In other words, a monopolist would produce less and more expensively than would be the case if there were a number of producers competing against each other.

Merit and demerit goods

All societies make judgements as to which products and services are desirable or undesirable. If markets were left to themselves these 'social valuations' might be ignored. Thus, it could be argued that sales of illegal drugs would increase if their supply were left to the market. Conversely, as there is little profit in providing health care to the poor, their needs might be ignored. Goods and services such as these which a society may judge to be 'good' or 'bad' are classified as merit and demerit goods.

Public goods

Whilst merit goods will be under provided if left to market forces, public goods may not be supplied at all. This is because it is difficult to identify who benefits from public goods and to stop those who do not directly pay for them from being able to consume them. They are non-excludable. It would, for instance, be very difficult to charge people directly for the benefit they receive from street lighting. In addition the benefit people gain from the light provided would not be reduced by more people walking down the road. They are non-rival.

Negative externalities

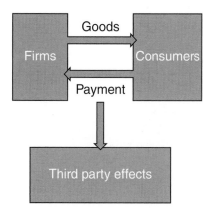

Figure 1: Third party effects

xternalities are another concept that is used to analyse possible market failure. They are defined by economists as third party effects of any transaction between a consumer and a firm. Externalities can either be positive or negative. It can be argued that if markets are left to themselves, too many goods and services will be produced which have harmful third party effects and too few goods and services will be produced which have beneficial third party effects.

The potential existence of externalities is illustrated in Figure 1.

Negative externalities

A whole range of industrial and commercial activities can give rise to negative externalities.

Pollution of various kinds is an obvious example. Some businesses may have scant regard to the effects of their activities on others. Clear and pure water might be used to cool and clean and wash, only to be returned to rivers and water courses as pollution. Forests are exploited for their timber giving rise to erosion, floods, infertility and even global warming. Anti-social behaviour by consumers of alcohol and tobacco can affect the well-being and health of 'innocent' third parties. These externalities are not just effects which are socially undesirable, they also represent additional costs for other members of society.

Negative externalities and market failure

Negative externalities are significant to economic arguments about the strengths and weaknesses of the market system because their existence places additional costs on other members of society. Thus, there are links between smoking tobacco and a range of serious diseases. Treatment of patients with these diseases means that the National Health Service and private health insurance companies are faced with additional expenditure. If markets operate freely and effectively, the price that a customer pays for a product or service should represent the actual costs involved in the production of that product or service. If production generates additional costs for other members of society, the market system can be said to have failed. This can be shown graphically. In Figure 2, S represents the costs of production faced by the producer of a good. These are known as private costs. S1 includes negative externalities and, therefore, represents the social costs which the production of this product creates. This is known as the marginal social cost and represents the full costs to society of producing the product or service.

If there were no government or other intervention, equilibrium would be reached at *a* and P would be the price charged for the product and Q would be the amount sold. However, if it were possible to calculate the external

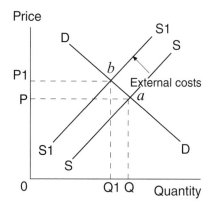

Figure 2: Negative externalities

Key concept

Negative externalities occur when social costs exceed private costs.

costs, if these were to be added to the private costs, and if consumers were required to pay the full social cost of production, a different equilibrium would prevail at b, giving a higher price of P1 and reduced sales of Q1. In other words, a freely operating market would lead to lower prices and higher outputs of goods which have harmful environmental and/or social consequences.

Producer and consumer surplus

The impact of negative externalities on producer and consumer surplus can be modelled using the diagrammatic approach outlined in Section 1.5. In Figure 3 it is clear that taking account of negative externalities results in a higher price and lower output. Comparison of the shaded areas shows that consumer surplus is reduced.

Summary

Negative externalities exist when the marginal social cost of production exceeds the private costs of production. If no account is taken of their existence, the price mechanism would result in the underpricing of such goods or services leading to higher levels of production than would be the case if the private costs reflected the full cost to society. Failure to take account of negative externalities would also mean that some members of society are faced with paying costs which they have not incurred.

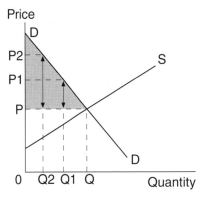

Figure 3: Consumer surplus

Positive externalities

Unintended external effects do not automatically lead to greater costs for society as a whole. Some economic transactions generate beneficial third party effects. Economists call these positive externalities. It can be argued that the price mechanism is likely to under-produce goods and services which generate positive externalities.

Positive externalities

Positive externalities are slightly more difficult to identify than their negative counterparts. They are often associated with government or charitable interventions in the market. Thus, in the mid-nineteenth century local government in many British cities invested in the provision of clean piped water. This had an obvious direct benefit to those who were given access to safe water supplies but also contributed to better standards of health, less illness and disease, and greater productivity. In this way employers and society in general benefited. Similarly, improvements to education and training may benefit society as a whole as well as those individuals who have directly benefited from the improvements.

More modern examples would include the benefits to urban regeneration that follow if a significant national retailer decides to open new branch in a particular city or suburb. Major stores like Boots or Tesco attract customers not just for themselves but also for other nearby retailers. Such increases in consumer spending will have other beneficial knock-on effects.

The existence of positive externalities can also be illustrated graphically. In Figure 1, D represents the demand from individuals i.e. the private benefits gained from purchasing a particular good or service and S represents the costs of providing that good or service. The market equilibrium is given at *a* with a price of P and sales of Q. If, however, it were possible to quantify the positive externalities associated with the provision of this good or service, these could be represented by D1, showing the full marginal social benefits that would benefit society as a whole. If these additional benefits were to be taken into account, the equilibrium would be at *b* with Q1 outputs selling for P1. In other words, more would be produced. If this were to apply, freely operating markets could be said to fail because less would be produced of socially useful goods.

The growth of particular industries in specific areas can create external economies of scale which will themselves contribute to positive externalities. Thus, the growth of financial services in the Bristol area attracts more supporting businesses, such as those involved in software production, and the concentration of a range of related businesses in a given area is likely to benefit all those involved.

Key concept

Positive externalities occur when social benefits exceed private benefits.

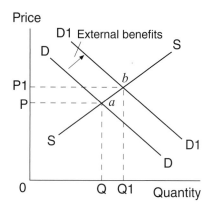

Figure 1: Positive externalities

Research task

Undertake an investigation of a market in which you consider there are significant positive externalities. How would you go about identifying and putting a price on the possible social benefits?

Summary

Positive externalities exist when the marginal social benefits of production exceed the private benefits. If no account is taken of their existence, the price mechanism would result in the over-pricing of such goods or services leading to lower levels of production than would be the case if the private benefits reflected the full benefits to society. Failure to take account of positive externalities would also mean that some members of society are gaining benefits for which they have not paid.

Quick check

Work in groups to brainstorm those economic activities which generate positive externalities. Choose three which your group consider the most beneficial to third parties.

Discuss as a class, and note if a consensus is reached or whether differences persist.

Market dominance 2.5

Introduction

The most extreme form of market dominance is monopoly by which one organisation is the sole producer or provider of a good or service. It is obvious that if an industry is made up of only one company, the monopoly concerned can exert tremendous power over that market. Often an industry is dominated by a small number of large firms. This form of dominance is called oligopoly, as illustrated in Section 1.21. In practice, a number of factors may give some firms more dominance than others. In particular there may be barriers to the entry and exit of firms from an industry. These include ownership and control of raw materials; patents; economies of scale; anti-competitive behaviour.

Ownership and control

If businesses are going to move freely in and out of industries in response to market pressures then they need access to the resources or factors required for production. If the ownership and control of raw materials is confined to a few companies, they can exert considerable control over that industry. Thus the De Beers group own a significant number of diamond mines and this has given them the means by which they can regulate the supply of diamonds and limit the impact of competitive behaviour. Similarly, oil reserves tend to be owned or controlled by a relatively small group of companies. This gives Exxon, Shell and the like great control of a series of oil-based industries.

Patents

Patents are issued by governments in order to help businesses enjoy the benefits from having invested in and developed new products. They simply mean that it is against the law for other firms to produce the same products. In most countries inventors of new products or processes can apply for patent status which can last for anything up to 25 years. It is said that Xerox took out hundreds of patents covering different working parts of their photocopiers to ensure that their monopoly lasted as long as possible.

Research task

Survey prices of TVs in local stores. What evidence does this reveal of competition in this particular market?

Economies of scale

The concept of economies of scale was introduced in Section 1.19. Put very simply, larger firms can often produce goods more cheaply. This can give larger companies a considerable competitive advantage compared with smaller producers. This particularly applies when large investments in expensive machinery and systems are required. Thus, it is very hard for independent film or music companies to compete with large companies like Sony and EMI.

Anti-competitive behaviour

Adam Smith described an idealised world in which competition ensured that the 'selfish' behaviour of individual firms ensured that everyone benefited. In reality, companies indulge in a range of behaviour designed to limit competition. This can range from legal activities associated with building up strong brand images to illegal price fixing and even strong-arm tactics. Firms with monopoly power can charge higher prices, incur higher costs, and restrict customer choice.

Higher prices

If a company has monopoly power, it will have the freedom to set its own prices. For example, prices are likely to be higher from a petrol station that has no local competitors. We pay more for branded goods than we do for non-branded goods. On the other hand, if there is lots of competition, individual companies will be strongly influenced by the prices charged by other businesses. Economists describe companies who have monopolistic power as price makers. If they know that the demand for their product is relatively inelastic they can boost revenue by putting up prices. In other words, a monopolist provides goods or services for which there are few close substitutes.

Another aspect of market power is that a monopolist can also charge different sets of customers different prices for the same product. Thus, a Mazda 323 is nearly £5,000 more expensive in the UK than in the rest of Europe. This particular form of monopoly power is called price discrimination and companies have used this technique to boost profits by charging higher prices to those with more inelastic demands and lower prices to those whose demand is relatively more elastic.

Higher costs

Moreover, a monopolist will have less incentive to keep costs low. Price makers can pass on additional costs to their customers. This lack of incentive to keep costs to their minimum is called 'x' inefficiency.

Restricted choice

Monopolies can exploit the dependence of their customers on their products by restricting choice. Henry Ford famously said that customers could buy a Model T Ford in any colour as long as it was black. Modern examples include limiting the number of retailers allowed to sell particular products.

Thinking like an economist

When you analyse a market ask yourself where you would place it on the following continuum:

Pure monopoly ——— Pure competition

Most markets will fall somewhere in the middle between these two extremes.

> **Puzzler**
>
> Who provides the greatest choice on television: BBC or ITV?

Private and public goods

2.6

arkets might be considered to fail if they result in the over- or under-production of certain types of goods or if they contribute to greater inequalities in society. The market system might lead to under-production of public goods as distinct from private goods.

Private goods

So far in this book, mention has been made of what have loosely been called goods and services, like computers and cars and sporting events. Technically speaking, these should be classified as private goods as they have two characteristics:

- rivalry
- exclusion.

Goods become private goods if there is competition or rivalry for their consumption. If you buy a moped or scooter you prevent someone else from enjoying the benefits of being transported by your Vespa or Honda. In theory, your purchase will prevent someone else from owning that particular vehicle. The principle of exclusion is similar in that once that good has been provided it is possible to exclude someone else from using it, unless they come to a special arrangement to do so. This will probably involve payment and in the case of the scooter, meeting legal requirements such as licensing and insurance.

Public goods

Economists have identified a range of goods to which these principles of rivalry and exclusion do not apply. Thus, there is also the principle of non-rivalry which means that if one person consumes a good or service others are not prevented from doing the same. Thus, one person enjoying Snowdonia will not stop someone else having a similar experience. Secondly, public goods are non-excludable, a related concept that means than once a public good is provided to one person it is not possible to stop others from enjoying it.

Public goods are likely to be under-provided by a free market system. These are products or services for which it is difficult to identify who benefits most. In a free market those who derive the greatest satisfaction from the consumption of a good or service are thought likely to be prepared to pay the most. In this way resources are rationed out to those who believe they will benefit most. In some cases it is impossible to predict who actually benefits from the production of particular goods and services. For example, it is hard to predict who needs the police and when, and it would be hard to work out a means by which consumers of police services would actually pay for the resources used for their benefit. Those who can consume a good or service paid for by others and without paying themselves are called 'free riders'.

Hot potato

Should we regard public transport as a public or merit good?

Research task

What would be the economic implications of leaving the provision of police to market forces?

Quasi public goods

Just to make things more complicated, economists have identified a third group of goods to which one of the principles of non-rivalry or non-excludability applies but not the other. Thus, one store may pay for CCTV security and others may benefit from lower levels of crime in that particular area. If goods fall into this category they might be provided by freely operating markets, or the state, or a combination of the two.

Government intervention

As has been implied in this section the existence of public goods is used as a justification for government or others to intervene in the price mechanism. It is just so hard to work out who benefits and, therefore, who pays. Lighthouses are a good example of a public good and they were first built by public subscription. The horrific consequences of shipwrecks made it possible in the eighteenth century for organisations such as Trinity House to raise sufficient funds from public donations to build lighthouses like the famous Bishop's Rock.

Quick check ✓

Decide whether the following are defined as public, private or quasi public goods:
Ambulance services; health care services; sports facilities.

Merit/demerit goods and imperfect information

Freely operating markets can also lead to market failure for other reasons. These include under-production of merit goods, over-production of demerit goods, and information failures.

Merit goods

The market system may lead to the under-production of particular goods or services. This might be something which society considers undesirable, or it might apply if production or provision were to create large positive externalities. Prior to 1947 health services in the UK were provided by a free market. Those needing a doctor had to pay and poor people often suffered ill health because of this financial barrier. As well as arguments about creating a fairer society, it was considered that the effects of ill health and lack of medical attention placed additional costs on society. Everyone would potentially benefit from a healthier work force. The Labour Government elected in 1945 was committed to the notion of a health service free at the point of use. Economists call this type of provision of something that is socially desirable a merit good. Other merit goods include the provision of library services, job centres, state education, and health and recreational services.

Demerit goods

Left to its own devices a free market could lead to the production of goods and services which a society might judge to be socially harmful. Consideration has already been given to circumstances in which companies will over-produce if private costs are far less than social costs, creating negative externalities. A free market system might also produce goods and services which society believes to be harmful and various measures are taken by governments to reduce the consumption of commodities such as alcohol and tobacco. The provision of other goods and services such as cannabis, prostitution and offensive weapons is banned. Goods which are judged to be harmful to society are called demerit goods.

Imperfect knowledge

If freely operating markets are going to lead to optimum allocation of resources, all consumers and producers need to be as well informed as possible about the markets in which they are involved. It may be unrealistic to assume perfect knowledge but in reality, knowledge and information may be very unevenly distributed. This concept is called asymmetric information, and economists have identified different examples of this possible imbalance. One of the clearest examples can be drawn from the work of the American economist, George Akerlof, who analysed the relationship between the buyer and seller of used cars. He argued that the potential buyer would have very little real understanding of the real quality of second-hand cars on sale whereas the seller would be far better informed. The potential transaction between the buyer and the seller would, Akerlof argued, be based on asymmetric information.

This principle can be applied to many different contexts, usually involving the superior knowledge of sellers at the expense of the ignorance of customers, and has been further developed in terms of the 'principal agent problem'. We do not always take economic decisions independently and often rely on the expertise of others. The person taking the decision is called the principal and the adviser is the agent. Thus, sorting out pension plans is difficult and it is logical to seek help from a financial adviser. This advisor or agent may not necessarily be acting in the best interests of the principal. In recent years in the UK misleading advice has been given by financial advisors because they have been paid incentives by particular companies to sell particular pension products. In this case there is asymmetric information between principal and agent

The effect of this factor is that a free market economy may allocate resources according to the preferences of those with most knowledge, or to the agent rather than the principal. For this reason markets could be said to fail.

Government intervention

Dealing with the possible under-provision of merit goods is relatively straightforward. Governments can use taxation to ensure that services such as education and health care are provided free at the point of use. In the mid-nineteenth century local government took on the responsibility for providing clean water and sewage systems. Government intervention increased during the two World Wars and accelerated in the 1940s and 50s, especially with programmes of road and council house building. In more recent years there has been vigorous political debate as to the effectiveness of such intervention. Conservative governments in the 1980s tried to reduce the role of the state, and the current government favours partnerships between the public and private sectors in the provision of health and some aspects of educational provision.

Information failure can be tackled by education, public awareness campaigns and a variety of bodies such as the Consumers' Association and Health Council.

Hot potato

Ask adults about pensions and see what happens.

Key concepts

Asymmetric information applies to unequal access to information between two or more parties in an economic relationship.
The principal agent problem arises because in an increasingly complex world we rely on others to help us make economic decisions.

Quick check ✓

What can be done to deal with the problem of asymmetric information?

Puzzler

It pays to deal with the causes of crime rather than its consequences.

Other sources of market failure

2.8

Freely operating marketing might not produce socially desirable or acceptable outcomes for other reasons. These include:

- Factor immobility
- Inequalities in the distribution of income.

Factor immobility

If markets are going to work freely to allocate resources most efficiently to those whose demand is greater, then all markets should respond to the push and pull of the price mechanism. If demand for a particular good increases, the good's price should rise and thus profits for producers should increase. Those producers will increase their demand for factors of production, and will offer higher wages for labour, higher rents for land, higher rates of interest for investment funds and greater profits to entrepreneurs. The increase in factor prices should act as a signal for the some of the owners of factors to 'sell to the highest bidder', and factors of production should move to those uses for which the demand is greatest. But will they?

This analysis assumes that factors move to the use wherever the return is highest. It is assumed that the profit motive outweighs other considerations. However, there is considerable evidence that humans do not behave solely in response to greater profitability. In practise it is often hard for workers to switch jobs or their work locations. Land and capital can be tied into particular uses. Managers and risk takers are not only motivated by salary increases. For these reasons factors may be slow to move between alternative uses and this means that freely operating markets rarely result in resources being used to produce those goods and services which are most in demand at a given moment.

Causes of factor immobility

Different explanations of immobility apply to each of the factors:

- land
- labour
- capital
- enterprise

Land

In some ways land can be treated as totally immobile. Although it is possible to think of imaginative ways in which more of the earth's crust can be used in human activity we are pretty much stuck with what we have got. However, land and the resources contained within it can be switched between different uses. Such mobility is likely to be constrained by planning and zoning laws and other government regulations governing the extraction of minerals and fuels.

Labour

Economists identify two forms of labour immobility:

- occupational
- geographical

Occupational mobility refers to the ease with which it is possible for people to switch jobs. This is usually much easier between similar jobs and those requiring general skills. Occupational mobility in and out of more specialist roles is much more limited. It is much harder for children of working-class parents to get professional jobs than it is for those whose parents are doctors, lawyers and the like.

Geographical mobility applies to the degree to which people are prepared to move away from low relative wage areas like Cornwall to high relative wage areas such as London and the South-east. Many factors limit the willingness of workers to move about the country, some of which are financial while others are social.

Capital

Capital in the sense of fixed assets of productive capacity can be completely immobile in the case of large, specific plant like power stations, or almost perfectly mobile in the case of portable machine tools.

Enterprise

The same considerations that apply to labour also apply to enterprise. However, an added dimension is related to the willingness to take risks. Not all people are equally disposed to the uncertainties that may be associated with truly entrepreneurial activity.

Income inequalities

Consumers need income to enter and take part in market transactions. Income is, in virtually every economy, unevenly distributed. Those with the most have a greater say in how resources are distributed. Freely operating markets will not allocate resources to those who cannot afford to pay the market price. This may create conditions which are socially unacceptable. Some would argue that there are direct links between poverty and crime and it follows that if freely operating markets fail to deal with poverty, society as a whole will be faced with enormous external or additional costs.

Key concepts

Geographic mobility refers to the preparedness of people to move about the country in responses to changes in labour markets.
Occupational mobility relates to movement between different jobs.

Hot potato

Do you agree with the contention that it is a good idea to make labour more mobile?

Quick check

What can be done to make land more mobile?

Cost benefit analysis

Introduction

Economists have long recognised the existence of externalities and have developed a range of statistical techniques in an effort to quantify both negative and positive externalities. This approach is called cost benefit analysis and involves attempting to give monetary values to externalities, and other forms of market failure.

Cost benefit analysis and market failure

Cost benefit analysis can be applied to new investments and also to existing markets. For example, there has been a long-running enquiry into the building of a new terminal at Heathrow airport. Supporters claim that it will aid economic growth not just of those directly concerned but also of firms and employees dependent upon the continued growth and expansion of Heathrow. Opponents to the development include a range of interested parties who have argued that noise pollution, congestion and the like will impose additional costs on the local community. As part of the process to decide whether or not permission should be given for this new development, cost benefit analysis has been undertaken. In this case, the purpose was to identify both the positive and negative externalities. A public enquiry was set up designed to reveal the full costs to society i.e. social cost of the new development and the full benefits i.e. social benefit.

The cost benefit process

Undertaking this calculation involves the following stages:
1. Identification and quantification of all private costs.
2. Identification and quantification of all external costs.
3. Calculation of social cost – this is the private and external costs added together.
4. Identification and quantification of all private benefits.
5. Identification and quantification of all external benefits.
6. Calculation of social benefit – this is the private and external benefits added together.

When all this has been done it is possible to make a direct comparison between the social cost of a project and the social benefit. In theory, if the social benefit exceeds the social cost, society as a whole would benefit from the development, and if this relationship were reversed, society would be economically worse off.

Problems with cost benefit

The challenge to those undertaking cost benefit analysis is to put a financial valuation on external costs and benefits. For example, it is difficult to

Key concepts

Social cost refers to both the private costs and negative externalities attributed to a particular use of economic resources.
Social benefit is the private benefits and positive externalities attributable to a particular use of economic resources.

quantify the monetary value of noise pollution. One approach might be to calculate the extent to which house prices and/or rents in the surrounding area might be affected, while another might involve working out the costs of additional soundproofing. Assessing the impact on environmental factors such as the disturbance to particular plants or animals is even more problematical. Similarly, valuing indirect benefits such as those which might accrue to local businesses requires a mixture of approximations, forecasts and guesswork.

Calculation problems are especially difficult when it comes to dealing with the costs faced by people. Thus, what would be the value of building a road that cuts 5 minutes off the typical journey time of a thousand road users per week? If improvements to road safety demonstrate that fewer accidents will occur, it is reasonably easy to put a value to the lower demand for hospital and medical care, but what value should be given to a saved limb, or even a saved life?

These practical difficulties are often made harder as cost benefit analysis is often used to assess the economic impact of controversial proposals. This was the case with the Heathrow extension mentioned above in which rival stakeholders challenged the data that each side and the inspector were using.

Using cost benefit analysis

Cost benefit analysis is used in a number of ways. These include public subsidy, regulation, and planning.

- Subsidy: If cost benefit analysis demonstrates that there will be greater social benefit than social cost, i.e. there are positive externalities, then this analysis might be used to justify government subsidy to ensure that resources are used in such a way as to maximise public welfare.
- Regulation: Similarly, if cost benefit analysis shows that negative externalities outweigh positive ones, a rationale is provided for government intervention to limit or control such outputs. This could involve direct controls, pollution taxes or the introduction of tradable permits.
- Planning: As in the case of the expansion at Heathrow, cost benefit analysis can be used to try to resolve the competing claims of different stakeholders. It can provide a more rational way of resolving controversial issues. It also provides government bodies such as the National Health Service and the Department of Environment with a means of deciding which investments in the public sector should be selected and which rejected.

Government intervention: negative externalities and demerit goods

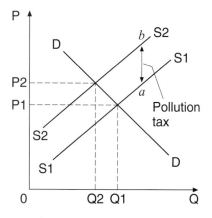

Figure 1: Taxing negative externalities

Introduction

The possible existence of market failure provides governments with a reason to intervene in the free working of markets. In reality there are very few markets in which governments do not intervene.

Negative externalities

If governments wish to prevent a negative externality such as pollution, or limit the consumption of a demerit good like tobacco, they can use:

- price mechanism
- direct controls
- persuasion
- tradable permits.

There are advantages and disadvantages to each of these approaches. One of the difficult tasks for governments (and economists) is anticipating the possible effects, intended and unintended, of particular actions.

Price mechanism

This approach can be illustrated diagrammatically as shown in Figure 1.

If a government is able to accurately calculate the external costs attributed to a polluting company, they could introduce a tax equal to the vertical distance $a-b$. This would force consumers of this product to pay a price which represented the full costs to society of its production. Output would be reduced to Q2 and the government would actually use the price mechanism to cure market failure.

One advantage of this approach is that if it worked, it would strengthen market-based solutions. If the right price were chosen it would be possible to ensure that customers actually paid for the true value of the resources used in the supply of the good or service. However, if this approach is applied to limiting traffic congestion in cities there could be considerable political opposition.

Direct controls

Governments can choose to pass laws and use the existing legislative framework in an attempt to control and constrain the behaviour of firms and industries which generate negative externalities. Thus, in the UK emissions of potentially dangerous chemicals are controlled by various regulations. Advertising by the tobacco industry is limited and car safety is promoted by annual car tests.

The difficulty with rules or controls is that they can be broken and that a regulatory framework is required to ensure that this does not happen. Direct controls are often applied to demerit goods. Do they work to stop young people consuming alcohol?

Persuasion

Some consider that changing customer and producer behaviour to ensure that greater account is taken of externalities is so complex and difficult that it is more effective in the long term to change the attitudes of those who demand and those who supply products and services which create negative externalities. Thus the UK government partially funds the Health Education Council whose role includes that of encouraging people to eat healthier diets. If these approaches are successful their effects will be fed through the market system. It is possible to argue that the demand for organic produce is a result of greater awareness of the importance of a healthy diet.

Pollution permits

Another market-based means of limiting some negative externalities involves the government giving or selling permits to polluters to emit a certain amount of waste. These permits can then be bought and sold. A company successful in cutting its pollution could sell its permit to one that was less successful. The company producing the lower emissions would gain and the heavier polluter would be forced to pay. By setting an overall limit on levels of pollution, governments could reduce this negative externality, but it would be left to market forces to determine where emissions would be reduced.

There is a big debate amongst economists as to whether or not such policies work as they may allow very profitable and powerful businesses to avoid creating negative externalities.

Research task

Undertake an investigation of a market in which you consider there are significant negative externalities. Try to estimate the monetary value on such externalities. Suggest possible government intervention strategies to take account of the externalities you have identified.

Quick check

Rank in order of effectiveness different strategies that could be used to reduce sulphur emission from power stations.

Puzzler

How would you deal with the negative externalities of car use in London and other large cities?

Weblinks

Check out:
http://www.foe.co.uk
http://www.oneworld.org
http://www.wiredforhealth.gov.uk

2.11 Government regulation: positive externalities and merit goods

A s outlined earlier, the existence of positive externalities and merit goods might provide a justification for government intervention to make markets work more effectively. They can choose from a range of strategies similar to those used to deal with negative externalities. In this case the following strategies might be used:

- price mechanism
- persuasion
- direct intervention
- vouchers

Price mechanism

Figure 1 illustrates a possible approach.

The government can work through the price mechanism to try to boost production of a product or service which a free market would over-price and under-produce. It could estimate the value of the positive externality and it would need to pay a subsidy to producers equal to this amount – shown by the vertical distance *cd*. The outcome would be production rising to Q1 and price falling to P1.

If this approach is being using to boost the sales of a merit good, its success or failure will be partly dependent on the elasticity of demand for the good or service. If the demand is relatively elastic any reduction in its market price will result in a more than proportionate increase in demand. On the other hand, if demand is relatively inelastic a cut in price will have a smaller relative impact on sales, making such a policy less effective.

These two possible outcomes are shown in Figure 2.

Direct intervention

If a government decides that the production of a particular good or service has significant positive externalities which society would not benefit from if markets were left to operate freely, it may intervene directly to provide that product or service. Thus, in many market-based economies, governments use taxation to directly provide public goods such as education and health services. In these cases the price mechanism is not used. In the UK everyone is entitled to free medical care. In terms of demand and supply, this means that the price is fixed at zero and whatever is demanded at that price is supplied. Waiting for operations or doctors' appointments means that we are all probably aware of the problems that this causes. Treatments are not rationed by price but by time, and it is very hard for the government and its agencies to predict what demand will be for particular services.

Education and other services are also free to the end user and it is likely that UK society would not approve of a more market-based system that used prices to allocate health care or education, because that would probably result in no health treatments or education for significant parts of the population.

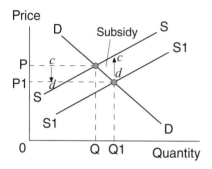

Figure 1: Using subsidies to account for positive externalities

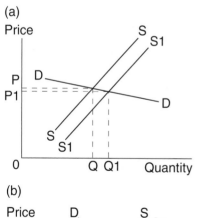

(a)

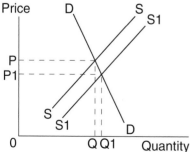

(b)

Figure 2: Price mechanism on (a) elastic demand (b) inelastic demand

Persuasion

It could be argued that much of any government's work is concerned with the function of persuasion in the form of advertising, political campaigning and the like. Changing attitudes to many aspects of our lives such as education, healthy living, sustainability, and preventive medicine can all be seen as attempts to change free market outcomes. These approaches, however, work through the price mechanism by boosting demand for particular services or treatments.

Vouchers

Both Conservative and Labour governments in the UK have experimented with the use of vouchers with the aim of producing greater consumption of merit goods or those with positive externalities. These vouchers are really an alternative form of money which can be given to those judged in need and used to purchase particular goods or services. They are, therefore, comparable to tradable permits as they are meant to use the price mechanism to produce socially desirable results. Thus, the government introduced 'Individual Learning Accounts' whereby adults were given a voucher up to the value of £150 to purchase additional education or training. This scheme succeeded in attracting a considerable number of adults back into education but was later found to have been used fraudulently. Some institutions providing training were able to claim that they had provided courses which had not taken place.

The Conservative party advocate the use of educational vouchers which parents could use to send their children to the school of their choice. The problem with schemes such as this is that the use of quasi-money can provide opportunities for fraud and misuse.

Summary

This section has been devoted to outlining strategies which governments could use to try to boost the consumption of those goods or services which are considered desirable, either because they benefit many people or because they are considered to be socially desirable. Each strategy has problems but it is unlikely that many people would consider that all resources should be allocated to those who can most afford to purchase them. Such arguments are partly about what we might call social justice, but as long as positive externalities exist, an economic case can be made for government intervention to ensure that the benefits of such production to society are maximised.

Research task

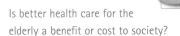

Undertake an investigation of a market in which you consider there are significant positive externalities. Try to estimate the monetary value of such externalities. Suggest possible government intervention strategies to take account of the externalities you have identified.

Hot potato

Is better health care for the elderly a benefit or cost to society?

Quick check ✓

Rank in order of effectiveness different strategies that could be used to encourage more adults to improve their literacy and numeracy skills.

2.12 Monopoly regulation

The UK and most other world governments pursue two strategies in order to reduce the possible distortions to the economy caused by the existence of monopoly power. These are:

- Limiting non-competitive behaviour by various constraints and controls
- Encouraging competitive behaviour by trying to create competitive conditions in markets

Limiting the power of monopolists

All western countries have policies which are intended to protect customers from exploitation by the exercise of monopoly power, and in the UK these are the responsibility of the Secretary of State for Trade and Industry. There is considerable legislation which is designed to protect the interests of consumers and possibly limit the power of monopolists. In law a monopoly exists if 25 per cent of sales in a given market are in the hands of one firm. There is a legal framework by which mergers which would result in the gain of a similar market share are investigated. These and other laws to protect customers are 'policed' by the Competition Commission which was created on 1 April 1999 by the government in an attempt to strengthen consumer protection. This government body took over from the Monopolies and Mergers Commission and is responsible for undertaking investigations.

Exam hint

You do not need to know the detail of all the legislation but you do need to understand that the government tries to establish what is in the public interest and doing this involves balancing the advantages and disadvantages of monopoly – just the sort of question examiners like to ask.

Research task

Check out http://www.competition-commission.gov.uk and find out which industries are currently under investigation. Why do you think these particular firms are under investigation?

The role of the Competition Commission

The Competition Commission's role is to investigate and report on matters referred to it relating to mergers, monopolies, anti-competitive practices, the regulation of utilities and the performance of public sector bodies. The Competition Commission cannot initiate its own inquiries. Most referrals are made by the Director General of Fair Trading (DGFT), the Secretary of State for Trade and Industry and the regulators of utilities. In almost all cases, the Competition Commission is asked to decide whether or not the matter referred was against the public interest.

The Competition Commission is a quasi-legal body which considers evidence prior to making judgements as to:

1. Whether or not a particular firm or group of firms has acted in such a way to violate any of the laws or regulations relating to that firm.
2. Whether a firm or group of firms has, for example, acted in an uncompetitive way, and whether their actions are against the public interest.

The notion of the public interest is a legal recognition that although firms may be judged to be uncompetitive there may be compensating benefits. Thus, the classic argument used by monopolists in defence of their activities is that, although competition is reduced, they are able to exploit economies of scale which lead to the supply of cheaper products than would otherwise be the case.

The Competition Commission reports directly to the Secretary of State for Trade and Industry and it is up to the government to decide on any action that needs to be taken. The Commission also has powers to investigate mergers, which would have the effect of creating monopoly power.

Such is the problem of monopoly that there is extensive legislation designed to limit this form of market failure. Table 1 should give you an idea of some of the legislative measures which have been passed.

Table 1 Laws and regulations to limit monopoly power

Activity	Legislation	Responsibility
Monopoly	Fair Trading Act 1973	Director General of Fair Trading, Secretary of State or certain Utility Regulators
Merger	Fair Trading Act 1973	Director General of Fair Trading, Secretary of State or certain Utility Regulators
Merger	Fair Trading Act 1973	Secretary of State
Newspaper merger	Fair Trading Act 1973	Secretary of State
Anti-competitive practices	Competition Act 1980	Director General of Fair Trading or certain Utility Regulators
Public sector	Competition Act 1980	Secretary of State
General references	Fair Trading Act 1973	Secretary of State
Restrictive labour practices	Fair Trading Act 1973	Secretary of State
Broadcasting	Broadcasting Act 1990	Independent Television Commission or holder of regional Channel 3 licence
Telecommunications	Telecommunications Act 1984	Director General of Telecommunications
Gas	Gas Act 1986 and 1995, Gas (N. Ireland) Order 1996	Director General of Gas Supply Director General of Gas Supply for Northern Ireland
Water	Water Industry Act 1991	Director General of Water Services
Electricity	Electricity Act 1989 Electricity (N. Ireland) Order 1992	Director General of Electricity Supply Director General of Electricity Supply for Northern Ireland
Railways	Railways Act 1993	Rail Regulator
Water merger	Water Industry Act 1991	Secretary of State
Airports	Airports Act 1986 Airports (N. Ireland) Order 1994	Civil Aviation Authority Civil Aviation Authority

Summary

Since the end of the Second World War, the UK Government has enacted legislation designed to limit the abuse of monopoly power especially in respect of protecting consumers from over-pricing, and a restricted choice of products. It has been argued that the existence of monopoly power tilts the balance of the economy away from meeting the interests of consumers to meeting those of large powerful companies. The existence of monopolies may, therefore, also make an economy less efficient both in terms of costs of production and in terms of customers being able to buy the goods and services which they demand.

Although the UK Government has extensive powers to investigate large firms, monopolistic behaviour is common in our economy. This may reflect the inadequacy of controls or the sheer impossibility of governments policing the activities of large firms.

Hot potato

Why is there so much legislation about monopoly?

2.13 Promoting competition

Another strategy followed by the UK and other governments to reduce the possible harmful effects of monopoly is to encourage greater competition. A variety of strategies have been followed which try to encourage the growth of new firms and the easier entry and exit of existing firms into particular industries. These include:

- Privatisation
- Regulation
- Creating internal markets
- Encouraging enterprise

Privatisation

In the early 1980s the Conservative government led by Margaret Thatcher tried to increase competition by transferring the ownership of businesses such as BP and ICL (Computers), from public to private ownership. In the mid-80s, Sealink, Jaguar, British Telecom and British Gas were also sold. At the end of the decade and during the early 1990s, more complicated sell-offs such as the water, electricity and rail industries were undertaken. The intention of these changes was to promote greater allocative and productive efficiency, and the success or failure of privatisation policies should be judged on the extent to which:

- prices have been cut
- output has been raised
- choice has been increased.

Governments believed that state ownership reduced the incentive for managers to be as efficient as possible, and the transfer to private ownership was meant to increase the importance that was attached to profitability. In addition to fitting in with the overall policy of encouraging more competition, privatisation created additional government revenue which has been estimated to exceed £60 billion.

Regulation

One of the problems of privatising industries, especially those that were said to be natural monopolies, was that all that was achieved was the replacement of a publicly owned monopoly with one owned privately. This was recognised by the Conservative governments in the 1980s and they tried to safeguard the public interest, by creating a series of regulators. These are independent bodies such as OFTEL (telecommunications), OFWAT (water) and OFGEM (Gas and electricity) with powers to regulate the actual behaviour of these industries by imposing pricing formulas, and insisting on customer service targets and levels of investment. The most important sanction available to most regulators is that regulating over-pricing. In many cases the freedom of newly privatised firms to raise prices is limited by formulae.

Internal markets

In the 1980s the Conservatives realised that the total privatisation of the public sector would be both politically unacceptable and very difficult to implement. They chose instead a variety of strategies designed to introduce or mimic market forces within industries and organisations.

The creation of internal markets involves the creation of individual cost centres and greater independence in financial decision-making. Thus in the NHS, budget-holding doctors were given the freedom to purchase medical care from those hospitals providing the most attractive service. Hospitals were expected to compete for business from GPs. This represented a radical change in established procedures which could have had devastating political effects had the government been prepared to allow failing hospitals to go 'bust' and close. The incoming Labour government abandoned these policies in 1997.

A version of an internal market still exists within the BBC in which independent programme makers have the freedom to employ camera operators, directors, costume designers etc. from within the BBC or from outside contractors.

Related developments include forcing local councils and other government agencies to put the provision of services out to tender. In other words, competition between the public and private sector is created.

Encouraging enterprise

UK governments have placed considerable emphasis on encouraging more people to start up their own businesses. They provide grants and advice to prospective small businesses and have tried to end practices which meant that the entry of new firms into the professions was limited. Thus, companies like Specsavers provide competition to traditional opticians.

Summary

Public policy associated with trying to prevent the abuses of monopolistic power has involved a mixture of 'carrot and stick' approaches. The previous section was devoted to legal controls on the ownership and structural aspects of large companies, and it implied that such policies had not been strictly or consistently applied in the UK, with few sanctions taken against firms whose actions might have been considered against the public interest. More recent developments have focused more on privatisation and the encouragement of greater enterprise and the growth of small businesses.

Thinking like an economist

Remember part of your job is to be objective. Do not rush to judgement as to the effectiveness of different government policies to counter market failure. Ask instead what evidence you require to evaluate the success or otherwise of government policies. Always be on the lookout for bias (even in this book!)

2.14 Government failure

Introduction

Government intervention to correct market failure does not always work. Policies might fail because of:

- Inadequate information
- Administrative failings
- Unintended effects
- Political conflicts

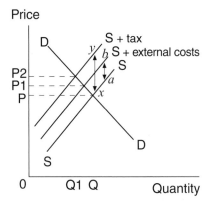

Figure 1: Effects of government over-taxing

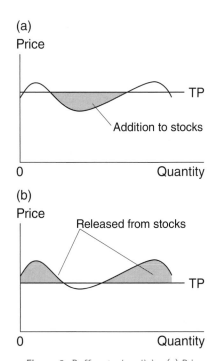

Figure 2: Buffer stock policies (a) Price is set too low (b) Price is set too high

Inadequate information

Many of the policy options outlined in the previous two sections rely on the government having excellent data and information on the markets in which they wish to intervene. Thus, if a government is using some form of tax to correct a negative externality, it has to be able to accurately estimate the external costs. If its estimates are too high then the market will be further distorted. This is shown in Figure 1 where the additional tax is set at *xy* rather than *ab*, with the result that consumers pay more than the product is worth in terms of resources used.

Similarly, failure to set target prices at the right level will result in the failure of buffer stock policies (see Figure 2).

In the first of these the target price (TP) is set too low resulting in ever bigger stocks, while in the second buffer stocks would soon run out.

Administrative failings

Governments and civil servants make mistakes. The imposition of any control or regulation provides scope for evasion. Policing emission controls is very difficult and in many cases the penalties for non-compliance are not very strong deterrents.

Changing the behaviour of people involves affecting complex and deep-rooted attitudes. Public relations campaigns do not always work in the ways in which they were intended. Some are far more successful than anticipated. Many depend upon the coincidence of other events. The problems that the British Government faced in 1999–2003 trying to gather more evidence as to the effectiveness of GM foods is an example of a government attempt to change attitudes that many believe failed.

Unintended effects

The growth of black markets is a good example of unintended effects, especially if the result of government policies is to create shortages of goods which are in demand. Black markets arise when maximum prices are set such that shortages of products or services are created. Some customers are prepared to pay more than the set price and this also creates a black market for such products. If governments introduce maximum prices in times of war, they usually outlaw black markets. As black markets are illegal, lawlessness is encouraged and this may have further repercussions. Much of modern gangsterism in the US is said to have developed in the 1920s and 1930s when many states banned the consumption of alcohol.

The incentive for black markets to develop is shown in Figure 3 in which the supply of a good is fixed at S1. Some customers are prepared to pay up to P2 which may indicate great profits from illegal activity.

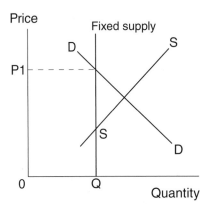

Figure 3: Government pricing and black markets

Political conflicts

Politics can be seen as a means of reconciling conflicts. Politicians need the votes of voters who may have different objectives. In 1999 the government announced that not all cigarette advertising was to be banned as quickly as originally intended. It has been argued that groups such as those promoting Formula 1 racing, who benefited from tobacco sponsorship, had been able to persuade the government to change its policies. In this case there was a conflict between the Labour Party raising revenue from corporate donors and its desire to reduce smoking.

The jobs of politicians can be made harder as a result of the pressure which can be put upon government by the media, various pressure groups and lobbyists. Sometimes politicians just cannot win.

Reconciling political differences is even harder in an international or global context. This is particularly significant in dealing with negative externalities. Pollution and pollutants do not recognise national boundaries. Countries need to agree common approaches. The failure of the United States government to cut greenhouse gas emissions is considered by some to be one of the biggest threats facing global society.

Research task

What would be the implications on the agriculture industry of moving towards a much more market-based economy by ending government indirect taxes and the provision of subsidies?

Quick check

Was Adam Smith right?

Hot potato

Will the railways ever work?

2.15 Activities

Activity 1

(a) Define a negative externality.
(b) Explain two possible negative externalities that may be caused by obesity.
(c) Discuss two measures a government could use to reduce obesity.

Activity 2

(a) State what is meant by the distribution of income
(b) Explain two costs of poverty to an economy.

Activity 3

(a) Distinguish between equity and efficiency.
(b) Discuss whether equity and efficiency conflict.

Activity 4

(a) Using a diagram, analyse the effect of granting a subsidy to train-operating companies.
(b) Discuss how a cost-benefit analysis could be used to decide whether a new rail line should be constructed.

Activity 5

(a) Define economic efficiency
(b) What are the arguments for raising the tax on petrol?
(c) Using a diagram, analyse the effect of increasing the tax on petrol.

Activity 6

(a) Distinguish between a merit and a public good.
(b) Is education a merit or public good?
(c) Discuss three ways a government could increase the consumption of merit goods.

Activity 7

(a) What is meant by information failure?
(b) Explain the connection between information failure and merit and demerit goods.

Activity 8

(a) Why would health care be under-consumed if left to market forces?
(b) Discuss the costs and benefits to society of an increase in government spending on health care.

Activity 9

(a) Define allocative efficiency.
(b) Explain why perfect competition may result in allocative efficiency.

Activity 10

(a) What is the optimal level of pollution?
(b) Discuss whether taxation or regulation is a more effective measure to reduce pollution.

The government is considering taking measures to correct what it sees as market failure in the provision of dental services in the UK. It is concerned that dentists are charging patients excessively high prices and carrying out unnecessary treatment.

The government provides some dental services on the NHS and requires all people offering dental services to be appropriately qualified. However, it is now considering taking further action including regulating the information dentists have to provide and imposing a maximum price dentists can charge for basic treatment. Some economists argue that the government should increase the number of public sector (NHS) dentists as the social benefit of dental treatment exceeds the private benefits. Other economists claim that the quality of dental services is higher and their prices lower in a competitive market.

(a) Define:
    (i) social benefit   (2)
    (ii) market failure.   (2)

(b) (i) Explain two causes of market failure which the passage implies is occurring in the case of dental services.   (6)
    (ii) Explain two reasons why dental services can be regarded as a merit good.   (6)

(c) (i) Using a diagram, explain the effect of setting a maximum price.   (10)
    (ii) Assess whether regulations are likely to correct market failure.   (7)

(d) Discuss whether consumers would benefit from a market becoming more competitive.   (12)

This exam has the same format as the Market System one. It is also one hour's duration and is marked out of 45. This module has a rather narrower range than the Market System but is rather more technical. Again you can expect to have to draw a diagram. The most common ones asked for relate to the effect of a tax, the effect of a subsidy, the impact of price fixing and the existence of positive and negative externalities.

(a) (i) In your definition it is important to mention not only that social benefit is total benefit but also that it consists of both positive benefits and external benefits.

(ii) Market failure occurs when the operation of free market forces does not achieve economic efficiency.

(b) (i) The passage touches on three causes of market failure. These are the abuse of market power, asymmetric information and the existence of positive externalities. You only have to explain two. You might select, for instance, the abuse of market power and the existence of positive externalities. The former can result in prices being higher and output being lower than the allocatively efficient levels. The existence of positive externalities is also likely to result in output being below the allocatively efficient level.

(ii) In considering whether a product is a merit or a demerit good you need to consider both information failure and the existence of externalities. Dental services can be regarded as a merit good because not all people are fully aware of the benefits they will gain from regular check ups and appropriate treatment and because they possess positive externalities including a healthier and so more productive labour force. Due to the lack of information and existence of positive externalities, dental services would be under-consumed and so under-provided if left to market forces.

(c) (i) As with all economic exams, draw a clear and appropriately labelled diagram. The effect of setting a maximum price will depend on where it is set. If it is set above the equilibrium, it will have no effect as producers will not want to charge such a high price. Mention this but then concentrate on analysing the effect of a maximum price being set below the equilibrium. As Figure 1 shows the strategy will cause a

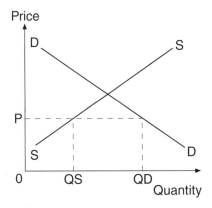

Figure 1

shortage, with demand exceeding supply. Those consumers who are able to purchase the product will experience higher consumer surplus. Others, some of whom would have been prepared to pay more, will not be able to obtain the product. There is a risk that a black market may develop and the government may have to ration the product.

(ii) This question requires you to make a judgement. In practice, regulations are likely to reduce but not completely correct market failure. You need to discuss how regulations should work and then mention their limitations, including the need to monitor, and that regulations do not directly compensate victims.

(d) The last question part is marked on the basis of levels. To reach the highest level you both need to analyse why consumers may do better in a competitive market and why they may not, and to come to some conclusions. In examining why competition may benefit consumers you should explain how it could lead to productive and allocative efficiency. In examining why consumers may not benefit you should discuss the possibility of market failure and the possible benefits of monopoly. In reaching a conclusion you might want to consider that most governments seek to promote competition, because of its perceived benefits, although they will intervene in markets if they consider that market failure is a problem or potential problem.

PART 3/AS

The national and international economy

The national and international economy – an overview

This Unit is concerned with macroeconomics, that is, the performance of the whole economy. How well the economy performs affects all our lives. It influences the quantity and quality of goods and services we can enjoy, our chances of gaining a job, and the prices we pay for products.

In this Unit you will first explore the nature of a government's key macroeconomic objectives. Then, in Sections 3.2 to 3.6, you will explore how output, economic growth, unemployment, inflation and the balance of payments are measured, what can cause changes in these key indicators of economic performance, and their consequences. In 3.7, you can test your understanding of this section.

The second part of the Unit, from Sections 3.8 to 3.12, concentrates on what is called aggregate demand and aggregate supply analysis. You will see some similarities with the demand and supply analysis you are familiar with from Unit 1, including the widespread use of diagrams. However, it is important to realise that there are differences, as you are now analysing total economic activity and not simply the market for one product. For instance, it is the price of the product that is measured on the vertical axis of a demand and supply diagram, whereas it is the price level that is measured on this axis on an aggregate demand and aggregate supply diagram. On the horizontal axis on aggregate demand and aggregate supply diagrams, it is real GDP (Gross Domestic Product, or national output) that is measured and Y is usually used to represent a particular level of output.

In the second part of the Unit you will come across two different schools of economic thought, Keynesian and new classical. Keynesian economists are named after the famous twentieth-century economist, John Maynard Keynes. Keynesians think that there can be significant market failure and that, in the absence of government intervention, the economy may experience significant macroeconomic problems. In contrast, new classical economists think that market failure is not significant and that the economy tends to move towards full employment in the long run. Because of their views on how economic forces work, Keynesians tend to favour government intervention, while new classical economists tend to urge a reduction in government intervention. Section 3.13 provides you with the opportunity to assess your understanding of the measures of aggregate demand and aggregate supply, and the determination of equilibrium national output and the price level.

The third part of the Unit focuses on the key policies that can be used in the management of the economy. In Sections 3.14 to 3.16, you will explore the nature of these policies, including what influences their effectiveness and, in Sections 3.17 to 3.20, you will consider which policy measures can be used to achieve specific objectives. In Section 3.21, there are a number of activities on macroeconomic problems.

The last part of the Unit moves from a national economy perspective to an international economy view. Sections 3.22 to 3.26 examine the causes and consequences of exchange rate changes, the pattern of international trade, the gains from international trade and the arguments for and against protectionism. Section 3.27 contains a number of activities designed to test your understanding of the international economy.

Section 3.28 provides you with a sample examination paper covering the whole module. When you have attempted this, you can read Section 3.29 to gain some useful examination guidance.

When you have completed this module you should be able to:
- explain how the performance of an economy is measured
- compare the performance of the UK economy with other economies
- explain the causes and consequences of economic growth, inflation, unemployment, balance of payments deficit and inequality of income
- apply aggregate demand and aggregate supply analysis to explore current economic behaviour and issues
- assess fiscal, monetary and supply-side policies
- explain the nature and key influences on international trade.

The spider diagrams on pages 94–97 give an overview of the four main parts of this module. It would be useful to review these again at the end of the module.

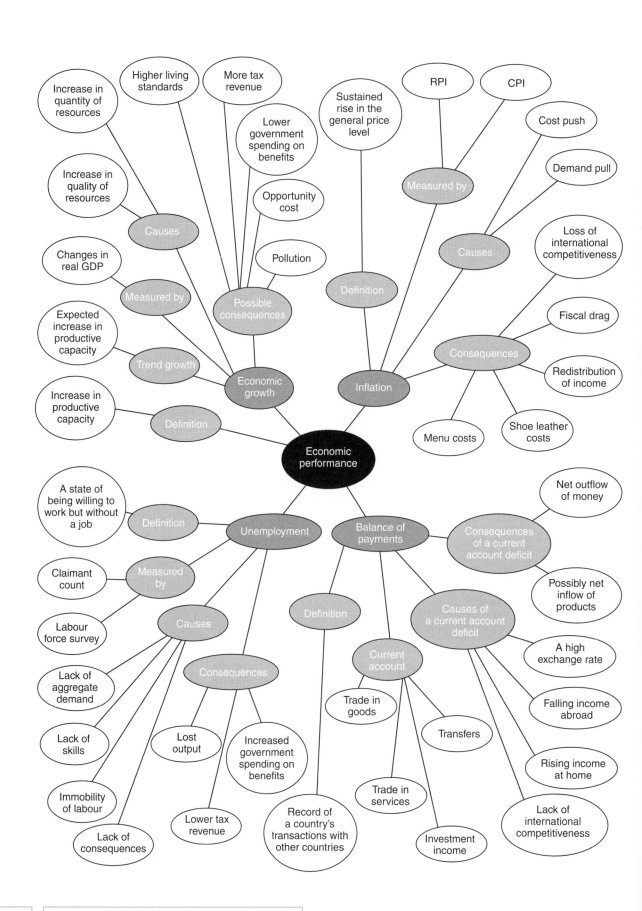

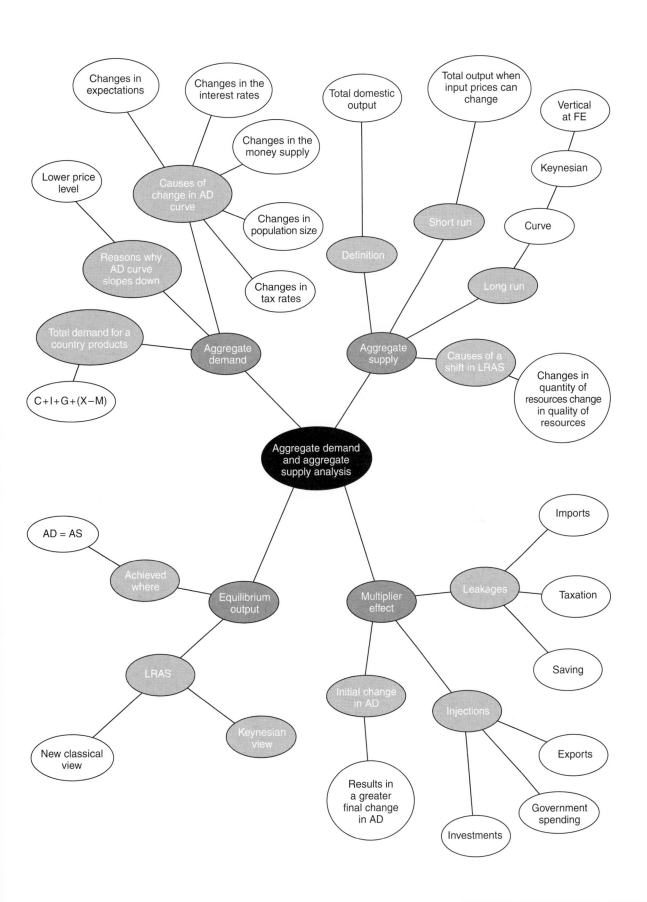

Changes in expectations

Changes in the interest rates

Changes in the money supply

Changes in population size

Changes in tax rates

Causes of change in AD curve

Lower price level

Reasons why AD curve slopes down

Total demand for a country products

C+I+G+(X−M)

Aggregate demand

Total domestic output

Definition

Total output when input prices can change

Short run

Long run

Vertical at FE

Keynesian

Curve

Aggregate supply

Causes of a shift in LRAS

Changes in quantity of resources change in quality of resources

Aggregate demand and aggregate supply analysis

AD = AS

Achieved where

Equilibrium output

LRAS

New classical view

Keynesian view

Multiplier effect

Leakages

Imports

Taxation

Saving

Initial change in AD

Results in a greater final change in AD

Injections

Exports

Government spending

Investments

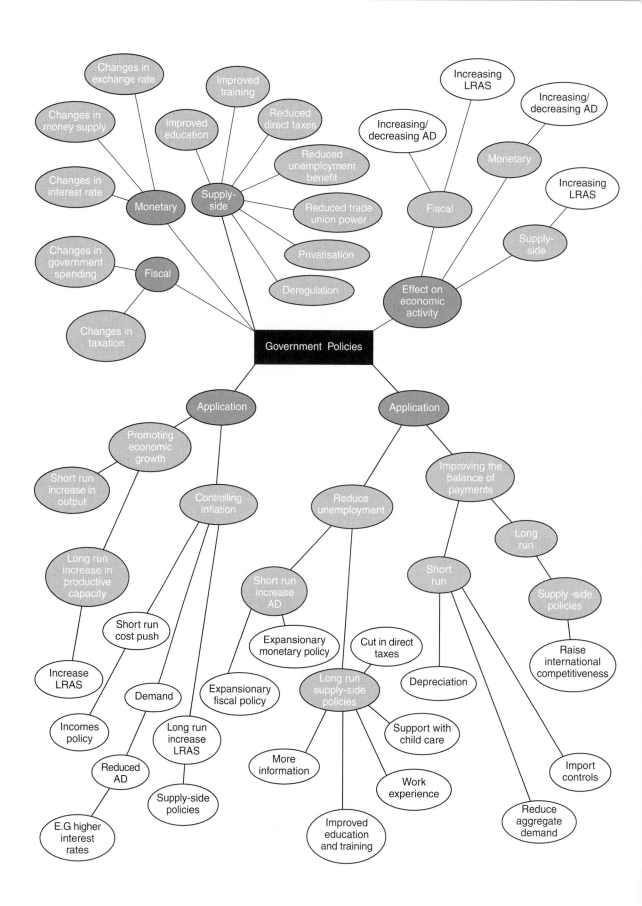

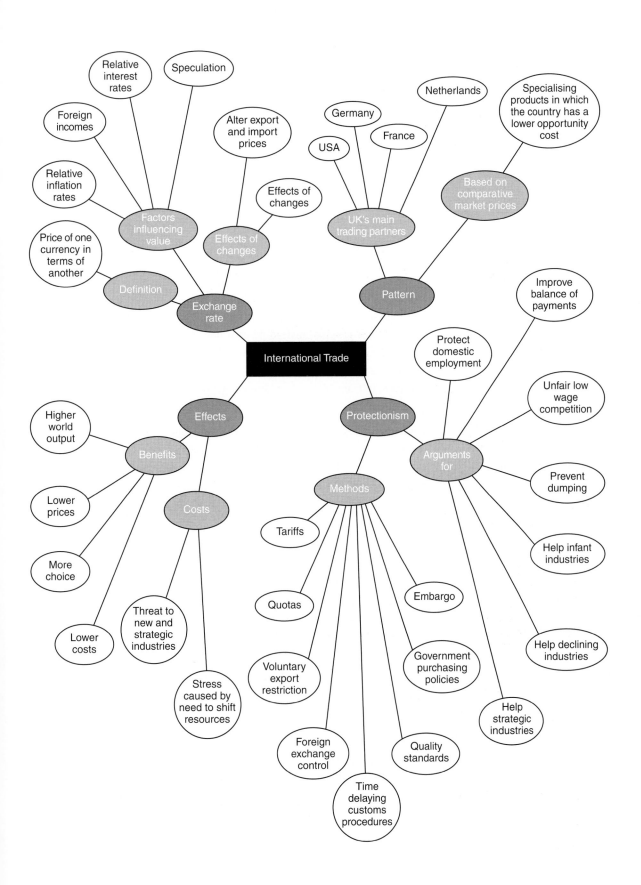

Macroeconomic policy objectives

Introduction

In managing the economy, governments usually pursue four main objectives:

- Full employment
- Low and stable inflation
- Steady rate of economic growth
- Satisfactory balance of payments position.

Of course over time, as economic circumstances alter and government administrations change, the priority given to these macroeconomic objectives also tends to change.

Full employment

The highest possible employment may be referred to as **full employment**. This term is somewhat misleading as it does not mean zero **unemployment**. It is often taken to be 3 per cent unemployed. Even during periods of high economic activity, some people will be out of work. These will be people who have left one job and are spending some time seeking a new job (i.e. people in between jobs).

A government is likely to want to achieve as high a level of employment as possible as it will confer a number of important advantages, including the possibility of high output and high living standards. In contrast, unemployment involves a waste of resources, a loss of potential output and can give rise to a number of social problems.

Definitions

Full Employment: a situation where those wanting to work can gain employment at the going wage rate.

Inflation: a sustained rise in the general price level.

Unemployment: a situation where people are out of work but are willing and able to work.

Low and stable inflation

Low **inflation** may be taken to mean that the general level of prices is rising at no more than, for example, 2 per cent a year. Stable inflation refers to the general price level rising at a consistent rate rather than at an accelerating rate, for example, 2 per cent this year and 2 per cent next year and not 2 per cent and 9 per cent next year.

A high and accelerating inflation rate can be harmful to an economy because it may reduce the international price competitiveness of the country's goods and services, may reduce the real value of people's incomes and savings and is likely to cause uncertainty.

However, zero inflation, with the general price level remaining unchanged has always been regarded as difficult to achieve and many economists now question whether it is desirable. A low level of inflation rather than zero inflation may bring benefits. For example, it may enable firms to reduce their costs by raising wages in line with inflation rather than by making some workers redundant.

Steady economic growth

Since 1950 the UK has had an average **economic growth rate** of 2 per cent. This means that the country's output has tended to increase at a rate of approximately 2 per cent a year. However, the rate of growth has not been steady. In some years output has increased by significantly more than 2 per cent, for example, in 1999, while in other years, for example, 1991, the amount produced actually declined. These fluctuations in economic growth cause uncertainty and make it difficult for the government, firms and households to plan for the future.

A steady rate of economic growth may confer a number of advantages on an economy including increasing material living standards. It also enables a government to reduce poverty without having to lower the living standards of the rich and middle income groups.

Satisfactory balance of payments position

The **balance of payments** is a record of a country's transactions with other countries over the period of a year. It shows the amount of money that has come into the country and the amount that has left. It is divided into a number of accounts. The account that receives the most attention in the media is the current account. This in turn is divided into four sections. The two best known are trade in goods and trade in services. These record the amount of money the country has earned from selling goods and services abroad and the amount it has spent on goods and services abroad.

In the long term, a government is likely to aim to match revenue with expenditure on goods and services. In the short term, however, it may be content, or indeed desire, to see a deficit (expenditure exceeding revenue) or surplus (revenue exceeding expenditure). For example, a deficit may be offset by a surplus in another section and it will mean that people are enjoying more goods and services than the country is producing.

Some economists argue that the balance of payments position is more of a constraint on its other objectives than an objective in itself. For example, if the UK is experiencing a deficit, the government may be reluctant to increase spending to help reduce unemployment. This is because it may believe that the higher spending will increase incomes and that some of this increase will be spent on imports of goods and services. If more is spent on imports the size of the deficit will get larger.

Quick check

1. Why will there always be some unemployment?
2. What is meant by stable inflation?
3. Identify a benefit of economic growth.
4. Identify two sectors of the current account of the balance of payments.

3.2 Output

Introduction

The level of output a country achieves has a significant impact on the lives of its inhabitants. It is important to measure and interpret output figures accurately.

Measuring output

One of the main measures of output is Gross Domestic Product (GDP). This is the total output of a country. It can be calculated by totalling up the output, income or expenditure of the country.

When using the output method, it is important to avoid double counting, that is counting the same output twice e.g. including the output of raw materials and then including them again in the value of the finished products. In the income method only incomes that have been earned in return for providing goods and services are included. So, for instance, job seeker's allowance and pensions are not included. With the expenditure method, it is important to remember to include exports (as they are produced by domestic firms) and to exclude imports (as they are produced by other countries' firms).

Real and nominal GDP

Government statisticians calculate both **real** and **nominal GDP**.

In assessing an economy's output performance it is important to make use of real GDP figures. This is because nominal GDP figures can be distorted by inflation. For example, the GDP of a country measured in the prices operating in the year in question (current prices) may rise from, for example, £500bn in 2003 to £550bn in 2004. This would appear to suggest that output has risen by:

$$\frac{£50bn}{£500bn} \times 100 = 10 \text{ per cent}$$

Money (or nominal GDP) has risen by 10 per cent. But at least part of this increase may be due to a price rise of the goods and services being produced. So to assess the rise in volume of output, the effects of price rises are taken out by using the following formula:

$$\frac{\text{Current year figure} \times \text{base year price index}}{\text{Current year price index}}$$

So if the price index in 2003 was 100 and 106 in 2004, real GDP was:

$$\frac{£550bn \times 100}{106} = £518.87bn$$

In real terms GDP has risen by $\frac{£18.87bn \times 100}{£500bn} = 3.4$ per cent

Production and productivity

As we have seen, real GDP is a measure of the total output of the economy. Output is the same as its production. Whereas **productivity** is output per worker hour. Changes in productivity are examined to assess a country's economic performance. If productivity rises by more than wages, then labour costs will fall and a country can become more price competitive. It is possible for production and productivity to move in opposite directions. When an economy is expanding, production will rise. If less skilled workers have to be recruited to make the extra output, productivity may fall. This would indicate that while the economy may appear to be doing well its ability to sustain rises in output may be in doubt.

Changes in real GDP and living standards

On the surface an increase in real GDP suggests that living standards are increasing but this may not be the case. One problem of interpretation that economists can eliminate is that a rise in output may be exceeded by a rise in population. If there is, for example, 4 per cent more output and 7 per cent more people to share the output between, on average each person will be worse off. So what economists often assess is real GDP per head. This is found by dividing real GDP by population.

In comparing a country's real GDP over time and between countries other problems can occur. One is the existence of the **hidden economy**. This term covers undeclared economic activity. The output of a country is likely to be higher than its official real GDP figure suggests. Some people selling goods and services may not include all the money they have earned on tax returns and those engaged in illegal activities will not declare any income earned.

In deciding how the level of, and changes in, real GDP affect people's living standards it is important to consider the composition of real GDP. If more is produced but the extra output consists of capital goods, people will not immediately feel better off although they will in the long run. If, for example, the rise in real GDP has been accounted for by increasing the police service to match rising crime people may actually feel worse off.

A rise in real GDP may not benefit many of the population if income is very unevenly distributed and if they are working longer hours, or working under worse conditions. In addition, the official figures do not include positive and negative externalities. So, for example, if pollution rises, real GDP does not fall even though people will experience a lower quality of life.

Quick check

1 What are the three methods of measuring national output?
2 Give two reasons why an increase in real GDP may overstate increases in living standards.

Exam hint

Remember that in assessing changes in a country's output, it is important to use real GDP rather than nominal GDP figures. This is because real GDP has been adjusted for inflation and so is not distorted by price changes.

Definitions

Labour Productivity: output per worker hour.
Hidden economy: undeclared economic activity.

Thinking like an economist

Economists and other social scientists make use of index numbers. These provide a measure of relative changes in a set of figures. It enables users of the data to assess quickly the percentage change from a previous year without having to undertake any calculations. The year against which such comparisons are made is known as the base year. It is given a value of 100. The year should be one in which nothing unusual has happened. To convert data into an index the following formula is used:

$$\frac{\text{Current year figure} \times 100}{\text{Base year figure}}$$

Economic growth

Introduction

In the short run, output can increase due to a rise in aggregate demand. In the long run, however, economic growth has to be supply-led. Figure 1 shows the productive capacity of the economy increasing.

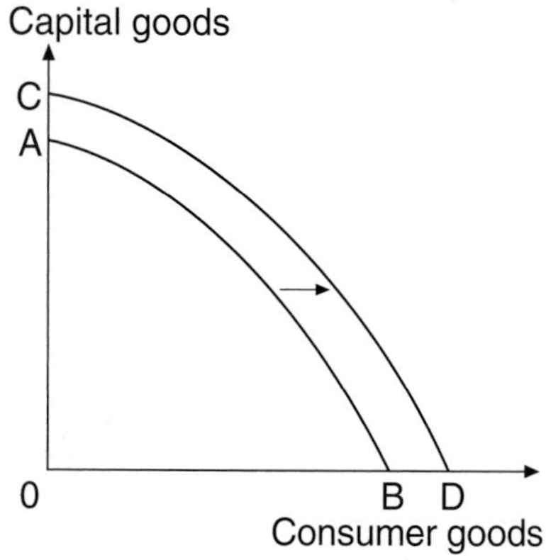

Changes in output

In the long run for output to continue to increase, the productive potential of the economy must rise. If not, the economy will hit a supply constraint, unable to produce any more with the given quantity and quality of resources and technological knowledge. Of course, there is no guarantee that an increase in the quantity and/or quality of a country's resources will mean that output will rise. For instance, the labour force of a country may increase but if there is no demand to use these resources output will not rise.

Capital goods

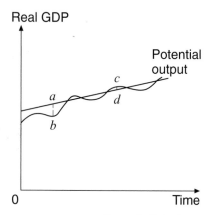

Figure 1: Economic growth

Trend growth

In practice, the productive potential of most economies increases each year. In industrialised economies this is due mainly to improvements in educational standards and technology. In some developing economies it is also due to rises in the size of the labour force.

Trend growth is the expected increase in potential output over time and is a measure of how fast the economy can grow without generating higher inflation. It is sometimes referred to as 'the economy's speed limit'.

Making connections

Use a production possibility curve to show (a) an increase in output resulting from using previously unemployed resources and (b) trend growth.

Output gap

When total demand matches the full employment level of total supply, actual output will match potential output. The economy will be making the maximum output it is capable of producing. However, when there is a lack of demand, there will be unemployed resources and an **output gap**. Figure 2 shows the growth in potential and actual output over time. The distance ab represents the output gap.

For short periods of time, high levels of total demand may push rises in output above the trend growth rate. Some of the extra output may be achieved by workers working overtime and routine maintenance not being undertaken on equipment. This is likely to lead to inflation and is referred to as 'overheating'. The distance cd on Figure 2 shows the economy overheating.

Definition

Output gap: the gap between potential and actual output.

Real GDP

Figure 2: Output gap

Benefits and costs of economic growth

The main benefit of economic growth is likely to be a rise in people's material standard of living. If real GDP per head rises, the population can enjoy more goods and services. The quantity, range and quality of goods and services available to people in the UK continues to grow.

Economic growth also enables poverty within a country to be reduced without having to redistribute existing income. Higher output raises tax revenue without having to increase tax rates, and some of this can be used to finance schemes to help the poor. Some of the higher tax revenue can also be used to improve public services, such as education and health care, and to improve the environment.

Economic growth raises the level of a country's real GDP and can thereby increase its status and power in international organisations and international negotiations. The United States, which has a very high level of real GDP per head, is a very powerful member of the United Nations (UN), the International Monetary Fund (IMF) and the World Trade Organisation (WTO).

Economic growth, depending on a country's circumstances and how it is achieved, however, can have costs. If an economy is currently using all its resources, and thus producing on its production possibility curve, the only way it can increase output is to switch resources from making consumer goods and services to making capital goods. So, in the short run, fewer consumer products will be produced. In the long run, though, the extra capital goods will enable more consumer products to be made. If economic growth is achieved in a way that is not **sustainable**, for example by the expansion of heavy industry without regard to controls on pollution, there will be damage to the environment. There is also the risk that economic growth may result in the depletion of non-renewable resources.

In addition, economic growth may reduce the quality of some people's lives. A growing economy is one which requires some people to adapt new skills and some to change jobs. The pace of work may also increase. Some people may find these changes stressful. Having more products also does not guarantee happiness. For example, the increase in the number of cars has increased people's flexibility of travel but has also resulted in more accidents, an increase in breathing-related illnesses and more noise.

Exam hint

Be careful when examining economic growth rates. For instance, in 2004 a country's economic growth may be 3 per cent and it may be 2 per cent in 2005. This does not mean that output is falling in 2005. It means that output is rising but rising at a slower rate than in 2004.

Definition

Sustainable economic growth: economic growth that does not endanger further generations' ability to expand productive capacity.

Quick check

1 What is meant by trend growth?
2 When is there an output gap?
3 What is the main benefit of economic growth?
4 Identify two possible costs of economic growth.

Unemployment

3.4

Introduction

Unemployment can have significant adverse effects on the economy and even more on the unemployed themselves. In this section you will examine the meaning of unemployment, how it is measured, what may cause it and the costs of unemployment.

Meaning of unemployment

Unemployment exists when people who are willing and able to work are without jobs. Some people aged between 16 and 65 are not in the labour market because, for example, they are homemakers, disabled, or have retired early. These people are said to be economically inactive and are not regarded as unemployed. However, there are other people who would classify themselves as unemployed despite not being prepared to take the jobs on offer.

Measuring unemployment

To assess how the economy is performing and whether unemployment is a problem, it is important to measure the number of people who are unemployed and the **unemployment rate**. In practice this is not as easy as it might appear. It can be difficult to decide which groups should be included and to assess who is genuinely looking for employment.

There are two main measures of unemployment used in the UK. One is the **claimant count**. This includes as unemployed anyone who is receiving unemployment related benefits, most significantly, job seekers' allowance. This is a relatively cheap and quick measure as the data is collected as benefits are paid out. But it misses some of those who are unemployed. This is because some of those who are willing to work and who are seeking employment are not receiving job seekers' allowance, for example, some married women.

The other measure, which now receives more government attention, is the **Labour Force Survey** measure. As its name suggests this is based on a survey. It is a household survey which collects a range of information on the labour force including employment, earnings, educational qualifications of the labour force as well as unemployment. In deciding who is unemployed from the responses given to them, this measure uses the International Labour Office (ILO) definition (and is sometimes referred to as the ILO measure). This defines as unemployed anyone who is without a job, available to start work, has been looking for work or is waiting to start a job they have already obtained. This is a more inclusive measure and, as it is used in many countries, it makes international comparisons easier. It is, however, slower and more expensive to compile and can be subject to sampling errors.

Definitions

Claimant count: a measure of unemployment which includes those receiving job seekers' allowance.
Labour Force Survey: a measure of unemployment based on a survey using the ILO definition of unemployment.
Unemployment rate: the percentage of people who are out of work. This is calculated by dividing the number of people unemployed by the labour force (i.e. those in employment and those unemployed) and multiplying by 100.

Causes of unemployment

Large-scale unemployment arises when the total demand for labour is below the full employment level. In this case, output is below the level that could be produced with all the labour force in work.

Unemployment can also occur when demand for labour is relatively high and there are job vacancies. This is because firms will not want to employ those people who lack the appropriate skills or who are not willing to work for the wages on offer. Unemployment may also arise if workers are geographically or occupationally immobile.

Costs of unemployment

The main cost of unemployment to an economy is the opportunity cost of lost output – a potential output that is lost forever. Figure 1 shows the production possibility curve of an economy experiencing unemployment.

As well as lost output, there are a number of other costs that unemployment imposes on an economy. When people are out of work they spend less so the government receives less revenue from indirect taxes such as VAT. Total income will also be below what it would be if there were full employment and so revenue from income tax will be lower than its potential level.

While tax revenue will be less, government expenditure will have to be higher. This is because the government will have to spend more money on job seekers' allowance. If there was less unemployment the government could spend more on other areas such as education or have lower tax rates.

Unemployment also generates other pressures on government spending. When people are out of work they are more likely to suffer from poor physical and mental health. This puts upward pressure on government spending on health care.

Of course, the people who bear the main burden of unemployment are the unemployed themselves. Most people who become unemployed experience a fall in income, loss of status and pressure on their relationships. The longer people are unemployed, the more they miss out on training, updating and promotion and, as a result, the more difficult they will find it to gain employment.

Quick check ✓

1. Identify two advantages of the claimant count measure of unemployment.
2. Why would improved training be expected to reduce unemployment?
3. Use a PPC to explain the effect of a reduction in unemployment on output.
4. Why would a rise in employment be likely to raise government tax revenue?

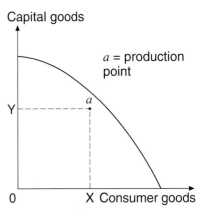

Figure 1: Output of an economy experiencing unemployment

Inflation

Introduction

In this section you will examine how inflation is measured in the UK and some of the effects of **inflation**.

Measuring inflation

The main measure of inflation in the UK is the **Retail Price Index** (RPI). This shows changes in the price of consumer goods and services purchased in the UK. There are three main stages in calculating the RPI. Government officials first seek to find out what people spend their money by carrying out a Family Expenditure Survey. From this, weights are given to different items of expenditure. If it is found, for instance, that 10 per cent of people's expenditure goes on food, this will be given a weighting of 10/100 or 1/10. Then how the prices of a variety of items have changed is checked. The final stage is to multiply the price changes by the weights in order to find the inflation rate.

The RPI aims to give a representative picture of what is happening to prices in the UK. However, this may not be a totally accurate picture. To assess whether prices are rising, the prices of the same goods and services should be compared. In practice, though, goods and services change, often improving in quality. So, for example, if the price of a vacuum cleaner rises by 6 per cent, this may reflect a higher charge to cover improvements in the model rather than the same cleaner becoming more expensive. Also, government officials do not monitor prices in charity shops, car boot sales and some other outlets. So the RPI may over-state the price rises which people face.

Measures of inflation

RPI is sometimes known as the headline rate of inflation as it has traditionally received so much attention. The government uses the data it collects in its compilation of the RPI to construct two measures of the underlying rates of inflation, RPIX and RPIY. These seek to provide a picture of the inflationary pressures building up in the economy.

RPIX is RPI minus mortgage interest payments and RPIY is RPI minus not only mortgage interest payments but also minus indirect taxes. RPIX was initially known as the target rate as this was the one that the government's target for inflation was first based on. RPIY is also sometimes known as the core inflation rate.

In April 2003 the Chancellor of the Exchequer announced his intentions to target CPI (Consumers Price Index) instead of RPIX. The CPI is an internationally recognised weighted consumer price index. It has a wide coverage but excludes housing.

Definitions

Inflation: a sustained rise in the general price level.
RPI: the Retail Price Index – a weighted consumer price index.
CPI: Consumers Price Index

Consequences of inflation

Inflation can impose a number of costs on an economy. Inflation creates what is known as 'menu', 'shoe leather', administrative costs and 'inflationary noise'.

'Menu' costs are the costs involved in changing prices in, for example, catalogues and advertisements, and 'shoe leather' costs relate to the extra time and effort involved in reducing holdings of cash and seeking the highest rate of interest. If money is losing its value at a high rate it cannot be left idle. Administrative costs are incurred as a result of staff time having to be devoted to adjusting accounts, assessing raw material costs, negotiating with unions about wage rises and estimating appropriate prices. The term 'inflationary noise' refers to the distorting effect that inflation causes. Without inflation, if the price of, for example, one model of television rises it can be concluded that it has become relatively more expensive. However, with inflation, consumers will be uncertain whether the rise in price does actually reflect a relative price rise or whether it is just in line with inflation.

There can be additional costs when the inflation rate is not correctly anticipated. These costs include what is called an arbitrary redistribution of income – some will gain and some will lose. For instance, some workers may fail to receive wage rises which keep pace with inflation, while borrowers may benefit if inflation reduces the real rate of interest. The government is likely to gain from inflation. This is because it is usually a large net borrower and if tax rates are not adjusted in line with inflation it may receive extra tax revenue. The tendency for people's income to be pushed into higher tax brackets as a result of inflation is known as fiscal drag.

One of the most serious disadvantages of unanticipated inflation is the uncertainty it creates. If firms are uncertain what their costs will be and what prices they will gain from selling their products they may be reluctant to invest.

Whether inflation is anticipated or unanticipated, it can have a harmful effect on a country's international trade position. If the country's inflation rate is above that of its main competitors, its goods and services will become less price competitive. This is likely to result in fewer exports being sold and more imports being purchased.

Research task

Using the *Economist* magazine, or any other appropriate source, compare the UK's inflation rate with that of the US, Germany and France. What effect do you think the UK's comparative inflation rate will have on its balance of payments position?

Quick check

1 Explain how the RPI is calculated.
2 Why may changes in the RPI overstate inflation?
3 Identify three costs of inflation.
4 Consider two benefits of a fall in inflation from 20 per cent to 5 per cent.

3.6 Balance of payments

Introduction

The balance of payments is a record of a country's economic transactions with the rest of the world. It contains a fascinating collection of information and enables us to see, for example, which products the country buys and sells, which countries it trades with, and which countries are buying factories and shares in the country.

Sections of the balance of payments

The main sections are the current account, the capital and financial accounts, and net errors and omissions.

The current account receives most media attention. It includes trade in goods, trade in services, investment income and transfers. Trade in goods records the earnings from exports and expenditure on imports of goods, for example, cars, food and chemicals. In recent years the UK has had a deficit in trade in goods. This means that it has spent more on imports of goods than it has earned from selling goods to other countries. Trade in services include e.g. travel (tourism), insurance, financial (banking) and computer and information services. The UK performs well in services. Since 1966 it has recorded a surplus every year. The UK also usually has a surplus on investment income. This means that its residents earn more in terms of profits, interest and dividends on their assets held in other countries than foreigners earn on their investments in the UK. Transfers covers the transfer of money made and received by the government and individuals e.g. government payments to and from the EU and money sent out of the UK by foreigners working in the UK.

The financial account shows the movement of direct investment, e.g. the purchase of a factory, and portfolio investment, e.g. the purchase of shares, and bank loans.

The last section, net errors and omissions, is added to ensure that the balance of payments balances. As the balance of payments is based on information relating to a vast number of transactions, it is not surprising that some mistakes are made and some items are initially left out.

Causes of a current account deficit

A deficit on the current account occurs when the country's expenditure abroad exceeds its revenue from abroad. This situation can arise because the country has spent more on goods and services and/or there has been a net outflow of investment income. In the UK's case, the most common reason for the current account to be in the red is for there to be a deficit on the trade balance.

This deficit may arise because the country is importing raw materials. This may be self-correcting as the raw materials may be converted into finished goods, some of which are exported.

It may also arise because the purchasers of the country's goods and services are experiencing economic difficulties and are not able to buy as many goods and services. When their economies improve the deficit may disappear. In contrast, the domestic economy may be booming and high demand may suck in more imports and cause some goods and services to be diverted from the export to the home market.

What is more serious is if the deficit is caused by a lack of price or quality competitiveness. If the country is charging too much for its goods and services, producing poor quality goods and services or making goods and services which consumers do not want to buy, the deficit will not be corrected without steps being taken to improve the performance of the country's firms.

Consequences of a current account deficit

The effects of a current account deficit will be influenced by its cause, its size and its duration. A small deficit which will be self-correcting is obviously of less concern than one which is large and which results from poor performance.

When a country spends more than it earns it is enjoying a higher living standard than it can afford. This may have to be financed by borrowing.

Causes of a current account surplus

A surplus on the current account is experienced when a country's revenue from abroad is greater than its expenditure abroad.

It may occur due to the country's revenue from exports exceeding expenditure on imports and/or because the country is a net earner of investment income.

Care has to be taken in interpreting a surplus on trade in goods and services. This is because it may arise from the strength or weakness of the economy. The country is likely to have a surplus if its products are very internationally competitive. But it may also have a surplus if the country is in a recession. This is because its citizens will not be buying many products, including imports, and because its firms, finding it difficult to sell at home, may be competing more vigorously in the export market.

Making connections

(a) Discuss the consequences of a current account surplus.
(b) Consider the effect of a fall in the UK's inflation rate on its current account position.

Quick check

1   What is meant by investment income?
2   Which section of the current account is most commonly in deficit?
3   Why might a fall in incomes in the USA have an adverse effect on the UK's balance of payments?
4   What is the purpose of the net errors and omissions section of the balance of payments?

Activities

Government macroeconomic policy objectives and indicators of national economic performance

Activity 1

In India since 1992 real income per head has been rising at over 40 per cent a year. If this rate is sustained, real income per head will have doubled by 2008. This would have a significant impact on the lives of the Indian population.

(a) Explain what is meant by 'real income per head'.
(b) Discuss three costs and benefits a country's population may experience as a result of economic growth.

Activity 2

In August 2002 UK unemployment fell to its lowest level in 27 years. The claimant count fell by 6,400 to just 943,300. This was the lowest level since October 1975. The UK's unemployment rate of 5.2 per cent was also among the lowest in the industrialised world.

(a) Define 'unemployment rate'.
(b) Explain the difference between the claimant count and the Labour Force Survey measures of unemployment.
(c) Discuss two benefits of a fall in unemployment.

Activity 3

In the first six months of 2002 the UK had a huge trade in goods deficit of £15bn. However, economists were not too worried. This was because it was offset in part by a trade in services surplus and inflows of capital from abroad and because the rest of the economy was doing relatively well.

(a) Explain what is meant by a 'trade in goods deficit'.
(b) Discuss what 'the rest of the economy was doing relatively well' is likely to mean.
(c) Discuss in what circumstances a trade in goods deficit is likely to be a cause for concern.

Activity 4

Inflation as measured by the RPIX rose from 1.9 per cent in August 2002 to 2.1 per cent in September 2002 and from 1.4 per cent to 1.7 per cent as measured by the RPI. The main forces behind the rise in inflation were new season increases in clothing prices at high street fashion chains and increases in the prices of services including insurance, foreign holidays and television licence fees. Food prices and petrol prices were expected to rise in the last quarter of the year.

(a) Distinguish between the RPI and RPIX measures of inflation.

(b) Explain what is meant by a rise in inflation.

(c) Discuss whether a change in food prices or television licence fees is likely to have a larger impact on the inflation rate.

Activity 5

| | 2002 | | |
	Inflation rate per cent	Unemployment rate per cent	Economic growth rate per cent
France	1.9	8.9	1.3
Germany	1.5	8.2	0.4
UK	1.2	5.2	1.8
USA	2.6	5.8	2.3

Table 1: Key economic indicators

(a) Using the evidence provided in Table 2, compare the UK's macroeconomic performance in 2002 with that of France, Germany and the USA.

(b) Identify another key economic indicator it would be appropriate to use.

Activity 6

Between 1998 and 2002 the price level in Japan was on a downward trend and in both 2001 and 2002 there was negative economic growth.

(a) Explain what is meant by:
(i) the price level was on a downward trend
(ii) negative economic growth.

(b) Consider what is likely to happen to unemployment when there is negative economic growth.

Aggregate demand

3.8

Introduction

In exploring what determines the level of economic activity in a country and in examining economic problems and issues, economists make frequent use of what is called aggregate demand and aggregate supply analysis.

Aggregate demand

Aggregate demand is the total demand for a country's goods and services at a given price level. Demand comes from:

- people buying products such as clothing and food (consumption (C))
- firms buying capital goods e.g. machines, delivery vehicles (investment (I))
- the government buying goods and services e.g. educational materials, medicines (government spending (G))
- foreigners buying the country's goods and services (X) minus domestic demand for foreign goods and services (M). Net exports is (X − M).

Aggregate demand (AD) is often expressed as: $AD = C + I + G + (X − M)$.

Consumption

Consumption is the largest component of aggregate demand. The main influence on consumption is income. As income rises consumption is likely to increase, although the proportion spent usually declines when people become richer. This is because they are able to save a higher proportion of their income. Other influences on consumption include the age structure of the country, inflation, the rate of interest and expectations about the future. For example, a fall in the rate of interest will encourage some people to spend more. This is because they will gain less from saving, it will be cheaper for them to borrow and they will have more money left to spend when they have made their mortgage payments.

Investment

Investment is the component of aggregate demand that fluctuates the most. Gross investment is the total amount spent on capital goods. Again, the main influence is income. When income is increasing, demand for consumer goods and services is also likely to be rising. So firms are likely to want to expand their capacity to meet this higher demand.

Investment is also influenced by expectations. Demand may be high and rising but if firms believe that the increase in demand will slow down or reverse in the near future, they will not buy capital goods to expand capacity and may not even replace all the capital goods that wear out.

A fall in the rate of interest should stimulate investment. It will reduce the cost of borrowing funds to spend on capital goods and will reduce the opportunity cost of using retained profits for investment purposes. Firms will

Thinking like an economist

Explain whether you would expect the following to shift the aggregate demand curve to the left or right:

1 a rise in expected profits.
2 a fall in income tax.
3 a world recession.
4 a rise in corporation tax (tax on firms' profits).

also be encouraged to buy capital goods if they fall in price, if advances in technology make them more productive than existing ones and if profits rise.

Government spending

A government purchases a range of goods and services including equipment and books for state schools and equipment for NHS hospitals.

The amount a government spends depends on a number of factors. These include its views on the extent of market failure and the ability of state intervention to correct it, the electorate's demand for health, education, roads etc., and the level of activity in the economy.

Net exports

Demand for a country's exports, relative to its demand for its imports, is influenced, for example, by the price and quality competitiveness of its goods and services, incomes at home and abroad, marketing and the exchange rate.

Aggregate demand curve

The AD curve slopes down from left to right indicating that aggregate demand will be higher the lower the price level. This is because a fall in price will:

- make the country's goods and services more price competitive at home and abroad. **So net exports** will rise.
- increase the amount the people's wealth can buy. This will encourage them to spend more and so raise consumption.
- lower prices cause interest rates to fall and lower interest rates to encourage a rise in consumption and investment.

Shifts in aggregate demand

If the aggregate demand curve shifts to the right it means that the total demand for goods and services has increased for some reason other than a change in the price level. A shift to the left represents a decrease in aggregate demand as shown in Figure 2.

You have already come across some of the reasons why the components of aggregate demand may change. For example, advances in technology will encourage firms to demand more capital goods. Other causes of changes in aggregate demand are changes in the size of the population and changes in the money supply.

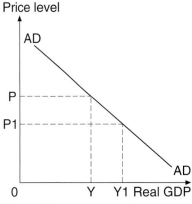

Figure 1: Aggregate demand curve

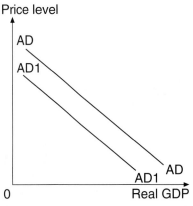

Figure 2: Decrease in aggregate demand

Exam hint

Be very careful with the labelling of AD diagrams. Remember it is the price level on the vertical axis, real GDP on the horizontal axis and the curve shows aggregate demand. You will not get any marks for micro labels.

3.9 Aggregate supply

Figure 1: Short run aggregate supply curve

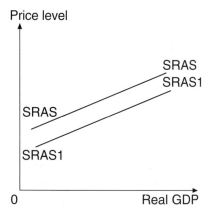

Figure 2: Decrease in short run aggregate supply

Introduction

Aggregate supply is the total quantity of goods and services that the country's firms and government concerns produce at a given price level. An aggregate supply curve shows the quantity of goods and services that would be produced at different price levels.

Economists distinguish between short run aggregate supply and long run aggregate supply.

Short run aggregate supply

Short run aggregate supply is the total quantity which will be supplied at different price levels when the prices of factors of production are assumed not to be changing. Figure 1 shows a short run aggregate supply (SRAS) curve.

This curve slopes up from left to right. There are two ways of looking at this. One is to explain why the price level rises when output goes up. The reason is because while, for instance, the wage rate is assumed not to be changing, average costs may rise with output. This is because to increase output overtime rates may have to be paid and machinery may have to be worked at a faster rate, leading to more breakdowns. The other is to explain why aggregate supply should rise when the price level goes up. If prices do increase while the prices of factors of production remain constant, production becomes more profitable.

Shifts in short run aggregate supply

A movement to the left of the SRAS curve shows a decrease in aggregate supply whereas a shift to the right shows an increase. Figure 2 illustrates an increase in short run aggregate supply.

The main causes of changes in short run aggregate supply are:
- changes in import prices
- changes in wage rates
- changes in the productivity of factors of production
- changes in taxation on firms.

These, of course, all change firms' costs of production.

Long run aggregate supply

Long run aggregate supply is the total quantity supplied at different price levels over a time period when the prices of the factors of production can change. For instance, the wage rate can move up or down.

Different views on the long run aggregate supply curve

Keynesian economists believe that the shape of the long run aggregate supply (LRAS) curve can be perfectly elastic at low levels of economic activity, less elastic at higher levels and perfectly inelastic when full employment is reached. This view is illustrated in Figure 3.

When the level of output is very low, and hence unemployment very high, between 0 and Y, any increase in output can be achieved by offering unemployed workers jobs at the going wage rate and paying the going price for materials and capital equipment. Between Y and Y1 shortages of workers, particularly skilled workers, and materials and equipment cause firms to compete for their services by offering to pay more for them. This raises costs and the price level. At Y1 all resources are employed and it is not possible to produce any more however high the price level rises.

In contrast, new classical economists believe that in the long run the economy will operate at the full employment level and the LRAS curve will be vertical, as illustrated in Figure 4.

Their thinking is that if, in the short run, aggregate demand falls, the workers who are made redundant will accept pay cuts and so price themselves back into employment in the longer run. So when the economy is operating at the long run equilibrium position, no one who is prepared to work at the going wage rate will be unemployed.

Shifts in long run aggregate supply

An increase in long run aggregate supply is illustrated by a shift to the right of the LRAS curve and a decrease by a shift to the left.

A move to the right of the LRAS curve shows that the productive potential of the economy has increased. With its resources fully employed an economy is capable of producing more goods and services. There are two main reasons why LRAS could increase. One is an increase in the quantity of resources. For instance, an increase in married women's participation in the labour force will increase the supply of potential workers and net investment will increase the quantity of capital goods available. So, for example, advances in technology and improvements in educational achievements will increase the quality of capital and labour and thereby raise their productivity.

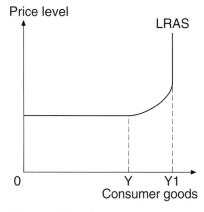

Figure 3: Keynesian long run aggregate supply curve

Figure 4: New classical long run aggregate supply curve

Exam hint

As with AD diagrams, be very careful with the labelling of AS diagrams – price level on the vertical axes, and real GDP on the horizontal axis.

3.10 Equilibrium output

Introduction

Having examined aggregate demand and aggregate supply you will now consider how they combine to determine output and the price level, and also consider the differences in the Keynesian and new classical views on long run **macroeconomic equilibrium**.

Equilibrium output and price level

In a market, equilibrium output and price occurs where demand and supply are equal. The same is true of **macroeconomic equilibrium**. This time, though, what we are considering is the equilibrium national output (real GDP) and the price level. This macroeconomic equilibrium occurs where aggregate demand and aggregate supply are equal. When aggregate demand and aggregate supply are equal there is no reason for national output and the price level to change. However if, for example, aggregate demand is higher than aggregate supply there would be a tendency for output to increase and the price level to rise.

Short run equilibrium

The short run equilibrium of output and the price level occurs where aggregate demand equals short run aggregate supply as shown in Figure 1.

At the price level of P all the output produced by domestic firms is sold and there is no reason for producers to increase or reduce their output and there are no pressures pushing up or lowering the price level.

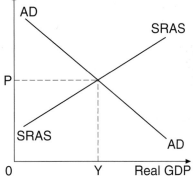

Figure 1: Short run equilibrium output

If, however, aggregate demand were higher than aggregate supply, there would be a shortage of goods and services. Consumers would bid up the price level and the higher prices on offer would encourage firms to expand their output until equilibrium was restored.

Aggregate supply exceeding aggregate demand would also lead to pressures that would move the economy back to equilibrium. This time, the existence of unsold goods and services would push the price level down. The lower price level would cause aggregate supply to contract and aggregate demand to expand until the two are equal.

Long run equilibrium

Economists agree that the long run equilibrium output and price level of an economy take place where aggregate demand equals the long run aggregate supply. However, they disagree about what this level of output may be.

New classical economists argue that in the long run the economy will operate with full employment of resources. As we saw in Section 3.9, they believe that the long run aggregate supply curve is vertical. Figure 2 illustrates their view on long run equilibrium with AD equalling LRAS.

Keynesians argue that aggregate demand may be equal to long run aggregate supply at any level of employment. They believe it is possible for an economy to be operating with spare capacity, i.e. with unused resources. Figure 3 shows long run equilibrium output occurring well below the full employment level. They also believe that the economy may be in equilibrium where it is experiencing shortages of resources and so where the price level is beginning to rise. They accept that it is possible for equilibrium output to be where full employment is achieved but that this is only one of a whole range of possible output positions.

Short run and long run equilibrium

Both Keynesians and new classical economists accept that it is possible for an economy to be in short run equilibrium but not necessarily in long run equilibrium. If, for example, aggregate demand rises to a very high level, in the short run domestic output may rise as a result of workers being prepared to work longer hours and low quality resources being used. However, in the longer run, the rise in costs which results will cause the short run aggregate supply curve to shift to the left and output to fall. Figure 4 uses the new classical version of the long run aggregate supply curve to illustrate this situation.

The economy is initially in short run and long run equilibrium at an output of Y. The increase in aggregate demand, illustrated by the shift in the aggregate demand curve from AD to AD1, causes output to rise in the short run. The economy moves to a new, higher level short run equilibrium output of Y1 and a higher equilibrium price level of P1. However, in the longer run, the higher costs that result from firms competing for increasingly scarce labour and raw materials raise costs of production. The short run aggregate supply curve moves to the left to SRAS1. Firms realising that in real terms, with the price rises they gained being offset by higher costs, they are no better off and reduce their output back to Y. The economy is now back to a position of both short run and long run equilibrium.

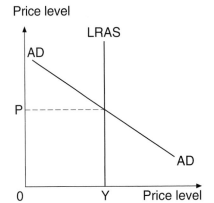

Figure 2: Long run equilibrium output

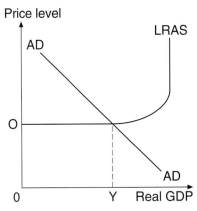

Figure 3: Keynesian long run equilibrium output below full employment

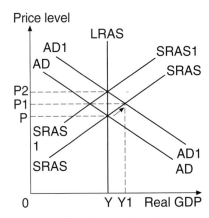

Figure 4: New classical view of the effects of an increase in aggregate demand

---

Quick check ✔

1   When is an economy not in macroeconomic equilibrium?
2   Explain why the economy tends to move towards macroeconomic equilibrium.
3   Distinguish between the Keynesian and new classical versions of the LRAS curve.
4   What does it mean if an economy is producing on the vertical part of the LRAS curve?

Changes in aggregate demand and aggregate supply

Introduction

In this spread you will examine the effects of changes in aggregate demand and aggregate supply, again exploring differences in the views of Keynesians and new classical economists.

Effects of shifts in aggregate demand

New classical economists believe that an increase in aggregate demand will cause a rise in output and the price level in the short run, but in the long run the only effect will be to increase the price level. Similarly, in the long run, a fall in aggregate demand will lower the price level but leave output changed. Figure 1 illustrates the new classical view of a fall in aggregate demand. Output initially falls to Y1 and the price level to P1. In the long run the workers made unemployed when output is cut back will be prepared to accept lower wages. This fall in costs encourages firms to expand their output and as a result, output rises back to Y but now with lower unit costs and price level.

In contrast, Keynesians argue that the effects of a change in aggregate demand will depend on where the economy is initially operating. If it is producing at the full employment level, then the long run effect of an increase in aggregate demand will be purely inflationary. Figure 2 shows aggregate demand rising from AD to AD1. This pushes up the price level but leaves output unchanged at Y.

If, however, the economy is producing with a high level of unemployment, an increase in aggregate demand will cause output to rise from Y to Y1 and have no effect on the price level. This outcome is illustrated in Figure 3.

The third possibility is that, before the rise in output, the economy may be experiencing some shortages of resources including, for instance, skilled workers. In this case, an increase in aggregate demand will raise both the price level and output as shown in Figure 4.

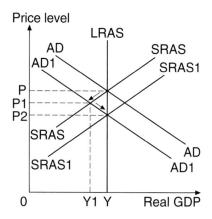

Figure 1: New classical view of the effects of a decrease in aggregate demand

Exam hint

Remember that spending on imports reduces a country's aggregate demand. This is because the spending is going on foreign and not domestic products.

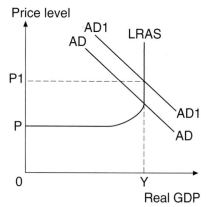

Figure 2: Keynesian view of an increase in aggregate demand occurring at the full employment level of output

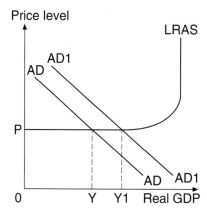

Figure 3: Keynesian view of an increase in aggregate demand occurring at a low level of output

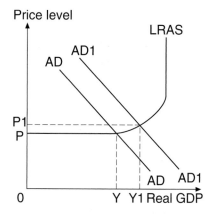

Figure 4: Keynesian view of an increase in aggregate demand occurring at a level of output where shortages start to be experienced

Effects of shifts in the short run aggregate supply curve

Economists agree that a decrease in short run aggregate supply will raise the price level, whereas an increase in short run aggregate supply will lower the price level. For example, a rise in the cost of imported raw materials will raise firms' costs of production. This will shift the SRAS curve to the left and, push up the price level and reduce output.

Effects of a shift in long run aggregate supply

There is again disagreement among new classical and Keynesian economists about the effects of a shift of the long run aggregate supply curve. New classical economists argue that an increase in long run aggregate supply will cause the economy to move to a new equilibrium position with a higher output and lower price level.

Keynesians, however, argue that it again depends on where the initial equilibrium position is. If the economy is operating at or near the full employment level, then an increase in LRAS will be likely to reduce the price level and increase output. However, if the economy is operating at a low level of economic activity, the increase in LRAS will increase the productive potential of the economy but the lack of aggregate demand will mean that it will not be used and output will remain at Y. Figure 5 shows the LRAS curve moving to the right but the price level and output staying at their initial levels.

Demand-side shocks

Demand-side shocks are unanticipated events that affect aggregate demand, shifting the AD curve and affecting the economy. These can be external or internal. External shocks start in other countries. For example, a US recession would reduce demand for imports from the EU. This would reduce aggregate demand in the UK and other EU countries. There can also be internal shocks. For instance, households may become more optimistic about the future and as a result increase the amount they spend – a consumer boom.

Supply-side shocks

These are again unanticipated internal and external events but this time ones that affect aggregate supply. For example, if key groups of workers gain a pay rise this may spread to other groups. Wage costs will rise and the short run aggregate supply curve will shift to the left and the price level will rise.

Sudden changes in aggregate supply may also result from external events. If the price of oil increases, those countries that buy their oil from abroad will face higher costs of production.

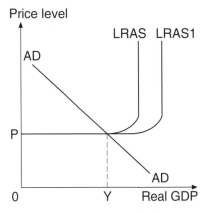

Figure 5: Keynesian view of an increase in long run aggregate supply occurring at a low level of output

Thinking like an economist

Using aggregate demand and aggregate supply analysis, explain what effect an increase in consumption would have on an economy currently experiencing a high level of unemployment.

Definitions

Demand–side shocks: unexpected changes in aggregate demand.
Supply–side shocks: unexpected changes in aggregate supply.

3.12 The multiplier effect

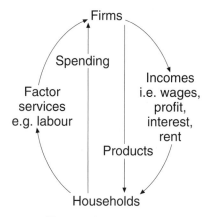

Figure 1: Circular flow of income

Definitions

Injections: additions to the circular flow.

Leakages: withdrawals from the circular flow.

Multiplier: the process by which any change in a component of aggregate demand results in a greater final change in real GDP.

The circular flow of income

The circular flow of income model illustrates how the macro-economy works. In the simplified version shown in Figure 1, there are two sectors, households and firms. Between these two flow income and products and factor services. Households provide factor services, e.g. labour and enterprise. In return households receive incomes. They use these incomes to buy products produced by firms.

Injections and leakages

In practice not all the income that is earned is spent and there are additional forms of spending that do not arise from the circular flow. Income which is not spent on domestic output leaks out of the circular flow. There are three **leakages** (which can also be called withdrawals). These are taxation, savings and spending on imports. Leakages reduce aggregate demand. In contrast, **injections** increase aggregate demand. Again, there are three: investment, government spending and exports. These are additional forms of spending, arising outside the circular flow of income. When the value of injections equals the value of leakages, output will not be changing and there will be macroeconomic equilibrium.

The multiplier effect

When injections exceed leakages, aggregate demand will increase. This rise in aggregate demand will have a greater final effect on the economy. This is because when households, firms and the government spend money, that expenditure becomes the income of those who sell them the products. They in turn will spend some of the money they receive. So there is a knock-on effect with aggregate demand rising by more than the initial amount. For example, if the government increases the value of pensions, the pensioners are likely to spend more on, for example, heating, housing and holidays. Those selling these products will receive more income. Some of this income will be spent and some will leak out of the circular flow. Spending will continue to rise until leakages match the initial injection.

Of course, the **multiplier** effect works in reverse. A rise in income tax, for instance, reduces disposable income and so reduces consumption. Lower spending causes firms to cut back on production, and reduces income. The lower income in turn reduces aggregate demand further.

Significance of the multiplier effect

The existence of a multiplier effect means that a government has to recognise that any change in government spending or taxation will have knock-on effects on the economy. So that, for instance, if the government wants to raise real GDP by £10bn and the multiplier has been estimated at 2, it would have to raise its spending by £5bn.

Quick check

1 What are the three injections?
2 Why is saving a leakage?
3 What effect would a rise in the rate of income tax have on aggregate demand?
4 If the multiplier is $2\frac{1}{2}$ and the government wants to raise real GDP by £150bn, how much would it have to raise its spending by?

Thinking like an economist

Using an AD and AS diagram, explain what effect an increase in expenditure on imports would have on output, employment and the price level.

Learning tip

The size of the UK multiplier is thought to be around 1.33.

Activities

3.13

Aggregate demand, aggregate supply and the determination of output, employment and price

Activity 1

What effect would you expect the following to have on a country's net exports?

(a) a recession in foreign countries
(b) a rise in the price competitiveness of foreign countries
(c) a major sporting event, for example, the Olympic games, being held in the home country.

Activity 2

A country's consumption is €200bn, investment is €60bn, government spending is €80bn, exports are €90bn and imports are €20bn. Calculate:

(a) net exports
(b) aggregate demand.

Activity 3

Figure 1 shows the output position of a country.

(a) Is the economy productively efficient? Explain your answer.
(b) Explain what effect a rise in consumption would be likely to have on output and the price level.

Activity 4

Figure 2 shows an economy's long run aggregate supply curve.

(a) Explain what is meant by the LRAS curve.
(b) Discuss two factors that could cause the LRAS curve to move to the right.

Activity 5

It has been said that increased investment allows an economy to grow without experiencing problems of inflation.

(a) What is meant by investment?
(b) Explain how increased investment can allow 'an economy to grow without problems of inflation.'

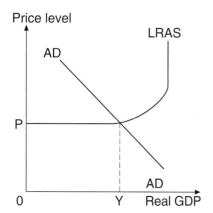

Figure 1: The output position of a country

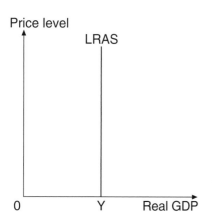

Figure 2: An economy's long run aggregate supply curve

Activity 6

A government increases its spending without raising taxes. This coincides with an increase in consumer spending caused by a rise in consumer confidence.

(a) Illustrate the likely effect on output and the price level of the events mentioned using:
  (i) the new classical version of the LRAS curve
  (ii) the Keynesian version of the LRAS curve.
(b) Discuss what factors may cause a rise in consumer confidence.

Activity 7

A country experiences a rise in its general price level.

(a) What effect will this have on aggregate demand?
(b) Explain one reason why the AD curve is downward sloping.

Activity 8

An economy moves temporarily from a position of equilibrium to disequilibrium as a result of a fall in consumption.

(a) What would have been the relationship between aggregate demand and aggregate supply in this case when the economy was in disequilibrium?
(b) Explain the forces which would cause the economy to return to equilibrium.

Fiscal policy

3.14

Introduction

Fiscal policy is one of the key economic policies that governments use to influence economic activity and achieve their macroeconomic objectives.

Fiscal policy is changes in taxation and government spending. The government can change the rate of taxes, the types of taxes it imposes, and the level, composition and timing of government spending.

Taxes

Taxes can be categorised in two main ways. One category includes direct and indirect taxes. Direct taxes are taxes on the income of people and firms, e.g. income tax and corporation tax. Indirect taxes are taxes on spending, e.g. VAT and excise duty.

The other category comprises progressive, proportional and regressive taxes. A progressive tax takes a higher percentage from the income of the rich, a proportional tax takes the same percentage from the income of all income groups and a regressive tax takes a greater percentage from the income of the poor.

Government spending

The main items of government spending are social security (including spending on pensions and job seekers' allowance), health, education and defence.

In recent years there have been a number of pressures on governments to spend more. One is the ageing population. With people living longer, there is an increasing demand for National Health Service treatment, pensions and residential care. Others include the increased length of time people spend in education, increased expectation of the range and quality of health care treatment, and advances in technology which have the effect of increasing the number and complexity of operations that are possible, and increasing the capital requirements of educational institutions.

Budget

The Chancellor of the Exchequer outlines government spending in its spending reviews and taxation plans in the annual budget. A budget deficit arises when government spending exceeds tax revenue, whereas a budget surplus occurs when tax revenue is greater than government spending.

Fiscal policy and aggregate demand

The government can raise aggregate demand either by increasing its own spending and/or by reducing taxes. Government spending is a component of aggregate demand. Government spending on, for example, computers in schools will directly increase aggregate demand. This higher spending will also have a multiplier effect causing AD to rise even higher.

Cuts in income tax will increase people's disposable income. This will raise consumption and/or again will have a multiplier effect. Rises in government spending and cuts in taxes are referred to as reflationary, expansionary or loose fiscal policy. In contrast, deflationary, restrictionist or tight fiscal policy involves measures that reduce aggregate demand i.e. cuts in government spending and/or rises in taxes. Figure 1 illustrates the effect of deflationary fiscal policy.

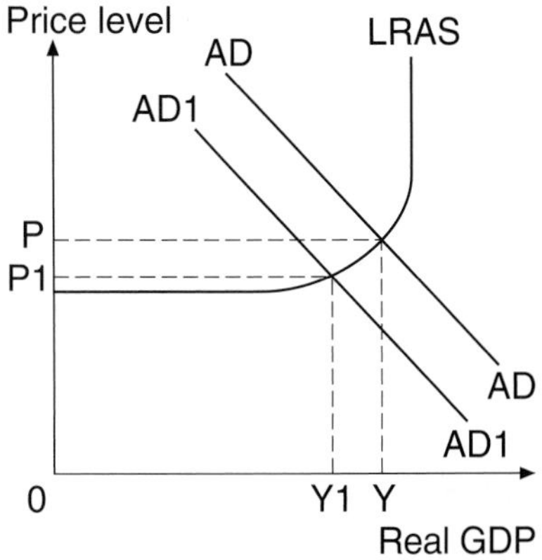

Figure 1: Effect of deflationary fiscal policy

Fiscal policy and aggregate supply

Changes in taxes and government spending can also affect aggregate supply. A cut in job seekers' allowance and income tax rates, for instance, will alter economic incentives that in turn may change the supply of labour. Government spending on education and training and investment grants may shift the LRAS curve to the right, as shown in Figure 2, if they succeed in improving the quantity of the labour force and the quality of capital goods.

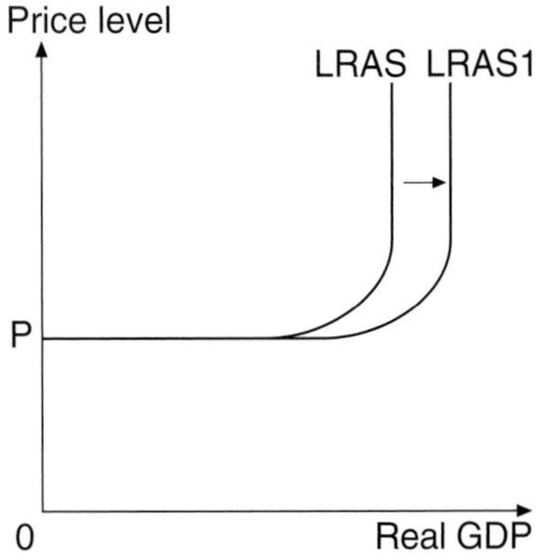

Effectiveness of fiscal policy

Fiscal policy has a number of advantages. It can be used to influence the performance of individual markets and the economy as a whole. Some forms of government spending and taxation, including cuts in corporation tax and training grants, have the potential to increase both aggregate demand and aggregate supply.

A number of taxes and forms of government spending adjust automatically to offset fluctuations in real GDP. For instance, government spending on unemployment benefits rises without any change in policy when real GDP falls.

However, fiscal policy also has a number of drawbacks. Changes in government spending and tax rates are not made frequently and they take time to have an effect on the economy. A number of forms of government spending are inflexible. It is, for instance, difficult to cut spending on health care and pensions. Fiscal policy measures can also have undesirable side-effects and people and firms may not react in the way expected. It is difficult to estimate the effects that changes in taxation and government spending will have on the economy. A rise in taxation designed to reduce inflation may cut aggregate demand too far and cause a rise in unemployment. It might, on the other hand, have little effect on aggregate demand if households and firms do not change their spending and investment plans despite the higher taxes.

Figure 2: Possible effect on LRAS of government spending on education and training

Exam hint

In examining the effects of fiscal policy measures, it is useful to illustrate your analysis with AD and AS diagrams.

Monetary policy

Introduction

Monetary policy measures include changes in the money supply, the rate of interest and the exchange rate. These measures are used to affect the economy by influencing aggregate demand.

Changes in the money supply

An increase in the money supply is likely to increase aggregate demand. If the government prints more money or makes it easier for banks to lend more money, people will have more money to spend. This will increase aggregate demand.

Changes in the rate of interest

A change in the rate of interest can affect the price level, output and employment by influencing three of the components of aggregate demand: consumption, investment, and net exports.

Effects on consumption

A higher interest rate is likely to reduce consumption as:
- higher mortgage rates will reduce the amount of money mortgage holders have to spend on other items
- higher mortgage rates will also be likely to reduce demand for houses. Lower demand will reduce the price of housing. For most people, their house is their most valuable asset. A fall in house prices will make them feel poorer and so discourage them from spending.
- lower house prices will reduce activity in the housing market. People often buy new carpets, curtains and new furniture and spend on decorating materials when they move.
- a higher return will be earned on saving. People will tend to save more and spend less.
- borrowing will be more expensive
- a higher interest rate is often accompanied by a fall in the value of financial assets, including shares. This again will discourage people from spending.

Effects on investment

A higher interest rate would be likely to lower firms' investment as:

- it will increase the costs of firms that have borrowed in the past
- investment will be more expensive as the cost of borrowing increases, i.e. the opportunity cost of investment will increase
- the expected lower consumption resulting from a higher interest rate is also likely to discourage investment.

Effects on net exports

A rise in the rate of interest is likely to encourage foreigners to place more money into UK financial institutions because of the higher return. They will exchange their currencies for pounds. This rise in demand for pounds will push up the value of the pound. Export prices will rise and import prices will fall, and as a result net exports are likely to fall.

Exchange rate

A government may seek to raise its exchange rate to reduce inflationary pressure. This may succeed in lowering inflation by:

- reducing the price of imported raw materials and so lowering firms' costs of production
- reducing aggregate demand by reducing exports and increasing imports
- putting pressure on domestic firms to keep their prices low in order to remain competitive.

Effectiveness of monetary policy

The main policy measure currently being used to influence short-term economic activity is the rate of interest. Changes in not only the rate of interest but also the exchange rate and the money supply can have a significant impact on aggregate demand.

However, it can take time for monetary policy measures to influence aggregate demand. It has been estimated that it can take eighteen months before a change in the rate of interest will alter consumption and investment plans.

In the 1970s and 1980s it was found that it is difficult to control the money supply especially as banks have a strong profit motive to increase bank lending.

Monetary policy measures may also have undesirable side effects. A rise in the exchange rate, designed to reduce inflationary pressures, may worsen the balance of payments position. Households and firms may also not react in the way expected. Lowering the rate of interest to stimulate rises in consumption and investment will not work if households and firms are pessimistic about future economic prospects.

The effects of monetary policy tend to be more concentrated on certain groups than changes in income tax, for example, tend to be. For instance, a rise in the rate of interest will hit firms that export a high proportion of their output more than other firms. This is because they will be affected not only by higher costs but also by a likely fall in demand resulting from a rise in the exchange rate. A government's ability to change its interest rate is also limited by the need for it to remain in line with other countries' interest rates, unless it is prepared to experience an inflow or outflow of funds.

Thinking like an economist

Work out how a fall in the rate of interest would affect consumption, investment and net exports.

Making connections

Compare monetary policy and fiscal policy in terms of how they work and their effectiveness.

Exam hint

In answering questions about how monetary policy works, concentrate on the rate of interest as this is currently the main measure used.

If a question asks you to discuss how effective monetary policy is in, for example, decreasing aggregate demand: identify what measures could be used; explain how one or two of these could reduce AD; assess the strengths and weaknesses of monetary policy.

Supply-side policies

Introduction

Supply-side policies, as their name suggests, seek to increase aggregate supply by improving the efficiency of markets. The term covers a range of measures, some of which are examined below.

Education and training

Improvements in education and training should raise productivity of labour. Output per worker hour will increase and the potential output of the economy will rise. This will shift the long run aggregate supply curve to the right as shown in Figure 1.

Reduction in direct taxes

As well as increasing aggregate demand, lower direct taxation may also increase aggregate supply. This would be achieved by increasing incentives to firms, workers and potential workers. A cut in corporation tax will increase the funds which firms have available to invest and the return from any investment undertaken. If investment does increase, the productive capacity of the economy will rise.

Some economists believe that a cut in income tax will encourage some existing workers to work overtime, be more willing to accept promotion and to stay in the labour force longer. In addition they believe it will persuade more of the unemployed to accept employment at the going wage rate as their **disposable income** will rise. However, others argue that lower income tax rates may encourage some workers to take more leisure time as they can now gain the same disposable income by working fewer hours. It is also argued that what stops the unemployed from gaining employment is not a lack of willingness to work at the going wage rate but a lack of jobs.

Reduction in unemployment benefit

Those economists who believe that market failure is a significant problem and favour government intervention do not support a cut in job seekers' allowance. They believe that what this will do is reduce aggregate demand, output and employment.

However, supporters of free market forces argue that lowering job seekers' allowance will, by widening the gap between employment and benefits, force the unemployed to seek work more actively and to accept employment at lower wage rates.

Definitions

Supply-side policies: policies designed to increase aggregate supply by improving the efficiency of markets.

Disposable income: income after direct taxation has been deducted and state benefits have been added.

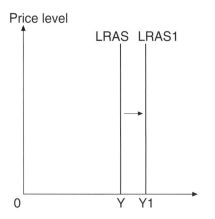

Figure 1: Increase in long run aggregate supply

Reduction in trade union power

Those who favour the operation of free market forces believe that reductions in trade union power will reduce imperfections in the labour market. They argue that trade unions reduce employment by pushing wage rates above the equilibrium level and by encouraging workers to engage in restrictive practices. These economists suggest that reducing the power of trade unions will increase labour productivity and reduce the cost of employing labour. As a result, firms will be encouraged to employ more workers and raise output.

Again, some economists disagree. They argue that trade unions act as a counter-balance to the market imperfection of very powerful employers. They also claim they reduce firms' costs by acting as a channel for communication between employers and workers on issues since it is cheaper to negotiate with one body than with individual workers.

Privatisation and deregulation

Supporters of free market forces argue that government intervention in the economy should be reduced. They believe that firms are in the best position to make decisions about what to produce, how to produce and what to charge. This is because they are subject to the discipline of the market. If they do not provide the products which consumers want at competitive prices, it is argued, they will go out of business. So these economists favour the removal of rules and regulations on firms and the transfer of firms from the public to the private sector.

However, again some economists disagree. Some argue that rules, regulations and/or government ownership of firms are beneficial in a number of circumstances where there is a high risk of market failure.

Research task

Identify two supply-side policies that could increase the quality of a country's capital goods.

Effectiveness of supply-side policies

Supply-side policies are now widely used. They have the advantage that they are selective, targeted at particular markets and are designed to raise efficiency. Economists agree that if the supply-side performance of the economy can be improved it will be easier for a government to achieve its objectives. Increasing aggregate supply enables aggregate demand to continue to rise over time without inflationary pressures building up. A higher quality of resources should also make domestic firms more price and quality competitive, and so improve the country's balance of payments position.

However, as noted above, there is disagreement about whether a free market or interventionist approach should be adopted, with differences of opinion about, for instance, how potential workers respond to cuts in benefits and whether firms operate more efficiently in the public or private sector. Some of the policies, for example, education spending, also take a relatively long time to have an effect.

Hot potato

What do you think is the best way of encouraging lone parents to enter the labour force?

Policies to reduce unemployment

Introduction

There is a range of policy measures a government may employ to reduce unemployment. The choice of measures will be influenced by the cause of the unemployment, the rate and duration of unemployment and the state of the other key macroeconomic objectives. In the short run, unemployment may be reduced by measures that increase aggregate demand but in the long run, supply-side measures may be more effective.

Short run

In the short run, with an economy operating below its productive capacity, unemployment may be reduced by increases in aggregate demand. In such a case, expansionary fiscal and monetary policy can be used to create jobs. A government, using fiscal policy, could increase its spending and/or cut tax rates in order to raise aggregate demand. In practice, a rise in government spending has the potential to have more of an impact on aggregate demand, and therefore unemployment, than cuts in taxes. This is because some of the rise in disposable income, which will result from lower taxes, may be saved and some may be spent on imports.

Increases in the money supply and lower interest rates are also likely to raise aggregate demand. For instance, a fall in interest rates and/or an increase in the money supply should stimulate consumption and investment. It may raise net exports if it causes a fall in the exchange rate.

Figure 1 shows the effect of a rise in aggregate demand on real GDP.

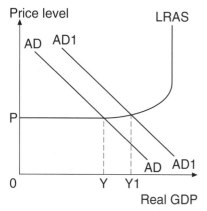

Figure 1: Effect of an increase in aggregate demand

Expansionary fiscal and monetary policies may have undesirable side-effects. One consequence of a rise in aggregate demand may be a rise in the price level as the economy approaches the full employment level. The higher level of spending may also increase any existing deficit on the current account of the balance of payments.

Long run

In the long run, if there is not a shortage of aggregate demand, the cause of unemployment will lie with supply-side problems. Those people who are out of work when the level of aggregate demand is high and there is no shortage of job vacancies, are likely to be in between jobs, lacking the appropriate skills, are geographically or occupationally immobile, have family circumstances which restrict their ability to work or are lacking the incentive to move off benefits and find employment.

There are a number of factors that determine such unemployment. The time people spend finding a job after they have left another job is influenced by the quantity of information they have about job vacancies. Many of the long-term unemployed lack qualifications, have poor communication skills and are geographically immobile. Some may have lost the work habit, some may be having difficulty affording child-care or overcoming prejudice in order to be permitted to work (for example, disabled people) and some may believe they are better off on benefits than in employment.

In these circumstances, it is unlikely that raising aggregate demand will succeed in reducing unemployment. What is needed is an increase in the attractiveness of work to the unemployed and an increase in the attractiveness of the unemployed to employers. Supply-side policies are likely to be more effective in achieving these objectives than demand-side policies.

Supply-side polices

Supply-side policies can be implemented to increase economic incentives and the quality of the labour services offered by the unemployed. They can increase the quantity and quality of information available to the unemployed about job vacancies and to the employers about those seeking jobs, to increase the skills of the unemployed, to make it easier for lone parents to work, to facilitate the employment of disabled workers, and to increase economic incentives.

Such measures include the provision of information, improved education and training, the provision of work experience, financial support for child-care, and a widening of the gap between the income received from employment and the income received in benefits. The latter measure can include, for instance, a reduction in the **marginal tax rate**.

The New Deal

The need to tackle the problems of long-term unemployment and youth unemployment lay behind the introduction of the New Deal by the Labour Government in 1998. This scheme provides help and advice to the unemployed in their search for a job during the first four months of unemployment. After this period has elapsed the unemployed have four options. These are to take up the offer of a job subsidised by the government, or a place on an educational or training course, or voluntary work or work with an environmental task force. The intention behind these options is to develop skills, confidence and work experience.

Unemployment and the full employment level

When the unemployment percentage is coming close to the full employment level, it tends to become increasingly difficult to reduce unemployment further. If, however, policy measures succeed in reducing the time people spend in between jobs and, in particular, in long-term unemployment, the unemployment percentage at the full employment level may possibly be reduced.

Hot potato

Would unemployment be more likely to be reduced by a cut in unemployment benefit or a rise in unemployment benefit?

Definition

Marginal tax rate: the proportion of extra income that is taken in tax.

Making connections

Discuss the benefits that would be experienced as a result of a fall in unemployment.

3.18 Policies to control inflation

Introduction

If a country is experiencing inflation, the measures it implements will be influenced significantly by what is thought to be causing the inflation. As well as tackling any current inflation, governments also implement measures which they hope will ensure relative price stability.

Causes of inflation

There are thought to be two main causes of inflation. One is known as **demand-pull** and the other is **cost-push inflation.**

Demand-pull inflation arises from aggregate demand increasing at a faster rate than aggregate supply. When the economy is producing at or near its productive capacity, increases in aggregate demand are likely to push up the price level.

In contrast, cost-push inflation arises when the general price level is pushed up by increases in the costs of production. A common cause of cost-push inflation is a rise in wage rates above increases in productivity.

Short run

Cost-push

There are a number of policy measures a government can take to control inflation in the short run. If a government believes that inflation is caused by excessive increases in wage rates, it may try to restrict wage rises. It can control wages in the public sector directly by restricting increases in government spending allocated to public sector wage rises. It can also restrict wage rises in both the public and private sectors by introducing an incomes policy. For instance, a government may place a limit on wage increases of 5 per cent or £2,000 a year. This measure does seek to reduce inflation without causing unemployment.

Demand-pull

To reduce demand-pull inflation, a government may adopt deflationary fiscal and/or monetary policy measures. These are ones that seek to reduce inflation by decreasing aggregate demand, or at least the growth of aggregate demand. A government could, for instance, raise income tax. This would reduce people's disposable income and their ability to spend.

The main short run anti-inflationary measure being employed in the UK, however, is currently changes in interest rates. Higher interest rates are likely to reduce aggregate demand by reducing consumption, investment and possibly net exports.

Making connections

To reduce inflation, a government introduces policy measures designed to lower aggregate demand. Consider what effect such measures may have on the government's other macroeconomic objectives.

Monetary Policy Committee

The Monetary Policy Committee (MPC) of the Bank of England sets the rate of interest with the main objective of achieving the government's target rate of inflation of 2 per cent, as measured by the CPI. Subject to meeting that objective, it has been instructed to support the economic policy of the government, including its objectives for employment and economic growth. The MPC consists of five members drawn from employees of the Bank of England, including the Governor of the Bank of England, and four economists nominated by the Chancellor of the Exchequer. It meets monthly to review evidence on the performance of the economy and indicators of changes in inflationary pressure. This information includes figures on the current and predicted growth of the money supply, the exchange rate, wage rates, employment, productivity, retail sales and surveys of business and consumer confidence. If the MPC believes that the information points to a risk that inflation will rise above the target, it will raise its interest rate.

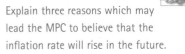

Thinking like an economist

Explain three reasons which may lead the MPC to believe that the inflation rate will rise in the future.

Monetary policy stance

A tight (restrictionist or deflationary) monetary policy is one that aims to reduce aggregate demand usually in a bid to lower inflation or to improve the balance of payments position. In contrast, an expansionary monetary policy approach (reflationary or loose monetary policy) is one that seeks to stimulate a growth in aggregate demand. So reducing the rate of interest would be regarded as an expansionary approach.

Long run

In the long run, a government is likely to seek to reduce the possibility of inflationary pressure by increasing long-run aggregate supply. If the productive capacity of the economy grows in line with aggregate demand, with shifts in the aggregate demand curve being matched by shifts in the LRAS curve, the economy can grow without the price level rising. This will enable people to enjoy more goods and services without the economy experiencing inflationary and balance of payments problems. As noted in Section 3.11, the policies used to increase long-run aggregate supply are supply-side policies. Improvements in education, training, increased incentives and other measures, if successful, should increase the quantity and quality of resources and so increase the maximum output the economy is capable of producing. Supply-side policies are, of course, a long-run approach to controlling inflationary pressure as they take time to have their full impact on productive capacity. They do, nonetheless, have the advantage that they do not run the risk of the adverse short-run side-effects on employment and output that deflationary fiscal and monetary policy may pose.

3.19

Policies to promote economic growth

Introduction

In this spread you will examine policy measures a government may use to increase output in the short run as well as the longer run measures that can be implemented to increase economic growth. You will also examine why governments seek to achieve stable economic growth and the nature of business cycles.

Short run

Increases in output in the short run can occur due to increases in aggregate demand if the economy is initially producing below its productive capacity. In a situation of low economic activity, aggregate demand may be stimulated by expansionary fiscal and/or monetary policy. Some measures of fiscal and monetary policies have the advantages that they may increase both aggregate demand and, in the long run, aggregate supply. For instance, a lower rate of interest is likely to stimulate consumption but also investment and higher investment will raise long-run aggregate supply. Increases in some forms of government spending, for example, spending on education and research and development, will also shift the long-run aggregate supply curve to the right.

Long run

In the long run, increases in output can continue to be achieved only if the productive capacity of the economy increases. This is why changes in long-run aggregate supply are so important. So for economic growth to occur, the quality and/or quantity of resources have to increase. Supply-side policies seek to achieve such an outcome. For instance, measures that raise investment will increase long-run aggregate supply. The extent of the increase will depend on the amount of investment, its type and how efficiently it is used. Capital deepening will be more effective than capital widening. Capital deepening involves increasing the amount of capital per worker. This should raise labour productivity. Capital widening occurs when investment increases to keep up with increases in the supply of labour.

To use capital efficiently it is important to have educated and healthy workers. Investment in **human capital** should increase the productive capacity of the economy but again, the extent to which this occurs is influenced by the appropriateness and the quality of the investment. For example, the function of training and one of the functions of education should be to develop the skills needed in the competitive world market. These include not only numeracy and literacy but also communication, interpersonal skills and literacy and computer technology skills. While increases in the quality and quantity of training and secondary education in a number of countries, including the newly industrialised countries, have come in for praise, the UK has been criticised for its low levels of training, educational standards and 'staying-on' rates. UK employers have been critical

Exam hint

Emphasise the importance of supply-side policies in improving the potential capacity of the economy.

Definition

Human capital: education, training and experience that a worker possesses.

of skill levels, particularly the communication and interpersonal skills, of the school leavers they employ. They, in turn, have been criticised in a number of reports for the poor quantity and insufficient training which they provide.

Stable growth

In seeking to promote economic growth, most governments aim for stable growth. Their objective is for actual growth to match trend growth and for that trend growth to rise over time.

They try to avoid aggregate demand increasing faster than the trend growth rate permits since this can result in the economy overheating, with inflation and balance of payments difficulties arising. They also try to stop aggregate demand rising more slowly than the trend growth rate, since this would mean an output gap developing with unemployed resources. So what most governments are trying to avoid is destabilising fluctuations in economic activity. The Labour government when first elected in 1997 gave as one of its objectives, the end of 'boom and bust'.

One way the Labour government is seeking to achieve greater economic stability is by creating stability of economic policy. It has, for instance, given the Bank of England independence to determine interest rates (subject to its need to meet the government's inflation target), sets three-year spending plans for government departments and has put limits on the level of government debt.

Effects of business cycles

Business cycles, which are sometimes referred to as trade cycles, describe the tendency for economic activity to fluctuate outside its trend growth rate, moving from a high level of economic activity (boom) to negative economic growth (recession). Governments seek to dampen down these cyclical fluctuations because of the harmful effects they can have on the performance of the economy. Uncertainty that aggregate demand will continue to rise will tend to discourage investment. It may also mean that firms are reluctant to increase employment opportunities. During an upturn some employers may also be reluctant to take on more workers for fear that the increased level of activity will not last, while during a downturn some may hoard labour.

Making connections

Discuss four supply-side policies that could be implemented to promote economic growth.

Thinking like an economist

Discuss what factors could cause real GDP to fall

Quick check

1 Identify a fiscal policy measure that can increase both aggregate demand and aggregate supply.
2 Why are supply-side policies so important in promoting economic growth?
3 Why do governments aim for stable economic growth?
4 Distinguish between an economic boom and a recession.

3.20 Policies to improve the balance of payments

Introduction

As with its other objectives, there are both short run and long run policy measures that a government can use to improve its balance of payments position. Again the short run measures tend to concentrate on demand while the long run measures focus on improving the supply-side of the economy.

Short run

In the short run there are three main policy measures a government can use to raise export revenue and/or reduce import expenditure in the case of a current account deficit. These measures are: the government reduces the value of the currency; reduces domestic spending; increases import restrictions. Each measure has the potential to improve the balance of payments position but also has its limitations.

Exchange rate adjustment

A country may seek to reduce its exchange rate if it believes that its current level is too high and as a result is causing its products to be uncompetitive against rival countries' products. A lower exchange rate will cause export prices to fall in terms of foreign countries' currencies and import prices to rise in terms of the domestic currency.

To succeed in increasing export revenue and reduce import expenditure it is important that demand for exports and imports is price elastic, that other countries do not devalue and do not increase their import restrictions.

If the fall in the exchange rate increases demand for the country's products, it is likely that employment and output will also rise in the short run. However, by increasing demand for the country's products and raising import prices it may lead to inflationary pressures.

Demand management

To discourage expenditure on imports and to encourage some products to be switched from the home to the export market, a government may adopt deflationary fiscal and monetary policy measures. Domestic spending may be reduced by higher taxation, lower government spending and/or higher interest rates. However, there is the risk that the resulting reduction in spending may cause output to fall and unemployment to rise.

Import restrictions

A country may seek to reduce expenditure on imports by imposing import restrictions including **tariffs** and **quotas**. However, such measures may have inflationary side-effects. For example, imposing tariffs will increase the price of some products bought in the country, raise the cost of imported raw

Making connections

Explain how a government could seek to reduce the value of its currency.

Definitions

Tariff: a tax on imports.
Quota: a limit on imports.

materials and reduce competitive pressure on domestic firms to keep costs and prices low.

Placing restrictions on imports also runs the risk of provoking retaliation. In addition, membership of a trade bloc, such as the EU, and of the **World Trade Organisation (WTO)** limits the independent action that a country can take on import restrictions.

Long run

If a deficit arises from a lack of quality competitiveness, lower labour productivity or higher inflationary pressure, then reducing the value of the currency, deflationary policy measures and import restrictions will not provide long-term solutions. In such a situation, the most appropriate approach would be to implement supply-side policies.

Supply-side policies

To raise international competitiveness, there are a number of supply-side policies a government may take, including:
- cutting corporation tax to stimulate investment
- cutting income tax to encourage enterprise and effort
- privatising industries if it is thought that firms will operate more efficiently in the private sector
- deregulating markets to promote competition
- promoting education and training to increase productivity and reduce labour costs.

A government may also give subsidies to **infant industries** in the belief that they have the potential to grow and become internationally competitive. It may also increase funds for research and development at universities to encourage invention and innovation.

How successful these measures are depends on the appropriateness of the measures, for example, the type of training provided, and how firms and workers respond to the incentives provided. The measures also can take a relatively long time to have an effect.

Current account surplus

A balance of payments disequilibrium may also arise because of a current account surplus. A government may seek to reduce or remove a surplus in order to avoid inflationary pressures and to raise the amount of imports it can enjoy. To reduce a surplus a government may seek to raise the value of its currency, introduce reflationary fiscal and monetary policy measures and/or reduce import restrictions.

Definition

World Trade Organisation (WTO): an international organisation which promotes free international trade and rules on international trade disputes.

Thinking like an economist

A country is experiencing a large balance of payments deficit. Identify a policy measure that in the short run could increase the country's output and improve its balance of payments position.

Definition

Infant industries: new industries which have not yet grown large enough to take full advantage of economies of scale.

Activities

The application of macroeconomic policies

Activity 1

Governments make use of a range of policies. Three of the most important policies are fiscal, monetary and supply-side.

(a) Distinguish between fiscal policy and monetary policy.
(b) Give two examples of supply-side policies.

Activity 2

At the end of the 1990s and start of the 2000s, the Japanese government was concerned about the level of aggregate demand in the economy. Consumption was falling and investment was low.

(a) What effect might low aggregate demand have on a government's policy objectives?
(b) Discuss what fiscal and monetary policy measures the Japanese government could have taken to raise aggregate demand.

Activity 3

In most EU countries VAT is imposed on food, but at present VAT is not charged on most food sold in the UK.

(a) Using a diagram, explain the effect of the imposition of VAT on food.
(b) Decide whether VAT is a progressive, proportional or regressive tax.
(c) Discuss the effect of the imposition of VAT on:
   (i) aggregate demand
   (ii) distribution of income.

Activity 4

UK firms have been criticised for being slow at developing new technologies, processes and products. A number of factors have been blamed for this shortcoming, including lack of management skills, poor educational performance and firms being more concerned with short-term profits than long-term profits.

(a) What effect is innovation likely to have on aggregate supply?
(b) Explain two measures a government could implement, apart from improved educational standards, to encourage innovation.

Activity 5

The MPC may decide to raise interest rates if it receives information that borrowing and house prices are rising to very high levels.

(a) Explain how high levels of borrowing and house price rises could cause inflation.
(b) Analyse the effect of higher interest rates on borrowing and house prices.
(c) Discuss one other policy measure the government could implement to control inflation.

Activity 6

A country is experiencing a high rate of unemployment and low economic growth.

(a) Explain two policy measures that could improve the country's economic performance in the short term.
(b) Explain two policy measures that could raise the country's economic performance in the long term.

Activity 7

A government receives £420bn in tax revenue and spends £405bn.

(a) Calculate the government's budget position.
(b) Discuss the effect a rise in economic growth would be likely to have on tax revenue.

Activity 8

Due to uncertainty about future economic prospects, Japanese citizens increased their savings at the end of the 1990s and start of the 2000s.

(a) What effect would an increase in savings have on aggregate demand?
(b) Explain what is meant by injections and leakages.
(c) Are savings an injection into, or a leakage from, the circular flow?

Exchange rate changes

Introduction

Changes in a country's exchange rate can have a significant impact on its economy. In this section you will examine the causes and consequences of such a change.

Determination of exchange rates

An exchange rate is the price of one currency in terms of another currency or currencies.

A country or area can operate a fixed or a floating exchange rate. If a **fixed exchange rate** comes under threat by market forces, the central bank, acting on behalf of the government, will step in to maintain the value by buying or selling the currency and/or changing the rate of interest.

Nowadays, though, most countries operate a **floating exchange rate**. This is one determined by market forces. If demand for the currency rises, this will raise the exchange rate whereas if the supply of the currency increases, the exchange rate will fall in value. If UK citizens' demand for imports increases, for instance, UK firms will sell pounds in order to gain the foreign currency to buy imports. This increase in the supply of pounds will reduce its value as shown in Figure 1.

Factors affecting exchange rates

A number of factors influence the value of a floating exchange rate and put upward or downward pressure on a fixed exchange rate. One is relative inflation rates. A country that is experiencing an inflation rate above that of its competitors is also likely to experience a decrease in demand for its exports and a rise in demand for imports. This would cause demand for the currency to fall and supply of the currency to rise and so tend to reduce the value of the currency.

Rises in income levels abroad, in contrast, will tend to increase a country's exchange rate. This is because foreigners will have more income to spend on the country's exports.

The exchange rate will also tend to rise if the country's products rise in quality relative to its competitors. This is because it will increase demand for the country's products and so increase demand for its currency. Improvements in marketing and after sales services will have a similar effect.

A key reason why the value of the currency may change is changes in relative interest rates. If a country's interest rate rises relative to other countries it is likely to attract an inflow of funds from abroad into its financial institutions. This will increase demand for the currency and is likely to raise its value.

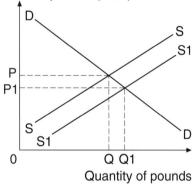

Price of pounds (in $s)

Figure 1: Effect of an increase in the supply of pounds

Speculation is also now an important influence on the exchange rate. A high percentage of the dealing in foreign exchange markets is accounted for by speculation. Speculators buy and sell currency hoping to make a profit from movements in interest rates and exchange rates. Speculation can have a stabilising or a destabilising effect on exchange rates. If speculators respond to a falling exchange rate by selling some of their holdings of the currency, they will drive the rate down further. But if they think the rate will soon start to rise they will purchase the currency now, thereby preventing a large fall.

Effects of exchange rate movements

A rise in the exchange rate will raise the price of the country's exports in terms of foreign currencies and reduce the price of imports in terms of the domestic currency. This will put downward pressure on inflation. This is because the price of imported raw materials will fall, thereby reducing the cost of production and the price of imported finished products that count in the calculation of the country's inflation rate. In addition, domestic firms, facing cheaper imported rival products at home and facing the prospect of their products becoming more expensive abroad will be under pressure to cut their costs in order to keep their prices low.

A rise in the exchange rate will improve the **terms of trade**. The sale of each export would enable more imports to be purchased. However, the change in prices will affect demand. If demand for exports is elastic, the revenue earned from selling exports will fall, thereby reducing the overall purchasing power of the country.

Higher priced exports and cheaper imports may also reduce the industrial base of the country. Some firms may not be able to compete at home and/or abroad as a result of the higher exchange rate and some may go out of business. This will reduce the rate of economic growth and cause unemployment.

Quick check

1   Explain what it means if the UK's exchange rate is £1 = $2.
2   What effect would a rise in UK interest rates have on the value of the pound?
3   Identify two causes of a fall in the value of the pound.
4   What effect would a rise in the value of the pound have on the price of UK exports and imports?

 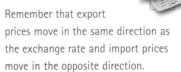

Pattern of international trade

nternational trade (external trade) involves the movement of goods and services across national boundaries. This section concentrates on the countries and products the UK trades in and recent UK trade performance.

Making connections

Using an aggregate demand and aggregate supply diagram, analyse the effect of a US recession on the UK economy.

The countries the UK trades with

The UK's main trading partners are the USA, Germany, France and the Netherlands. We tend to buy from and sell to mainly industrialised countries with which we have economic and social ties. As Tables 1 and 2 show, European Union countries figure prominently in our top trading partners.

Table 1: Main destination of UK exports 2001

	£m
1. USA	29,643
2. Germany	23,907
3. France	19,462
4. Netherlands	14,761
5. Irish Republic	13,896
6. Belgium and Luxembourg	10,009
7. Italy	8,526
8. Spain	8,429
9. Japan	3,815
10. Switzerland	3,079

Table 2: Main source of imports 2001

	£m
1. USA	29,805
2. Germany	28,407
3. France	19,135
4. Netherlands	14,975
5. Belgium and Luxembourg	13,026
6. Italy	9,743
7. Irish Republic	9,334
8. Japan	9,241
9. Norway	5,630
10. Switzerland	4,638

Thinking like an economist

Consider the impact that the entry of Poland and East European countries will have on the UK's pattern of trade.

Source: Table 15.8, Monthly Digest of Statistics, ONS, April 2002

The UK's performance

The UK usually has a surplus in oil, chemicals, beverages and medical products but a deficit in most other categories of goods including clothing, consumer goods, food, motor cars and plastics.

In contrast, the country usually records a surplus on most of the categories in the trade in services section.

The performance in the different categories reflects the competitiveness of different UK industries. There are a number of industries in which the UK is very internationally competitive. These include pharmaceuticals, business services, computer software, civil aviation and financial services. The industries in which the UK is least competitive tend to be those heavily dependent on heavy capital investment or cheap labour and which are facing strong competition from developing countries. They include footwear, iron, steel and textiles.

Research task

Using the Monthly Digest of Statistics or UK Balance of Payments, the Pink Book, find out this year's top ten destinations of UK exports and top ten sources of UK imports and compare them with the 2001 lists.

Quick check

1 Identify the UK's four main trading partners.
2 Why is it expected that Poland will become more important as a trading partner for the UK in the future?
3 Identify three products in which the UK is internationally competitive.
4 How many countries are in the EU?

The effect of international trade

Introduction

Free international trade can bring a number of significant advantages but it may also impose a number of costs. In this section you will examine the nature of free trade, what determines which products countries specialise in and export, and the advantages and disadvantages of free international trade.

International free trade

As its name suggests, international free trade occurs when there are no restrictions imposed on the movement of goods and services into and out of countries. The fewer the restrictions on imports and exports, the greater the value of international trade is likely to be.

The basis of international trade

A small amount of international trade is based on what is called **absolute advantage**. A country is said to have an absolute advantage in producing a product when it is better at producing it than other countries. More technically, it means that it can produce more of the product from each unit of resource than other countries – it has greater productivity.

Most international trade is now, however, based on **comparative advantage**. A large proportion of the UK's trade, for example, is with countries producing products the country is either making or could make in fairly similar quantities per worker.

Comparative advantage, as its name suggests, is concerned with relative efficiency. A country is said to have a comparative advantage in a product when it is even better at making that product or not so bad at making the product. This can be expressed in terms of opportunity cost – a country has a comparative advantage if it can produce a good or service at a lower opportunity cost than another country.

The principle or theory of comparative advantage states that both of two countries will benefit from specialisation and trade even if one country is more efficient at making both products as long as there is a difference in their relative efficiencies.

For example, assume that each worker in the USA can make either six cars or 120 toys and each worker in China can make either two cars or 80 toys.

Definitions

Absolute advantage: the ability to produce output using fewer resources than other regions or countries.

Comparative advantage: relative efficiency – ability to produce a product at a lower opportunity cost than other regions or countries.

	Cars	Toys
USA	6	120
China	2	80

Table 1: Position before specialisation and trade

The USA has the absolute advantage in the production of both of the goods. Its comparative advantage, however, lies in the production of cars. It can produce three times as many cars as China but only one and a half times as many cars. Opportunity cost ratios also confirm this. The opportunity cost of one car in America is lower than in China, 20 toys as opposed to 40 toys.

Benefits and costs of international trade

In theory, if countries specialise and trade, total output will be greater. The resulting rise in living standards is the main benefit claimed for free international trade.

Consumers can benefit from the lower prices and higher quality that result from the higher level of competition that arises from countries trading internationally. They also enjoy a greater variety of products including a few not made in their own countries.

Although firms will face greater competition in their domestic markets, they will also have access to larger markets in which to sell their products and from which to buy raw materials (enabling them to take greater advantage of economies of scale).

Despite all these advantages and increasing trade liberalisation, restrictions on exports and, more particularly, imports still exist. This can be because governments are concerned that, for example, certain undesirable products may be imported, that the continued existence of new and strategic industries may be threatened and other countries will not engage in fair competition.

International trade poses challenges for countries. Competition from other countries and access to their markets results in some industries contracting and some expanding. This requires the shifting of resources that can be unsettling and may be difficult to achieve due to, for example, occupational immobility of labour.

Protectionism

Definition

Protectionism: the restriction on the free movement of products between countries.

Thinking like an economist

Assess the effect the imposition of tariffs may have on aggregate demand.

Introduction

Protectionism refers to the deliberate restriction of the free movement of goods and services between countries and trade blocs. A government engages in protectionism when it introduces measures to protect its own industries from competition from the industries of other countries.

Protectionist measures

The best-known protectionist measure is tariffs (which can also be called customs duties or import duties). They are taxes on imported products. They can be imposed with the intention of raising revenue and/or discouraging domestic consumers from buying imported products. For example, the European Union's common external tariff, which is a tax on imports coming into the EU from countries outside, does raise revenue, but its main purpose is to encourage EU member countries to trade with each other.

Tariffs can be ad valorem (percentage taxes) or specific (fixed sum taxes). The effect of imposing a tariff is to raise prices for domestic consumers and, in the absence of any retaliation, shift demand from imports to domestically produced products.

Figure 1 shows the effect of a specific tariff. Before the country engages in international trade, price is P and the quantity purchased is Q, all of which comes from domestic suppliers. When the country engages in international trade, the number of producers in the market increases significantly. The increase in competition drives price down to P1.

The quantity demanded extends to Q1. Of this amount QX is now bought from domestic suppliers and QX–Q1 from foreign firms. Therefore, domestic supply falls from Q to QX.

The imposition of a tariff causes the world supply to decrease to WS1. It raises the price to P2 and causes the quantity to be purchased on the domestic market to fall to Q2. Domestic supply rises to QY and imports fall to QY–Q2. Domestic producers gain but this is at the expense of domestic consumers.

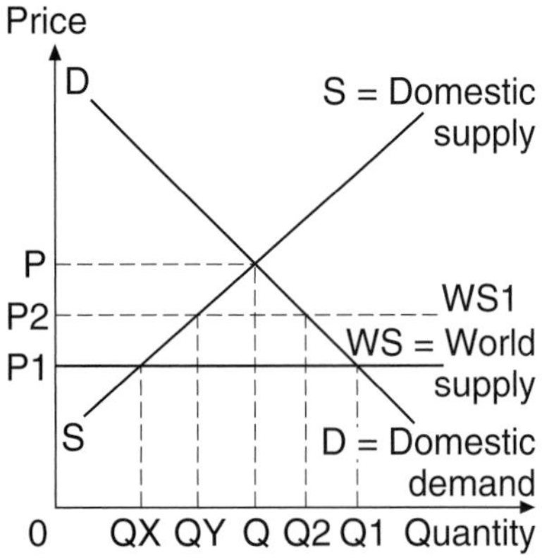

Another well-known measure is a quota. This is a limit on the supply of a good or service. It can be imposed on exports. For example, a developing country may seek to limit the export of food during a period of food shortages. However, quotas on imports are more common. For example, a quota may place a restriction on the imports of cars to, for example, 40,000 a year or alternatively, to, for example, £400,000 worth of cars. The effect of a quota is to reduce supply. This is likely to push up price. Foreign firms will experience a reduction in the quantity they can sell but they may benefit from the higher price if demand for their products is inelastic and if the quotas are not operated via the selling of import licences.

Figure 1: Effect of a tariff

A voluntary export restraint or restriction (VER) is similar to a quota but this time the limit on imports arises from a voluntary agreement between the exporting and the importing country. A country may agree to restrict its exports in return for a similar limit being put on the exports of the importing country or to avoid more damaging import restrictions being imposed on its products. VERs have been used frequently by the EU and the USA. For example, the EU entered into several VERs with Japan which restricted the sale of Japanese cars.

A government or an area may also seek to reduce imports by limiting the amount of foreign exchange made available to those wishing to import goods and services or to invest or to travel abroad. This is a measure which was used by a number of European countries, including the UK, in the 1960s and 1970s and is still found in some developing countries.

Another measure is an embargo. This is a ban on the export or import of a product and/or a ban on trade with a particular country. For example, a country may ban the export of arms to a country with a poor human rights record, may prohibit the importation of hard-core pornography and is likely to break off trading relations with a country during a military conflict.

Time-delaying customs procedures may be used to discourage imports. If it takes time to complete long and complex customs forms it will be more expensive to import products.

Two additional measures are quality standards and government purchasing policies. Quality standards may set high and complex requirements with the intention of raising the costs of foreign firms seeking to export to the country. A government may also try to reduce imports by favouring domestic firms when it places orders even when the domestic firms are producing at a higher cost or lower quality.

Making connections

Consider the effect that import restrictions may have on efficiency.

Quick check

1 Identify two reasons for imposing a tariff.
2 What effect will a reduction in a tariff on an imported product be likely to have on its price, and the amount of it consumed?
3 What is meant by a voluntary export restriction?
4 What is the most extreme method of protectionism?

Arguments for and against protection

Introduction

There are a number of arguments put forward for imposing restrictions on free trade. Some of these are for protecting most industries and some are for restricting a few, specific industries. In assessing these arguments it is important to understand the case for and against such moves.

Arguments for general import restrictions

One traditional reason for imposing import restrictions is to protect domestic employment. Some argue that imposing import restrictions will mean that the country's citizens will purchase more domestic products and thereby raise domestic employment. Imposing import restrictions, however, is likely to reduce other countries' ability to buy exports and may revoke retaliation. So the country's exports may decline and any jobs created by imports may be offset by jobs lost due to the fall in imports. Indeed, the level of unemployment may rise if the imposition of tariffs results in a trade war with other countries raising their tariffs higher and higher – building 'tariff walls' around their countries. There will also be a welfare loss resulting from countries not being able to specialise to any greater extent in those products in which they have a comparative advantage.

Countries also sometimes impose import restrictions in order to improve their balance of payments position. The intention is to switch domestic expenditure from imports to expenditure on domestic products. However, again, such a policy may provoke a trade war and may reduce the degree of specialisation. In addition, just imposing import restrictions in the absence of any other policy measures does not solve the cause of any current account deficit. If domestic consumers are purchasing imports because their quality is higher, for example, they may still continue to buy imports even after the restrictions have been imposed.

Another argument advanced is to protect the country's industries from 'unfair low wage competition' from abroad. This would involve putting restrictions on the imports from certain countries. Some argue that if the wages paid to workers in developing countries are very low then firms in industrialised countries will not be able to compete unless they reduce wages to unacceptably low levels. However, low wages do not always mean low unit wage costs. Due to a lack of capital equipment and education, labour productivity in a number of countries is low.

Being able to sell products without restrictions to industrialised countries may enable income levels to rise in developing countries. This may result in their levels of investment, education, wages and purchases of products from industrialised countries rising.

The competition from low-wage countries may also reflect the fact that those countries have a comparative advantage in low-skilled, labour-intensive industries. In which case, unemployment in certain industries may rise but the rise may be temporary if the labour can move into industries in which the country does have a comparative advantage.

Where the case has more justification is where the wages are being held below the equilibrium rates, the working conditions are poor and child or slave labour is employed.

Arguments for protecting particular industries

These include the prevention of **dumping**. Foreign firms may engage in dumping because government subsidies permit them to sell at very low prices or because they are seeking to raise profits by price discriminating. Domestic consumers may benefit in the short run from lower prices but in the long run, if domestic firms are driven out of business, they may face less choice and higher prices.

Governments also often seek to protect **infant industries**. These may find it difficult to grow because their average costs may be higher than their well-established foreign competitors. If they are given protection in their early years, they may be able to grow and thereby take advantage of economies of scale, lower their average costs and become competitive. At this stage the protection could be removed. This argument is thought to be particularly strong in the case of high technology industries that have high fixed costs and which have a potential comparative advantage. There is, however, a risk that the industries may become dependent on protection.

It is also argued by some that declining industries and strategic industries should be protected. If industries which no longer have a comparative advantage go out of business quickly there may be a sudden and large increase in unemployment. Protection may enable an industry to contract gradually, thereby allowing time for resources, including labour, to move to other industries. Protecting strategic industries allows countries to have a degree of self-sufficiency in those industries, (for example, arms and agriculture) in case disputes or military conflicts cut off supplies.

Quick check

1 What is meant by a trade war?
2 Identify two arguments for general import restrictions.
3 What are the motives behind dumping?
4 Explain the argument in favour of protecting infant industries.

Definitions

Dumping: the sale of products at less than cost price.
Infant industries: newly established industries that are also called sunrise industries.

Exam hint

Remember that the arguments against protection are based on the benefits of free trade.

Hot potato

In recent years there has been something of a trade war between the EU and the USA. The EU has banned all hormone-treated beef largely because of public concern about food safety. This has hit US farmers in particular, as there is widespread use of hormones in US beef farming.

3.27

Activities

Structure and essential determinants of international transactions

Activity 1

	Output per worker per day	
	Country X	Country Y
Televisions	10	20
Bottles of lemonade	80	240

(a) Which country has the absolute advantage in producing televisions?
(b) What is the opportunity cost of producing a television in both countries?
(c) Which country has the comparative advantage in producing televisions?

Activity 2

In 2002 the USA imposed tariffs of up to 30 per cent on imported steel. The US government claimed that other countries were dumping steel and damaging its domestic industry.

(a) Define a tariff.
(b) Explain what is meant by dumping.

Activity 3

In August 2002 the UK exported goods and services worth £21bn but imported goods and services worth £23bn.

(a) Comment on the trade in goods and services position.
(b) Explain another component of the current account.

Activity 4

The high value of the pound sterling at the end of the 1990s and start of the 2000s led to some concern among economists and business people. One of their worries was that the value of sterling would fall suddenly and abruptly. While exporters would benefit from a lower exchange rate, a large fall would raise the price of imported raw materials significantly and could feed through to domestically generated inflation.

(a) What might cause the value of the pound to fall?
(b) Explain why a fall in the exchange rate may create inflation.
(c) Discuss the advantage of a lower exchange rate.

Activity 5

In the early 2000s, the UK's trade position came under a number of pressures. One was the US recession and the sharp slowdown in the German and other large European economies. Another pressure was the strength of spending by UK citizens. Both these pressures contributed to a trade in goods deficit.

(a) Explain why the events outlined above would have been likely to have led to a trade deficit.

(b) Discuss one other possible cause of a trade deficit.

Activity 6

| | UK international trade by area 2001 £m | |
	Exports	Imports
European Union	110,832	115,538
Other western European countries	7,182	12,548
North America	33,867	35,156
Other OECD countries	10,925	17,417
Oil exporting countries	6,483	4,003
Rest of the world	21,693	39,594

(a) With which area of the world did the UK trade most in 2001?

(b) Comment on the UK's trade position with the different areas.

Activity 7

Many economists and politicians throughout the world emphasise the benefits of free trade and yet tariffs, quotas and other trade restrictions are imposed by many countries.

(a) Explain the likely effects of imposing a quota.

(b) Discuss one trade restriction, apart from a tariff and a quota.

Activity 8

In recent years, UK's exports to Spain have been increasing while the country's exports to Australia have been declining.

(a) Explain two reasons why exports to a country may change.

(b) Identify the UK's four main trading partners.

Question

Ireland is a major trading partner of the UK. Trade between the two countries continues to rise, with both exports and imports increasing. Both countries have witnessed increases in their aggregate demand and long-run aggregate supply. However, there has been a difference in their economic performance.

Ireland's economic growth rate declined from 11.5 per cent in 2000 to 5.3 per cent in 2003 but remained above that of the UK. However, while UK unemployment fell in this period, Ireland's unemployment rose and the economy experienced a higher rate of inflation than the UK (see Table 1).

In a bid to improve the UK's economic growth rate, the government introduced a number of fiscal policy measures and supply-side policies in the early 2000s.

Table 1

		Inflation rates (per cent) 2000–2003	
Year	UK	Ireland
2000	0.8	5.2
2001	1.2	4.0
2002	1.2	4.4
2003	1.6	2.8

(a) Define:
   (i) aggregate demand   (2)
   (ii) fiscal policy.   (2)

(b) (i) Consider two causes of a rise in UK exports.   (4)
   (ii) Using an aggregate demand and aggregate supply diagram,
        analyse the effect of an increase in exports on an economy.   (6)

(c) (i) State what is meant by a decline in a country's economic
        growth rate.   (2)
   (ii) Explain two supply-side policies a government could use to
        increase its economic growth rate.   (4)

(d) (i) Using Table 1, compare the changes in the UK's price level
        from 2000 to 2003 with that of Ireland's price level over the
        same period.   (4)
   (ii) Explain two possible costs of inflation.   (4)

(e) Discuss the effectiveness of one monetary policy measure in
    reducing unemployment.   (12)

Exam guidance

T he examination lasts for one hour. The number of marks allocated is 45. Remember you should first read through the questions, then examine the data and then look through the questions again. The amount you should write on each question part is indicated by the space provided in the answer booklet.

(a) (i) The key directive word here is 'define'. This means you should provide the meaning of aggregate demand (total demand for the economy's products) and in this case, state that it consists of C + I + G + X − M.

(ii) Again, the word 'define' indicates that you must provide the meaning of fiscal policy (changes in government spending and taxation).

(b) (i) 'Consider' means to give your thoughts on the question. Here you need to identify two causes and briefly explain why they would lead to arise in UK exports. For instance, a rise in incomes abroad increases foreigners' ability to buy UK products. Also a rise in UK product quality would increase their willingness to buy UK.

(ii) You need to both draw a diagram to illustrate the effect of an increase in exports and provide an explanation. Exports are a component of AD. An increase in exports will shift the AD curve to the right. The effect that this has on the economy will depend on the extent of the increase in exports and the initial output position.

Draw a diagram of at least a third of a page and label it. In Figure 1, the Keynesian LRAS curve has been used, and AD is shown to be shifting from a position of relatively low output to one that intersects LRAS near to full capacity.

In commenting on the effect on the economy, examine the impact on output, price level and employment. If the economy is not initially operating at the full employment level, an increase in AD would be expected to raise output, employment and the price level.

(c) (i) The key directive word 'state' means that you must make something clear. Here you need to show that you know that a decline in a country's economic growth means the country's output, as measured by real GDP, is increasing at a slower rate. For instance, the rate of economic growth may decline from 5 per cent to 3 per cent. This would mean that in the previous year output increased by 5 per cent whereas this year it only rose by 3 per cent.

(ii) You should identify two appropriate supply-side policies, e.g. cuts in direct taxes and increased spending on training, and explain how they could increase the country's economic growth rate. Cuts in direct taxes

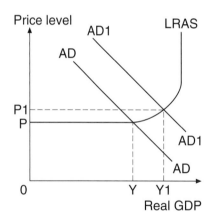

Figure 1: Effect of an increase in exports on an economy

may encourage some workers to work more hours, some people to enter the labour force, and some firms to undertake more investment. Such a response would increase the quantity of resources and shift the LRAS curve to the right. Increased spending on investment and training would also be likely to shift the LRAS curve to the right – this time because the quantity of resources would increase.

(d) (i) It is important when commenting on statistical data that you draw conclusions and do not just describe the data. In this case, you should recognise that inflation rates show percentage increases in the price level. There are a number of comparisons you could make. In both countries the price level rose throughout the period but more slowly in the UK. The price level in the UK rose steadily over most of the period shown but the price level in Ireland was rising more slowly at the end of the period than at the start.

(ii) You need to identify two costs of inflation and to explain how inflation generates these costs. For example, inflation, if higher than rival countries' inflation rates, will reduce the price competitiveness of the country's products. This might result in balance of payments problems. Inflation may also create uncertainty which can discourage investment and so reduce economic growth.

(e) The last question part is marked using what are called 'levels'. Answers are classified into four levels with Level 1 receiving the lowest marks and Level 4 the highest marks. To gain Level 1 you have to show knowledge and understanding of the topic of the question. In this case you need to identify a monetary policy measure that could be used, i.e. interest rates, the money supply or the exchange rate.

Level 2 requires you to use application skills. Here you would need to apply a monetary policy measure to the policy objective. This would involve you stating what should be done with the measure in order to reduce unemployment. For instance, interest rates could be reduced.

At Level 3 it is necessary to analyse. This involves explanation. In this case, if you have selected interest rates you should explain how a fall in interest rates would be expected to raise aggregate demand by considering how they will affect consumption, investment and net exports.

At Level 4 you need to evaluate. This involves making judgements. In this case, you might mention, for instance, that lowering interest rates might not be very effective in reducing unemployment if confidence is low.

Part 1

Sections 1.1–1.17, 1.21 C.Bamford and S.Munday, *Markets*, Heinemann, 2002, Chapters 1, 2, 3, 4, 5, 6, 7

Sections 1.1, 1.4 S.Munday, *Markets and Market Failure*, Heinemann, 2000, Chapter 1

Sections 1.2, 1.8, 1.10 G.Hale, *Labour Markets*, Heinemann, 2001, Chapters 1, 2, 4

Sections 1.18–1.21 A.Griffiths and S.Ison, *Business Economics*, Heinemann, 2001, Chapter 1, 2, 3–7

Part 2

Sections 2.1–2.14 S.Munday, *Markets and Market Failure*, Heinemann, 2000 Chapters 1, 2, 3, 4, 5, 6, 7, 8

Section 2.9 C.Bamford, *Transport Economics*, 3rd edn., Heinemann, 2001, Chapter 4

Section 2.13 A.Griffiths and S.Ison, *Business Economics*, Heinemann, 2001 Chapter 9

Part 3

Sections 3.1–3.12, 3.16–3.20, 3.22–3.26 C.Bamford and S.Grant, *The UK Economy in a Global Context*, Heinemann 2000, Chapters 1, 2, 3, 4, 5, 6, 7, 8

Sections 3.2, 3.3 S.Grant, *Economic Growth and Business Cycles*, Heinemann, 1999, Chapters 1-6

Sections 3.3, 3.4, 3.14, 3.16, 3.18, 3.19 D.Smith, *UK Current Economic Policy*, 2nd edition, Heinemann, 2003, Chapters 2, 3, 4, 5, 6.

Section 3.4 G. Hale, *Labour Economics*, Heinemann, 2001, Chapter 5

Sections 3.11, 3.16 M.Cook and N.Healey, *Supply-side Policies*, Heinemann, 2001, Chapters 1, 3-7

Sections 3.15, 3.18 M.Russell and D.Heathfield, *Inflation and UK Monetary Policy*, Heinemann, 1999, Chapters 6-9

Section 3.19 S.Grant, *Economic Growth and Business Cycles*, Heinemann, 1999, Chapters 2-4

Section 3.22 C.Bamford and S.Munday, *Markets*, Heinemann, 2000, Chapter 6

PART 4/A2

Work and leisure and transport economics

Work and leisure and transport economics – an overview

Introduction

Candidates have to sit either Paper 2884 (Economics of Work and Leisure) or Paper 2885 (Transport Economics). These modules are built on the work you undertook at AS level, particularly the work you did on the first two, largely microeconomic topics.

There are similarities between the two modules in their context – see the spider diagrams that follow. Both include trends in their markets, theories of market structure and competitive behaviour, how resources are allocated and market failure. Obviously what is different is the markets which have been chosen as the contexts for study.

Both markets are interesting ones. Whichever one you study you should enjoy finding out more about the market and applying relevant economic concepts and analysis in examining key issues in the market. You will already have some knowledge and understanding of both markets. We are all consumers of leisure, most of us are workers and we all use a variety of transport modes.

In both modules you will make use of what you learned at AS on price determination, the characteristics of market structures and the causes and consequences of market failure. You will learn new concepts and explore familiar concepts in more depth; particularly market structures.

The examination

The module is assessed in a I $1\frac{1}{2}$ hour examination paper. The examination counts for 15% of the total A' level marks. It consists of one data response question and one structured essay from a choice of three.

Maximising your grade

To achieve a high grade, it is particularly important to develop your analytical, evaluative and essay writing skills. In assessing labour or transport market issues you need to apply not only relevant economic concepts, but also to explain the points you are making using appropriate economic analysis and, for the higher marked questions, to make judgements supported by economic evidence and analysis.

The first part (a) of the structured essay questions is likely to begin with the word 'explain' to emphasise to you that you must analyse. The second part (b) will probably start with the word 'discuss' and will require you to evaluate.

There is a widespread coverage of labour market and transport market issues in newspaper articles, magazines, and websites. So try to keep in touch with developments in the market you have selected by regularly reading relevant articles and visiting appropriate websites. Also regularly check and analyse labour market and transport market data. Such data can be found in ONS publications and on its website. The sections in Social Trends are particularly informative.

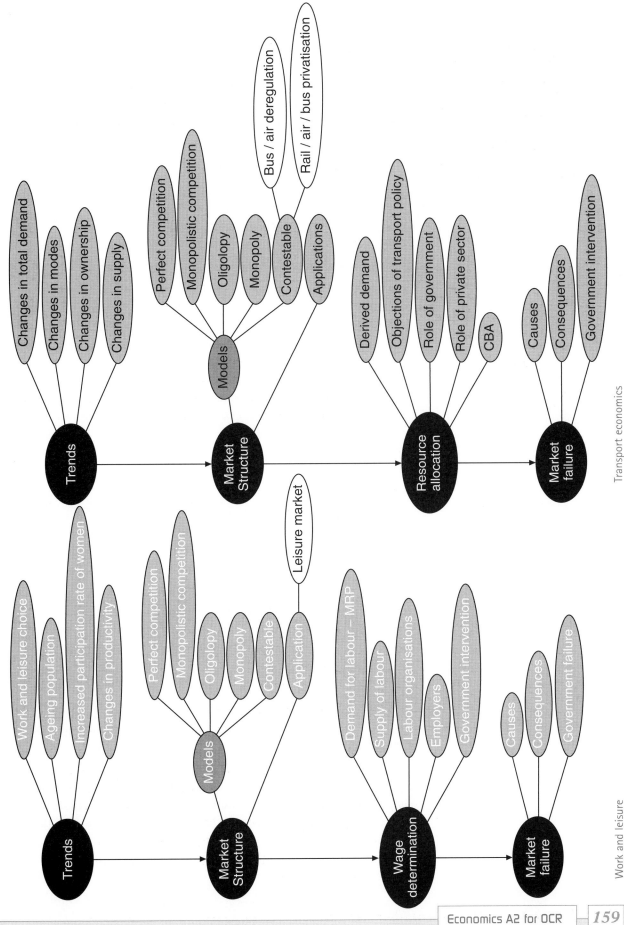

Transport economics

Transport economics map:

- **Trends**
  - Changes in total demand
  - Changes in modes
  - Changes in ownership
  - Changes in supply
- **Market Structure**
  - Models
    - Perfect competition
    - Monopolistic competition
    - Oligolopy
    - Monopoly
    - Contestable
      - Bus / air deregulation
    - Applications
      - Rail / air / bus privatisation
- **Resource allocation**
  - Derived demand
  - Objections of transport policy
  - Role of government
  - Role of private sector
  - CBA
- **Market failure**
  - Causes
  - Consequences
  - Government intervention

Work and leisure

Work and leisure map:

- **Trends**
  - Work and leisure choice
  - Ageing population
  - Increased participation rate of women
  - Changes in productivity
- **Market Structure**
  - Models
    - Perfect competition
    - Monopolistic competition
    - Oligolopy
    - Monopoly
    - Contestable
    - Application
      - Leisure market
- **Wage determination**
  - Demand for labour – MRP
  - Supply of labour
  - Labour organisations
  - Employers
  - Government intervention
- **Market failure**
  - Causes
  - Consequences
  - Government failure

Earnings and employment 4.1

Introduction

This is an interesting time to study the UK labour market. Changes are occurring in a number of aspects of employment and earnings. This Section also shows that age, gender, ethnicity and location all influence the chances someone has of gaining a job and the pay they receive.

Age

UK workers are getting older. In 1991, the average age of people in the labour force (also called the workforce) was 37.5 years. This had risen to 39 years by 2001, and there is now also a higher proportion of workers aged between 50 and 64 years of age.

Older workers tend to change their jobs less frequently and be less geographically and occupationally mobile than young workers. They are less likely to lose their jobs but if they do become unemployed, they take longer to return to work. They also participate less in training. An ageing labour force has a number of implications for both the labour market and the wider economy. It tends to raise employers' wage costs. As older workers change their jobs less frequently, they reduce firms' turnover costs, including recruitment and initial training costs. Their experience may also have positive effects on productivity. This downward pressure on wage costs is, however, usually more than offset by the tendency for pay rising with age.

The lower mobility of older workers makes the labour market less flexible. At a time of considerable technological change and globalisation, it is increasingly important for workers to be able to move smoothly from one job to another and from one area to another area. Work experience may raise productivity but older workers may still be less productive than their younger counterparts due to their knowledge and skills becoming dated and due to a greater risk of ill health.

In the UK and many other industrialised countries, this ageing population is putting ever greater strain on the health service and pension provision. In 2003, 3.5 people in the labour force were supporting each person over 65 but in 2038 there will be only 2.4 workers for each pensioner.

Gender

Women are continuing to form an increasing proportion of the UK's labour force. In 1971, women formed 38.5 per cent of the labour force but this had risen to 44.7 per cent by 2002. This rise reflects an increase in the participation rate of women and a decline in the participation rate of men. In 1986, 88 per cent of males of working age were **economically active** and 68 per cent of females. By 2001 this had changed to an economic activity rate for males of 83 per cent and 72 per cent of females.

Synoptic link

This section builds on the knowledge and understanding of labour markets you gained in AS Section 1.16.

Thinking like an economist

What effect would an increase in the number of women entering the labour force have on the country's productive potential?

Hot potato

Should the retirement age be raised?

The major rise in the participation rate of women has come in the 25 to 44 age range. In 1971, just over half of this group were economically active. By 2002, this had risen to over three-quarters. There are a variety of reasons why women are participating more. These include increased job opportunities for women, increased pay, changing social attitudes, increased expectations of living standards. Women are also tending to have children later and returning to work more quickly.

Women are less likely to be unemployed than men but they are less well paid than men. In 2002, the hourly earnings of women working full time were 81.5 per cent that of men, although there were considerable variations between different occupations as shown in Table 1.

Table 1: Gender pay gap by occupation, 2002

	Female full-time hourly earnings as a percentage of male earnings
Company financial managers	59.9
Marketing/sales managers	67.9
Computer operators	75.7
Doctors	80.8
Solicitors	84.4
Waiters/waitresses	85.9
Police officers	90.2
Nurses	98.0
Retail cash desk/checkout operators	99.4

There are a number of reasons why women are, on average, paid less than men. These include older women having fewer qualifications than their male counterparts, women workers being concentrated in lower-paid occupations, and **discrimination**. The trend is for the gap to narrow as women's qualifications are rising, women's ambitions are rising and discrimination is being overcome.

Ethnic minorities

People from ethnic minorities are also, on average, less well paid. This is partly because of discrimination. They are also disadvantaged by having higher unemployment rates. Unemployment rates for black, Pakistani and Bangladeshi people are currently three times higher than that for white people. For all ethnic minority groups, unemployment is much higher among young people aged 16 to 24 than for other age groups. Nearly one in three of young black people are unemployed.

Definitions

Economically active: those in employment plus those unemployed.
Discrimination: treating one group differently than other groups.

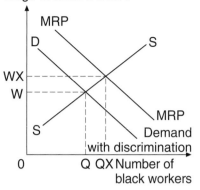

Wage of black workers

Figure 1: A discriminating employer labour market

Thinking like an economist

Discuss whether the pay gap between white workers and workers from ethnic minorities is likely to narrow over time.

The lower wages and higher unemployment arise in part from discrimination. If employers believe through prejudice that the productivity of black workers is lower than it actually is, the wage rate paid to those workers and their employment will be below the allocatively efficient level as Figure 1 shows.

Asian and Asian British women are the least economically-active members of the population. Bangladeshi women are particularly unlikely to be part of the labour force. In 2002, Bangladeshi women had an economic activity rate of only 22 per cent. This low rate reflects, in part, language difficulties as well as cultural influences.

People from ethnic minorities, particularly Chinese, Pakistani and Bangladeshi people, are more likely to be self-employed than the population as a whole. Many of these work in the distribution, hotels and restaurants sector.

Sectors

There continues to be a decline in the numbers employed in the manufacturing sector and an increase in the numbers employed in the tertiary sector. In recent years, the largest increase in employment for both men and women has been in financial and business services.

Wage rates vary between industrial sectors. For instance, workers in agriculture, distribution, hotels and restaurants are relatively low paid while people in financial services are well paid.

Region

In recent years, total employment has been increasing in most regions. The largest rise has been in London, the West Midlands and the South-East. Employment has fallen, however, in the Yorkshire and Humberside region, the East Midlands and the East regions.

In 2002, the average gross annual pay for full-time employees was £24,603. London had by far the highest average earnings and the North East the lowest. High earnings in London reflect high levels of employment and the high quality of jobs there.

Other changes

While most people still work on a full-time basis, the number of people working part-time increased by more than 30 per cent between 1986 and 2002. Now more than one-fifth of those in employment are working part-time. More women than men work part-time. The reasons why men and women work part-time differ. Most women choose to work part-time in order to spend time looking after their children. However, surveys indicate that only about a quarter of male employees in part-time employment have chosen to do so. Most are working part-time while seeking full-time employment.

The proportion of the labour force that is self-employed continues to rise. A report from the Department of Trade and Industry (1999) predicted that four out of ten workers will be self-employed. The main industrial categories in which people are self-employed are construction, distribution, hotels and restaurants, banking, finance and insurance. The fastest growth, however, is in artistic and literary creation, hairdressing and other beauty treatments.

Unit labour costs

Unit labour costs are wages per unit of output. Changes in the nature of the labour force will influence unit labour costs. The two key influences on unit labour costs are wage rates and productivity. If productivity rises by more than wage rates, unit labour costs will fall. A rise in the quality of the labour force, through improved education and training, would put downward pressure on unit labour costs and would be likely to raise the country's international competitiveness. With an ageing population, regular on-the-job training is likely to become increasingly important.

Quick check

1　Explain three effects of an ageing population.
2　Why are more women entering the labour force?
3　Why, on average, do people from ethnic minorities earn less than the white population?
4　Identify two industries that are experiencing increases in employment and two that are experiencing decreases in employment.

Puzzler

Which occupations will be in high demand and highly paid in 2020?

4.2 Work and leisure

Synoptic link

In this section you can apply your understanding of demand and supply analysis to leisure.

Introduction

Section 4.1 concentrated on employment, unemployment and earnings. People, however, do not spend all their time working or seeking work. This Section looks at the issue of how people spend their free or leisure time. It starts by defining leisure and examining different forms of leisure. It discusses the demand and supply of leisure and recent developments in the leisure market.

The meaning of leisure

Leisure is an experience that occurs outside working hours within the time when people are free to select what they do. People's time can be divided into three main categories:

- work/education
- maintenance time, for example, time spent looking after children, sleeping, bathing, eating and undertaking domestic work – the activities necessary for existence
- leisure.

So leisure time is the time which people have left to spend in ways they wish after they have completed their work/educational and maintenance commitments. Leisure can also be regarded as a product – something we consume. We demand leisure products. Some we pay for, such as a ticket to a football match, and some we are not charged directly for, such as jogging.

Of course it is not always clear-cut as to what constitutes leisure. Someone may regard time spent gardening as maintenance time while another person may regard it as leisure time. Similarly one person studying an A level subject might be doing so for 'leisure reasons' while another might be doing it as part of a course with the intention of using the qualification to gain access to higher education. In addition, while some people, for example, play football for fun others are paid to play.

Leisure time is not evenly distributed between people. Retired people have the most free time while women working full-time have the least.

Choice between work and leisure

A key determinant of how much leisure time many adults have is how long they spend working. This is affected by the income and substitution effects which are discussed in Section 4.7. The trade-off between work and leisure also explains why overtime rates are usually above the standard pay rates. If employers ask their workers to work longer hours, they are also asking them to have less leisure time. The fewer the hours of leisure that people have the more valuable those hours become to them and the more they have to be compensated to give them up.

Forms of leisure

Leisure activities can be divided into categories in a number of different ways. One category is home-based activities, such as reading, listening to CDs and gardening; another is out-of-home activities, such as eating out, visiting a disco and going to the cinema. In the UK, the most popular home-based activity is watching television. On average in 2000, people spent 25 hours a week watching television. The most common leisure activity outside the home in the UK is visiting the pub.

Another form of categorisation is into broad categories such as educational and cultural, sporting, social and caring, and nature and environmental. The most detailed form of categorisation is into particular activities, such as music, film, tourism, theatre.

Demand for leisure

The key influences on demand for leisure include the following.

- Disposable income: Leisure is a normal good. As incomes rise, demand for leisure increases.
- The price of leisure: The demand for leisure is influenced by its opportunity cost i.e. what has to be given up to gain the free time.
- The pattern of working hours: Over time the standard working week in most countries has tended to decline giving rise to more free time.
- Technological developments in domestic appliances: The increased efficiency of, for example washing machines and vacuum cleaners, has reduced the amount of time people need to spend on domestic tasks.
- The range and quality of leisure activities and equipment: The development of new forms of leisure activities, for example surfing the Internet, have increased demand for leisure.
- Population size and age distribution: Obviously a rise in population size increases demand for leisure. An increase in the proportion above retirement age may also increase demand for leisure.

Thinking like an economist

How would you expect the income elasticity of demand for theatre tickets and demand for tickets to darts competitions to differ?

The supply of leisure

Leisure is supplied by:

- the private sector: Private sector firms supply a range of leisure activities through, for example, health clubs, travel agents, cinemas, theme parks and professional football clubs. The most common aim of these firms is to maximise profits so a rise in price will usually result in more being supplied.
- the public sector: Local authorities and agencies acting on behalf of the government, such as the Arts Council, also directly supply a range of leisure activities including libraries, public playing fields, sports centres, museums and art galleries. They charge either no price or, more commonly, a low price for these activities. The state also subsidises some

leisure activities by giving grants including grants from National Lottery funds to private sector companies supplying leisure services. The motive behind the state's intervention is linked to the merit good nature of many leisure activities and the question of equity.

- voluntary sector: A number of voluntary organisations supply leisure services, for example tennis clubs, angling clubs and craft societies. These are usually self-financed through subscriptions and charges.

Factors influencing demand for a particular leisure activity

These include:

- the price of the activity: Some leisure activities are provided free to the consumer such as walking, watching hockey on local playing fields, and making use of public libraries. Other activities involve fixed and variable costs. For example, someone who plays tennis has to buy rackets and balls and may pay to belong to a tennis club (fixed costs). They may also then have to pay each time they use a court (variable cost).
- the price of complementary goods and services: Someone who enjoys visiting the theatre may also have to pay to get to the theatre in which case a taxi or bus service is a complementary good.
- the price of substitutes including not only other leisure activities, but also work.
- tastes: Tastes in leisure activities change over time. For example, in recent years the popularity of line dancing has increased while the popularity of tenpin bowling has declined.
- age composition: The increase in the average age of the population has lead to a rise in the demand for holidays specially designed for the over 50s and an increase in spending at garden centres.
- gender composition: For example, a higher percentage of men engage in DIY and gardening than women, and a higher percentage of women read books and knit than men.
- Advertising: Advertising can be a potent force. Advertisements for films and concerts can help to raise attendances.
- major events: A major event can generate demand for related activities. For example, attendances at football matches usually rise after a World Cup and a concert by a group can help sell the group's CDs.
- exchange rate: A fall in the exchange rate makes the country or area's products more price competitive in terms of other countries' currencies. This can result in a rise in the number of tourists visiting the country/area.

Changes in the leisure market

In recent years there have been a number of changes in the market.

- There has been a rise in the proportion of home-based leisure activities. For example, the ownership of home computers has increased from 16 per cent in 1986 to 26 per cent in 1996-1997 and more people now order deliveries of, for example, pizzas and Chinese food to their homes.

- There has been a rise in gambling. This is largely accounted for by the introduction of the National Lottery in November 1994. It has been estimated that 94 per cent of the adult population have bought a lottery ticket.

- There has been a rise in expenditure on leisure activities. This has been the result of rising income and more leisure time. Some of this rise in expenditure has gone on merchandise associated with leisure activities. For example, anglers buy magazines on angling and football supporters buy football shirts sold by their clubs.

- There has been an increase in the influence of the United States. Trends in leisure activities in the UK and the EU are increasingly being influenced by developments in the leisure industry in the United States. For example, theme parks and private health clubs have spread from the US to Europe.

Quick check

1   Distinguish between work and leisure.
2   What are the key influences on demand for leisure?
3   Which sectors supply leisure?
4   How are advances in technology affecting leisure?

Puzzler

Why is the London Eye such a popular attraction?

Leisure and the national economy

4.3

Synoptic link

This section is limited to a range of aspects from the AS *National and International Economy* module (Part 3). It also draws on the knowledge and understanding of merit goods in AS Sections 2.6 and 2.7.

Introduction

The leisure sector is making an increasing contribution to the country's GDP, employment and export revenue. In assessing how the leisure sector affects the national economy, we use tourism and sport as examples in this Section.

Tourism

Tourism involves people moving from their usual place of residence to a destination in which they make use of facilities and undertake activities. People can be tourists in their own countries as well as in other countries.

People from the UK, and from a wide range of other countries including the USA, Japan and Germany, visit tourist sites such as the Tower of London, Madame Tussauds and Edinburgh Castle.

In the UK and most other countries, tourism has grown significantly in the last two decades and is now the largest industry in the world. Nevertheless, its market is volatile, with significant fluctuations in demand according to the time of the year, the type of weather experienced and changes in income levels.

Tourism affects the national economy via its effects on income, employment, the balance of payments and the environment.

The growth of tourism

The tourist industry has increased because of:
- an increase in disposable income
- a reduction in working hours
- early retirement
- a reduction in the time spent on domestic tasks
- improved transport
- increased advertising
- increased awareness of the benefits of holidays and travel.

The effects of tourism

Income and employment
The growth of the tourist industry has increased income and employment in a number of countries. This effect can be greater than it first appears. Obviously tourists create income and employment directly for the hotels, restaurants and attractions that cater for tourists. However, they also create income and employment in a wide range of other industries. Some of these are ones that supply goods and services to the tourist industry, for example, insurance firms, farms and taxi firms. Others are ones that benefit from the spending by local people and firms arising from the income brought in by

the tourists. So an initial rise in income of, for example, £30m in an area and the creation of 2000 extra jobs, may eventually lead to a rise in income of £90m and 5000 more jobs. This knock-on effect on income and employment is referred to as the tourism income multiplier.

However the initial jobs created in the tourist industry may not be of a very high quality as many are unskilled. Workers in the tourist industry also tend not to be very well paid. In addition, the effect on income and employment will not be very great if a significant proportion of the goods and services used in the tourist industry are bought in from abroad. For example, a hotel in Petra in Jordan run by a UK company may buy some of its furniture and linen from the UK. Some of the senior staff it employs may also come from the UK.

The balance of payments

The effects on the country's balance of payments position will also be influenced by where the firms in the tourist industry obtain their materials and food from, and the national origin of the firms. The UK firm running the hotel in Petra will send profits back to the UK.

Countries not only have tourists visiting them but also their own citizens are tourists in other countries, so in the trade in services section of the balance of payments there is both a credit and a debit item.

Culture

Where there are notable differences in the income levels and culture of the tourists and the local inhabitants, social tensions can arise. Tourists may act in such a way, for example getting drunk and gambling, which upsets the sensibility of the locals and their greater spending power may result in resources being switched from meeting the needs of locals to meeting the needs of the tourists. For example, houses for locals may be demolished in order to build hotels.

Local culture may be threatened by the presence of tourists in a number of ways. One is referred to as the demonstration effect. This is where the locals, particularly the younger locals, copy the culture of the tourists especially in terms of clothes, films, music, food, drink and social attitudes. The presence of tourists, especially wealthy tourists, changes the type of goods and services demanded and thereby changes the skills and working patterns of the locals. The process whereby contact with tourists actually changes the culture of a county is called acculturation.

Environment

Tourism may damage the environment in a number of ways including:

- visual pollution: the building of hotels, funfairs etc. can reduce the visual attractiveness of an area
- noise and air pollution caused by the planes and coaches transporting the tourists

- waste generated by the tourists
- congestion arising from the influx of tourists and people catering for the needs of tourists
- destruction of the natural environment to, for example, build golf courses and ski slopes for tourists
- heavy use of water supplies often in areas where the locals are short of water.

The ability of an area to cope with tourists in such a way that it does not damage the features that attract the tourists in the first place is referred to its carrying capacity.

Sport

Sport is another major component of the leisure sector. It covers a range of activities including games, outdoor pursuits, dance and movement and keep-fit. It can also be divided into participatory and spectator sports. For example, many more people watch football, including both on the television and at football games, than actually play football.

Consumption and investment benefits

Those people who take part in physical activity gain both consumption and investment benefits. People may enjoy, for example, playing hockey. It can give them a sense of well-being and the competitive element may provide them with mental stimulation and satisfaction. This is the consumption benefit.

The investment benefit refers to the increased productivity and income potential which results from the improvement to health. Those who take regular exercise live longer, feel fitter and have fewer days off work. This increases the amount they are capable of earning. In the case of professional sportsmen and sportswomen, there is a clear investment benefit as an increase in the quality and quantity of their training should improve their performances and hence their earnings.

Of course the benefits vary between different activities. For example, walking provides high investment benefits but, for some, low consumption benefits. In contrast snooker provides high consumption benefits for some but relatively low investment benefits. There are also possible harmful effects arising from participating in sport in the form of injuries and deaths but for the vast majority of people the benefits exceed the harmful effects.

Market failure and sport

Governments encourage and sponsor participation in sport and indeed some governments make it compulsory in schools. This is because they believe

Thinking like an economist

Discuss two arguments that could be used to support the case for the UK government promoting tourism.

Thinking like an economist

Analyse the possible consumption and investment benefits of attending a horseracing meeting.

that participation in sport would be below the allocatively efficient level if left to market forces. Sport may be regarded as a merit good. Some people undervalue the investment benefit it provides. In addition, sport provides not only private benefits but also external benefits. By raising the productivity of workers, it increases the output and the income of the country. It also has the net effect of reducing the burden on the NHS and some suggest it reduces vandalism.

Another reason for government intervention is that some sporting activities may be regarded as quasi-public goods. For example, participating in water sports on a large lake may be non-rival until the number of participants reach a certain number.

Spectator sport

People watch a range of sporting activities. One sport that has become more popular in recent years has been watching football. The football clubs which had the highest average attendances in the 2002/03 season in England were Manchester United, Liverpool and Arsenal, and in Scotland they were Glasgow Rangers and Glasgow Celtic.

League football clubs raise revenue in a variety of ways.
- Merchandise sales: Clubs have sold items such as shirts and scarves for some time but now most have branched out into a whole range of items which have the club's name attached to them such as duvet covers and watches.
- Sponsorship: League football clubs are sponsored by firms and their players wear the sponsor's name on their shirts. The competitions they play in are also sponsored.
- Selling TV coverage: In recent years the amount of money received by the top clubs from TV companies paying for the right to screen their games has increased dramatically. This has enabled the clubs to raise their players' wages to unprecedented levels.
- Ticket sales: Clubs are faced with the problem of a fixed supply of seats. In recent years a number of the top clubs have built new stadia, but nevertheless demand for tickets still frequently exceeds the supply. To increase their profits clubs charge different prices according to:
  - the age of the spectators
  - where people sit in the stadium
  - the quality of the seating – for example charging people more to hire a box
  - the expected quality of the game – for example charging their fans more for watching their team play Chelsea than for playing Coventry.

The first example may be regarded as price discrimination but it could be claimed that in the case of the last three a different service is being provided to the different groups.

Hot potato

Might sport ever be regarded as a demerit good?

The national economy and leisure

As well as leisure having an impact on the national economy, changes in the national economy also has an impact on leisure. When the economy is expanding, with incomes rising, demand for most leisure products rises.

Expansionary monetary and fiscal policies benefit most leisure sectors. For example, a lower rate of interest will reduce firms' costs and increase aggregate demand. Lower income tax will also increase aggregate demand by raising disposable income. Leisure products tend to be disproportionately affected by changes in disposable income as many have positive income elasticity of demand and a significant number have positive income elasticity of demand greater than one (superior or luxury goods).

A fall in the exchange rate particularly benefits the home tourist industry as it makes the cost of holidays in the domestic country relatively cheaper, in terms of foreign currency, and makes foreign holidays, in terms of the domestic currency, relatively more expensive.

Thinking like an economist

Compare the effect a rise in income tax would be likely to have on bingo and on yachting as leisure pursuits.

Quick check

1 Why is tourism growing?
2 How is the growth of tourism likely to affect the UK economy?
3 Why does participation in sport tend to raise productivity?
4 How do league football clubs raise revenue?

Introduction

Firms in leisure markets, as in all markets, operate under a variety of competition conditions. Economists identify four main market structures:

- perfect competition
- monopolistic competition
- oligopoly
- monopoly.

As well as examining the level of actual competition in markets, economists now also examine the level of potential competition.

Perfect competition

Perfect competition is said to exist when there are many buyers and sellers, no barriers to entry and exit, identical products, perfect knowledge and no attachment between buyers and sellers.

Firms in this market structure are price takers. Price is determined by market demand and supply. Any individual firm has to accept the market price. It cannot charge above the market price as consumers would just switch to rival producers. As it can sell all of its produce at the market price, it has no incentive to charge less.

Two of the key characteristics of perfect competition make this market structure very responsive to changes in consumer demand and ensure that firms earn only **normal profit** in the long run. These are the absence of barriers to entry and exit and the existence of perfect knowledge.

In the short run, if market demand increases, the firms will earn **supernormal profit**. Figure 1a shows market demand increasing, price rising and supply extending. Figure 1b shows the effect on an individual firm. The rise in price encourages the firm to supply more and raises its average revenue above average cost.

Synoptic link

In AS Section 1.21 you were introduced to market structures. In this section and Section 4.5 you will examine these market structures in more depth.

Definitions

Perfect competition: a market structure with many buyers and sellers, free entry and exit and an identical product.

Normal profit: the level of profit needed to keep a firm in the market in the long run.

Supernormal profit: profit earned where average revenue exceeds average cost (which includes normal profit).

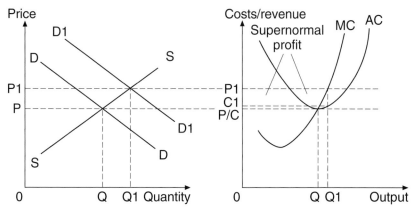

Figure 1a): The effects of an increase in demand on the market

Figure 1b): The effect on an increase in demand on an individual firm

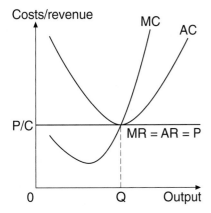

Figure 2: A perfectly competitive firm earning normal profit

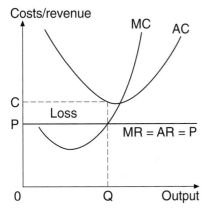

Figure 3: A perfectly competitive firm experiencing a loss

Firms outside the market will be aware of the supernormal profits being earned and will be attracted into the market. Their entry will cause the market supply curve to shift to the right. New firms will continue to enter until market price falls low enough that firms again earn **normal profits**. Figure 2 shows a perfectly competitive firm earning normal profit.

A decrease in demand will have the opposite effect. The market price will be driven down. Firms will make a loss as shown in Figure 3.

If firms cannot cover their variable costs, they will leave the industry. In practice very few market structures can be described as perfectly competitive.

Monopolistic competition

This market structure is characterised by a large number of firms, easy entry and exit, product differentiation and non-price competition. As each product is slightly different, each firm faces a downward sloping demand curve and is a price maker.

The lack of barriers to entry and exit, as with **perfect competition**, means that normal profit is again earned in the long run as shown in Figure 4.

In this market structure firms seek to benefit from **supernormal profit** in the short run not just through an increase in market demand but also through increasing the attractiveness of its product. It may seek to do this by, for example, small-scale advertising, after sales service, better location of outlets and improved style.

Monopolistic competition is a common market structure and a number of leisure markets may be identified as operating under conditions of monopolistic competition.

Oligopoly

Most firms operate under conditions of either monopolistic competition or oligopoly. An **oligopoly** is a market dominated by a few large firms. There are barriers to entry and exit, the product may be differentiated or non-differentiated and firms are price makers. A key feature of this market structure is that firms are interdependent. In making its decisions a firm considers the reaction of its rivals and constantly watches what its rivals are doing.

Due to the existence of barriers to entry and exit, firms in an oligopolistic market may earn supernormal profits in the long run.

Monopoly

A pure **monopoly** is a market structure in which there is just one seller. There are significant barriers to entry and exit, the product is unique and the firm is a price maker.

As with oligopoly, a monopoly can earn supernormal profit in the long run. Figure 5 shows a monopolist producing where MC = MR (and so maximising profits) and where AR > AC (and so enjoying supernormal profit).

Assessing market structures

In deciding in which market structure firms operate, economists examine a number of key indicators. One is the market concentration ratio. This shows the market share of the largest few firms. The figure will be high under conditions of oilgopoly, for instance, and lower under conditions of **monopolistic competition**. Economists also look at whether there are barriers to entry and exit, the market power exercised by firms, the type of profits earned in the long run and the behaviour of the firms – see Section 4.5.

Contestable markets

Contestable market theory suggests that the behaviour and performance of firms is influenced not by the level of actual competition in the market in which they operate, but by the level of potential competition. A **contestable** market is one in which there are no barriers to entry and exit. In such a market, which might only contain one or a few firms, the threat of a new firm or firms entering the market may make the current firm/firms behave in a competitive way.

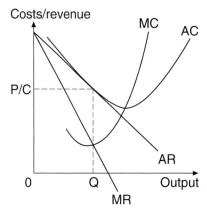

Figure 4: The long run output position of a firm operating under conditions of monopolistic competition

---

Quick check ✓

1 In which market structures are firms price makers?
2 What are the differences between perfect competition and monopolistic competition?
3 In which market structures can firms earn supernormal profits in the long run?
4 In which market structures do most leisure industries operate?
5 Research the market structure for TV broadcasting and explain why it does not operate under conditions of perfect competition.
6 Explain how a city pub could seek to attract extra customers.
7 Air travel in the UK is largely an oligopolistic market. Identify two barriers to entry into the market and consider whether the market is likely to remain an oligopoly.
8 The National Lottery is a monopoly. What are the barriers to entry and exit in this market?
9 Explain what effects advances in technology should have on the contestability of the publishing market.

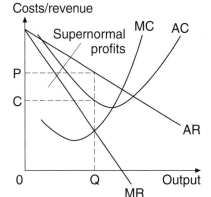

Figure 5: A monopolist experiencing supernormal profits

Behaviour and efficiency in leisure markets

Synoptic link

See Section 4.4

Introduction

Firms are likely to behave in different ways in different market structures. The ways that firms behave has implications for consumers and the economy as a whole.

Perfect competition

It was noted in the previous section that firms operating under conditions of perfect competition are very responsive to changes in consumer demand. This market structure should ensure that firms achieve both allocative and productive efficiency in the long run. Figure 1 shows a perfectly competitive firm producing where MC = AR (allocative efficiency) and where MC = AC (productive efficiency).

Monopolistic competition

As under conditions of perfect competition, firms operating under conditions of monopolistic competition do not make excessive profits in the long run. Monopolistically competitive firms, though, are not economically efficient. As Figure 2 shows, a firm in this market structure produces an output at which price (AR) exceeds marginal cost (and so does not achieve allocative efficiency). It also produces below the productively efficient level (failing to achieve productive efficiency) and operates with excess capacity.

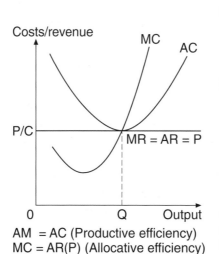

AM = AC (Productive efficiency)
MC = AR(P) (Allocative efficiency)

Figure 1: Economic efficiency being achieved under conditions of perfect competition

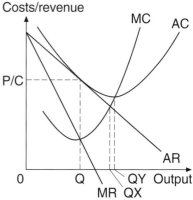

Q = Profit maximisation output
QX = Allocatively efficient output
QY = Productively efficient output

Figure 2: Monopolistic competition

It is thought, however, that consumers may gain from the existence of production differentiation, which occurs under conditions of monopolistic competition. Many consumers like differences in products. In a bid to differentiate their products, firms may also innovate and so raise the quality of their products and possibly reduce their prices.

Oligopoly

Analysing the behaviour of firms operating under conditions of oligopoly is a relatively complex process. This is because the firms may adopt a variety of strategies.

One possible strategy is to cut price in a bid to gain a larger share of the market. Such a move is likely to provoke a price war, with rival firms matching price reductions. Price wars have broken out in the newspaper and other markets on a number of occasions.

Price cutting, though, is not a popular strategy as it is high risk and often does not bring long-term benefits. The disadvantages of altering price are emphasised in the kinked demand curve diagram as illustrated in Figure 3

Above the current price of P, the firm expects its demand curve to be relatively elastic. This is because it is likely to think that its rivals will not follow any price rise it initiates and so choosing to raise price will lose it a significant number of sales. Below the current price, demand is relatively inelastic as the firm anticipates that its rivals will match any price cuts so that a lower price will not result in many more sales.

The kinked demand curve suggests price rigidity is likely to exist in oligopoly and that firms are likely to put more reliance on non-price competition rather than price competition. This non-price competition takes a variety of forms including large-scale advertising, competitions, free gifts and brand names.

Firms may also seek to reduce the risks of a price war by colluding with its rivals. Formal collusion involves firms forming a cartel. In such a situation the firms produce separately but sell at one agreed price. Cartels are illegal in most countries, including the UK, but nevertheless some firms take the risk. However, tacit collusion is more common than formal collusion. Tacit collusion usually takes the form of price leadership. This involves firms following the price strategy of one firm. This firm may be the dominant firm in the market, the firm with most experience in setting price or a barometric firm, i.e. the firm most sensitive to changes in market conditions.

Monopoly

Monopolies do not provide choice and are traditionally seen as inefficient. The lack of direct competitive pressure may indeed mean that:
- price is set above marginal cost
- average costs are not minimised
- monopolies do not innovate
- the quality of the product produced is poor.

Thinking like an economist

Publishing operates under conditions of monopolistic competition. Analyse the possible benefits and costs consumers might experience from the market moving towards perfect competition.

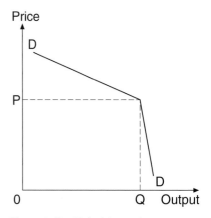

Figure 3: The kinked demand curve

Thinking like an economist

How do package holiday operators seek to attract customers?

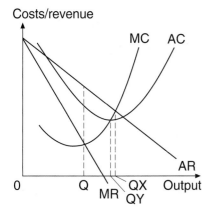

Costs/revenue

Q = Profit maximising output
QY = Productively efficient output
QX = Allocatively efficient output

Figure 4: Monopoly

Research task

What effect would a move from perfect competition to monopoly be likely to have on producer and consumer surplus?

Figure 4 shows a monopoly firm producing below the allocatively and productively efficient levels.

However, where economies of scale are significant, prices may be lower under conditions of both monopoly and oligopoly. In addition monopolies may innovate. This is because, due to their ability to earn supernormal profits in the long run, they are likely to have significant funds to undertake research and development and to develop new products and methods. They may also consider that the existence of barriers to entry and exit will enable them to protect any supernormal profit they make from introducing new products and methods. The theory of creative destruction also suggests that the existence of barriers will encourage firms outside the market to develop superior products and methods, since doing so may enable them to overcome the barriers.

Contestable market

A contestable market should, in theory, enable consumers to reap the advantages of both perfect competition and monopoly. Where economies of scale are significant, one or a few firms operating in a market may mean that average costs are low. The threat of competition may also ensure that the firm or firms earn only normal profits in the long run and achieve economic efficiency.

The potential benefits arising from contestable markets have led the government to seek to increase the contestability of a number of markets, including some leisure markets. For example, independent TV companies have to bid for franchises. If their performance is not up to standard their franchises will not be extended and may even be withdrawn.

Quick check

1 Distinguish between productive and allocative efficiency.
2 Are monopolistically competitive firms economically efficient?
3 What does the kinked demand curve show?
4 Identify two possible advantages and two possible disadvantages for consumers of a monopoly market.

Introduction

The demand for labour is influenced by its function as a factor of production. Firms will demand more labour if demand for the products they produce rises. Marginal productivity theory seeks to explain what determines the number of workers a firm employs. A change in the wage rate obviously has an impact on the demand for labour. Elasticity of demand measures the extent to which demand responds to a change in the wage rate.

Derived demand

As with the demand for all the factors of production, demand for labour is a **derived demand**. Factors of production are not wanted for their own sake but for what they can produce. So the number of workers that firms wish to employ depends principally on the demand for the products produced. If demand rises, firms will usually seek to employ more workers.

The aggregate demand for labour

The aggregate (total) demand for labour depends mainly on the level of economic activity. If the economy is growing and firms are optimistic that it will continue to grow in the future, employment is likely to be rising. However, if output is declining or even growing at a slower rate than the trend growth rate and firms are pessimistic about future levels of aggregate demand, employment is likely to be falling.

A firm's demand for labour

How many workers, or working hours, a firm seeks to employ is influenced by a number of factors. These include:

- demand and expected future demand for the product produced. This is again the key influence.
- productivity: the higher the output per worker hour the more attractive labour is.
- complementary labour costs: as well as wages, firms incur other costs when they employ labour. So, for example, if national insurance contributions rise, demand for labour is likely to fall.
- the price of labour: a rise in wage rates above any rise in labour productivity will raise unit labour costs and is likely to result in a contraction in demand for labour.
- the price of other factors of production which can be substituted for labour. If capital becomes cheaper firms may seek to replace some of their workers by machines.

The demand for labour

4.6

Synoptic link

Look back at AS Sections 1.5, 1.7 and 1.16.

Key concepts

Derived demand: demand for one item depending on the demand for another item.

Thinking like an economist

1 Why is the demand for vets increasing?
2 Why may economic growth be below the trend rate?

Marginal productivity theory

Definitions

Marginal productivity theory: the view that demand for a factor of production depends on its marginal revenue product.
Marginal revenue product of labour (MRP): the change in a firm's revenue resulting from employing one more worker.
Elasticity of demand for labour: the responsiveness of demand for labour to a change in the wage rate.

Marginal productivity theory suggests that demand for any factor of production depends on its **marginal revenue product** (MRP) and that the quantity of any factor employed will be determined by where the marginal cost of employing one more unit of the factor equals the marginal revenue product of that factor.

The marginal product of labour is the change in total output which results from employing one more worker. As more workers are employed, output may initially rise rapidly as increasing returns are experienced, so marginal product may increase. However once a certain level of employment is reached marginal product may fall as diminishing returns set in. Marginal revenue product of labour is the change in a firm's revenue resulting from employing one more worker. It is found by multiplying marginal product by marginal revenue. In a perfectly competitive product, market marginal revenue will be equal to price. Table 1 shows how marginal revenue product is calculated.

Table 1: Marginal revenue product

No. of workers	Total output	Marginal product	Marginal revenue (price £)		Marginal revenue product	Total revenue
1	20	20	× 10	=	200	200
2	80	60	× 10	=	600	800
3	160	80	× 10	=	800	1600
4	220	60	× 10	=	600	2200
5	260	40	× 10	=	400	2600
6	280	20	× 10	=	200	2800

If the wage rate is constant at £400, the firm will employ five workers since this is where the marginal cost of labour equals MRP. At this level of employment, the total cost of workers will be 5 x £400 = £2000. This level of employment is the one where the gap between total revenue and total cost of labour is greatest, i.e. £2600 - £2000 = £600.

The marginal revenue product of labour curve shows the quantity of labour demanded at each wage rate as shown in Figure 1.

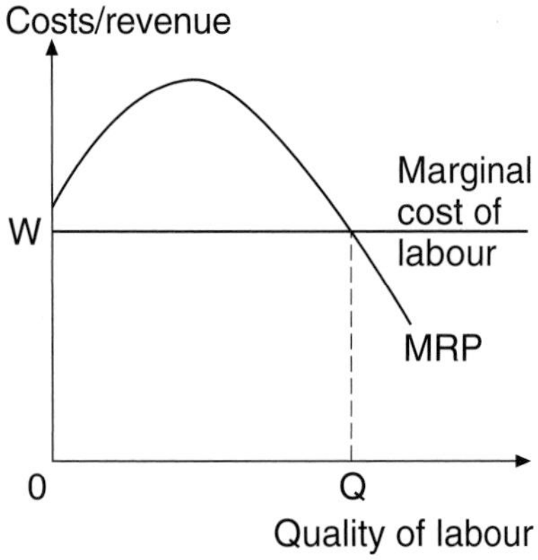

So the marginal revenue product curve of labour is the demand curve for labour. The MRP and hence the demand curve for labour will shift out to the right if the marginal product of labour and/or marginal revenue increase. For example the demand for electricians will increase if the productivity of electricians rises, perhaps due to increased training, and/or if the price of their services rises due to, for example a switch from gas to electrical appliances. This increase in MRP is illustrated in Figure 2.

Figure 1: Marginal revenue product

In practice it can be difficult to measure MRP. This is because workers often work in teams so it can be difficult to isolate the contribution one worker makes to changes in output. In addition, it is difficult to measure the marginal product of a number of people who work in the tertiary sector. For example, is a doctor who treats twenty people in a day for varicose veins more productive than one who carries out one multiple-organ transplant?

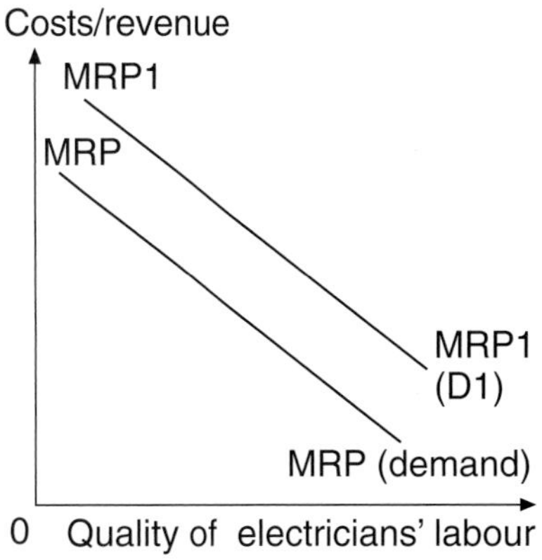

The elasticity of demand for labour

While a change in marginal productivity or marginal revenue will shift the demand curve for labour, a change in the wage rate will cause a movement along the demand curve for labour. The extent to which demand will contract or extend as a result of a change in the wage rate is measured by the **elasticity of demand for labour**. The formula is:

Elasticity of demand for labour = $\dfrac{\text{percentage change in demand for labour}}{\text{percentage change in wage rate}}$

There are a number of factors which influence the elasticity of demand for labour. These include:

- the price elasticity of demand for the product produced. If demand for the product is inelastic, demand for the labour that produces it is also likely to be inelastic. This is because the rise in the price of the product that will result from a rise in the wage rate will cause a smaller percentage fall in demand for the product. So as output will not change by much, employment will not fall significantly.
- the proportion of wage costs in total costs. If wages account for a significant proportion of total costs, demand will be elastic. The reason is because a change in the wage rate will have a large impact on total costs. If the wage rate falls, total costs will fall by a noticeable amount and demand for labour will rise by a greater percentage.
- the ease with which labour can be substituted by other factors. If it is easy to substitute capital for labour, demand for labour will be elastic. A rise in the wage rate will cause workers to be substituted by machines. Demand for labour will fall by a greater percentage than the rise in the wage rate.
- the elasticity of supply of complementary factors. If wages fall and it is easy to obtain more of the factors that are used alongside labour, demand for labour will be elastic.
- the time period. Demand for labour is more elastic in the long run when there is more time for firms to reorganise their production methods.

Costs/revenue

Figure 2: An increase in MRP

Quick check

1   What effect will a rise in vegetarianism have on demand for butchers?
2   Explain two possible causes of an increase in the MRP of hairdressers.
3   Why is it difficult to measure MRP?
4   Why is the demand for pilots more elastic than demand for air stewards?

The supply of labour

Synoptic link

Before starting this section it would be useful to review AS Sections 1.10 and 1.11.

Introduction

The supply of labour can be examined on a number of levels, from what influences how many hours an individual works to the total supply of labour in an economy.

As with the supply of goods and services, there are a number of key influences on the supply of labour. One of the main influences is the price of labour, i.e. the wage rate. Due to its importance, economists measure the elasticity of supply of labour.

The individual supply of labour

The number of hours a worker decides to work is influenced by the number of hours on offer and the relative importance that the worker attaches to income and leisure.

Many workers are unable to alter the number of hours they work in their main jobs. They are contracted to work, say, 38 hours a week and are not offered the opportunity to vary these hours. However, with increasing flexibility in labour markets, more workers are now being provided with a choice as to how many hours they work.

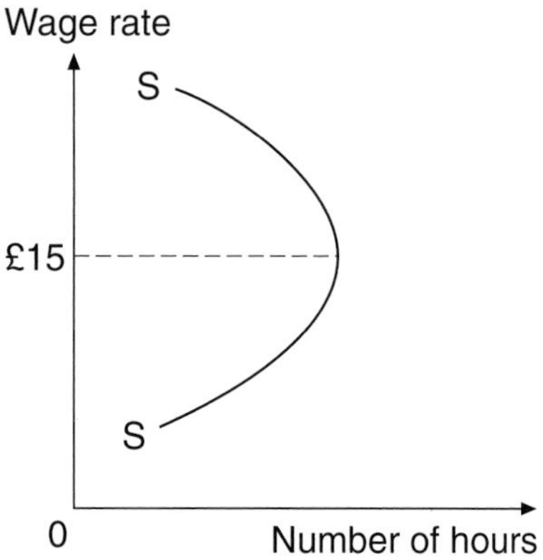

It thought that, at low wages, a rise in the wage rate will cause an extension in supply with a worker being prepared to work more hours. After a certain wage is reached, however, the offer of a higher wage rate may cause a worker to choose to work fewer hours. She or he may decide that a given income level is sufficient to meet his or her financial requirements and may be keen to have more leisure time in which to enjoy her or his earnings. For example, a worker may currently work 40 hours at £15 per hour. This gives a gross income of £60 per week. A rise in the wage rate to £20 would enable the worker to earn the same wage rate by working 30 hours, giving 10 hours more leisure time. This change in response to an increase in the wage rate gives rise to the backward sloping supply curve as illustrated in Figure 1. Up to the wage rate of £15, the supply of labour extends, but any rise above £15 causes supply to contract.

The behaviour of the worker can be explained by the income and substitution effects. The **income effect of a wage** rise is to reduce the number of hours a person works. This is because, as the wage rate rises, she or he buys more of most goods and services, including leisure. In contrast, the **substitution effect** of a wage rise is to increase the number of hours worked. A higher wage rate increases the return from working and increases the opportunity cost of leisure, so the worker selects to work more hours.

At a low wage rate, it is thought that the substitution effect is likely to outweigh the income effect. The worker will work more hours in order to raise her or his material living standard. However, once the wage rate has reached a certain level, in our example £15, the income effect may

Figure 1: The backward sloping supply curve

Definitions

The income effect of a wage change: the effect on the supply of labour caused by the change in the ability to buy leisure time.
Substitution effect: the effect on the supply of labour influenced by a change in the opportunity cost of leisure.

outweigh the substitution effect. The worker is now able to afford to buy more leisure time.

The aggregate supply of labour

The total supply of labour is influenced by three key factors:
- the size of the population
- the size of the **working population** (labour or workforce)
- the hours worked.

Population

The larger the population size, the greater the potential supply of labour. So, for example, the United States with a population of 280 million has a greater supply of labour than France with a population of 60 million. As well as the total size of population, the age distribution of the population, school leaving age and retirement age influence the size of the labour force. The higher the proportion of the population in the working age range, the greater the supply of labour. In the UK, the population of working age consists of those aged between 16 and 65. This proportion could rise as a result of a rise in the birth rate that occurred sixteen or more years before, net immigration (since most immigrants are aged between 20 and 40), a lowering of the school leaving age or a raising of the retirement age.

The working population

The **working population** or labour or workforce consists of those in employment and those seeking employment. This is not the same as the population of working age. Some of those who are older than the school leaving age and younger than the state retirement age may not be economically active. The main groups who are not actively participating in the labour force (**economically inactive**) are those still in full-time education, those who have retired early, those who are long-term sick or disabled and those who are homemakers.

There are various factors that influence the **participation rate** of the population of working age in the labour force.
- Wage rates: higher wage rates will tend to encourage more people to seek to enter or stay in the labour force.
- Employment opportunities: the greater the number and quality of jobs on offer the higher the participation rate is likely to be.
- Social attitudes to women working: countries in which it is acceptable for women and, in particular, married women to work have a large pool of workers to call on.
- Provision for the care of the very young and the elderly: those countries in which there is state and private provision will tend to have a higher participation rate than those in which the very young and the elderly are looked after solely by relatives at home.

Thinking like an economist

Explain the income and substitution effects of a rise in income tax.

Definitions

Working population: those who are economically active, i.e. in employment or unemployed.
Economically inactive: people who are neither in employment nor unemployed
Participation rate: proportion of those of working age in the working population (labour or workforce)

The hours worked

As well as the number of workers, the hours they work influences the supply of labour. The hours worked in turn is influenced by the length of the working week, the number of days holidays and the number of days lost through industrial action. The more hours worked, the greater the supply of labour in terms of quantity. However when workers work long hours, with few holidays, the quality of what they produce may decline.

The supply of labour to a particular occupation

The number of people willing and able to work in a given occupation is influenced by both pecuniary (financial) and non-pecuniary benefits including:

- the wage rate: the higher the wage rate, the more people are likely to want to do the job. For example, a relatively high number of people seek to become accountants because of the high wages on offer.
- the convenience and flexibility of hours: long and unsociable working hours are likely to discourage potential workers. Nursing homes find it difficult to recruit night-time nursing staff. Whereas flexibility of hours may attract people to a given occupation. For example, salesmen and women may be able, to a certain extent, to decide when they work.
- status: the high status achieved by pilots, for example, makes it an attractive job.
- promotion chances: some people are prepared to work initially for relatively low wages, for example in the media, in the hope than they will progress on to high paid jobs.
- flexibility of location: it is becoming increasingly possible in certain occupations such as architects and designers to work at least some days from home. This increases the attractiveness of the occupations.
- qualifications and skills: the higher the qualifications and skills required, the fewer the number of people who are able to undertake the occupation. While the supply of sales assistants is relatively high, the supply of brain surgeons is low.
- job security: the more secure a job, the more attractive it is likely to be. University lecturers and professors in the UK used to be given tenure for life. This made some people willing to enter an academic life even though pay was not very high. However, security of tenure has now ended and this has coincided with a decrease in the numbers wanting to become university lecturers.
- pleasantness of the job: everything else being equal, more workers will be attracted to more pleasant jobs. It might be expected that the supply of, for example sewage workers, would be low as it is not a particularly pleasant job. However, the unpleasantness is more than offset by the low level of qualifications required. Some of the sewage workers may not be

Thinking like an economist

Discuss two policies a government could employ to increase the participation rate of disabled adults.

particularly keen to work in the occupation but they may not have the qualifications to switch to alternative jobs.

- holidays: long holidays are likely to attract workers. Some people may be encouraged to become teachers because of the relatively long holidays on offer. However, this benefit is likely to decrease. Already lecturers in further education have experienced reductions in their holiday entitlement.
- perks and fringe benefits: company cars, paid trips abroad, profit sharing schemes, free private health care, good company pension schemes are likely to make a given occupation more attractive. For example, pilots receive a number of benefits including very cheap flights for their families, good company pension schemes and the opportunity to retire early.

The supply of labour to a particular firm

Some of the same influences as in the case of the supply of labour to a particular occupation come into play here including:
- the wage rate offered
- the length and convenience of the hours
- promotion chances
- flexibility of location
- job security
- working conditions
- holidays
- perks and fringe benefits.

In addition supply is influenced by:
- the quality and quantity of training on offer. The greater the quality and amount of training that workers can gain from the firm, the greater the number of workers that are likely to be attracted.
- the location of the firm. Firms based in major cities have a greater pool of labour to select from.
- the level of employment. Firms often find it difficult to recruit workers when there is a low level of unemployment.
- the reputation of the firm. This is similar to the status of an occupation.
- the recent performance of the firm. Potential workers are encouraged to apply to firms which are doing well and expanding. This is linked to previous influences as an expanding firm may be expected to offer higher wages, more training, greater promotion chances and more job security than static or declining firms.
- the opportunity to work overtime. Some people are keen to raise their incomes by working extra hours at higher rates.

Thinking like an economist

Why are UK farmers finding it difficult to recruit fruit pickers?

The elasticity of supply of labour

As already noted, the wage rate on offer is a key influence on the supply of labour. The extent to which the supply of labour changes as a result of a change in the wage rate is measured by the **elasticity of supply of labour**. The formula is:

$$\text{Elasticity of supply of labour} = \frac{\text{percentage change in supply of labour}}{\text{percentage change in wage rate}}$$

The factors which influence the elasticity of supply of labour are:

- the qualifications and skills required. The supply of skilled workers is more inelastic than the supply of unskilled workers as there are fewer skilled than unskilled workers. For example the supply of vets is more inelastic than the supply of pet shop assistants.
- the length of training. A long period of training may discourage some people from undertaking the occupation. So a rise in the wage rate will not attract many new workers.
- the level of employment. If there is high unemployment, supply of labour to many occupations is likely to elastic. This is because the wage rate will not have to be raised by much to attract a high number of applicants from people seeking employment.
- the mobility of labour. The easier workers find it to switch jobs (occupational mobility) and the easier they find it move from one area to another (geographical mobility) the more elastic the supply will be.
- the time period. As with demand, supply will be more elastic the longer the time period involved. A rise in the wage rate of barristers, for example, may not have much effect on the supply of barristers in the short run. However, in the long run it is likely to as more students will be encouraged to study law and undertake the necessary training.

Quick check

1 Distinguish between the income and substitution effects of a fall in the wage rate offered to a worker.
2 What factors determine the size of the working population?
3 What may cause a shortage of truck drivers?
4 What effect does a fall in unemployment have on the elasticity of supply of labour?

Introduction

Why did the pay of barristers increase in 2002? Why are financial advisers paid more than checkout assistants? In examining how wages are determined and why they differ between groups of workers, it is important to consider the demand for, and supply of labour.

Wage determination

The market forces of demand and supply play a key role in determining relative wages. The wage rate of a group of workers will rise if either the demand for their services increases or their supply decreases. For example, the wages of computer programmers have risen as the spread of information technology has increased the demand for their services. This effect is shown in Figure 1.

In contrast, the wage of clerical workers has fallen relative to other groups as their supply has increased and demand for their services has fallen.

Economic rent and transfer earnings

The level of demand and their supply and their elasticities determine not only the level of wage rates but also the proportion of wages which consist of economic rent and the proportion which consist of transfer earnings.

Transfer earnings are what a worker can earn in her/his next best paid job – the opportunity cost of performing the current job. They are the equivalent to the minimum which has to be paid to keep the worker in her/his current job.

Economic rent is the surplus over transfer earnings and is total earnings minus transfer earnings. For example, a woman may earn £580 a week as an optician. If the next best paid job she is willing and able to do is as an advertising executive earning £494 a week, her economic rent is £86 and her transfer earnings are £494.

Figure 2 shows that the total earnings received by the workers is 0WXQ. Of this YWX is economic rent and 0YXQ is **transfer earnings**. This figure shows that economic rent is the area above the supply curve and below the wage rate. The amount of economic rent earned by the workers will vary. The first worker employed would have been prepared to work for considerably less than the wage rate actually paid. So a relatively high proportion of her/his earnings will be economic rent. Whereas the last worker employed would have be prepared to work only for the going wage rate and so earns no economic rent.

The proportion of earnings which constitute economic rent depends on the elasticity of supply. Economic rent will form a large proportion when supply is inelastic. For example, many of the footballers playing in the premier leagues of England and Scotland are thought to earn a large amount of

Synoptic link

Look back at AS Sections 1.12–1.16 to help your understanding of this section.

Wages of computer programmers

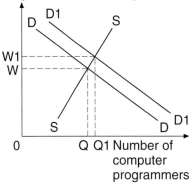

Figure 1: An increase in demand for computer programmers

Definitions

Economic rent: a surplus paid to a factor of production above what is needed to keep it in its current occupation.

Transfer earnings: the amount a factor of production could earn in its next best paid occupation.

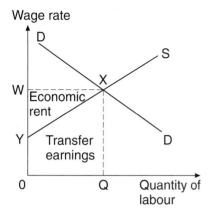

Figure 2: Economic rent and transfer earnings

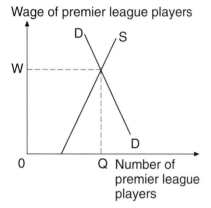

Figure 3: The market for premier league football players

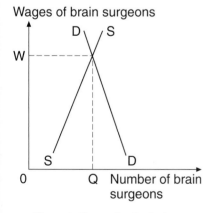

Figure 4: The market for brain surgeons

Hot potato

Should economic rent be taxed?

economic rent. Supply is inelastic since most footballers enjoy playing football and would continue to play even if their wage rate was cut as most would earn considerably less in their next best paid jobs. These footballers are also highly paid. Demand for their skills is high since they attract not only large attendances at matches but also promote high merchandise sales. The supply of skilled players is limited. Figure 3 shows the market for premier league players.

Other influences on wage determination

In practice, demand and supply are not the only influences on the wages of many workers. The other influences include the relative bargaining power of employers and workers, government policy and public opinion. Wages are likely to be higher when workers have strong bargaining power relative to their employers (see Section 4.14).

Government policy affects wages both directly and indirectly. The government is a major employer, it passes legislation which affects the bargaining power of workers and employers (trade union reform) and which directly affects wage rates (the National Minimum Wage).

Attitudes towards 'what people deserve to be paid' influence wages via the amounts that workers ask for and employers offer. Public opinion tends to value highly sacrifice in the form of being prepared to undergo long periods of training and study as well as certain groups. In many societies, work dominated by white, middle-class males is held in higher esteem than work undertaken mainly by the working class or women or people from ethnic minorities. For example, most top barristers who are highly paid are still mainly middle class, male and white.

Demand and supply

Wages are likely to be high when demand is high and inelastic and supply is low and inelastic. In contrast, wages are likely to be low where supply is high relative to demand and both demand and supply are elastic.

For example, brain surgeons are paid considerably more than waiters and waitresses. The supply of brain surgeons is low relative to demand. It is limited by the long period of training involved and the high qualifications required to start that training. These features also make supply inelastic. A rise in the wage rate will not attract many new brain surgeons in the short run. Demand is also inelastic as brain surgeons are a vital part of an operating team and there is no viable substitute. Figure 4 shows the market for brain surgeons.

In contrast, the supply of waiters and waitresses is high and elastic. The job requires no qualifications and the minimum of training. So there is a large number of people capable of doing the job and a rise in the wage rate will attract a greater percentage extension in supply. The marginal revenue productivity of waiters and waitresses is also low and so demand is low. Figure 5 shows the market for waiters and waitresses.

Wage differentials

Wage differentials are differences in wages. Wage differentials occur between occupations, industries, firms and regions and within these categories. Table 1 shows the differences in pay earned by workers in a number of occupations.

Table 1: Highest and lowest paid occupations in Great Britain, April 2000

Occupation	Average gross weekly pay (£)
Highest paid	
Treasurers and company financial managers	1059
Medical practitioners	964
Organisation and methods and work study managers	813
Management consultants, business analysts	812
Underwriters, claims assessors, brokers, investment analysts	775
Police officers (inspector or above)	766
Computer systems and data processing managers	757
Solicitors	748
Marketing and sales managers	719
Advertising and public relations managers	690
Lowest paid	
Educational assistants	212
Other childcare and related occupations	205
Counterhands, catering assistants	196
Launderers, dry cleaners, pressers	196
Hairdressers, barbers	190
Waiters, waitresses	189
Petrol pump/forecourt attendants	189
Retail cash desk and check-out operators	185
Bar staff	184
Kitchen porters/hands	184

Source: Table 5.8, Page 93, Social Trends 2002, ONS.

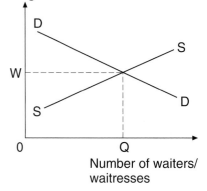

Figure 5: The market for waiters and waitresses

Other influences

The gap in pay between brain surgeons and waiters and waitresses can also be explained in terms of the other influences on wage rates.

- Relative bargaining strength: Most brain surgeons are members of the British Medical Association (BMA), a strong professional organisation. The Association has large funds and has built up a close relationship with Ministers of Health. Any industrial action it may take would have significant consequences and brain surgeons cannot be replaced by capital equipment or other types of doctors. By contrast, waiters and waitresses have low bargaining power. Very few belong to a trade union and they can usually be replaced by unemployed workers.

- Government policy: An ageing population, advances in technology and increasing expectations have increased public spending on health care and increased demand for brain surgeons. The government has also granted relatively large pay increases for surgeons. Government policy has also had an impact on the pay of waiters and waitresses via the introduction of the National Minimum Wage. This has raised the wage rate of some waiters and waitresses but not all of those aged under 18.

- Public opinion: Surgeons are held in high public esteem. They are perceived as providing a vital service, of having undergone a long period of training and of being well qualified and highly skilled. Most of the top surgeons are still male and middle class, whereas a high proportion of the people who serve on tables are female; a significant proportion are also from ethnic minorities. The job they perform is not held in particularly high regard and it is generally thought that anyone could do the job.

Wage differentials between particular groups

- Skilled and unskilled workers. Skilled workers are paid more than unskilled workers principally because the demand for skilled workers is higher and their supply is less. The marginal revenue productivity of skilled labour is high because the skills possessed by the workers will lead to high output per worker. The supply of skilled labour in many countries is below that of unskilled workers. It is also more difficult to substitute skilled labour with machines and unemployed workers than is the case with unskilled labour. Figure 6 shows the markets for skilled and unskilled workers.

- Male and female workers: Despite equal pay legislation, men are still paid more than women. When comparing weekly pay, part of the explanation lies in the fact that more women work part-time than men. However, even when hourly paid rates are compared, men still earn more than women.

There are a number of reasons why women still earn less than men. One is that, on average, the marginal revenue productivity of women is lower than that of men. In the past a significant reason was that the qualifications of men was greater than that of women. More males went to university than

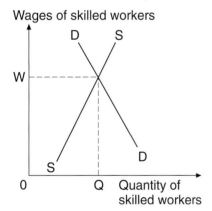

Figure 6: The market for skilled and unskilled workers

females. The gap in the qualifications and hence the marginal productivity of the genders is now narrowing. However, the marginal revenue productivity of women remains below that of men because women are disproportionately concentrated in low-paid occupations which generate low marginal revenue. In addition, a smaller percentage of women belong to trade unions and professional organisations and so have lower bargaining power. Some women also lose out on promotion chances because of leaving the labour markets at crucial times in their career in order to bear and raise children. Another factor that still exists is discrimination with some employers undervaluing the services of female workers.

- Part-time and full-time workers: Part-time workers, on average, receive less pay per hour than full-time workers. Again there are a number of reasons which explain this. One is that the supply of people wanting to work part-time is high relative to the demand. Part-time work is convenient for a number of people bringing up children, pursuing university studies and other interests and careers. Part-time workers are also less likely to receive training, both on and off the job, than full-time workers so their productivity tends to be lower. In addition, a smaller proportion of part-time workers belong to trade unions and professional organisations and a higher proportion are women.

- Ethnic groups: As noted In Section 4.1, people from ethnic minorities tend to be lower paid than white workers. One particular group which receives low pay is workers of a Bangladeshi origin. There are again a number of reasons for this. One is that a high proportion of Bangladeshis work in the catering industry, which is low paid. Another is that the qualifications of Bangladeshis, particularly Bangladeshi women, are currently, on average, below those of the rest of the population. Another factor is discrimination.

Explain how discrimination creates inefficiency.

Quick check

1 Distinguish between economic rent and transfer earnings.
2 What is the significance of elasticities of demand for, and supply of, labour in wage determination?
3 Why are skilled workers paid more than unskilled workers?
4 Why is the gap between male and female wage rates narrowing?

Labour market failure

Synoptic link

This section links back to AS Sections 2.1–2.8.

Thinking like an economist

What policies might a government employ to reduce unemployment?

Introduction

Labour market failure occurs when the market forces of demand and supply do not result in an efficient allocation of resources. Evidence of labour market failure occurs in a number of forms. The most obvious is unemployment. Other examples include shortages of skilled labour, workers being in jobs that they are not best suited for, a lack of training and wage rates being above or below their equilibrium rate.

Unemployment

Unemployment means that labour markets are not clearing. Some of those willing and able to work cannot obtain a job. The existence of unemployment means that a country is not making all that it is capable of. It will not be producing on its production possibility curve and so will not be achieving productive efficiency.

The extent to which unemployment causes labour market failure is obviously influenced by the number of people who are out of work. It is also influenced by how long people are out of work. The longer someone is unemployed, the more they get out of touch with the skills required and the greater the risk that they may give up hope of gaining a job.

Dominant buyers and sellers

Trade unions may push the wage rate above the equilibrium and thereby cause unemployment, although a trade union would not push up the wage rate indefinitely since such a policy would result in one paid member. Trade unions may also engage in restrictive practices such as job demarcation in which workers will only undertake tasks outlined in their job descriptions. This will influence the flexibility of the labour force.

In labour markets monopsonists and oligopsonist employers have the power to determine the wage rate and employment, both of which are likely to be lower than in a perfectly competitive labour market.

Lack of information

Workers may be in jobs which are less well paid and which they enjoy less than other jobs they are capable of doing because they are unaware of suitable vacancies. Similarly, employers may not appoint the most productive workers because they are not in touch with all the potential workers. Obtaining information on job vacancies and potential workers, applying for jobs and interviewing workers involves a variety of costs. For workers it takes time and effort and money to look for a new job, fill out application forms and attend interviews. Employers incur costs in advertising jobs, assessing applications, interviewing people and inducting new staff. So both groups have to consider the benefits of searching for a better situation against the costs of searching.

Immobility of labour

Labour immobility comes in two main forms. One is **geographical immobility**, which is the obstacles that workers experience in moving from jobs in one area to jobs in another area. When this occurs, shortages of workers in one area and surpluses in other areas are not corrected and regional unemployment and geographical wage differentials continue to exist. Geographical immobility arises for a number of reasons. These include differences in the availability and price of housing in different areas and social ties.

The other type of immobility is **occupational immobility**. This is concerned with the obstacles that workers experience in changing occupations. These obstacles contribute to occupational wage differentials and structural unemployment. Occupational immobility arises because of differences in qualifications, skills and social barriers.

There are a number of barriers that exist to the free movement of workers between different sections of the labour market. Indeed in practice there are a number of different labour markets with many workers' choices of jobs being restricted to the segment in which they are currently operating. For instance, it is still difficult for men to get jobs as nannies and for journalists to retrain as doctors. This means that the competition for jobs in any particular labour market can be limited.

Other causes of labour market failure

- Attachment between workers and employers: Some workers may stay in less well-paid jobs because they like working for their employers – they have a good working relationship. Employers may also feel a sense of loyalty to their existing workforce. This attachment reduces the mobility of labour and makes supply more inelastic.
- Inertia: Workers may not move to higher paid jobs and employers may not seek to replace less productive workers by more productive workers out of laziness.
- Externalities: Training is a merit good. It has positive externalities and if left to market forces too few resources would be devoted to it. This is because some workers and some firms take a short-term view and underestimate the benefits of training. In addition, some firms are afraid that other firms may reap the benefits of their expenditure by poaching their staff.

Discrimination

Discrimination results in an inefficient allocation of resources and inequitable wage differentials. Its costs include:

- the group discriminated against clearly suffers. They are likely to be paid less than other workers doing the same job and to find it harder to gain employment. In addition, some may have to settle for less demanding jobs than they are capable of undertaking, may be overlooked for promotion and may not be selected to go on training courses. The existence of discrimination may also discourage members from the discriminated group from applying for well-paid jobs and from seeking to gain higher qualifications.

- producers who discriminate have a smaller pool of labour to select from. They may also not make the best use of, for example, any black workers they do employ. This will raise their costs of production and make them less competitive against rival firms at home and abroad.
- consumers will experience higher prices if producers discriminate. They will also experience higher prices and less choice if they themselves discriminate against firms which employ workers from a particular group.
- the government may have to pay out more welfare benefits to groups which are discriminated against and may have to spend time and money introducing and monitoring legislation to end discrimination and tackle social tension.
- the economy will lose out as a result of the misallocation of resources. Output will be below the potential output which could be achieved if the group were not discriminated against in terms of employment, pay, promotion and training.

Theories of discrimination

A number of theories have been put forward to explain negative discrimination.

- Becker's theory: Gary Becker, Professor of Economics at Chicago University, argues that some people may be prepared to experience higher costs rather than come into contact with members of a particular group. In effect, the individuals pay in the form of lower profits to avoid employing, for example, women workers and in the form of higher prices to avoid buying from firms employing female workers.
- Statistical discrimination: This arises because of imperfect information. Some economists argue that employers discriminate as a result of seeking to reduce their costs. They do not know in advance the productivity of job applicants and may find it difficult to measure the productivity of existing workers. So when deciding who to employ, how much to pay and who to promote and train they make decisions on generalisations about groups of workers. For example, an employer may assume that workers aged 50 and over are less productive and will have a shorter time with the firm than younger workers. As a result s/he may use age as a screening device when deciding on job applicants, may not promote older workers or send them on training courses and if deciding on redundancies may select older workers first.

Thinking like an economist

1 Apart from legislation, identify two other ways a government could seek to reduce discrimination.
2 Why might a worker not leave her current job for a better job for which she is qualified?

Introduction

In practice, many wages are not determined in competitive labour markets. In these markets, factors, in addition to the free market forces of demand and supply, play a role in determining wages and the level of employment. One such factor is labour organisations. Workers may join together to sell their labour through one body. This may be a **trade union** or professional body.

The role of labour organisations

Labour organisations seek to promote the interests of their members. Probably their best-known function is to negotiate pay and conditions of employment with employers. Negotiations can take place both at a national and at a local level. For example, the AUT (Association of University Teachers) negotiate lecturers' pay at a national level with the Higher Education Funding Council and will negotiate with individual universities over possible redundancies. Unions lobby the government through the TUC (Trades Union Congress), the national body of the trade union movement.

In addition to their negotiating role, labour organisations also carry out a number of other functions. They provide a channel for communication between workers and employers. The presence of a trade union or a strong professional body reduces labour turnover and raises the level of training.

A number provide benefits and services for their members including financial services and legal advice. Some are also involved in lobbying national government on behalf of their members and setting minimum qualification standards.

The effect of labour organisations on wages and employment

If all the workers in a labour market are members of a trade union or a professional organisation, the body will act as a monopoly seller. This will alter the supply curve of labour.

Figure 1 shows the effect of a trade union forcing the wage rate up from W to W1. The supply curve now becomes W1XS. All workers would be prepared to work for W1 or above. The diagram also shows employment falling from Q to Q2. This may occur if trade unions force up the wage rate paid by firms producing under conditions of perfect competition or monopolistic competition in the product market. In these two market structures firms earn only normal profit in the long run. So a rise in their costs will cause marginal firms to leave the industry causing output and employment to fall.

The trade union may seek to avoid loss of jobs by supporting measures to increase labour productivity (for example, participating in training initiatives) or measures to increase demand for the product (for example, participating in an advertising campaign). In both cases, if the measures are

Synoptic link

A2 Section 4.8 explained how wages and employment are influenced by market forces. This section focuses on another key influence.

Definition

Trade union: an association of workers.

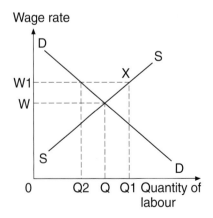

Figure 1: The effect of a trade union on the labour market

Thinking like
an economist

What factors will limit how
high a labour organisation seeks to
push up the wage rate of its
members?

successful, the marginal revenue productivity and hence the demand curve will shift to the right. A union may be in a stronger position to raise the wage rate of its members if the employer operates under conditions of monopoly or oligopoly in the product market. This is because the firms may be earning supernormal profits in the long run.

Factors influencing a labour organisation's bargaining strength

A labour organisation will be stronger, the:
- greater the financial reserves of the organisation
- higher the proportion of workers in the organisation
- more inelastic the demand for the firm's product
- lower the degree of substitution between capital and labour
- lower the proportion of labour costs in total costs
- lower the rate of unemployment
- greater the support the workers have from the general public
- more legislation favours the rights of workers and the more disruption any industrial action would cause.

Thinking like
an economist

Why are labour organisations
stronger during an economic boom
than during a recession?

Trends in trade union membership

The trend in trade union membership is downwards. Table 1 shows that membership has fallen by more than 2.1 million between 1990 and 2000. In the early years of the 1990s, one reason for the decline was the rise in unemployment – there were fewer people in jobs to join trade unions. An increase in employment, in part, explains the short time rise in membership between 1997 and 2000.

Table 2 Trade union membership, 1990-2000

Year	No. of members (millions)
1990	9.96
1991	9.56
1992	9.17
1993	8.85
1994	8.30
1995	8.11
1996	7.98
1997	7.84
1998	7.89
1999	7.94
2000	7.82

Source: Table 7.26 (page 115), Annual Abstract of Statistics, 2003, ONS

Union membership as a proportion of the labour force has also fallen from 58 per cent in 1984 to 34 per cent in 2002. The reasons why trade union membership has been declining are thought to include a change in the composition of the working population and a decline in union power.

There has been a fall in the number of workers employed in areas which are heavily unionised and a rise in the number of workers employed in areas with low union density. For example, the number of workers in the public sector, engineering, large companies has declined while the number of workers in the private sector, small companies, self-employment and part-time work has increased.

Unions have become less powerful because of legislation introduced in the 1980s and 1990s, which restricted their rights, and by the rise in the number of companies deciding not to recognise unions. The fall in the power of unions is reflected in the decline in the gap between union and non-union members which has occurred since the mid-1990s.

When a company does not recognise a union it means that the union does not have the right to negotiate on behalf of its members. This would make it difficult for the union to recruit members. In recent years more new establishments have chosen not to recognise unions.

Labour disputes

In the last two decades there has been a noticeable decline in labour disputes. This is reflected in the three measures of labour disputes:
- the number of stoppages arising from labour disputes
- the number of workers involved in the stoppages
- the number of working days lost through stoppages (probably the main measure)

In 1980, for example, there were 1330 stoppages and 11.97m working days lost as a result. This contrasts with 212 stoppages and 499,000 working days lost in 2000.

In comparison with other EU countries, the UK has recently had a good record in labour relations. In 2000, for instance, the UK lost 11 days per 1000 employees to labour disputes, compared with the EU average of 50.

Quick check

1 What are the key functions of a labour organisation?
2 In what sense may a labour organisation be a monopoly?
3 Explain three factors that influence the bargaining power of a labour organisation.
4 Why is trade union membership declining?

Hot potato

Does a reduction in labour disputes necessarily imply an improvement in labour relations?

4.11 Monopsony employer

Introduction

In some labour markets, employers exercise considerable market power. In such markets the wage rate and employment level may be driven below the efficient levels.

Synoptic link

A2 Section 4.10 examined market power in the sale of labour. This section examines market power in the *purchase* of labour.

Definitions

Monopsonist: a single buyer.
Oligopsonist: one of a few dominant buyers.

Employers with labour market power

Those employers who employ a high percentage of workers in a particular labour market can influence the wage rate. In a labour market, a **monopsonist** is a firm which is the only buyer (i.e. employer) and an **oligopsonist** is one of a few dominant firms buying a certain type of labour. An example of a monopsonist employer is the Ordnance Survey, which is the main employer of map-makers in the UK. In some areas where there are only a few veterinary practices, vets and veterinary nurses sell their labour in an oligopsonistic market.

The determination of wages and employment

Monopsonists and oligoposonists are price makers. They influence the wage rate. To employ more workers they have to raise the wage rate. So the marginal cost of labour (MCL) will exceed the average cost of labour (ACL), which is equivalent to the wage rate.

Table 1 shows how the average cost of labour exceeds the marginal cost of labour. For example, to attract a fourth worker costs the employer an extra £25 since s/he not only pays that worker £16 but also pays an extra £3 to each of the first three workers employed. In this circumstance, a union can raise the wage rate without causing unemployment.

Table 1

No. of workers	Average cost of labour (wage rate) per hour	Total cost of labour per hour	Marginal cost of labour per hour
1	10	10	10
2	11	22	12
3	13	39	17
4	16	64	25
5	20	100	36
6	25	150	50

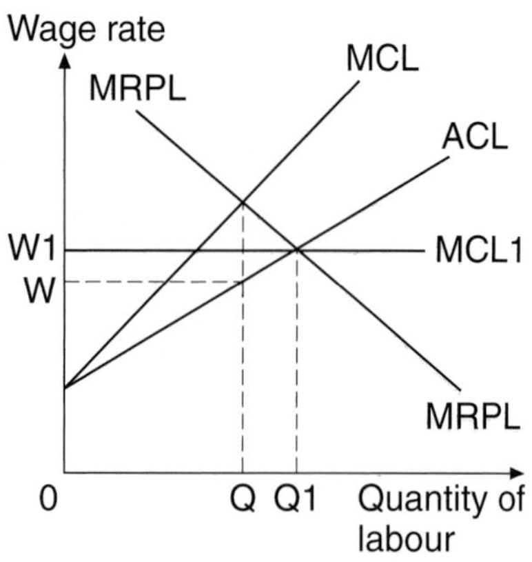

Figure 1: A monopsony labour market

Figure 1 shows that, in the absence of union action, the number of workers employed will be Q (where MRPL equals MCL) and the wage rate will be W (found from the ACL curve).

The union may then raise the wage rate to W1. This then becomes the new marginal cost of labour (MCL1) as there will be one wage rate for all union members. Employment now rises to Q1. It also means, however, that once the wage rate has been settled by negotiation the monoposonist will not have to increase the wage rate to attract labour.

Bilateral monopoly

When a monopoly trade union negotiates with a monopsonist employer, the situation is referred to as a **bilateral monopoly**. In this case, the wage rate will be determined by the relative bargaining strengths of the two sides. If the monopsonist is very powerful, the outcome will be a wage rate close to that which the monopsonist would have chosen to pay without any trade union intervention. The upper limit will be the maximum the monopsonist can pay without threatening the existence of the firm. The stronger the trade union is, the closer the wage rate will be to this limit. Figure 2 shows the lower limit and a possible upper limit.

Factors influencing an employer's bargaining strength

An employer will be stronger the:
- greater the financial reserves it has with which it can last out any dispute
- lower the proportion of its workers are in the union
- greater the degree of substitution between capital and labour
- higher the rate of unemployment since this will mean it can substitute existing workers with unemployed workers
- lower the support workers have from the general public
- lower the disruption any industrial action would cause to the productive process
- the more branches the firm has which employ either non-union labour of labour in different unions – so that production can be moved in the case of a dispute
- the more legislation favours employers.

Quick check ✔

1 Why, in the case of a monopsonistic labour market, does the marginal cost of labour exceed the average cost of labour?
2 Why might employment rise if a union negotiates a pay rise for its members from a monopsonist employer?
3 Identify three factors which could increase the strength of an employer's bargaining power?
4 How does social convention influence wages?

Hot potato

Will the working conditions of people working for a monopsonist employer be better or worse than those of people working for employers in a competitive labour market?

Definition

Bilateral monopoly: a market with a single buyer and seller.

Thinking like an economist

1 What effect is globalisation having on employers' bargaining strength?
2 What would be the characteristics of a perfect labour market?

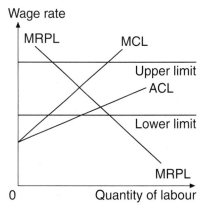

Figure 2: Bargaining limits

4.12 Government intervention in labour markets

Synoptic link

In AS Sections 2.10–2.13 you examined a variety of forms of government intervention. This section concentrates on some of the most common forms of intervention in labour markets.

Thinking like an economist

Why is discriminating against a particular group of workers likely to raise a firm's costs?

Introduction

Government intervention affects wages and employment in a number of ways. These include the government's employment of public sector workers, its general macroeconomic and microeconomic policies and specific labour market policies.

Government intervention in the economy

Despite the major privatisation programmes of the 1980s and 1990s, the government remains a major employer. The pay and number of people working in the public sector, such as nurses, civil servants and teachers, is affected by the level of government expenditure.

Government policy measures which increase aggregate demand tend to stimulate employment, at least in the short run, and to raise wages. Changes in tax rates and welfare benefits can also affect wage rates. New classical economists believe that cuts in tax rates and benefits will stimulate a rise in the supply of labour and reduce upward pressure on gross wages. In contrast, Keynesians believe the effects of tax cuts are more uncertain and that reductions in benefits may reduce employment by lowering aggregate demand.

Government policies on particular markets can affect wage rates and employment in those markets. For example, raising tax rates on cigarettes is likely to result in a fall in demand for cigarettes and thereby put downward pressure on wages.

The government also operates the Advisory, Conciliation and Arbitration Service (ACAS), which conciliates in disputes between employers and employees.

Labour market information

To offset the lack of labour market information the government provides information in a variety of forms. There is a state funded careers service that provides details about requirements, working conditions and pay of a variety of occupations. Careers education is also part of the curriculum of state schools and most private sector (public) schools. Government job centres provide information about job vacancies and welfare benefit officials discuss with the unemployed what jobs are on offer and how to apply for them.

Regional policy

Regional policy seeks to influence the distribution of firms and people. To reduce the problem of geographical immobility of labour and regional unemployment, governments employ a variety of measures. Financial assistance may be given to workers to relocate to areas where there are vacancies requiring their particular skills. More commonly, however 'work is taken to the workers' by providing financial assistance for firms to locate and relocate in areas of high unemployment.

Training

A government can seek to raise the level of training to the allocatively efficient level in a variety of ways.

- It can provide training itself directly to its own employees and to the unemployed and those changing jobs.
- It can subsidise individuals to engage in training and/or firms to provide training.
- It can pass legislation requiring firms to engage in a certain level of training.

Education

Increases and improvements in state educational provision should raise the qualifications and skills levels of workers. This should increase the occupational mobility of the labour force, reduce the shortage of skilled labour and raise the productivity of labour.

Measures to raise the qualifications and skills of workers are referred to as investment in human capital. If there is investment in developing the abilities of a wide range of people the problem of social exclusion (people not feeling a part of society) should also be reduced.

Minimum wage legislation

Minimum wage legislation is introduced to help raise the pay of low-paid workers. To have any effect, the minimum wage has to be set above the market equilibrium wage rate.

New classical economists argue that such government intervention in the operation of free market forces raises firms' costs of production and results in higher unemployment. Figure 1 shows that the setting of a minimum wage of WX above the equilibrium wage rate of W causes an extension in the supply of labour but also a contraction in the demand for labour causing a shortfall of employment of QS-QD. Compared with the situation before the intervention of the government, employment falls from Q to QD.

However, some Keynesian economists argue that the introduction of a national minimum wage may not result in higher unemployment. Low-paid workers often have low bargaining power relative to their employers, some of which are monopsonists and oligopsonists. In these cases, the introduction of a minimum wage could raise both the wage rate and employment. Figure 2 shows that a minimum wage of WX becomes the new marginal cost of labour and raises employment from Q to Q1.

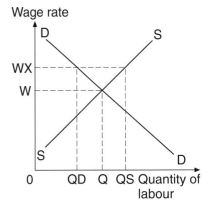

Figure 1: The effect of the introduction of a minimum wage

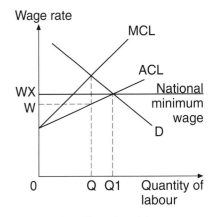

Figure 2: The effect of a minimum wage in a monopsony labour market

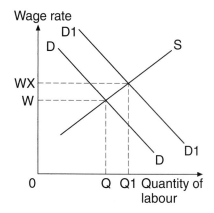

Figure 3: An increase in demand resulting from the introduction of a minimum wage

Thinking like an economist

How might the ending of age discrimination benefit society?

There are other reasons why a national minimum wage may not cause unemployment. One is that the first effect of its introduction is to raise wages. This, in turn, raises demand for goods and services which, in turn, may increase demand for labour. The higher wages may also raise the morale and productivity of those affected. Productivity will also increase if employers seek to gain higher returns from the now higher-paid workers by providing more training. Rises in demand for products and increases in productivity will shift the marginal revenue productivity (demand for labour) to the right and increase employment as illustrated In Figure 3.

A national minimum wage, affecting the pay of 1.8 million workers, was introduced in the UK in April 1999. The minimum pay for adults was initially set at £3.60 per hour; £3.00 for eighteen to twenty-one year olds (which rose to £3.20 in June 2000). Sixteen and seventeen year old workers were made exempt. The minimum is reviewed regularly. In October 2003 it was £4.50 for adults and £3.80 for eighteen to twenty-one year olds.

Discrimination legislation

A government can pass legislation making discrimination against a particular group illegal. In the UK, the Equal Pay Act of 1970, which was implemented in 1975, sought to end differences in pay between men and women undertaking the same or broadly similar work, or for work rated as equivalent under a job evaluation study. The Sex Discrimination Act made unequal treatment on the grounds of gender or marital status in aspects of employment other than pay, which was already covered, illegal. In 1983, both Acts were consolidated and broadened under the Equal Pay (Amendment) Regulation. The Race Relations Act of 1976 makes it illegal to discriminate on the grounds of colour or race. In 1995, the Disability Discrimination Act came into force which made discrimination on the grounds of disability illegal.

Such legislation may change attitudes over time. Employers may find that a group which they had previously discriminated against is more productive than they first thought. However, at least in the short run, employers may seek to get round any such legislation by, for example, claiming that workers from a certain group are less well suited than others for the jobs on offer and redefining jobs undertaken by workers from different groups. In practice it can often be difficult to prove that discrimination has occurred.

Trade union reform

If it is thought that the power of trade unions has been weakened by previous legislation and that bargaining power had been reduced too much in relation to that of employers, a government may repeal some of the legislation. The Labour government that came to power in May 1997 changed a number of the measures that previous Conservative governments had introduced. For example, it removed the ban on government employees at GCHQ at Cheltenham from joining a union.

Agreement on the Social Chapter

In 1997, the newly elected Labour government reversed the UK's opt out from the Social Chapter of the Maastricht Treaty. It adopted various EU directives on employment legislation, for example on the right to paternity leave and paid holidays, maximum working hours and minimum standards of health and safety at work.

Workers in the UK work longer hours than those in most other European Union (EU) countries. On 1 October 1998, the Working Time Directive came into force. This requires employers to 'take all reasonable steps' to ensure that employers do not work, against their will, more than an average of 48 hours a week. Despite this, in 2003, more than one-fifth of UK workers worked more than 48 hours a week in their main jobs. At the time employers expressed concern that this directive might raise their labour costs and reduce the flexibility of their labour force. There is evidence, however, that reducing long working hours raises labour productivity.

Quick check

1   How does discrimination affect the wages and employment of those discriminated against?
2   Why is anti-discrimination legislation not always successful?
3   Which poor groups do not benefit from the National Minimum Wage (NMW)?
4   What effect may a NMW have on employment?

Puzzler

Should the National Minimum Wage be raised?

Labour market flexibility

Introduction

Labour market failure reduces the flexibility of labour markets. For example, a lack of information and labour mobility will make it difficult for expanding firms to recruit new workers. The government seeks to promote labour market flexibility in a variety of ways.

Flexibility of the labour force

A flexible labour force is one that adjusts, with ease, in terms of the number of hours worked and the amount of pay received to changes in market conditions.

The flexibility of labour is influenced by how easy it is for firms to 'hire and fire' labour and how easy workers find it to adapt to new tasks and technology. It can be interpreted in terms of numerical flexibility (ability to change the numbers of workers), temporal flexibility (ability to change the hours people work), locational flexibility (ability to change where people work – at home or their place of employment), functional flexibility (ability to change the tasks workers perform) and wage flexibility (the ability to raise or lower wages).

Flexibility allows firms to respond to increased demand without encountering capacity constraints and without putting upward pressure on wages and allows them to adjust smoothly and quickly to falls in demand. However, it can create greater insecurity for workers. For example, if they are working on a casual contract, they may find it difficult to obtain a mortgage.

The UK's performance

The UK has a more flexible labour market than many industrialised countries, including most EU countries. Recent years have seen an increase in temporary employment, part-time employment, flexible hours, out-of-hours working and more workers working from home. These changes have contributed to a more flexible labour force but they have not been the main cause. The main cause is actually the fewer legal restrictions on the hiring and firing of people in regular jobs and the deployment of labour at different times. The USA is one of the few countries that has a lower level of employment protection than the UK.

Government policies

There are a number of measures a government can employ to increase the flexibility of the labour force. Increased labour information, improved training and education should all make labour more mobile and therefore raise the responsiveness of labour to changes in the pattern of demand. In addition a government may employ other supply-side policies in order to increase the responsiveness of workers to changes in the demand for labour.

Cutting marginal tax rates

Firms will find it easier to adjust to changes in demand if the supply of labour is responsive to changes in wage rates. New classical economists believe that reducing marginal direct tax rates will raise the incentive for existing workers to increase the number of hours they work, for the unemployed to seek work more actively and for those considering retiring early to stay in the labour force for longer. They think that the substitution effect of any rise in net pay resulting from a tax cut will exceed the income effect. However, studies have shown that a large proportion of workers are not free to alter the hours that they can work, and of those who can as many choose to work fewer hours as work more hours.

However, cuts in marginal tax rates do seem to have some influence on people's decision as to when they will retire if they have some choice in the matter.

The effect on unemployment is a controversial matter. Keynesians believe that the main cause of unemployment is a lack of aggregate demand and hence job vacancies. They do not think that people remain unemployed because they are not prepared to work for the going wage rate.

Reducing unemployment benefit

Some new classical economists have suggested that, in addition to cutting marginal tax rates, the gap between paid employment and benefits (such as job seekers' allowance) should be increased by reducing benefits. They believe that this makes unemployment a less attractive prospect and so reduces the time that the unemployed spend searching for a job.

Again Keynesians argue that the unemployed are not voluntarily unemployed. They also believe that cutting job seekers' allowance will actually increase unemployment by reducing aggregate demand. The unemployed spend a high proportion of their income. A cut in their benefits will reduce their spending which will have a knock-on effect on the spending of the people they buy goods and services from and so on.

The New Deal

The government has introduced a welfare-to-work strategy – providing benefits to people not to remain unemployed but to support them while they actively seek employment. This particularly targets those most prone to long-term unemployment, including lone parents with dependent children, people from ethnic minorities, people with disabilities and those living in disadvantaged areas.

When people are first unemployed, they receive careers advice and guidance and help with developing job search skills. Those who are still out of work after six months, then have to move onto one of four options. They can enter subsidised employment, undertake work experience with a voluntary organisation, join an environmental taskforce or participate in full-time education. If at the end of this experience a person is still unemployed, she or he will receive more guidance and, if necessary, more training.

Trade union reform

New classical economists believe that trade unions can cause unemployment by pushing up the wage rate above the equilibrium level and reduce the flexibility of labour by engaging in restrictive practices. The Conservative administrations of 1979 to 1997 passed a number of Acts limiting the power of trade unions.

Quick check

1   What is meant by the flexibility of labour?
2   Why may locational flexibility reduce firms' costs?
3   What are the benefits of a more flexible labour force?
4   How might cuts in income tax increase the flexibility of labour?

Introduction

Throughout most of the twentieth century, income and wealth became more evenly distributed. However, the last two decades of the twentieth century saw a reversal of this trend and now, at the start of the twenty-first century, a quarter of the UK population live in households with incomes below half the national average.

Wealth

Wealth is a stock of assets that have a financial value. Economists distinguish between marketable and non-marketable wealth. Marketable wealth is wealth that can be transferred to another person, such as houses and shares, whereas non-marketable wealth is wealth which is specific to a person and cannot be transferred, such as pension rights.

The distribution of wealth can be considered in terms of how it is distributed between the population (size distribution), the forms in which it is held and according to the characteristics of those holding wealth.

The size distribution of wealth

Wealth is very unequally distributed among the UK population. Table 1 shows the size distribution of marketable wealth in the UK in 1986 and 1999.

Table 1: Distribution of wealth in the UK

Percentage of marketable wealth owned by:	1986 (%)	1999 (%)
Most wealthy 1%	18	23
Most wealthy 5%	36	43
Most wealthy 10%	50	54
Most wealthy 25%	73	74
Most wealthy 50%	90	94
Total marketable wealth (£ billion)	955	2752

Source: Table 5.25 Social Trends 30 and 32, ONS, 2000 and 2002.

The table shows that wealth has become more unequally distributed between 1986 and 1999. It also shows the extent of inequality. In both years, the wealthiest 10 per cent of the population owned half or more than half of the country's wealth.

Synoptic link

Income inequalities were touched on in AS Section 2.8. The workings of labour markets discussed in the previous A2 sections influence the distribution of income and wealth.

Wealth distribution between assets

Wealth can be held in a variety of forms including life assurance and pension funds, property, securities and shares, banking and building society deposits and cash.

Life assurance and pension fund holdings have, in the past, accounted for the largest percentage of wealth held, forming more than a third of all household wealth in 1997. This form of wealth is more evenly distributed than property, securities and shares.

The proportion of a particular asset in the wealth of the household sector is influenced by not only the amount accumulated but also by changes in its value. For example, in the late 1980s the share accounted for by property in the form of residential houses rose as a result of increases in owner-occupation and rises in the price of houses. Conversely, in the early 1990s the fall in property prices was reflected in a decline in property as a percentage of the wealth of the household sector.

Wealth distribution between different groups

As would be expected, wealth is unevenly distributed between age categories. For example, people in their 40s and 50s have had more time to accumulate savings than people in their 20s and 30s and do indeed have greater wealth.

However the amount of wealth held also varies between ethnic groups and genders. White adults have more wealth than adults from ethnic minorities. The group which currently has the lowest holding of wealth per head is people of a Bangladeshi background. Men also have more wealth than women.

Sources of wealth

A person can become wealthy in four main ways.
- Inheritance: This is the main way someone becomes wealthy.
- Saving: A person could accumulate wealth by saving. However, to achieve significant wealth saving has to be on a large scale. This is easier to achieve by people with high incomes that may themselves be generated by significant holdings of wealth. Indeed wealth creates wealth.
- The use of entrepreneurial skills: Some people are self-made millionaires as a result of building up a business. For example, Bill Gates of Microsoft has built up a fortune in excess of £36.25 billion.
- Chance: Lottery winners receive a considerable amount of publicity and a number of people are made 'instant millionaires'. However, for example, even a £2 million lottery win pales into insignificance when compared with the approximately £1750 million that the family of the Duke of Westminster stand to inherit.

Thinking like an economist

Explain the effect a rise in wealth is likely to have on consumption.

Causes of the inequality of wealth

The causes of the inequality of wealth are obviously linked to the sources of wealth and include:

- the pattern of inheritance: In the UK, significant holdings of wealth have traditionally been passed on to the next generation on the basis of primogeniture (the right of the eldest son to inherit to the exclusion of others). In the UK, major estates and the connected titles are still passed on to the eldest son, whereas in countries where property and other assets are distributed amongst the children on the death of the parents, wealth becomes more evenly distributed over time.
- Marriage patterns of the wealthy: The wealthy tend to marry other wealthy people. This further concentrates wealth in the hands of the few.
- Inequality of income: As already noted, people with high incomes are more able to save and earn interest.
- Different tendencies to save: Those who save a higher proportion of their income will accumulate more wealth than those who save a smaller proportion.
- Luck: This plays a part in terms of the success of businesses which people start and in terms of who wins money.

Wealth and income distribution

Wealth is more unevenly distributed than income. While a person can survive without owning any assets by, for example, renting a house, it is not possible to survive without any income. In addition, due to inheritance the highest amount of wealth a person can hold at any one time exceeds the highest amount a person can earn.

Distribution of income

Within a country the distribution of income can be considered in terms of how income is shared out between the factors of production (functional distribution of income), between households (size distribution) and between geographical areas (geographical distribution of income).

The functional distribution of income

Income is a flow of money over a period of time. Income can be earned by labour in the form of wages, by capital in the form of interest, by land in the form of rent and by entrepreneurs in the form of profits. In the UK, wages still account for the largest percentage but the percentage is falling. In 1987, 61 per cent of household income came from wages, but by 2000, it was down to 57 per cent. In contrast, income from dividends, interest and rent (collectively known as investment income) has been rising.

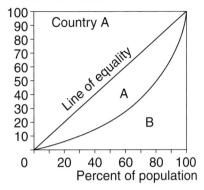

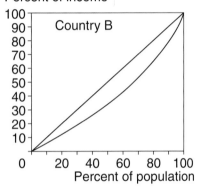

Figure 1 A comparison of inequality

In addition to earned income and investment income, households can receive income in the form of social security benefit. The relative shares of earned income, investment income and transfer payments depend on a variety of factors but principally on the level of employment and the relative power of labour and capital.

Measuring the size distribution of income

A common method of measuring the degree of inequality of income and wealth distribution between households is the Lorenz curve. This is named after the American statistician, Max Otto Lorenz.

Lorenz curves can be used to compare the distribution of income and wealth over time and between countries. The horizontal axis measures the percentage of the population starting with the poorest. In the case of income distribution, the vertical axis measures the percentage of income earned. A 45° line is included. This is called the line of income equality as it shows a situation in which, for example, 40 per cent of the population earned 40 per cent of the income and 80 per cent of the population earned 80 per cent of the income. The actual cumulative percentage income shares are then included on the diagram. In practice this will form a curve which starts at the origin and ends with 100 per cent of the population earning 100 per cent of income but which lies below the 45° line. The greater the degree of inequality the greater the extent to which the curve will be below the 45° line. Figure 1 shows that income is more unevenly distributed in Country A than in Country B.

For example in Country A, the poorest 20 per cent of the population earn only 5 per cent of the income whereas in Country B they earn 12 per cent.

The distribution can be measured in terms of, for example, fifths of the population (quintiles) or deciles (tenths).

The Gini coefficient is an international measure of inequality. It measures precisely the degree of inequality shown on a Lorenz curve. It is the ratio of the area between the Lorenz curve and the line of inequality and the line of income inequality to the total area below the line. On Figure 1A, this is the ratio of A/(A+B). Complete equality would give a ratio of 0 and complete inequality a ratio of 1 (100 per cent). So in practice the ratio will lie between 0 and 1 (100 per cent) and the nearer it is to 1 (100 per cent) the more unequal the distribution of income.

The size distribution of income in the UK

In recent years, the distribution of income has become more unequal. The widening of the gap between those with high incomes and those with low incomes was particularly noticeable between 1980 and 1990. In the first half of the 1990s, income distribution appeared to stabilise, but since then there appears to have been a further small increase in inequality.

Thinking like an economist

The Gini coefficient for the UK increased from 29 per cent in 1985 to 35 per cent in 2002. Explain what this means.

There are a number of reasons for this rise in income equality. One was the cut in the top tax rates in the 1980s and 1990s that obviously benefited the rich most. Another is the rise in top executive pay which was sparked initially by privatisation. At the other end of the income range there has been a decrease in the real value of benefits, particularly job seekers' allowance and a rise in the number of lone parents. The percentage of families with dependent children that are headed by lone parents is doubling. It more than doubled between 1971 and 2002. The lack of support in bringing up the children means lone parents are often not in work or only in part-time jobs.

The causes of income inequality between households

These include:

- unequal holdings of wealth: As wealth generates income in the form of profit, interest and dividends, differentials in wealth cause differences in income.
- differences in the composition of households: Some households may have, for example, three adults working whereas other households may contain no one in employment. Indeed low income is closely associated with a dependency on benefits.
- differences in skills and qualifications: Those with high skills and qualifications are likely to be in high demand and hence be likely to be able to earn high incomes.
- differences in educational opportunities: Those who have the opportunity to stay in education for longer are likely to gain more qualifications and develop more skills and so, as indicated above, are likely to increase their earning potential. Indeed lifetime earnings of graduates are noticeably higher than those of non-graduates.
- discrimination: The income of some groups are adversely affected by discrimination in terms of employment opportunities, pay and promotion chances.
- differences in hours worked: Most full-time workers earn more than part-time workers and those who work overtime earn more than those who work the standard hours.

The geographical distribution of income

Income is unevenly distributed between the regions of the UK. For example in 1999, the GDP per head in London was 130 per cent of the UK's average, while it was 77 per cent in the North East and Northern Ireland.

Regional income differences are even greater in Germany and Italy. Germany has a very wide gap between the former East Germany and the former West Germany. There is a north-south divide in Italy, where the southern Mezzogiorno region is much poorer than the north.

Hot potato

Is the current distribution of income equitable?

There are a number of causes of differences in the geographical distribution of income, including differences in:

- unemployment rates
- the proportion of the population claiming benefits
- the qualifications and the skills of the labour force
- industrial structure
- occupational structure
- living costs such as London allowances.

Of course there are variations within regions. Even though London as a whole has a high income per head, it has some of the most deprived districts in the UK.

Government policies

The extent to which a government intervenes to affect the distribution of income and wealth depends on the extent to which it believes that the free market distribution would be inequitable, the effects such inequality will have on society and the effects it believes any intervention will have on incentives and efficiency.

New classical economists do not favour significant intervention. This is because they believe that differences in income act as signals encouraging workers to move jobs and differences in wealth promote saving and investment. They also think that the provision of benefits above a minimum level for those who cannot work such as the disabled and sick can encourage voluntary unemployment.

In contrast, Keynesians believe that intervention is justified as market forces will not ensure an efficient allocation of income and wealth and that low levels of income and wealth can cause considerable problems for the households involved, including having a detrimental effect on the educational performance of the children. They also think that significant differences in income and wealth can cause social division with the poor feeling socially excluded.

Ways in which governments affect the distribution of income and wealth

Governments influence the distribution in a number of ways including:

- taxation: To assess the effects of taxation on the distribution of income and wealth pre- and post-tax distribution can be compared. In the UK, the overall effect of the tax system is to reduce inequality. However while progressive taxes, such as income tax which take a higher percentage of the income or wealth of the rich, make the distribution more equal, regressive taxes, such as VAT which take a higher percentage of the income of the poor, make the distribution more unequal.

- the provision of cash benefits: There are two types of cash benefits – means tested and universal. Means tested benefits, such as family credit, are available to those who claim them and who can prove their income is below a certain level. Universal benefits are available to everyone in a particular group irrespective of income. For example, all families with young children receive child benefit. Means tested benefits reduce inequality and universal benefits form a larger percentage of the income of the poor.
- the provision of benefits in kind: These include the provision of, for example, health care, education, school meals. The take up of these benefits depends on the age composition of the household (for example the elderly make the most use of the National Health Service) and attitudes and opportunities to access the provision (with, for example, more middle-class children staying on in education after 16 than working-class children).
- labour market policy: The Minimum Wage Act of 1999, the anti-discrimination acts and government subsidising of training reduce income inequality.
- macroeconomic policy influences the distribution of income and wealth in a number of ways. For example, measures to reduce unemployment may benefit low-income households and regional policy reduces geographical inequalities of income and wealth.

Research task

Using the most recent Social Trends, assess the effects of state benefits and taxes on the distribution of income.

Quick check

1   What are the main ways people can become wealthy?
2   What are the main causes of wealth inequality?
3   How are wealth and income inequality related?
4   Identify three ways in which the government influences the distribution of income and wealth.

Poverty

Introduction

It is estimated that a third of children in the UK, 4.5 million, live in poverty. In understanding the problem of poverty it is important to consider the meaning, measurement and consequences of poverty and the policy measures that a government can take to reduce poverty.

Absolute poverty

Economists distinguish between **absolute** and **relative poverty**. People are said to be in absolute poverty when their income is insufficient for them to be able to afford basic shelter, food and clothing. Even in rich countries there are some people who still do not have any housing. It has been estimated that in 2000 there were 1600 people sleeping rough in England. Of course the problem of absolute poverty is more extensive in poor countries.

Relative poverty

While someone in the UK may consider themselves to be poor if they are living in poor accommodation, have a television but no video recorder and can only afford to go out once a week, someone in Mali, for example, might regard themselves as well off if they had the same standard of living. This reflects the difference between absolute and relative poverty.

People are relatively poor when they are poor in comparison to other people. They are those who are unable to afford a certain standard of living at a particular time. As a result they are unable to participate in the usual activities of the society they live in.

The concept of human poverty, introduced in the Human Development Report 1997, sees poverty as a situation where people not only lack material goods but also lack access to those items needed to enjoy a long, healthy and creative life including self-esteem and the respect of others.

Relative and absolute poverty

Relative poverty varies between countries and over time. Someone who is regarded as poor in the USA might be regarded as relatively rich in, for example, Ethiopia. Fifteen years ago in the UK a personal computer might have been regarded as something of a luxury for a household but now, to participate in the activities of society, it might be viewed as a necessity. If a country experiences a rise in income, absolute poverty may fall. However, if those on high incomes benefit more than those on low incomes, relative poverty may rise.

Measuring poverty

To assess the extent to which poverty is a problem, it has to be measured. Economists often define as poor those whose income is less than 60 per cent

The last section examined the distribution of income and wealth. This section looks at those with low incomes and little or no wealth.

Definitions

Absolute poverty: the inability to purchase the basic necessities of life.
Relative poverty: a situation of being poor relative to others.

of the average income (adjusted to take account of family size). The current Labour government has set itself the task of eradicating child poverty by 2020, and now publishes a poverty audit. This includes poverty statistics and assesses the government's performance against a set of indicators. Among the indicators included are:

- an increase in the proportion of working-age people with a qualification
- improving literacy and numeracy at age 11
- reducing the proportion of older people unable to afford to heat their homes properly
- reducing the number of households with low incomes
- reducing homelessness
- reducing the number of children in workless households.

Particular groups are more prone to poverty than others. These include the old, the disabled, the sick, lone parents with children, the unemployed and those from ethnic minorities. For example in 1999-2000, 35 per cent of lone parent families were in households below 60 per cent median income.

Causes of poverty

Essentially the amount of poverty experienced depends on the level of income achieved and how it is distributed. The reasons why particular people are poor include:

- unemployment: This is a major cause of unemployment with some households having no-one in employment.
- low wages: Some workers in unskilled, casual employment earn very low wages. For example, a significant proportion of workers in Northern Ireland and the North East are on low wages. However just because someone earns low wages does not necessarily mean they are poor. It is possible that they could live in a household with a high income earning partner or parents.
- sickness and disability: Most of the long-term sick and disabled are dependent on benefits and this takes them into the low-income category.
- old age: For pensioners, state benefits are the largest source of income. However, occupational pensions and investment income are forming an increasing proportion of the income of some of the older population.
- the poverty trap: This arises when the poor find it difficult to raise their disposable income because any rise in gross income results in them having to pay more in taxes and receiving less in benefits.
- being a lone parent: Not having a partner to cope with the raising of a child may make it difficult for someone to obtain full-time employment.
- reluctance to claim benefits: A number of people, either because they are unaware of their entitlements or because of fear of social stigma, do not claim benefits which could help to supplement their incomes.

Thinking like
an economist

Explain how studying might
enable someone to escape poverty.

The effects of poverty

Poverty, especially absolute poverty, has a number of serious adverse effects on those who experience it. The poor tend to suffer worse physical and mental health and indeed have a lower life expectancy. The children of the poor suffer in terms of receiving less education, and it is often of a lower quality. They are less likely to stay in full-time education post-16, have few books at home and attend low performing schools. They are also less likely to have a personal computer in the home and to travel abroad. All these factors tend to result in them gaining fewer qualifications and a vicious circle of poverty developing. The poor can also feel cut off and even alienated from society, unable to live the type of life that the majority can experience.

Government policy measures to reduce poverty

Governments may seek to reduce absolute policy by introducing measures which raise the income of the poorest groups. They may also try to reduce relative policy by introducing measures which also reduce the gap between the rich and the poor. Among the various measures which they might use are:

- operating a national minimum wage: If set above the equilibrium rate, this will help the low paid who stay in employment. However, there are disputes about the effect that such a measure may have on the employment of unskilled workers. Also, as mentioned above, not all the low paid are poor and of course not all the poor are in low-paid jobs, such as the old and the disabled. In addition, if over time the minimum wage is not raised in line with earnings, it will cease to have any effect.
- cutting the bottom rates of income tax: This is something the Labour government has done in order to reduce the extent of the poverty trap and provide a greater incentive for people to work. However, in addition to the incentive, there also has to be the jobs available.
- increasing employment opportunities: This is thought to be significant as a major cause of poverty is unemployment. However, economists disagree about the best methods of increasing the number of jobs on offer.
- improving the quantity and quality of training and education: This is a long-term measure but again is an important one as it will increase the productivity and potential productivity of those affected and thereby improve their job prospects and earning potential.
- making use of the trickle down effect: This is a more controversial measure favoured by some supply-side economists. The idea is to cut the rate of corporation tax and the high rates of income tax with the intention of encouraging entrepreneurs to expand and thereby create employment for the poor. It is also thought that the higher spending which the rich may undertake may also stimulate the economy. However, it is debateable how the rich will react and whether the poor will benefit from any expansion that does occur. For example, will they have the skills for any new jobs created and what about the poor who are unable to work?

Thinking like an economist

Assess the arguments for and against raising benefits to reduce poverty.

- increasing benefits: Economists differ on their views about the effects of raising benefits for the unemployed. Keynesians think that it can raise aggregate demand and thereby create jobs, while new classical economists believe it will increase voluntary unemployment. However, there is more agreement on increasing benefits for those unable to work or who are retired. Those dependent solely on state sickness or disability benefit or the state pension fall into the lowest quintile of income and many of these would be unable to take out private insurance or invest to raise their income.
- increasing the provision of affordable child-care: This would enable more lone parents to undertake full-time employment and raise themselves out of poverty.

Hot potato

Should an income tax rate of 50 per cent on those with incomes over £100,000 be introduced to combat poverty?

Quick check

1   Why might absolute poverty fall while relative poverty increases?
2   What are the main causes of poverty?
3   What are the main costs of poverty?
4   Explain three measures a government could employ to reduce poverty.

4.16 Transport, transport trends and the economy

Synoptic link

For this and the following sections you will need to make sure that you are on top of:
- derived demand
- private and public sectors
- the general principles of demand and supply.

This section is designed to help you make links with the economic concepts that you have already learned and to be able to apply them to the transport sector of the economy. It includes information on:
- defining transport in economic terms
- identifying different modes of transport
- ownership of different transport operations
- identifying and understanding the implications of recent broad trends in the demand and supply of transport.

Learning tip

Although you should be used to it, the use of the terms private and public can be confusing. In this context, public transport refers to mass rather than individual transport, and some of this is publicly owned (by us), for example London Underground.

Transport defined

Transport can be defined most literally as the movement of resources and goods from the point of supply to the point of use. This can range from the extraction of timber from the middle of equatorial forests to the weekly delivery of your groceries by Tesco.

People move for a variety of reasons, including getting to and from work (commuting), as part of their work, to shop, to go to the cinema and other places of entertainment, to visit friends and relations and to go on holiday.

Categories of transport

Transport can be categorised and measured as follows.

According to what is being transported: Freight transport is the movement of goods. Demand for freight transport is usually measured in terms of tonne kilometres or number of journeys. Passenger transport is the movement of people and is measured in terms of passenger kilometres or, again, number of journeys.

The mode or means of transport: These are the methods or forms of transport. The modes can be divided into:
- road
- rail
- sea
- inland waterways
- pipeline (in the case of freight only).

Road transport can be further broken down into transport by lorry, van, car, taxi, bus, coach, motorbike, bicycle and walking.

Private or public transport: Private transport is usually taken to include transport by lorry, van, car, taxi, motorbike and bicycle. Public (mass) transport is transport by rail, bus and coach, all of which involve moving freight and people in 'bulk'.

Each mode of transport has particular advantages and disadvantages.

Transport of goods: The main criteria that would be used to evaluate the relative merits of different modes of transport are as follows:
- speed
- flexibility of routes
- capacity
- cost.

This can be summed up in a crude fashion in Table 1. However, it must always be remembered that it is necessary to examine the particular characteristics of what is being transported, and for what reason, to make judgements as to the best mode of transport in the UK.

Table 1: The advantages and disadvantages of different modes of freight transport

Mode	Advantages	Disadvantages
Road	Flexible, especially for small loads	Cost Congestion
Rail	Can be fast	Fixed routes Decaying infrastructure
Sea	Relatively cheap	Relatively slow
Inland waterways	Cheap	Very slow Fixed routes
Pipeline	Low variable costs	High sunk costs Fixed routes

Transport of people: Similar criteria can be applied to the choice of mode of transport for people but they might be phrased slightly differently:

- speed
- convenience
- cost
- convenience
- distance.

The principle choice that has to be made for domestic transport is between the use of the car and public transport, whereas if the transport of people is looked at globally, the benefits of air transport are likely to outweigh its relatively high cost. The choice of modes of travel within Europe is much more finely balanced.

Significance of demand for transport being derived

Demand for the vast majority of transport is, like the demand for labour, a derived demand. It is not wanted for its own sake but for what it enables companies and households to do. So, demand for transport is influenced by, for example, the distance people live away from their work, the number of holidays they take and the number of goods companies sell. This will have a crucial impact on the choice of mode of transport.

Thus if goods are being transported which are high in value the significance of the cost of transport is relatively small. Similarly if speed of supply is important to the purchaser of the final good then this characteristic will be most important.

From the people point of view, the derived nature of the demand for transport explains the significant fluctuations in demand that occur during the day and between seasons. For example, demand for a number of forms of transport is much higher between 7.30 am and 9 am and between 3.30

pm and 6 pm than in other periods of the day because a high number of people are taking their children to school or going to work at these times.

Ownership

The ownership of different modes of transport and the supporting infrastructure in the UK is complicated and involves a mixture of private and public ownership. Thus, the railway infrastructure is overseen by the government but run semi-independently as a not-for-profit organisation. Rail operating companies, bus transport companies and airlines all have publicly regulated owners in the private sector.

Almost all roads in the UK are regarded as public goods and are provided by the state and financed directly from taxation, but they tend to be built and maintained by private sector firms competing for government-supervised contracts. Whether or not truck owners and car owners pay the real cost of the resources that they consume is a controversial issue.

In most other countries, the whole of rail operations and many airlines are state owned. In the UK, airports and ports are privately owned but again abroad many are owned by national and local governments. These issues are explored in greater depth in Section 4.28 Promoting competition in transport markets.

Trends in transport in the UK

In recent decades there have been three major trends.

An overall increase in demand for transport

This reflects a variety of factors, including the increased importance of international trade, increased economic activity, people living further away from their place of work and relatives, people undertaking more holidays and holidays further a-field, hypermarkets and places of entertainment being built outside city centres and increases in output.

Changes in the organisation, ownership and scale of businesses in the UK

In broad terms there tends to be an increase in the degree of concentration in key UK industries such as food and other forms of retailing, newspaper and media, motor vehicle manufacture. These changes are inter-related with the process of globalisation, which has created new markets for UK-produced goods and new sources of partly-finished and finished products and services. Increasingly, large producers are able to source production from any part of the world, and manufacturing processes have tended to move to those countries with lower labour costs. These changes increase the need and frequency of transport of both goods and people. At the same time the relative cost of international transport has fallen, which again contributes to increased use.

A significant shift from public to private transport

One noticeable feature is the rise in car travel and the fall in bus travel. Figure 1 shows the rapid growth in car, van and taxi transport and the fall in bus and coach transport (as a percentage of total passenger transport). This is also reflected in the switching of the transport of goods domestically and in Europe to privately-owned road hauliers, and away from railway use. In June 2003, the Royal Mail announced that it was no longer using trains to transport mail.

Significant increases in the use of air transport for both goods and services

It is estimated that over 50 per cent of UK households will travel by air this year, primarily to European short-haul destinations. This expansion in air travel is partly related to the impact of low-cost airlines so much so that the Irish-based airline, Ryan Air, is now the third largest airline in the world.

The significance of these trends is explored more fully in the following Sections.

Summary

In terms of demand, transport can be seen to be a superior good in that expenditure tends to increase more than proportionately than income. This generalisation does not appear to apply to all forms of transport in the UK, and some forms of public transport appear to be characterised by a negative income elasticity of demand.

These shifts in demand are both an effect and a cause of other effects on the whole economy. They reflect an increase in demand for a wider range of goods produced more widely in many different global locations, and they also cause significant externalities as the actual private cost of many forms of transport does not always reflect the social costs imposed upon the economy as a whole.

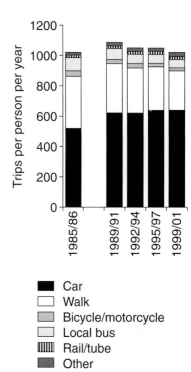

Figure 1: Average number of trips made, by main mode: 1985/86–1989/2001
Source: Department for Transport

Quick check ✓

1 Draw demand and supply diagrams to show the effects of:
   a) the recent series of rail accidents
   b) 9/11 and the transatlantic air passenger market
   c) negative externalities associated with road congestion

Changes in UK transport

Synoptic link

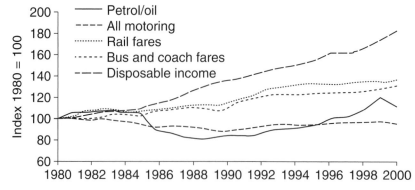

This section builds directly on the previous introduction to Transport, transport trends and the economy, and deals in greater detail with changes in UK transport. Numerous statistics are used to analyse the economic implications of the following changes:

- the growth in road transport
- the relative decline in bus transport.

Road transport

Increases in the demand for road transport come from the movement of both people and freight.

Passenger transport

The car is the preferred mode of passenger transport and its dominance is increasing. In 1961, only 30 per cent of UK households had a car and only 2 per cent had two or more. However by 1998, 70 per cent of households had at least one car and 25 per cent had two or more. Cars now account for 60 per cent of all journeys, whereas in 1975 they accounted for only 25 per cent. The rise in importance of car transport is illustrated in Figure 1.

It should be noted that this figure shows that total passenger distance travelled has increased between 1980 and 2001 from 491 to 734 billion passenger kilometres, and the bulk of this increase occurred during the 1980s. In the last decade of the twentieth century, the rate of growth in car travel slowed to 6 per cent.

The following reasons account for the rise in demand for car transport.

- A fall in the price of car use relative to other forms of transport. This has occurred because the cost of using a car has risen less than bus, coach and rail fares. This is illustrated in Figure 2.
- A rise in real incomes. Car use has a high-income elasticity of demand. Car travel is regarded as the most flexible, comfortable and convenient of all the transport modes. It enables people to travel when they want, from door to door and in some cases to areas not served by other forms of transport, apart perhaps from taxis. In the 20 years since 1980, the overall cost of motoring in real terms has remained at its 1980 level while average disposable income is 80 per cent higher, again measured in real terms.
- Changes in tastes, such as concerns about personal safety and child safety, retail habits as the popularity of shopping malls has grown, and the expectation that many young people have about car ownership.

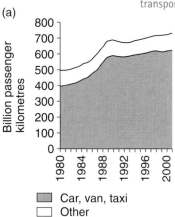

(a)

Car, van, taxi
Other

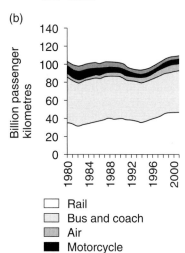

(b)

Rail
Bus and coach
Air
Motorcycle
Bicycle

Figure 1: (a) Passenger travel by car and other modes (b) Passenger travel by modes other than car.

Source: *Department for Transport*

Figure 2: Changes in the real cost of transport.

Source: *Office for National Statistics*

Freight transport

The transport of freight by road has grown in the last 20 years by 69 per cent since 1980, and this accounts for the bulk of the increase in total tonne kilometres transported. The use of rail for freight transport has fallen by two per cent, and that by water and pipeline has stayed relatively stable.

For most goods road transport is the preferred mode. The main exceptions to this are movements of petroleum products, of which nearly three quarters are transported by sea, and coal and coke, of which 70 per cent is transported by rail.

Some of the reasons for the popularity of road for freight transport were given in the previous Section.

- As notions such as '**just in time**' become significant in helping many suppliers distribute their goods more efficiently, road transport is most flexible in transporting goods from a variety of origins to a variety of destinations.
- Growing relative efficiency. Goods are now transported by bigger trucks, which carry bigger payloads reducing the cost per ton of transport. These trucks are also used more intensively as shown by a reduction in the number of trucks run empty which has fallen from a third 20 years ago to around 25 per cent today.
- Decreases in the relative importance of the extractive and heavy manufacturing sectors compared with higher unit value trade in consumer goods and a wide range of electronic and IT-based trade.
- A largely non-unionised and highly competitive road haulage industry helps ensure that transport costs are driven down.

The implications of the increasing popularity of road transport include:
- falling relative demand for other modes of transport
- greater mobility
- potential congestion.

Other modes of transport

In terms of passenger travel, urban and local bus services have been faced with decreasing demand and the number of bus journeys has declined considerably since the 1950s. Distances travelled by bus fell during the 1980s by around 17 per cent but have increased by around 7 per cent in the 1990s. In recent years the number of journeys has stabilised but, as a percentage of passenger transport, it continues to fall in importance. It is important to make the point that it is urban and local bus travel for which the demand has fallen most greatly as shown in Figures 1 and 2, which gives the average number of trips per year by mode.

Again, there are a number of reasons behind this trend, including the following.

- A rise in real incomes. As noted earlier, bus transport is perceived as an inferior good. Passengers are restricted by timetables. Buses are

Definition

Just-in-time: a business concept to minimise the costs of holding stocks, which describes the practise of ensuring the required supplies are received as close as possible to the time that they are needed for production or supply to the final consumer.

perceived as providing a low quality of service. They do not usually carry passengers from door to door, which is a particular disadvantage during bad weather, passengers are not guaranteed a seat, there can be delays and buses are not always as clean and comfortable as passengers would like.

- A rise in price. Bus fares have risen more in real terms than the cost of using a car.
- An increase in the length of journeys undertaken. People are more likely to undertake long journeys by car, rail or coach because of the greater speed and comfort.

Another significant factor related to increasing car use is the decline in number of journeys made on foot or by cycle or motorbike. This could have implications for health and spending on medical services, as well as those employed in affected industries.

Greater mobility

Obviously greater use of road transport can contribute to the mobility of factors of production within the economy. The distances that people travel by car have risen steadily over the last 20 years. The average person now travels nearly 5500 miles a year, an increase of 41 per cent since 1985. This has many implications for:

- the location of retail outlets
- taking short holidays in the UK
- choice of schools
- labour mobility.

Research task

Interview someone involved with the road haulage industry, the railways or the emergency services and find out what they think the government should do in terms of a transport policy.

The last of these is probably very significant in contributing to greater flexibility in the workforce. People expect and are expected to travel to find work. Many workers in the building and related trades commute weekly from the north of the country to London and the South East to take advantage of higher rates of pay relative to those in their home areas.

Similarly, the increased use of road transport has contributed greatly to increased efficiency in retailing and other service industries. Both private and business customers have become used to the notion of the overnight or next day delivery. These developments have also been fuelled by the intense competition that there is in some sections of the haulage industry.

Finally improvements in technology and the widespread use of containers has meant that long distance transport of goods is now highly automated and companies can take advantage of the relative merits of different modes for the transport of different types of goods over any distance. Road hauliers in the UK have been the principal beneficiaries of these developments, which speed the transport of internationally-traded goods.

Congestion

The growth in road traffic is not without its problems as the demand for road transport has risen more quickly that the supply of suitable roads. Since 1980 the length of the UK's road system has increased by 10 per cent while at the same time total traffic use by passengers and freight has risen by 73 per cent. This has resulted in reduced average speeds and longer journey times. Congestion tends to be concentrated on particular motorways such as the M1 and M6 and the M5 in summer, and in the larger urban areas especially London (see Figure 3).

Congestion is also a problem when there are accidents and road works and it has become increasingly difficult to maintain and repair the major road arteries without causing massive disruption to traffic flows.

Economists differ in their predictions as to the future demands for road transport. Some models predict that journey times will get slower and slower and that particular combinations of events could result in gridlock by which traffic becomes frozen. Thus Department for Transport data indicated a projected increase in demand for roads of 48 per cent by 2026. Other forecasts from the Commission for Integrated Transport suggest that road congestion is likely to rise by 65 per cent by 2010 and on motorways by 286 per cent by the same date. These projections make future planning for the growth of road traffic particularly difficult. Should more roads be built or the use of road transport limited?

Summary

The demand of both people and goods for road transport has increased significantly over the last 20 years. Road transport can appear to offer flexibility to the business user and personal freedom to the consumer. If these trends continue, road congestion is likely to be an increasing problem and the demand for road space is fast outstripping its supply. However, the demand for road transport tended to slow in the 1990s making it especially hard to predict future patterns and develop appropriate policies.

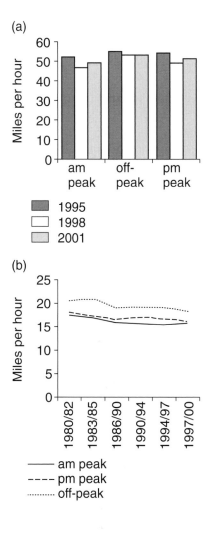

Figure 3: (a) Average traffic speeds on trunk roads: 1995, 1998, 2001
(b) Average traffic speeds in Greater London: 1980/82 – 1997/2000.
Source: *Department for Transport*

Quick check ✓

1   Identify:
    a) four factors leading to an increase in the demand for passenger transport by road
    b) four factors contributing to a increase in the demand for goods traffic by road
    c) four negative externalities which might be associated with growing road use.

4.18 Costs of production

Introduction

All firms, irrespective of their mission statements, objectives, ownership and what they might say about themselves, have to make decisions about two key factors: costs and revenue. If firms are going to survive they need to ensure that one way or another their revenues are at the very least the same as their costs. Most businesses strive to ensure that revenue exceeds costs. This positive difference is described by economists as profit. Should costs exceed revenue, a loss is made. The economic analysis contained in this and the following Section is based on this very simple reasoning.

Thus, examination of data about costs and revenue is important in helping you develop a better understanding of the behaviour of firms within the transport industry.

Short-run costs of production

All payments made by a firm in the production of a good or provision of a service are called costs. Economists' use of the convention, followed by many businesses, distinguishes between overheads and running costs. Overheads are costs of production that businesses have to pay irrespective of their level of output. Thus, a bookstore is likely to be faced with bills for rent, business rates, and repayment of loans that will remain the same irrespective of how many books are sold. These expenditures are classified as fixed costs and the convention is that these do not change in the short run, which is defined as that period of time in which it is not possible to change the quantity of an input of a particular factor of production (usually called factor input). Running costs, such as payment of wages, stock purchases and the like that will change as sales change in the short run, are classified as variable costs. In practice, it is not always easy to decide whether a particular cost should be classified as fixed or variable. For example, contracts and salaries might be agreed to cover a particular length of time, making them fixed, whereas maintenance costs might change considerably as output changes making them variable.

The addition of fixed and variable costs gives total costs, which include all the costs faced by a firm in the production of a good or a provision of a service.

The total cost divided by the output of the business gives the short run average total cost, which is usually abbreviated to short-run average cost, or even just average cost. This is probably the most useful of these measures as it indicates the cost of producing each item or providing a service. The average cost is sometimes referred to as the unit cost.

Finally economists and business people make use of the concept of marginal cost, which is the additional cost of producing an extra unit of output of a particular good or service. Thus, if a clothing manufacturing company were to produce an extra suit, it would be faced with the costs of additional

Synoptic link

This section and the following eight sections are designed to develop your understanding of the main characteristics of different market structures. You need to make sure that you can describe the main characteristics of the following models:

- perfect competition
- monopolistic competition
- oligopoly
- monopoly.

You also need to make sure you can remember the different ways costs can be analysed. This will include work that you did for AS on:

- average costs
- marginal costs
- average revenue
- marginal revenue
- normal profit.

Thinking like an economist

Think cars and trains and the relative importance of the balance of fixed and variable costs in each. Any conclusions?

materials and labour but would not have to pay out any more for design or machine setting costs.

Short-run costs

Economic analysis of the behaviour of firms focuses on either the short or the long run. In the short run, as has already been indicated, a firm can change only the input of variable factors such as labour. In the long run they can change the inputs of any factor. This Section is concerned with the analysis of changes in the short run, and a series of logical deductions can be made on the basis of this classification.

In Table 1 it is easy to work out the monthly total costs (total variable cost plus total fixed cost) of running the taxi service (column 2 plus column 4). From this it is possible to derive the average daily cost of providing the taxi service, which is run for seven days a week. If we assume that there are 30 days in the month, the average cost of providing the service will be £295 per week.

Table 1: Average monthly costs of running A2B taxi service

Fixed Costs	£	Variable Costs	£		
Rent	2000	Fuel and repairs	2000		
Uniform business rate	1000	Postage	300		
Bank loan repayment	750	Telephone	200		
Depreciation of computer and other equipment	50	Overtime	500		
Insurance	50				
Wages	2000				
Total fixed cost	£5850	Total variable cost	£3000	Total cost	£8850

Graphing average costs

If it were possible to continue to collect cost data relating to different levels of output or sales, then it would be possible to construct graphs illustrating the relationship between costs and different levels of sales.

Output is measured on the horizontal axis and average costs of production on the vertical. This (short -run) average cost curve is U-shaped. As output expands, efficiency increases and short-run average costs fall. They reach a minimum or 'optimum' point and beyond that short-run costs rise indicating

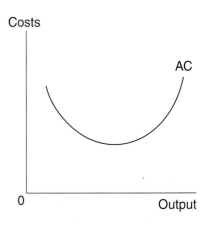

Figure 1: Short-run average costs

declining efficiency. This will apply to the short-run costs of any firm, and is known by economists as the **law of diminishing marginal returns**, which will always occur if the use of a variable factor is increased while another factor input remains fixed. In the example of the taxi service consisting of only one vehicle, cars and number of drivers output can be increased by increasing the hours drivers work, but overtime payments and the extra costs of employing more drivers will eventually drive up costs. Similarly if a factory manager wanted to increase production in the short run he/she would not be able to rapidly expand the size of the factory, nor buy new machines. Employees could be asked to work overtime, and more workers could be taken on. If this process were to be continued, a point would be reached when overcrowding and the sheer mass of workers would contribute to rising short-run average costs.

Graphing marginal costs

As indicated earlier, any change in costs brought about by changing production by an additional unit is described as a marginal cost. These can be calculated by looking at how total costs change according to changes in output. Table 2 relates to total costs incurred on a daily basis by a garage specialising in undertaking MoTs.

Table 2: Total daily costs of a garage specialising in undertaking MoTs

Daily number of MoT tests	Total daily costs	Average costs	Marginal costs
0	150		
1	150	150	150
2	180	90	30
3	196	65.30	16
4	211	52.75	15
5	224	44.80	13
6	236	39.30	12
7	247	35.30	11
8	257	32.10	10
9	266	29.50	9
10	274	27.40	8
11	280	25.40	6
12	285	23.75	5
13	292	22.50	7

14	301	21.50	9
15	311	20.70	10
16	331	20.70	20
17	355	20.90	24
18	385	21.40	30
19	423	22.30	38
20	471	23.60	48

In this example, the garage owner is faced with fixed costs of £150 a day – rent, business rates, wages, loan repayment and so forth. As more and more MoTs are carried out, resources are used more efficiently which is reflected in both falling average cost and marginal costs. As in the earlier example, the garage owner will find that costs will bottom out and then begin to increase. In this example undertaking 16 rather than 15 MoTs causes a big rise in costs – perhaps because extra labour is required. As work increases the garage becomes more crowded and congested, and both average and marginal costs rise.

The data contained in the table is illustrated graphically in Figure 2. Marginal costs are plotted against the midpoint of each unit change in output, and the marginal cost curve will cut the lowest point of the average cost curve.

What is important is that average and marginal cost curves will always have the same relationship to each other in the short run. The application of the law of diminishing marginal returns means that any attempt to increase output by changing the use of one factor while the use of others remains fixed will initially lead to falling average and marginal costs. An optimum will then be reached where average costs are at a minimum, and thereafter growing inefficiency will lead to rising average costs, This observation that short-run average cost curves are U-shaped is one that all students of economics become familiar with.

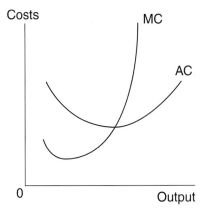

Figure 2: Marginal and average costs

Quick check

Assume the A2B taxi service gets a new contract to take and collect students from school. What will be the effect on:
1   fixed costs
2   variable costs
3   average costs
4   potential profits, by implication?

Long-run costs

Synoptic link

The central concept which you need to understand to analyse long-run costs is that of economies of scale. Look back on your notes on market failure for AS and make sure you understand what the following are and why they might occur.

- Internal and external economies of scale.
- Internal and external diseconomies of scale.

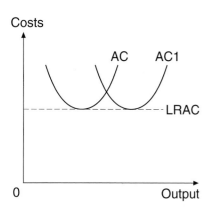

Figure 1: Constant economies of scale

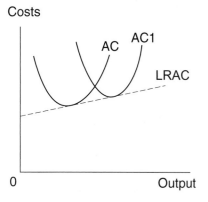

Figure 2: Diseconomies of scale

Introduction

The previous Section focused on short-run costs. The long run is defined as that period of time in which it is possible for a firm to alter any or all of its factor inputs. This links directly to the work that you did for AS on economies of scale. Traditionally, economists have considered the distinction between the long and the short term as being very important in analysing costs and the behaviour of firms. There is now more debate about this approach and at the end of this Section there is an outline of alternative approaches. You need to understand both traditional and newer approaches to the analysis of costs.

Traditional theory

This builds on the analysis in the previous Section. Thus, in the example of A2B taxis, the long run is about the firm purchasing new taxis or moving to a bigger office. The effect of expanding production on long-run average costs is likely to depend on a number of factors.

The following three scenarios apply to the long-run expansion of A2B involving the purchase of one more taxi, effectively doubling the size of the business.

Scenario 1

Suppose the new cost structure facing A2B was similar to that which applied before. For example, the cars are equally efficient, drivers' wages do not change, but twice as much work can be taken on. In this context, the effect of expansion on efficiency would be neutral and the daily average cost of operations would remain much the same. However, twice as many passenger/hours can be provided; in theory 48 per day rather than 24.

This is illustrated by the two short-run average cost curves, Figure 1, which show unchanged average costs of production, and a possible long-run average cost curve.

Scenario 2

In this case, the cost of acquiring the extra car might be greater than the previous one. New drivers might need extra training or the record keeping system might not be able to cope with the extra business. In this situation, long-run costs would be rising as illustrated in Figure 2. At his optimum level of output, the short-run average costs of providing each passenger/hour would be greater than was the case with the optimum level running just one taxi giving a rising long-run average cost curve.

Scenario 3

In contrast to the previous scenario, the newly-acquired taxi might be more fuel efficient, have a larger capacity making it cheaper to run and more productive. In this case, optimum short-run costs of production would fall and not only would A2B be able to take on more business but its average weekly or dialing costs would be lower. In this case the two short-run average cost curves clearly indicate that long-run costs are falling.

Factors affecting returns to scale in the transport industry

Unlike short-run costs there is no law or certainty governing the shape of the long-run average cost curves. Some factors such as more bureaucracy and paperwork are likely to push up costs whereas technical economies often contribute to falling long-run costs. The following sources of economies and diseconomies of scale have to be balanced against each other.

Sources of internal economies of scale

- Technical factors: Generally speaking, larger forms of transportation are more fuel-efficient but there is usually a point at which these technical advances no longer apply.
- Organisational factors: Larger transport businesses are like any other. They can afford to employ specialists, have dedicated marketing teams etc.
- Market power: There are clearly great advantages in transport of building a monopoly of a particular mode of transport as in the case of companies such as Stagecoach.

Sources of external economies of scale

- Growth and concentration of particular industries in defined geographical areas leading to greater efficiencies in the supply chain, for example aircraft component manufacture in the Bristol, Swindon and Gloucester triangle.
- This also theoretically improves the local supplies of appropriately-skilled labour.

Diseconomies of scale

A similar analysis can be applied to diseconomies of scale. The most important being the growth of bureaucracy and loss of responsiveness as evidenced in large organisations such as the Strategic Rail Authority.

Summary of traditional approaches to long-run costs

The positives and negatives from the above factors have to be weighed up against each other such that in traditional economic theory there is no automatic formula that can be applied to long-run average costs. In some industries, such as in motorcar manufacture, potential economies of scale that benefit firms able to produce in large scale for a global market are

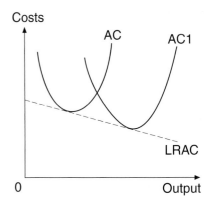

Figure 3: Economies of scale

Exam hint

Sorting out the balance between economies and diseconomies of scale is a good lead into an assess/discuss/evaluate question and using technical and organisation factors provides a way of structuring your answer to such high scoring questions.

Weblink

Using other texts and journal articles, research different approaches to modeling average costs. Is the modern approach outlined above more helpful to you in making sense of the behaviour of firms? You may find http://bizednet.bris.ac.uk helpful in locating suitable articles.

Research task

Choose a transport business which you are confident you can find out more about. Identify their main fixed costs, variable costs, the length of time it takes to vary inputs of land, labour and capital, and the existence of significant economies or diseconomies of scale.

enormous. In others, especially where more traditional methods of production are used, diseconomies of scale may be more significant.

Modern approaches to costs

Some economists have questioned the wisdom of making a rigid distinction between short- and long-run costs, while others have researched the actual nature of costs faced by firms in different industries, as follows.

1. In many businesses, flexible working and modern technological developments mean that the distinction between short and long run can become blurred. Thus, modern technologies can link factories in one country to others in the world. If more machine parts are needed it is not necessary to construct a new factory or plant, new orders can be sub-contracted to suppliers in other parts of the world. Similarly, improvements in the transportation of materials mean that individual components can be shipped around the world quickly and relatively cheaply.

2. Many firms find that initial growth in output and sales is accompanied by dramatic cost savings, i.e. economies of scale are significant. Thereafter unit or average costs remain similar irrespective of output, until a point is reached at which average costs rise dramatically.

If these two sets of research findings are applied to traditional approaches of classifying costs, they have a significant effect on how the behaviour of firms is analysed. This is shown in Figure 4. There is no short-run average or long-run average cost, just an average cost 'curve' which might be 'trench' shaped.

Summary

This section presented two different ways of treating costs faced by firms. Traditional economic analysis is based on a rigid distinction between the short- and the long-term, and this provides a rationale for the existence of the U-shaped average cost curve, and the concept of returns to scale. Alternative treatments regard the distinction between short- and long-run as artificial, and consider that firms can be much more flexible and responsive in their reactions to changing market conditions.

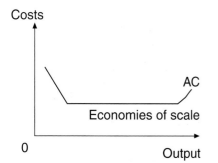

Figure 4: Modern approaches to average cost curves

Quick check

Draw a long-run average cost curve that shows gradual economies of scale followed by both internal and external diseconomies of scale

Introduction

This section is devoted to developing an understanding of different measures of revenue and how this appears in graphs. This analysis will be added to the previous two Sections on costs to provide a means of graphically modeling firms operating under different market structures.

Revenue

Revenue is the term used by economists to describe those flows of money which are received by a firm, as distinct from costs which refers to those payments made by firms. Different firms earn 'revenue' in different ways. For example, A2B taxi service's revenues will be largely determined by the number of customers it gets plus any longer-term contracts for the transport of students etc. All firms need revenue from somewhere. The analysis in the Section is based on an example of a firm operating in the private sector but it can also be applied to public and voluntary sector organisations.

Calculating average and total revenue (AR and TR)

Calculating average and total revenue is straightforward for those businesses that rely on the sales of a good or service. The demand curve shows the relationship between sales and different prices. In Figure 1, P is the price that will be paid if Q is sold. In other words P is the average revenue. Total revenue is simply price multiplied by the number of items which are sold P × Q, therefore, the shaded area abcd represents the total sales revenue earned.

Marginal revenue (MR)

Marginal revenue is defined as the change in revenue which occurs if sales are changed by one unit. In Figure 2, if sales are increased from ten units to eleven units, revenue will rise by £28. (Ten units sell for £50 each giving a total revenue of £500 but to sell eleven units the firm has to accept a lower price of £48 per unit, giving a new total revenue of £48 x 11 = £528). If sales are further increased the marginal revenue will continue to decline. In other words if the demand curve is downward sloping to the right more goods can only be sold at a lower price, which means that MR will always be less than AR. Thus, if the demand curve for a product or service is represented by a straight line then the marginal revenue curve will bisect the angle formed by the average revenue (or demand) curve and the vertical axis as illustrated in Figure 2. Note that the marginal revenue is plotted against the midpoints of sales represented on the horizontal axis.

Total, average and marginal revenue

Synoptic link

Make sure you have reread AS Section 1.8. You should remember that if the price elasticity of demand for a product is relatively inelastic any cut in price is likely to decrease total revenue, whereas if demand is relatively elastic a cut in price will raise total revenue.

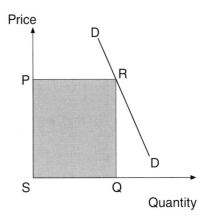

Figure 1: Total revenue

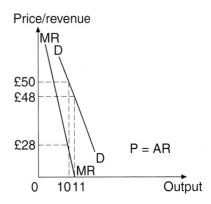

Figure 2: Derivation of marginal revenue

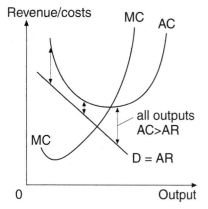

Figure 3: Loss maker

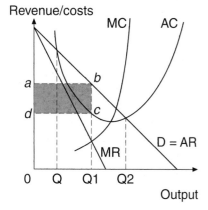

Figure 4: Profit maker

Definitions

Marginal cost: the change in cost brought about by changing production by one unit.
Marginal revenue: the change in revenue brought about by changing sales by one unit.

Putting costs and revenue together

The basic figure showing short-run costs which was developed in Section 4.18 (remember the U-shaped curve and Nike swoosh) can be superimposed on top of the average and marginal revenue figure developed above. This is done in Figure 3.

It should be clear that Figure 3 illustrates a business that would not be likely to survive. At any point on the figure, average costs are above average revenue or price. This firm is clearly making a loss in the short run. On the other hand, Figure 4 shows a range of outputs in which average costs being above and below revenue. This means that between Q1 and Q2 this business would be making some level of profit.

Profits

At this stage in the analysis of a firm's behaviour, it is important to clarify how economists define the term profit. They use the term normal profit to define that amount of additional return once all other costs have been met which is just sufficient to keep a business producing its current level of production. Anything above this is called supernormal or abnormal profit. If a firm is making less than normal profits, it is making a loss.

Business objectives

The work that you did earlier on business objectives needs to be brought into the analysis as understanding these is useful in helping determine the level of output chosen by an individual firm. Three scenarios will be considered:

- survival
- sales maximisation
- profit maximisation.

In order to survive, a business must choose an output between Q1 and Q2. If a business wanted to sales maximise it would produce Q2. Finally using graphical analysis to identify the profit maximising output is slightly more complicated. Profit maximisation quite simply means producing the largest profit possible and this output is found by applying what is known as the profit-maximising rule. This means choosing the output Q1 at which marginal costs and marginal revenue are equal. At this output, the gap between average revenue and average costs is maximised. If a firm chose this output, total profits equal to the shaded area abcd would be earned. As AR > AC these would be called supernormal or abnormal profits.

If the firm decided on an output to the right of Q1, **marginal costs** would exceed **marginal revenue**, in other words, expanding production beyond Q1 would raise costs by a larger amount than any increase in revenue, reducing total profits. On the other hand any point to the left of Q1 would mean that marginal costs were less than marginal revenue, meaning that if output were expanded, revenue would grow by more than costs. Only at the point at which MR=MC will profits be maximised.

Summary

The revenue earned by a firm will be determined by the interaction of price and the demand for their good or service. Data on revenue and costs can be put onto the same graph and this can be used to predict the levels of output chosen by different types of firms according to their business objectives. This Section provides an introduction to what is known as the 'theory of the firm'.

Quick check

Suppose a business is known to want to maximise profits. How will it change production if:

- demand increases
- variable costs increase
- fixed costs increase?

Thinking like an economist

Normal profits is a relative rather than an absolute term. In high-risk industries, firms will expect a higher level of normal profit than in low-risk industries. Normal profit is often indicated by a firm's mark up, that is the percentage that is added to costs to determine price. High street fashion stores mark up from 100 to 200 per cent, but for fruit and vegetables the mark up is probably nearer 30 per cent.

Exam hint

Understanding this section is absolutely vital. Read it through at least three times. Shut your textbook and then make your own summary of the main points, including the figures.

4.21

Perfect competition and the transport industry

Synoptic link

To further develop your understanding of how, given certain assumptions, perfect competition can lead to an optimum allocation of resources, re-read Section 2.1 on productive and allocative efficiency. Make sure you understand the argument that that if we lived in a perfectly competitive economy, goods and services would be produced at the lowest possible cost (productive efficiency) and that they would be produced in accordance to the demands of consumers (allocative efficiency).

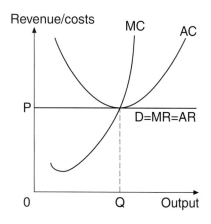

Figure 1: Perfectly competitive equilibrium

Introduction

This Section builds on the work that you did for AS by using diagrams to analyse the behaviour of firms acting under conditions of perfect competition. When you have done this you should be able to show off your higher order skills by critically assessing this proposition that perfect competition could result in the optimum allocation of resources.

Although this Section is mainly theoretical in nature, it is important to have a firm grip on this underpinning knowledge and understanding to do well in this Unit and so get a top grade from OCR.

Productive efficiency

The starting point for this analysis is to consider the equilibrium of the perfectly competitive firm and industry. This is illustrated in Figure 1. It is important to note that, given the assumptions of perfect competition, the individual firm in the transport or any other industry will be obliged to produce that output at which average costs are minimised. The profit-maximising rule of equating MC with MR has to apply if the firm is to avoid making a loss and that coincides with the lowest or optimum point on the average cost curve.

Just suppose that the owner of one firm operating in this industry has a 'eureka moment' and discovers a new, quicker, cheaper way of making the product. If the new production technique is quicker and cheaper the average cost curve will shift downwards to the right dragging the marginal cost curve with it. The profit maximising firm will expand production and will now be making supernormal profits shown by the shaded area in Figure 2.

This situation will only persist in the short run as all competitors have perfect knowledge of what is going on within the industry. They will find out how the innovating firm has been able to cut production costs and copy the more efficient means of production. New firms might enter the industry. This long-run change will involve an increase in the industry-wide supply of the product. This rise in supply will force prices down and the firm who started the process off with its eureka moment will be back to earning normal profits as shown in Figure 1.

An added twist to this argument is that if particular firms are slow in copying the more efficient means of production they will find themselves making losses as output in the industry increases. Loss making firms will be forced out of the industry. This scenario is illustrated in Figure 3.

The logic of this analysis is that if the assumptions underpinning the perfectly competitive model were to be met, competition between large numbers of firms producing identical goods would ensure that there would be a continuous incentive to develop cheaper, more efficient ways of producing goods and providing services. The reward for this would be short-term supernormal profits and the sanction for not keeping up with competitors would be losses and business failure. The real beneficiaries would be the public who would be assured of a constant stream of newer, better, more cost-effective products and services.

Allocative efficiency

This refers to consumer sovereignty. Allocative efficiency is achieved when firms produce where P=MC. In a perfectly competitive market, it is consumers who ultimately determine which of the world's resources are used to produce what products and services. This can be analysed diagrammatically by considering what happens if consumers' tastes change for some reason. Suppose there is an increase in demand for diesel cars at the expense of those with petrol engines. Two changes will take place: there will be a shift to the right in the demand curve for diesels and a shift to the left in the demand for petrol engine cars. This will lead to a rise in price to P1 for diesels and a fall in price to P for their substitute. This is shown in Figure 4.

When translated into changes in demand facing the perfectly competitive producers of diesels and petrol engines, the latter will be faced with potential losses, as in Figure 4, and the former with supernormal profits (see Figure 2).

The long-run response to this situation is that losses will force some firms to drop out of the petrol engine market while new firms will be attracted into the diesel market. New long-term equilibriums will be reached in which both sets of firms earn normal profits but the industry output of diesels will have increased while the production of petrol engines will have been reduced. The essence of the analysis is that if the assumptions are true, perfect competition will force businesses to adjust and change production decisions in line with customer demands. If they fail to respond they are likely to go out of business.

The analysis, however, does not stop here. More successful companies will make larger short-run profits. They will be able to pay more to attract scarce factors of production. Owners of these factors will sell their capital, land, labour or enterprise to the highest bidder and resources will be diverted to the production of goods that are most in demand.

Thus, if all industries were perfectly competitive there would be an optimum allocation of resources. Consumers would determine what is produced and these goods and services would be produced at the lowest possible cost.

Critically assessing the perfectly competitive model as applied to transport

Assessing the perfectly competitive model can be done by asking two sets of related questions.
- Are the assumptions valid?
- What is the effect on the model if any of the assumptions are relaxed?

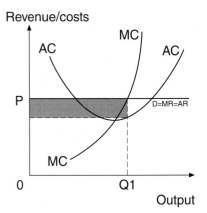

Figure 2: Perfectly competitive supernormal profit

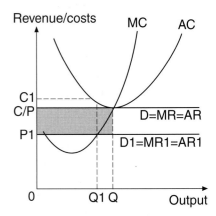

Figure 3: Loss making firms

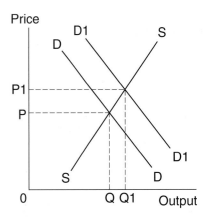

Figure 4: Increase demand for diesel cars

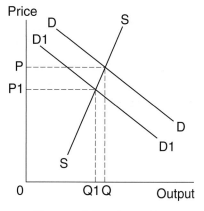

Figure 5: Falling demand for petrol
engined cars

- homogenous outputs
- many firms
- perfect consumer knowledge
- perfect producer knowledge
- freedom of entry and exit.

Homogenous outputs

Another way of testing this assumption is to ask the question 'can a particular product or service be identified with an individual producer?' Clearly branding is designed to ensure that we differentiate most consumer products one from another. Companies use branding to build up brand loyalty, which ultimately means that customers are prepared to pay more for one brand rather than another. Take away the packaging or label, and goods become much more homogonous – one car is much like another. Similarly, stripped to the essentials, most competing transport products are similar to each other. However, almost all transport services are heavily branded so they do not appear to be homogenous. The crucial question is 'if the assumption of absolute homogeneity is relaxed, and the other assumptions are held in place, will the perfectly competitive model result in productive and allocative efficiency?'

Many firms

This assumption partly relates to the production of homogenous products and is crucial in determining the shape of the demand curve facing the perfectly competitive firm. It is not hard to think of industries that are made up of very many individual suppliers who are forced to accept the price set by the market. Most suppliers of small-scale transport services, which can be set up with relatively little capital or expertise, probably fall into this category. But large-scale provision of networks has tended to become increasingly concentrated in the hands of fewer producers.

Perfect consumer knowledge

This is not a very realistic assumption. It is argued that the average consumer knows only the likely price of less than 20 different items in a supermarket stocking 15,000 different products. How many people know the price of a train ticket between London and Birmingham? Individually we may be expert about some products and services but collectively the evidence is such that we might be nearer to perfect consumer ignorance than we are to perfect knowledge. This is particularly true of the passenger transport market but probably less of the freight transport market.

Perfect producer knowledge

This is harder to assess. Successful businesses need to have a good knowledge of developments within their industry. By the same token it is in the interest of firms to keep things secret. Sometimes secrecy is protected by law, as with patents. Although there are exceptions, such as the formula for making Coca Cola, it is probably reasonably safe to assume that over a long period of time producers have relatively good knowledge of their industry.

Freedom of entry and exit

Some economists argue that this is the crucial assumption and there is no clear yes or no answer as to its validity. Three factors are likely to be important: the cost of entry or exit, attitudes of businesses within a given industry and the legislative framework. The cost of entering many modern transport industries, such as air transport, road maintenance or vehicle production, are likely to provide an enormous barrier to entry, and existing business will tend to be hostile to incomers. On the other hand, barriers will be fewer in industries where smaller-scale production is the norm.

Quick check

Use diagrams to predict what will happen to short-run supernormal profits of an individual A2B taxi firm under the following conditions.
- New entrants are attracted to the industry.
- Demand for the product increases.
- Customer ignorance is reduced.

Hot potato

Has the development of the Internet encouraged greater competition in the European air passenger market?

Monopoly and the transport industry

4.22

Synoptic link

In AS you will have spent some time understanding monopoly. Make sure you now know:
■ how to define a monopoly
■ different types of behaviour that you would expect from a monopolist
■ the possible effects of monopoly power in terms of prices, outputs and choice
■ the possible benefits of monopoly.

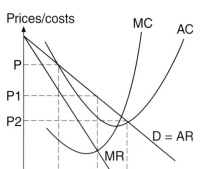

Figure 1: Demand and cost conditions facing a monopolistic firm

Hot potato

Is the monopolistic model as much help as the perfectly competitive one in helping us to understand how businesses operate in the 'real' world?

Introduction

The model of monopoly is built up in a similar way to that of perfect competition and it is based on two related simplifying assumptions.
■ Production of a whole industry is in the hands of one firm.
■ Complete barriers prevent the entry and exit of firms.

Thus when the railway network was in the public sector and known as British Rail, the demand they faced for rail services as an individual firm would have been the same as that for the industry as a whole. Moreover, there is no distinction, as there is with perfect competition, between the short and the long run. If a monopoly is total, barriers to entry are absolute and prevent other firms competing away excess profits. British Rail were able to set the price or the number of services provided and, theoretically, had considerable freedom to pursue a range of economic and social objectives.

Possible price, sales and output levels can be analysed graphically as is illustrated in Figure 1, where demand and average revenue are above average costs at outputs between Q and Q2. This means that a monopolistic firm could set a price anywhere between P and P2 and make more than normal profits.

In this case, a profit maximising monopolist would produce at Q1, a sales maximiser at Q2 and barriers to entry would ensure that this short-run situation was also the long-run position.

Changing market conditions

Although the diagrams get a little complicated, the analysis of increases or decreases in demand for average costs are quite straightforward. Thus if the demand for the output of a monopolist increases, the demand curve will shift to the right dragging the MR curve with it. This is illustrated in Figure 2.

If the monopolist is a profit maximiser, MC meets the new MR curve at Q1 output. P1 will be charged for the product and abnormal profits will increase. In other words an increase in demand will lead to an increase in sales, prices and profits.

If, on the other hand, the costs of raw materials were to rise, the average and marginal cost curves would move upwards to the left. This situation would result in lower sales, output and profit levels.

Conclusions

If transport markets conform to this model:
■ average costs of production will not necessarily be minimised
■ excessive profits could be earned in the long run
■ firms would not have to attempt to maximise profits
■ firms would not necessarily have to respond to changes in demand
■ there would be little incentive to innovate
■ customer choice could be restricted.

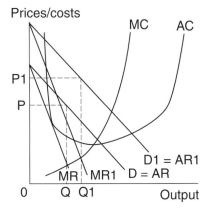

Figure 2: Increasing demand

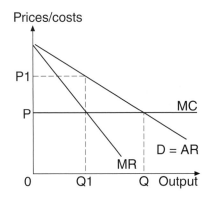

Figure 3: Monopoly and perfect competition compared

Comparisons with perfect competition

Graphical analysis can be used to demonstrate that, in the short run, prices under monopoly will be higher than those if perfect competition were to apply and that output would be lower. This is illustrated in Figure 3.

Under perfect competition, firms are forced by competitive pressures to produce where MC equals price. If this is applied to a whole industry, perfectly competitive output would be at Q and price P, whereas a profit-maximising monopolist would charge P1 for an output of Q1.

This conclusion depends on one implicit assumption – that both monopolist and perfectly competitive firms would be faced with the same average and marginal cost conditions. One argument that has been used to justify the existence of monopolies is that they are able to enjoy the benefits of economies of scale that may arise from increasing size, which then leads to falling long-run average costs. The effects of this possibility are illustrated in Figure 4 where MC1 represents lower long-run costs which might be generated by economies of scale enjoyed by the monopolist. In this case the profit maximising monopolist will charge P for output Q, compared with P1 and Q1 for the perfectly competitive industry.

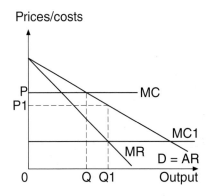

Figure 4: Monopolist benefiting from economies of scale

Summary

This section develops the descriptive treatment of monopoly and competition developed in Sections 2.12 and 2.13 of your AS book. Graphical analysis has been used to compare output, prices and profits under the two extremes of perfect competition and monopoly. The use of this analysis indicates that prices might be lower and outputs higher under conditions of perfect competition than under monopoly. However, this simple comparison ignores the existence of economies of scale and the greater freedom that a monopolistic firm has to pursue differing objectives. You will appreciate that this analysis is particularly valuable to understanding large sections of the transport market.

Thinking like an economist

Do not jump to conclusions based on the analysis in this Section. In the real world it is hard to find pure monopoly or perfect competition. However, you will find that firms behave in some of the ways that have been described in this section.

Quick check

Which of the following are closest to being monopolies as defined in this Section:
- Stena-Sealink
- Virgin Rail
- British Airways?

Puzzler

How might a rail operating company respond to an increase in fixed costs charged by the Strategic Rail Authority? (This may require some detailed analysis and lots of logic.)

Introduction

It is hard to find industries and firms in transport markets to which it is possible to apply the assumptions that underpin the models of monopoly and perfect competition. Common sense tells us that most markets lie between these two extremes. This view is supported by the many economists who have sought to develop theories which are modelled more accurately on the characteristics of businesses operating in the real world.

This Section is devoted to monopolistic competition – a term used to describe market structures which lie between the theoretical extremes of perfect competition and monopoly.

Monopolistic competition

In the 1930s, two economists, Joan Robinson and Edward Chamberlain, both developed similar models which they both considered were more realistic than the extremes of monopoly and perfect competition. Chamberlain, an American, called his theory 'monopolistic competition' while Robinson, an Englishwoman, preferred the term 'imperfect competition'. Although there are differences between these two approaches for A level they can be treated as one and OCR prefer the term 'monopolistic competition'.

The following underpinning assumptions, which are borrowed from the theories of perfect competition and monopoly, are used to build up this model.

- Freedom of entry and exit – as with perfect competition, it is assumed that there are no barriers preventing firms from joining or leaving the industry in question.
- Independent decision-making by firms, i.e. individual firms decide about sales levels, product design and the like without reference to the behaviour of potential competitors. In this respect firms are expected to behave in a similar way to perfectly competitive firms.
- Product differentiation – it is assumed that each firm operating under conditions of imperfect competition will seek to make its product or service different to that of its competitors. Such differences might be in packaging or branding, but could also include more fundamental differences in design or construction. This characteristic has more in common with monopoly that it does with perfect competition.

Equilibrium under conditions of monopolistic competition

The second assumption above means that the demand curve facing the monopolistically competitive firm will slope downwards to the right (like monopoly). This means that the marginal revenue curve will also slope downwards to the right (also like monopoly). In other words a firm operating in these conditions is to some degree a price maker rather than a price taker. These features are both illustrated in Figure 1.

Synoptic link

AS Part 1 The market system was devoted to how freely operating markets might work and in *AS Part 2 Market failure and government intervention* you will have learned about uncompetitive markets. This understanding has been developed for A2 in the Sections 4.20 to 4.24. You must know features that make a market:
- perfectly competitive
- monopolistic.

You should also be aware of the arguments for and against the application of these models to transport markets.

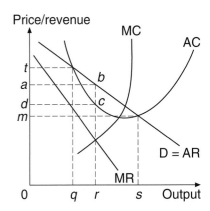

Figure 1: Short-run equilibrium of a monopolistically competitive firm

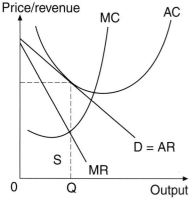

Price/revenue

Figure 2: Long run equilibrium of a monopolistically competitive firm

If market conditions are like those illustrated in Figure 1 there will be a range of profitable outputs between Q and Q1, and prices between P and P1 in which average costs would exceed average revenue. A profit maximising firm would choose to produce at OR where MC=MR, and abnormal profits equivalent to the area abcd would exist.

Long-run equilibrium of the firm under conditions of monopolistic competition

The situation in the long run will be determined by the application of the first assumption made in building up this model. Other firms will realise that abnormal profits can be made by copying the behaviour of the firm managing to produce with AR>AC. They too will increase production or be attracted into the industry leading to a long-term increase in supply, which will result in a decrease in the price. Prices will fall and the short run abnormal profits will be eroded away until a situation as depicted in Figure 2 develops.

The converse of this analysis also applies. If demand falls for the outputs of a firm operating in an imperfectly competitive industry, the demand and marginal revenue curves will shift to the left, resulting in losses irrespective of the chosen output.

In this case the least efficient and/or less well-resourced businesses will go out of business first, leaving the remaining firms to compete for shares in a larger market. The exit of some firms should result in the reestablishment of a long-run equilibrium as shown in Figure 2.

Imperfectly competitive firms

If firms in an industry satisfy the assumptions of this model, then it is likely that:
- supernormal profits can only be earned in the short run because low barriers to entry will attract new firms into the industry and competitors will expand production
- there is a constant incentive for firms to innovate and differentiate their product from that of competitors. In essence, monopolistically competitive firms will want to try to make the demand for their products or services more inelastic
- advertising and branding become important as these represent strategies aimed at both boosting demand and creating brand loyalty
- in the long run firms will not be maximising their efficiency, as they will not be producing at the lowest point on their average cost curve. In fact output will be lower and a monopolistically competitive firm will have spare or excess capacity
- if firms are to survive in the long run they are obliged to maximise profits.

Critical evaluation

How well do transport markets meet the assumptions which underpin this model? Is it more realistic? Consider the original assumptions in the context of air passenger transport.

- Numbers of firms: Taken globally there are a large number of airlines but they tend to operate in restricted markets and, generally speaking, there are relatively few airlines competing on exactly the same routes.
- Slightly differentiated products: This appears to apply as the basic service is very similar but it is often presented in very different ways, for example, the difference between First and Club class seats and travel on budget airlines.
- Advertising: Major British-owned airlines advertise heavily.
- Freedom of entry and exit: The answer to this is yes and no. The demand for landing slots at major airports, such as Heathrow, is greater than the supply, and existing carriers such as BA 'own' slots making this a difficult barrier to penetrate. Less popular airports are more accessible and new entrants to the business, such as Ryan Air and easyJet, have used this to enter the market. The other major barrier is the scale of investment needed to provide an effective service. This barrier is significant, but leasing and sub-contracting arrangements are highly developed reducing **sunk costs**, which would otherwise be considerable.

If this model is applied to the air passenger market it should lead to particular long-run outcomes.

- Long run normal profits: Over the last decade BA's profitability has been falling while that of RyanAir has been rising.
- Lower levels of efficiency than in more competitive markets: This appears not to apply as the real cost of air passenger traffic continues to fall and less efficient carriers are being driven out of the market.
- The importance of advertising: This appears to be significant.

The model of monopolistic competition does have some relevance in helping us understand the air passenger transport market but there appears to be a gap between the predicted assumption of the model and actual practice. What is your judgement?

Definition

Sunk costs: are fixed costs required to enter an industry.

Research task

1 Outline the principal features of monopolistic competition and apply them to a transport market (not air passenger!).
2 How useful is this model in explaining the behaviour of businesses in your chosen market?

Quick check ✓

Which of the following industries comes closest to satisfying the assumption of imperfect competition:

- car manufacture
- car component manufacture
- car hire companies?

Oligopoly and the transport industry

Synoptic link

This section is all new, but it builds on your understanding from AS of:
- perfect competition
- monopoly.

It also covers A2 graphical treatments of different market structures.

Introduction

Oligopoly literally means competition among the few, and there are two principal assumptions underpinning this model.

- The existence of barriers of entry to and from the industry. These will vary from industry to industry but their existence makes the analysis of oligopoly more similar to that of monopoly. As has been indicated earlier, most transport industries are characterised by the existence of some barriers to entry. The key question is judging the degree to which they cannot be overcome.

- The interdependence of decision-making. The assumption is unique to this model and means that individual firms make decisions about prices, marketing, product design etc. with reference to how they perceive their competitors will respond. Each firm is affected by the actions of others. This would appear to apply to most large-scale transport markets.

Barriers to entry

The first assumption has especial importance in understanding the likely behaviour of oligopolists. In theory a monopolist's market dominance is secure. Barriers to the entry of other firms are absolute. Perfectly competitive firms can, in theory, try to maintain short-run barriers but in the long run the assumption of perfect knowledge should ensure that any form of product differentiation could be copied. Oligopolists, on the other hand, are protected by barriers and are likely to constantly erect new barriers in order to maintain long-term market share and profits. Barriers to entry and exit are likely to include the following:

- capital costs especially in capital and technology intensive industries such as ticketing systems
- high levels of sunk costs, i.e. those fixed costs attributable to capital equipment which cannot be transferred to other uses, such as in the Channel Tunnel
- national and global branding; the degree to which the promotion a global or national image can be applied to transport is debatable compared with more specific final products such as Coca Cola or Ralph Lauren
- patent, copyright and external regulation. The last of these is especially significant as issues of safety are particularly relevant to the transport of people and goods. Most transport markets are regulated and this can provide barriers to entry, for example all ships reaching UK ports are meant to meet minimum safety standards
- takeover – dominant firms often respond to the threat of new entrants by taking them over, for example Stagecoach.

Interdependence

The second assumption is very significant because it makes it much more difficult for economists to model the behaviour of an oligopolistic firm. The behaviour of one firm will depend upon its perceptions of how other firms will react to changes. The responses of other firms will depend upon their perceptions of the responses of others. It is harder, therefore, to predict how oligopolistic firms are likely to behave. The models developed by economists to analyse perfectly competitive and monopolistic markets may be of little use, and different ways have been developed to aid our understanding of the behaviour of oligopolists. The crucial issue is because pricing and output decisions can be interdependent; oligopolistic firms may choose to compete but it may well be in their interest to collude. This describes a situation in which firms find some way of agreeing with each other to avoid the risks associated with competition. Colluding firms may seek to set common prices or levels of output for each. This topic is dealt with in more detail in Section 4.26 Other aspects of oliopolistic behaviour.

Game theory

As indicated earlier, predicting the outcomes of decision making by oligopolists is difficult. To take a current example, Volkswagen needs to decide on the recommended selling price for its new Polo. It is currently selling a basic version of the Polo for £8,999, but some competitors like the Nissan Micra are available more cheaply while others like the Vauxhall Corsa are more expensive. There are fears in the automobile industry that car prices are likely to fall, what should Volkswagen do? If they cut their price and competitors follow suit they will end up with the same market share. If they cut their price and competitors fail to respond, Volkswagen's market share may increase. What if Vauxhall or Nissan make larger price cuts? One approach used by economists to try to make sense of such competitive behaviour is by use of game theory, first developed by psychologists when trying to predict human responses in similarly unpredictable situations. At a simple level this can be restricted to looking at the behaviour of one firm and the possible responses of another. This is illustrated in the matrix shown in Figure 1.

To start with, assume that the market for small cars is shared equally between Volkswagen and Nissan. They charge the same price of £8,999 for cars with similar specifications, and they both receive £200 million. This is depicted in box A of the matrix. The outcomes of Volkswagen cutting £1000 from its recommended price will depend upon the responses of Nissan. If they keep their original price, Volkswagen will gain a bigger market share and a larger proportion of the industry profit. This is illustrated in box B. Alternatively, Nissan could copy Volkswagen, leaving both with an equal market share but reduced profits because of the price cut. This is shown in box D. A fourth alternative is that Volkswagen maintain their price at

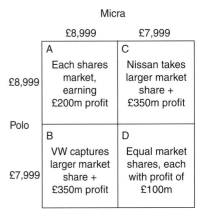

Figure 1: Game theory matrix

£6,999. In this case both Volkswagen's market share and profits will be cut as shown in box C.

This approach to the analysis of the behaviour of oligopolists yields an important prediction. For Volkswagen, option B would give the best possible return but is also the most risky. It depends on Nissan ignoring an aggressive price cut. Option C is the worst outcome, while D and A are the least risky. Logic dictates that Volkswagen ought to collude with Nissan.

The essence of game theory is that there are a range of possible outcomes in response to market changes or changes in the behaviour of firms. Game theory focuses on alternative strategies which firms may pursue. Cautious firms will elect a strategy which is least risky. This is called a maximin strategy, whereas an approach which involves taking greater risks to gain higher levels of profit is called a maximax strategy. If both approaches lead to the same outcome firms are said to be playing a dominant strategy game.

Competitive oligopolists

If oligopolist firms decide to pursue competitive strategies they may well try to drive weaker competitors out of their market. Predatory pricing policies are sometimes used to achieve this objective. Those firms which are larger and better resourced may be prepared to sell output at a loss if this enables them to undercut the prices charged by competitors. The attraction of this strategy is that competitors are faced with a stark choice. Cut their prices to retain market share or stick tight and hope that demand for their product is relatively inelastic. If the former response is preferred then there is every chance of a price war breaking out. This might not be attractive as competitive price-cutting could result in losses which none of the firms in the industry could sustain.

Nonetheless price wars do happen. Ryanair and Easyjet have used predatory pricing not only to gather major market shares but also to force competitors like Buzz and Go out of business.

Kinked demand curves

An alternative theoretical treatment of the behaviour of oligopolists is that associated with another American economist, Paul Sweezy. He observed that even if oligopolists were in competition with each other, prices in such markets tended to be stable. He used a simplified form of game theory by reasoning that as pricing decisions by oligopolists were interdependent, an individual firm would be very reluctant to raise its prices as it would fear that none of its competitors would follow suit. On the other hand he argued that an individual firm would be reluctant to cut its prices as competitors would copy this decision. In other words the oligopolist would be faced with an elastic demand curve in terms of price rises and an inelastic curve for price cuts. This is illustrated graphically in Figure 2.

Hot potato

Construct a matrix to predict possible outcomes of interdependent decision making in a transport industry of your choice (not cars!).

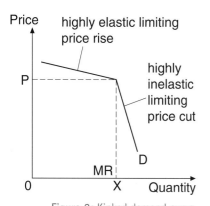

Figure 2: Kinked demand curve

Although this theory provides a convincing argument for why price stability can be a feature of oligopoly, Sweezy's theory has been attacked by a number of economists as lacking in any empirical evidence.

Summary

Analysing the behaviour of oligopolistic firms is far more complex than for firms operating in other market structures. Graphical analysis is less helpful as outcomes in terms of pricing, output and profits are less predictable. Some transport markets are characterised by high levels of competition resulting in price fluctuations. Others might more closely resemble monopoly and be characterised by high but stable prices and little or no direct competition. Some industries may alternate between periods of intense competition and periods of stability and collusion. However, a number of generalisations can be made about the behaviour of oligopolists.

- There can be strong incentives to use predatory pricing strategies to drive competitors from a particular market.
- Price competition will generally be avoided as non-price competition in terms of advertising and customer service is less risky.
- Oligopolistic firms will tend to maintain and strengthen barriers to entry to their industry.

Thinking like an economist

What evidence would you search for to try to establish the validity of the following models to analyse the behaviour of large firms operating in transport markets?

- Maximin gaming strategy
- Maximax gaming strategy
- Kinked demand curves

Quick check

Which of the following industries comes closest to satisfying the assumptions of oligopolistic competition:

- train operating companies
- airlines
- companies operating sea cruises?

Behaviour in transport markets

Synoptic link

Look back at AS Section 1.5 for producer and consumer surplus.

Introduction

Economic theory demonstrates that firms which are monopolies or oligopolies have considerable market power to set prices, determine customer choice, limit competition and prevent new market entrants. These firms are also often very large, commanding turnovers greater than many countries in the world, and are able to use their economic power to influence the behaviour of governments. Economists differ in their assessments of the impact of such large firms but have developed further theories and techniques to help measure market power and advise governments of possible intervention strategies. This Section is devoted to:

- price discrimination
- consumer and producer surplus.

Price discrimination

One method of assessing the degree of power which any firm has in the market place is to establish the degree to which it is able to charge different customers different prices for the same product or service. This is called price discrimination and is an aspect of market power used by firms to boost revenue and profits. Most of us are used to being charged a range of different prices for particular goods or services. Airfares are a good example; customers flying from London to New York can pay between £200 and £1000 for the same seat in the same aircraft. In order to benefit from price discrimination, airlines need to ensure that the following conditions must be fulfilled.

- The firm must have some degree of market power and be a price maker.
- Demand for the good or service will be spread between different customers each with differing price elasticities of demand for the product or service.
- These different market segments have to be separated from each other.
- The proportion of fixed to total costs is likely to be high.

Market power

Only those firms who are facing a downward sloping overall demand curve for their product or service will be able to charge different prices to different customers. The more monopoly power a firm enjoys, the more it can price discriminate. On the other hand, those firms who are closer to being perfectly competitive will have only a limited opportunity to charge different prices to different customers. Clearly there are only a limited number of airlines flying between London and New York and those that offer the most flights will be able to set prices rather than having to accept the 'market' price.

Differing price elasticities of demand

A discriminating monopolist will wish to charge higher prices to some of its customers and will be prepared to sell the same product or service to others at a lower price as long as this boosts overall revenue. Airlines exploit this by charging those who have to fly at particular times and those whose airfare is likely to be part of an expense account, much higher fares. Other market segments, such as young people travelling around the world, are likely to be much more price sensitive and will only be attracted by lower fares. Another important segment for some airlines is the holiday market. Holiday companies may make block bookings of seats but will expect significant discounts. Finally, seats which are hard to sell can be sold through 'bucket shops' and those travel agencies dealing in last minute bookings.

Separation of markets

Elaborate strategies, such as those outlined above, will only work if it is impossible for one set of airline customers to sell on its cheaper tickets to passengers who would otherwise be prepared to pay higher fares. This is relatively easy for the airlines as tickets are usable only by a named person. Other price discriminators use time to separate markets. Train tickets bought at different times of the day cost different amounts and can be used only on specified trains.

Relatively high fixed costs

The bulk of the costs of flying from London to New York are fuel, maintenance, and debt repayment. Once committed to the flight, the airline has low levels of variable costs. Put another way, marginal costs of carrying additional passengers are low. It costs very little more to carry 350 passengers than it does to carry 349. Hence, the airline will add to its profits once it has covered the costs of extra meals, ticketing and costs associated with the 350th passenger.

If variable costs are relatively more significant, marginal costs will be higher and a profit seeking company would be more limited in its opportunities to discount.

Consumer and producer surpluses

Another way in which economists attempt to assess the impact of non-competitive behaviour by firms is by the use of two concepts:
- consumer surplus
- producer surplus.

Consumer surplus

This concept uses graphical analysis to illustrate the benefits that customers gain from consuming a particular product or service. Figure 1 illustrates consumer surplus and P represents an equilibrium price with the level of sales at Q2.

Hot potato

How might consumer and producer surplus be affected by the following:
- reduction of barriers of entry in the airline industry
- the establishment of a cartel by car manufacturers?

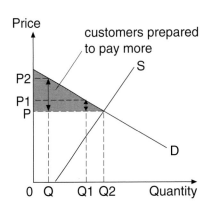

Figure 1: Consumer surplus

Producer surplus

A similar analytical approach can be made to gains made by producers of a good or service.

This concept is applied to understanding the impact of monopoly power. Figure 2 shows that a profit maximising oligopolist or monopolist will produce at Q1 and charge P1 for its output, whereas a perfectly competitive industry facing the same cost structure will produce at Q and charge P for its output. Consumer surplus under monopolistic conditions will be the equivalent of area *a*, but under perfect competition it would be larger and equal to *a + b +c*. Producer surplus on the other hand is bigger under monopoly consisting of *d + b* compared with a perfectly competitive producer surplus of *d + e*. In other words, this graphical analysis shows that producers gain while consumers lose. Overall *c + e* represents losses under monopoly of both producer and consumer surpluses. This area is known as deadweight welfare loss of monopoly.

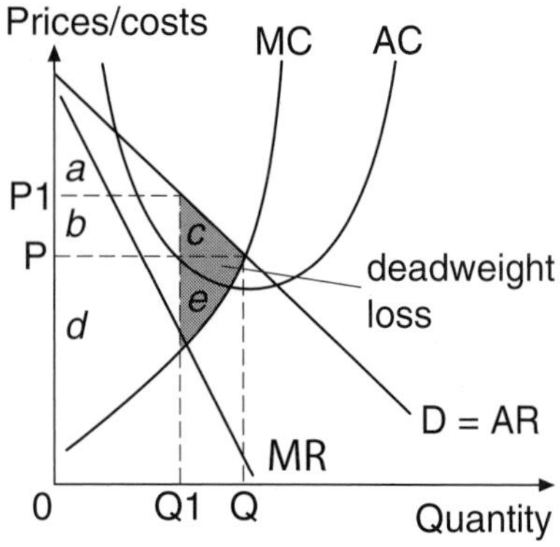

Figure 2: Deadweight welfare loss of monopoly

Summary

This section has been devoted to an explanation of some of the techniques which economists use to measure the extent and possible effects of the exercise of monopoly power, and the ability of firms to charge different prices to different sections of their markets was also considered. Graphical analysis has been used to indicate the possible harmful affects of monopoly power.

Exam hint

There is plenty of scope in this Section for questions which test your higher order skills. Be prepared to assess, evaluate or discuss the degree of competition in a given transport market. Remember to develop a number of arguments and make a clear conclusion based on the analysis that has gone before.

Quick check

Which of the following operates the most comprehensive policies of price discrimination:

- the Italian Railway company
- package holiday suppliers
- Easyjet?

Collusion

Reaching agreements to limit competition can take place in different ways:
- open or overt
- informal or covert
- tacit.

Open agreements

Open or overt agreements are public'y made formal collective agreements. Those making such an agreement are called a cartel and they may enter into binding agreements to set agreed price levels and/or production quotas. This will almost always involve pushing up prices and cutting down on output. If cartels are going to work, it is important that agreement is reached about both prices and outputs. If this is not done there is a great incentive for individual members of a cartel to secretly produce more and benefit from the higher agreed prices. There is a clear conflict of interest between the members of a cartel and consumers and, with some exceptions, cartels are illegal in the UK and in most other western countries.

Cartels are, however, more commonly agreed in the global trade of particular commodities. The most famous cartel is that of some petroleum exporting countries, OPEC, who have had varying degrees of success in regulating the world price of crude oil. It can be argued that countries which are heavily dependent on the export of commodities such as oil, sugar, coffee, will suffer greatly if there are regular price fluctuations. Indeed poverty in a number of developing nations is directly attributable to the low prices for crops such as coffee and sugar. In this context there is a clear conflict of interest between the producer countries and those in which the commodities are consumed.

Informal or covert agreements

These are naturally much more difficult to find out about. They occur both nationally and internationally and almost always involve illegal activities by which firms try to find ways of keeping prices high and competition low. As prices for many consumer goods are relatively higher in the UK than in the rest of Europe and the US, there is evidence that manufacturers in this country inflate prices and stop retailers from selling at discounted prices. It is likely that firms in the UK have informal agreements especially in the markets for electrical goods, cars and perfumery, but, as this form of activity might be the target of government investigation and intervention, it is hard to find evidence of secret agreements.

Tacit agreements

The interdependence that characterises the behaviour of individual oligopolists can mean that they arrive at common pricing and output

Synoptic link

This section builds on the one immediately before it (4.25) and focuses on two contrasting aspects of oligopolistic theory and behaviour. Firstly, consideration is given to extending the game theory introduced in A2 Section 4.24. This showed that it can be in the interests of oligopolistic firms to collude, that is, form agreements to reduce the risks attached to competition, especially price competition.

The remainder of this section is devoted to contestable market theory, which can be used to argue that firms dominated by a small number of firms may actually behave in a competitive rather than a collusive way.

policies without formal or informal agreements. This makes it much more difficult to demonstrate or prove that firms may be acting illegally. Some industries are dominated by a particular firm and others will follow its pricing decisions. In the UK, ESSO is seen as a leader in terms of petrol prices, Kellogg for breakfast cereals, and Nike for trainers. It was noted in earlier Sections that firms might adopt common pricing formulas and pay similar amounts for factor inputs. Most pubs mark up the price of beers and lager by 100 per cent, and local stores add 40 per cent to the cost price of confectionery and similar products, while restaurants add 500 per cent to the cost of ingredients to price their menus. This can lead to competitive firms charging similar prices for the same meals. The use of these cost plus pricing strategies is more likely to result in stable prices and greater importance being attached to non-price competition.

Another related pricing strategy which can be either tacit or overt is that of limit pricing, where oligopolists will try to set their prices at the highest possible level without leading to new entrants into the industry. Often existing businesses have different forms of competitive advantage, which might mean that new entrants are faced with relatively higher costs. Limit pricing is designed to reduce the incentive effect of excessive profits.

Collusion, though attractive to oligopolists as a means of reducing risks and safeguarding profits, has particular dangers. It may:

- attract unwelcome government intervention
- create a poor public image
- lead to broken agreements leading to competitive advantage being gained by rival firms or countries.

Exam hint

Examiners like argument, and the two approaches to oligopoly contained in this Section can easily lead to assess, evaluate, compare-type questions. Make sure you understand the subtleties of these 'trigger' words.

Contestable market theory

This is an alternative approach developed by economists in the 1970s and 1980s which has had significant influence on government policies in the UK and US towards monopolies and oligopolists. Contestable market theory can be seen as an adaptation of traditional theory to assess the degree of competition that may occur within an industry. It is based on the premise that firms will operate competitively if they fear competition in some way. There are a number of variants of this theory and it is argued that a firm with monopolistic power will behave like a competitive firm if:

- there is a fear of take-over
- there are zero entry and exit barriers
- industries are dynamic.

Fear of take over

No PLC in the UK is free from the fear of take-over and senior managers of such firms have to compete with other businesses on the stock market. Rising share prices are associated with business success and will be fed by stock market perceptions of potential profits, levels of customer service,

Hot potato

Contestable market theory is just a fig leaf for big bad capitalists. Do you agree?

responsiveness to changes in demand and so on. Monopolistic and oligopolistic firms who fail to pursue those and other objectives associated with competitive behaviour will, the theorists argue, be punished by the stock market and share prices will fall, making such firms more liable to take-over. It could be argued that this described the position of Marks and Spencer in 2000-2001, and the position of Safeway in 2002-2003.

Zero cost entry and exit

A slightly different treatment of contestable markets is that which concentrates on entry and exit as you will have studied for perfect competition. A market is said to be perfectly contestable if barriers to entry and exit are zero. If this were to be the case, other firms would be attracted to those industries in which supernormal profits are being made. In order to prevent increased competition, firms operating in a contestable market will keep prices down, and ensure that profits are kept to normal levels. To be contestable barriers need also to be minimised. If sunk costs are significant, firms already in an industry will be deterred from leaving as they cannot transfer such resources to other uses. Moreover, new entrants will be deterred if they were unable to transfer capital elsewhere.

Although there must be a strong temptation for oligopolists to avoid unnecessary risks by colluding with each other, some businesses are likely to be more aggressive and confrontational. Stable relationships between oligopolist firms can be upset by:
- new technologies
- changes in ownership .

Dynamic industries

If technologies and the ownership of firms are relatively dynamic, then these changes are likely to result in more competitive behaviour.

The ways in which goods and services are produced is constantly changing and as this process is likely to occur unevenly across firms making up an industry; some firms are likely to find themselves producing goods more cheaply than their competitors. For example, digital technologies are revolutionising the printing and media industries. Those businesses in the forefront of this change are likely to try to use their lower production costs to drive competitors out of the industry. But the fear of the introduction is new technological change may encourage existing firms to act competitively.

As with technology, the ownership of companies, especially of PLCs, in the UK is not always static. Changes at the top can lead to changes in business strategy, especially if the goal is to drive up shareholder value. The hostile acquisition of rivals and aggressive behaviour in building up market share are non-collusive strategies. In particular, some firms may start price wars by deliberately selling close to or below costs of production with a view to driving out competitors.

Summary

This Section has been devoted to two different theoretical treatments of the behaviour of large firms. Firstly, evidence was provided to support the contention that oligopolists are likely to collude, either openly or in secret, to keep prices high and outputs lower than would be the case in more competitive markets. Contestable market theory provides a theoretical case for firms that have monopoly power to act competitively. The changing nature of some markets may have the same effect.

Quick check

1   Which firms operating in a transport market do you suspect of collusion?
2   What is your best example of a transport market which might be contestable?

Introduction

This Section deals with:

- ways of measuring market concentration
- different forms of non-competitive behaviour
- assessing the effectiveness of government intervention.

Measuring concentrated markets

Governments make use of a simple device developed by economists to illustrate whether or not production in a given market is in the hands of a few or many firms. They are called concentration ratios and involve the calculation of the share of output of the leading firms in a given market. Thus, a three-firm concentration ratio would involve adding together the market shares of the three largest firms. The government uses a five-firm ratio to produce a measure of competitiveness in key economic sectors. This is shown in Table 1.

Table 1

Industrial sector	Five-firm concentration ratio (per cent)
Tobacco	99.5
Iron and steel	95.3
Motor vehicles	82.9
Cement	77.7
Water supply	49.7
Footwear	48.2
Bread and biscuits	47.0
Carpets	21.8
Clothing	20.7
Plastics processing	8.8

Examination of these ratios reveals the possible existence of two inter-related influences determining levels of competitiveness.

- Differing levels of economies of scale, for example steel and cement.
- Differing extent of barriers of entry, for example clothing and water supply.

However national ratios such as these do not indicate the level of global competitiveness, for example motor vehicle manufacture, nor do they account for the existence of local monopolies, for example water supply.

Synoptic link

You should have covered much of the content required in this A2 Section in the work that you did for AS. Make sure you know about the Competition Commission and various policies to promote competition:

- privatisation
- regulation
- creating internal markets
- encouraging enterprise.

The case for government intervention

The more detailed theoretical treatment of the significance of market structures in Sections 4.25 and 4.26 tends to indicate that, subject to crucial assumptions, customers and societies will be better off if markets are competitive rather than monopolistic. However, there is growing evidence that concentration ratios in key industries tend to be increasing and that many firms develop strategies to avoid competitive pressures. This divergence between what might be seen as socially desirable and the actual behaviour of an increasing number of larger firms provides a challenge both to economists and to governments. This rest of this Section explores how governments have attempted to promote competition and limit the adverse effects of firms able to exercise monopoly power.

The case against monopolies is summarised in the Thinking like an economist box. The economic arguments against the exercise of monopolistic power are not conclusive and they provide a particular challenge to governments in developing policies which guard against the potential excesses of monopolistic power while trying to ensure that possible benefits are not lost.

Government policies towards monopolies

The UK government has not always been suspicious of the motives and behaviour of firms perceived to have monopoly power. In the 1930s, the government promoted development of larger and more powerful companies as it was considered that they would provide a more secure business environment. However, since the passing of the Monopolies and Restrictive Practices Act in 1948, successive governments have looked more critically at the activities of large firms. The Act, which has been amended and strengthened by the addition of additional powers, has provided the basis of government control which continues today. The government Trade Minister, the President of the Board of Trade, is advised by what is now known as the Office of Fair Trading. In particular, the Office of Fair Trading recommends cases of possible abuse of monopoly power that should be investigated more fully. This function is carried out by the Competition Commission (formally known as the Monopolies and Mergers Commission). The Commission is a quasi-legal body which hears evidence prior to coming to a judgement about suspected abuses of monopoly power. Its findings are reported to the minister, who is then responsible for taking or not taking action. The minister, therefore, has the final say.

The law defines a monopoly as being any firm which has a 25 per cent or more share in a local or national market, or two or more firms supplying 25 per cent of the total market if it is suspected that they are colluding informally. The 1980 Competition Act identified various types of un-competitive behaviour, including the following:

■ price discrimination

Thinking like an economist

Economic theorists have argued that monopoly power can result in:

■ higher prices
■ lower outputs
■ less customer choice
■ fewer innovations
■ less efficient production both allocatively and productively.

On the other hand, it can be argued that firms with large market shares:

■ are able to exploit economies of scale
■ can compete more effectively in the global market place
■ have the resources to devote to research and development
■ can be socially responsible.

- selective distribution by which a firm may refuse to supply particular companies
- predatory pricing when firms deliberately cut prices below costs in an attempt to force competitors from a market.

The job of the Competition Commission is to establish whether or not uncompetitive behaviour is taking place and to balance this against possible benefits in order to make a judgement as to whether or not the firm in question is acting in the public interest. This is especially hard in some transport markets which have been called natural monopolies by some economists. In other words, efficiency dictates that the scale of provision is so large that the particular good or service can only be provided by a monopoly. Thus, it makes economic sense to run the railway network as one network. Similarly it would be hard to imagine competing pipelines. Large infrastructure systems tend to be natural monopolies. This issue is considered in more detail in the section of the privatisation of the railways in Section 4.28. At the end of their investigation the Commission can make recommendations relating to:

- price cuts
- reduced expenditure on advertising
- reducing barriers of entry
- breaking up monopolies.

Control over mergers

In 1965, Parliament enacted legislation which strengthened government controls over the potential abuse of monopoly power by compelling companies to give notice to the Office of Fair Trading of any proposed merger which would result in the creation of a monopoly as defined by the legislation. The Office of Fair Trading can recommend to the minister that conditions may be attached to giving permission for the merger to take place or reference can be made to the Competition Commission to investigate the likely outcomes of the merger in terms of the framework developed for investigating the abuses of monopoly power. The Commission, having considered evidence, recommends to the minister whether or not the merger should proceed.

In practice only a tiny minority of mergers in transport industries have been referred to the Commission. Practically all of these proposals have been rejected by the minister or abandoned by the companies in question. This apparent contradiction may indicate that government policies towards mergers have lacked consistency. It is not clear on what basis referrals are made to the minister and analysis of the outcomes indicates that mergers tend not to be in the public interest.

The present government has given greater powers and independence to the Office of Fair Trading. Its Director is now empowered to decide which mergers are investigated by the Competition Commission.

Control over monopolistic and oligopolistic abuses

The legal framework used to curb the abuse of power by monopolists and oligopolists is tougher than that relating to their existence and creation. Restrictive Trade Practices is the legal terminology used to describe various forms of collusion. All such agreements have to be registered with the Office of Fair Trading and they are banned unless the participants can prove that they are in the public interest. The law recognises that collusion can bring benefits such as:

- protecting employment
- promoting exports
- ensuring safety standards are met.

But even if it is possible to prove the existence of such benefits before the Restrictive Practices Court, firms still have to demonstrate that possible benefits outweigh any harmful effects.

Similarly a tough stance is taken towards limiting the power of manufacturers to set and enforce minimum retail prices for their products. Over the years formal price fixing agreements have been ended, and currently only exist for some medical products.

European Union legislation

The development of the single European market has meant that member states have been forced to adopt a common approach to competition policy, especially in respect of those firms which have monopoly power within the EU. There is no minimum market share which triggers investigation. Firms who behave unfairly towards consumers by their pricing policies or other activities can be referred to the European Court of Justice, and if found 'guilty', they can be fined as well as being debarred from acting uncompetitively.

EU policies towards mergers and collusive behaviour are similar. The focus is on investigation of uncompetitive behaviour rather than market share or such like.

Summary

Governments in most countries intervene to limit the power of monopolies and oligopolies. The existence of considerable numbers of laws, regulations, and a quasi-court structure indicate that this is a complex aspect of economic policy over which it is difficult to legislate. However, the legal framework in this country is designed to try to ensure that government intervention promotes the public interest. Whether or not governments have been successful is a big question.

Research task

Use this Section and other sources to plan and research an essay in which you assess the effectiveness of government attempts to limit the harmful economic effects of the abuse of monopoly power within a transport market.

Weblink

Weblink to competition Guardian/economist/FT for commentaries on effectiveness of government policies.

Introduction

Industrial relations, production and the international competitiveness of the UK economy in the late 1970s were seen to be poor. Margaret Thatcher came to power in 1979 with the slogan 'Getting Britain back to work'. She was strongly influenced by 'right-wing' economists who argued that the performance of the UK economy was poor because it was not competitive. They argued that economic performance would improve if:

- monetarist polices were followed (see Section 3.15)
- trade union power was reduced (see Section 3.16)
- some publicly owned organisations were privatised
- organisations remaining in public ownership should be made more competitive
- enterprise and market based strategies were encouraged.

This Section is devoted to:
- privatisation
- deregulation.

Privatisation

Prior to 1979, partly because they were natural monopolies or key infrastructure investments, a large number of transport industries were in public ownership. Along with businesses such as BP, ICL (Computers) British Sugar, Jaguar and British Telecom, transport businesses such as Thomas Cook, Sealink and BA were sold to the private sector. At the end of the 1980s and the early 1990s more complicated sell-offs such as the water, electricity and rail industries were undertaken. The current Labour government has tended to continue these policies by privatising Air Traffic Control, but it has undone some of changes made by the Conservatives by winding up Rail Track and replacing it with the not for profit 'Strategic Rail Authority'.

The privatisation process

Transferring ownership from the public to the private sector has usually involved the following process:
1. valuation of assets to be sold off
2. publication of prospectus, detailing the form and nature of the share offer including the determination of number of shares to be issued
3. setting an individual share price
4. publicising the sell-off
5. flotation, i.e. selling shares.

From the government's point of view, stage 3 is crucial. If the business is undervalued the government loses potential revenue, but if it is overvalued the actual flotation could fail.

Synoptic link

Section 4.28 follows directly from the previous one, which looked at how government policies decided to limit the power of monopolists and oligopolists in transport markets. The difference is that the focus of this Section is on government policy to promote competition. This approach has been preferred by governments over the last 20 years and there has been a significant attempt to deregulate transport markets. There are direct links between these public policies and the theory of contestable markets covered in Section 4.26.

Hot potato

Will rail privatisation result in the creation of a privately owned monopoly?

The Conservative governments of the 1980s recognised that the transfer of ownership from the public to the private sectors would not be sufficient to protect the public from the abuse of monopoly power. In order to safeguard the public interest, legislation to permit privatisation also contained provision for the creation of regulators. These are independent bodies such as OFCOM (media and telecommunications), OFWAT (water) and OFGEM (gas and electricity markets) with powers to regulate the actual behaviour of these industries by imposing pricing formulas, insisting on customer service targets and levels of investment. The most important sanction available to most regulators is over pricing. In many cases the freedom of newly privatised firms to raise prices is limited by formulae. Although its application varies between industries, the regulator's formula can be represented as RPI - X + Y + K. In this formula, RPI stands for the retail price index; X is a percentage representing costs saving which the regulator expects to be reflected in lower customer prices; Y stands for unavoidable cost increases and K applies to the water companies as an allowance to cover the costs of environmental improvements, for example cleaner rivers.

These regulatory powers are in addition to the legal constraints outlined earlier, and are particularly relevant in the case of natural monopolies.

Research task

Select a transport industry that has been privatised or deregulated and evaluate the economic effectiveness of these changes.

Natural monopolies

Industries such as water, electricity supply and the railways can be described as natural monopolies and it has been more difficult to sell these off in such as way as to promote competition and the other benefits which private ownership is meant to bring.

Privatising British Rail

As indicated earlier, it was harder to devise ways of privatising natural monopolies without losing the efficiencies that characterise the large scale of their provision. No more so than in the case of the railways, which were one of the Conservative's last privatisations and one that was especially problematical. On the advice of economists, the government created an imaginative plan to try to introduce competition into this natural monopoly. They split the industry into three parts:

- the railway and station network
- rolling stock provision
- rail operating companies.

Each Section was privatised differently.

Railtrack
The government accepted that this was a natural monopoly that could not be broken up and sold it into private ownership for slightly less than

£2billion in 1996. Its market value in January 2000 was £3.25 billion. In the event, Railtrack ran into financial difficulties and after a period in which government subsidised their activities they were wound up and replaced by Network Rail in 2002.

Rolling stock

Three rolling stock companies were created whose job was to compete in order to supply engines and carriages to the train operating companies.

Train operating companies

Investors were encouraged to bid for franchises to run trains over regional and inter-city routes. Successful companies would then pay Railtrack to use 'their' stations and track, and lease rolling stock as required. At the end of seven to fourteen years new bids would be invited to run services in the future.

Regulation

A powerful independent regulatory regime was introduced to ensure that minimum service levels were met, that profits were not excessive and that government guidelines were followed.

Assessing performance of the privatised rail network

The general perception of the public as revealed in surveys is that the privatisation of the railways has yet to be successful.

- Train operating companies have used their market power to introduce complicated discriminatory pricing policies.
- Prices on some services have been dramatically increased.
- Punctuality and customer service are thought to have deteriorated.
- Safety may have been given less priority.

The long-term test of the success of this particular privatisation will be the degree to which a natural monopoly re-establishes itself through merger and take over within the industry. This has already started to occur in the electricity generation and supply industry.

Deregulation

For various reasons that have already been outlined, other transport markets have been either publicly owned or very closely regulated at a local, national and international level. Governments in the UK and in other parts of the world have been anxious to create more competitive markets by removing some of the regulations that could act as barriers to entry. The impact of these moves can be seen in the following transport industries.

Road transport

Elements of road haulage were state owned until 1982 but some elements of regulation were removed before this. There are still regulations relating health and safety such as limiting the number of hours at the driving wheel without breaks, but the industry is now highly competitive with relatively low barriers to entry.

Bus travel

This followed a similar pattern of the sale of national networks and the deregulation of local services involving the removal of agreements about routes and frequency of services. This has tended to result in competition for profitable routes and the abandonment of services of those that are less profitable. This together with the removal of subsidies has badly hit the provision of bus services in rural areas.

Air transport

Air transport has been deregulated both nationally and internationally. Historically, airlines have been publicly owned and often a source of national pride and prestige, protected from competition by all manner of restrictions. Many of these were abandoned first in the US, then in the UK and some European counties and now internationally. Domestic air services in Europe are now open to competition from airlines owned by other countries. These changes have allowed the entry of low-cost carriers which have led to significant price cuts and a large increase in passenger miles.

Whether or not these changes can be sustained is open to debate as there are strong market forces to encourage take over and a return to more concentrated markets.

Sea transport

Sea transport is now practically unregulated and real costs of sea transport have fallen but so have safety standards as competition forces prices down and results in very low pay for many foreign crews. The UK once had the largest share of this market but now is a minor player.

Summary

In recent years, governments in the UK have also attempted to encourage the development of more competitive markets through privatisation and the deregulation of transport markets. These policies appear to have had very mixed results in terms of prices and sales of transport products, which may be related to the degree to which the industry might be regarded as a natural monopoly. It could be argued that is too early to assess the long-term impact of these changes on society as a whole.

Introduction

The first part of this Section is meant to help you understand the broader context in which economists consider market failure and government intervention. The second part explains the significance of property rights, while the last part is devoted to further consideration of the possibility of government failure.

Social efficiency

In your AS course you will have assessed the effectiveness of the price mechanism as a means of allocating resources. You will have also learned that if markets are competitive and/or if there are no externalities, the price mechanism will achieve an optimal allocation of resources. In other words, the world's resources will be used as efficiently as possible to meet the demands of customers in the market place. This theoretical state is known as Pareto Optimal. Vilfredo Pareto (1848–1923) was an Italian economist who argued in favour of positive economics. He contended that social efficiency was reached in an economy when it was not possible to make any individual better off without making someone else worse off. Conversely, if it was possible to make someone better off without making someone else worse off, an economy would be described as operating sub optimally, i.e. it would be socially inefficient.

This analysis depends upon consumers and producers behaving in a rational way, which means that consumers will go on consuming, for example Coca Cola, as long as the marginal benefit (the satisfaction gained from the last mouthful) is greater than the marginal cost (the cost of that last mouthful). If, on the other hand, the additional cost is greater than the additional pleasure the rational consumer will cut down the consumption of Coca Cola. Thus, the rational consumer will stop consuming Coca Cola when its marginal cost is equal to its marginal benefit.

You will also be familiar with the behaviour of a competitive firm wishing to maximise profits. It will go on producing until the marginal cost of production is the same as the marginal revenue gained from sales. If marginal cost is less than marginal revenue, production will be expanded whereas the profit-maximising firm will cut output if marginal costs exceed marginal revenue.

Finally, when studying factor markets you will have learned that in a competitive labour market a profit maximising employer will go on employing more of an individual factor of production until the last unit adds as much to marginal revenue product as it does to costs.

Still with it? This is meant to be a *gestalt* moment in your understanding of economics. If all economic agents are rational, and all attempt to equate marginal benefits with marginal costs, private efficiency will be maximised,

Government intervention and transport markets

Synoptic link

This section is designed to pull together several themes which have been developed throughout your economics course and also in your deeper study of transport issues. You need to have a broad understanding of the micro part of your AS course which dealt with market systems and market failure. You need to ensure that you are comfortable with the following:

- positive and negative externalities
- public goods
- merit and demerit goods
- market imperfections
- monopoly power
- imperfect knowledge
- factor immobility
- government use of:
  □ indirect taxation
  □ subsidies
  □ price control
  □ buffer
  □ stocks
  □ pollution permits
  □ state provision
- government failure
- imperfect knowledge
- conflicting objectives
- administrative costs.

You should also be developing an understanding of the particular nature of transport markets and the possible rationale for government intervention. Finally, you should be able to evaluate the effectiveness of such interventions.

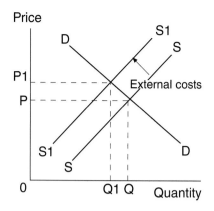

Figure 1: Negative externalities

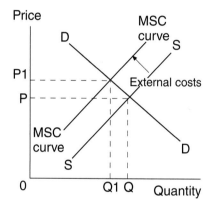

Figure 2: The MSC curve

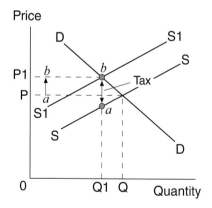

Figure 3: Taxing away negative externalities

i.e. it would not be possible to make someone better off without making someone worse off.

Last lap – this analysis can be extended to considering social efficiency, i.e. if the marginal social benefit of any activity is equal to the marginal social cost then society as a whole is achieving Pareto optimality. You may find this hard going, but you should have undertaken very similar analysis for AS. Do you remember Figure 1?

This uses an extra supply curve to represent a negative externality, congestion being an obvious example in transport economics. The graphical analysis can be used to show that if the government could calculate the additional costs on society of road congestion and were to introduce a tax equivalent to the vertical distance ab it would be able to ensure an optimum allocation of resources because at P and Q an equilibrium is reached at which customers are paying the total cost to society for the road space that they are using. The same analysis can be used but at A2 level you need to get used to calling the S2 in this context **the MSC curve** (Figure 2).

A similar change can be made to the diagram you will have studied to identify the effects of positive externalities and the possible use of government subsidy to achieve an optimal allocation of resources. Thus again it is possible to argue that having an efficient means of bringing workers quickly to work in London or any other major city might have significant positive externalities: more leisure/work time, happier, less stressed workers, less pollution. Again, in theory, if the government could put a monetary value on these benefits it might be possible to achieve a socially more desirable allocation of resources (Figure 3).

Property rights

An additional theoretical approach to dealing with negative externalities can be by the introduction of tradable permits whereby governments can encourage individual firms to reduce pollution by creating a market in which those firms who cut pollution the most have the most to gain. This is an extension of one approach to dealing with externalities without the necessity of government intervention. This approach is associated with an American economist, Ronald Coase. In 1960, he argued that government intervention was not required to deal with negative externalities as long as property rights are well defined and that transactions costs are relatively low. Coase argued that it is possible to extend rights to define who owns what property, to what uses it can be put, and what rights others have over. If they could be extended to cover each and every resource, then the owners would have an incentive to ensure that the value of their property was protected. Thus, if something that I own is damaged it would be logical for me to sue who ever caused the damage. Clearly if the legal or transaction costs to this action were relatively large, I might be dissuaded from seeking compensation.

The difficulty of applying this approach to internalising external costs is that it is hard to establish property rights in relation to many of the environmental resources directly linked to transport markets. Who owns the air above my house, the water that flows from mountains to sea, and what happens when it is difficult to identify the perpetrator of some perceived negative externality?

Nonetheless, it is clear that the development of legal systems which include establishing the terms and conditions associated with contract law, the rights of buyers and sellers, the liability of particular types of businesses and the importance of insurance have all contributed to the development of economic systems which at least go some way in trying to ensure that resources are used effectively. Indeed, great damage has been done to less developed and former communist countries in applying market-led solutions in contexts where property rights were both ill-defined and ill-protected.

Government failure

In the final part of your AS Unit on markets and market failure you were introduced to the concept of government failure which is a concept that recognises that government intervention in markets may lead to unintended outcomes. Thus, it can be argued that the government does not impose taxes on motorists and road uses such that the marginal social cost of using roads equals that of marginal social benefits leading to a higher demand for road space than is socially desirable. Even worse there are no taxes on the supply of airplane fuel – one of the major sources of pollutants which are thought to damage the ozone layer and contribute to global warming. Misplaced price intervention may create surpluses or shortages. Direct government controls can lead to the creation of new unregulated markets such as the distinction between black cabs and minicabs or private cabs. Taxes and subsidies may distort the signals given by the price mechanism. Such arguments are often used by economists who favour the working of free market forces who sometimes suggest that there is a straight choice to be made between free market or capitalist solutions and interventionist or socialist solutions.

The winner of the Nobel Price for Economics in 2001, Joseph Stiglitz, has suggested that much of this debate is misplaced. He has argued that free market ideology is fundamentally flawed as 'whenever information is imperfect and markets incomplete, which is to say always, then the invisible hand works most imperfectly'. He goes on to argue that government interventions 'can improve upon the efficiency of the market' and that one of the roles of government is to try to remove imperfections in information flows. He suggests that it is more useful to discuss the appropriate balance between governments and markets.

Hot potato

Are all transport markets imperfect and incomplete?

It has been said a number of
times, but do not forget the work
you covered for this at AS. The
examiners can set questions on
anything that you did for AS as well
as for A2.

Summary

Transport markets are likely to fail because of the existence of significant externalities both positive and negative. Market-based solutions based on the extension of property rights are unlikely to work because of the environmental aspect of transport markets. Governments often intervene in transport markets to improve the efficiency and effectiveness of resource use and this may improve or exacerbate the efficient allocation of transport resources.

Quick check

What assumptions have to be made for the free market system to ensure the optimum allocation of transport resources?

Government policies

Investment in infrastructure, such as road and railways, has largely been the responsibility of UK governments. Historically the UK government has failed to invest sufficiently to cope with the increasing demand for road transport and failed to invest sufficiently to maintain the quality of the rail network. It has also been slow to improve air traffic infrastructure especially air traffic control.

The reasons for these failings are complex, but during the 1980s and early 1990s successive conservative governments relied almost exclusively on market based solutions to economic problems. As has been demonstrated, many transport markets are failing markets largely because of the 'externality' problem.

Under-investment has been highlighted in a series of highly publicised rail disasters and in failing standards of service and punctuality on the railway. At the same time the public perceive that problems of congestion on the roads have got worse and there are also worries about safety and congestion in our UK and European air routes. In this context the government has produced a ten-year transport plan. This was first announced in the White Paper 'A New Deal for Transport – Better for Everyone' which was published in 1998 and involves spending £180 billion over the period 2000 to 2010 to improve transport in the UK. This is split three ways between the railways, roads and local transport. The government set the following targets:

- reduced congestion on our roads
- modern trains with better services and reduced fares
- a 50 per cent increase in passenger use of the railway
- resources to enable the Mayor to reduce overcrowding on the London Underground and congestion in London – with £3.2bn investment in the first three years
- 100 new bypasses
- 360 miles of trunk road and motorway widening
- big improvements in rural transport
- better bus services and a 10 per cent growth in passenger use
- up to 25 new light rail projects in major cities
- safer roads and railways
- lower emissions and better air quality.

These objectives provide a considerable challenge to economists; many can be considered to be normative. Thus it is hard to answer the question 'how safe is safe'. Moreover, it has to be recognised that any government plan has significant political dimensions. In this particular case, transport problems are perceived by the government to be a high priority with electors. The current government is sensitive to the charge that although Labour have been in office since 1997 they have achieved little in reforming and improving major public services like education, the health service and transport. Moreover, the government was badly shaken by the blockades and

Synoptic link

Individual aspects of government polices towards transport have been dealt with in preceding sections.
- Controls on monopolies and oligopolies
- Privatisation
- Deregulation

These have been attempts to introduce market-based solutions to the distribution of resources, in particular UK transport markets. The previous section considered some of the theoretical reasons why transport markets might be considered to fail and this section is devoted to consideration of attempts by UK governments to develop an overall policy towards transport. By the end of this section you should be able to start to evaluate the effectiveness of such policies.

civil disobedience that occurred in 2000 as some truckers tried to get the government to cut taxes on road haulage companies. In short it is possible to argue that government responses to transport problems are likely to be influenced more by political considerations than economic ones.

Three aspects of these policies are particularly significant:
- targets to increase the use of public transport
- the integration of transport services
- funding.

Increased use of public transport

Government projections, as outlined in earlier Sections, indicate that problems of traffic congestion are likely to increase. The government appears to have at least partially rejected one solution, which would be to simply increase the supply of road space by building more roads. Evidence suggests that the act of building more roads generates more traffic thus making the problems of congestion worse. It is generally recognised that public transport is more efficient and enables better use to be made of available road space. However, the public perception of some public transport provision is that it is dirty, unreliable and uncomfortable. Hence the need to invest more heavily in the provision of better quality trains, and to facilitate the movement of buses and coaches.

The responsibility for provision and improvement of local public transport has been delegated to local authorities and this has created conflicts between local councils, who claim that they are given greater responsibilities but denied the resources to improve services, and government, for example the well-publicised differences between the Mayor of London and the government.

Issues about the railways are extremely complex. Privatisation in the early 1990s has made the formulation of national policies more difficult and the government has intervened to set up the Strategic Rail Authority and has encouraged a reduction in the number train operating companies, as well as extending the length of individual franchises.

Hot potato

Our love affair with the motor car has got to end. Do you agree?

The other half of such a policy would logically involve making road transport more expensive through the tax system or other forms of control. This is dealt with in greater detail in Section 4.32, but it appears that the government is very frightened of alienating car users and the haulage industry.

The integration of services

As part of its proposals to improve transport contained in the 1998 White Paper, the government set up an independent advisory body, the Commission for Integrated Transport. This is led by Professor David Begg, an economist.

The fragmentation of all transport services is a particular problem in the UK compared with many other European countries. By encouraging greater competition, limiting subsidies to public transport, deregulating services and extensive privatisation, the government has intensified this fragmentation of services. This has many effects:

- railway stations are not necessarily linked to local bus services
- rural areas are badly served
- through ticketing on the rail network is difficult
- the breaking up of markets makes it easier for companies providing transport services to use price discrimination at the expense of consumers.

The government now expects local authorities to use the planning process to contribute to more closely integrated services.

In 2001, Professor Begg published his assessment of transport in the UK, and his stark judgement was that we had the worse transport in Europe. He noted that in the UK:

- rail fares are the third highest in Europe
- 25 per cent of main roads are jammed for an hour a day
- fuel tax is the highest in Europe
- there is the lowest rail subsidy in Europe.

But Professor Begg also indicated that government plans appeared to offer some chance of tackling these problems.

Funding

As indicated earlier, many of the problems associated with transport are the result of under-investment. Historically the benefits and potential profits which might accrue from investment in transport infrastructure projects have been so long term as to deter private sector investment. It is especially true in the UK when financial markets tend to be more short-termist than in other countries. Traditionally, government spending was used to fill this gap, but since the mid-1970s successive governments have tried to cut down on government spending and the present government has promised not to increase the burden of income tax. This poses a major dilemma for the government in how to finance the much-needed improvements in transport infrastructure. The present government has developed a new approach which involves private/public partnership; meeting its transport objectives is dependent upon the success of this particular strategy. This is illustrated in Table 1.

Table 1

(£billion, outturn prices)	Public investment	Private investment	Total	Public resource spend	Total
Strategic roads	13.6	2.6	16.2	5.0	21.3
Railways	14.7	34.3	49.1	11.3	60.4
Local transport	19.3	9.0	28.3	30.6	58.9
London	7.5	10.4	17.8	7.4	25.3
Other transport	0.7	n/a	0.7	1.5	2.2
Unallocated	9.0	n/a	9.0	n/a	9.0
Charging income	n/a	n/a	n/a	2.7	2.7
Total	64.7	56.3	121.0	58.6	179.7

Private Funding Initiative (PFI) as it is known, is designed to make investment in public services more attractive by reducing the risks faced by private capital. Returns are guaranteed as long as various targets and budgets are met. The government argues that the private sector is a better manager of such investment projects and that this approach offers better value for money. Many government-financed initiatives have gone seriously over budget.

These arguments are fiercely contested by the main trade unions and some economists who argue that public money is being spent to boost the profits of private investors. Recent reports by the government's audit commission have thrown some doubt as to whether or not PFI works in the way that the government claims.

Summary

Developing strategies which might improve transport in the UK is one of the biggest challenges facing the present government. They are committed to improving public transport and encouraging a switch away from the use of roads. They hope that the use of PFI will speed up investment in major infrastructure projects but there are some doubts as to whether these policies with improve the worst transport system in Europe.

The political challenges are underlined by the sacking of one minister, Stephen Byers in 2002, to be followed by an announcement of an expanded road-building programme. In December 2002, the Transport Department admitted that some of its objectives to cut road use by 2010 would not be met. Make sure you keep up-to-date with political developments.

> ### Quick check
>
> What will the theoretical effects of the £3billion plan to increase spending on roads, announced in December 2002, be on:
> - the demand for cars
> - the demand for road space
> - the price of rail journeys?

Introduction

Cost benefit analysis is one of the statistical techniques developed by government economists to try to:

- quantify both negative and positive externalities
- determine possible levels of government subsidy
- establish levels of taxation
- help reconcile the interests of different stakeholders.

Cost benefit analysis and market failure

Cost benefit analysis can be applied to new investments and also to existing markets. For example, there has been a long running enquiry into the building of a new terminal at Heathrow Airport. Supporters claim that it will aid economic growth, not just of those directly concerned, but also for firms and employees dependent upon the continued growth and expansion of Heathrow. On the other hand, a range of interests opposed to the development have argued that noise pollution, congestion and the like will impose additional costs on the local community. As part of the process to decide whether or not permission should be given for this new development, cost benefit analysis was undertaken. In this case the purpose was to identify both the positive and negative externalities. A public enquiry was set up to reveal the full costs to society, i.e. the **social cost** of the new development, and the full benefits, i.e. **social benefit**. At the end of the day the government decided that the social advantages outweighed the social disadvantages and gave the green light to one of the largest civil engineering projects ever undertaken.

The cost benefit process

Undertaking this cost benefit analysis usually involves the following procedures.

1. Identification and quantification of all private costs. These are the fixed and variable costs which the company or organisation undertaking the project would normally be expected to pay. In the case of the new Heathrow Terminal this might involve the cost of land, design, building, labour costs and many others.

2. Identification and quantification of all external costs. In other words putting a monetary value to all the negative externalities. This is more difficult. It is relatively straightforward to estimate the additional costs of improving soundproofing for those living in the vicinity, but much more difficult to find monetary values for matters relating to environmental damage and degradation.

Synoptic link

You will have covered cost benefit analysis for your AS course. This section repeats some of this and considers the contribution that this analytical tool can make to resource decisions in transport markets.

Definitions

Social costs refers to both the private costs and negative externalities attributed to a particular use of economic resources.

Social benefits are the private benefits and positive externalities attributable to a particular use of economic resources.

3. Calculation of social cost. This simply involves adding the private and external costs together to estimate the full cost to society of the project in question.

4. Identification and quantification of all private benefits. These are all the benefits which customers are prepared to pay for. Sometimes such calculations are straightforward if the people who benefit actually have to pay for a new service.

5. Identification and quantification of all external benefits. As with negative externalities this is more tricky as it involves identifying all those who are likely to benefit in some way and putting a monetary value on their benefit. What is the benefit of a business person getting to a meeting in a foreign country on time? How do you assess the positive effects on the local economy?

6. Calculation of social benefit. These are the private and external benefits added together.

When all this has been done it is possible to make a direct comparison between the social costs of a project and the social benefits. In theory if the social benefit exceeds the social cost, society as a whole would benefit from the development, but if this relationship were reversed society would be economically worse off.

Problems with cost benefit

The big challenge to those undertaking cost benefit analysis is to put a financial valuation on external costs and benefits, and this requires a mixture of approximations, forecasts and guesswork.

Calculation problems are especially difficult when it comes to dealing with the costs faced by people. Thus what would be the value of building a road that cuts five minutes off the typical journey time of a thousand road users per week? If improvements to road safety demonstrate that fewer accidents will occur it is reasonably easy to put a value to the lower demand for hospital and medical care, but what value should be given to a saved limb, or even a saved life?

These practical difficulties are sometimes made harder as cost benefit analysis is often used to assess the economic impact of controversial proposals. This was the case with the Heathrow extension mentioned above in which rival stakeholders challenged the data that each side and the inspector were using.

The development of cost benefit analysis

The development of techniques of cost benefit analysis is partly linked to the development of models to help make effective decisions in respect of transport. As noted earlier, large negative and positive externalities are one of the characteristics of transport markets. Similarly, because of the high fixed cost of many infrastructure projects, private investors have been reluctant to provide funds, and provision has depended upon government intervention to build roads, airports, docks and the like. The Department of Transport has developed a series of models to help determine priorities in road building. Until the late 1990s they used a system called COBA (Cost Benefit Appraisal) which compares the user cost on the old road network to the estimated user cost of the improved network to establish the benefits that users would gain. This is set against the cost of construction to give a net value to the net benefits of a particular scheme (NPV). This model was useful in helping sort priorities but compared with cost benefit analysis was a very limited approach as it excluded attempting to quantify:

- negative externalities especially in relation to environmental damage
- positive externalities especially in relation to knock on effects on local businesses.

COBA has now been replaced by more sophisticated models which attempt to remedy these shortcomings.

Using cost benefit analysis

Cost benefit analysis is used in a number of ways. These include:
- public subsidy
- regulation
- planning.

Subsidy

If cost benefit analysis demonstrates that there will be greater social benefit than social cost, i.e. there is a net social gain, then this analysis might be used to justify government subsidy to ensure that resources are used in such a way as to maximise public welfare.

Regulation

Similarly if cost benefit analysis shows that negative externalities outweigh positive, a rationale is provided for government intervention to limit or control such outputs. This could involve direct controls, pollution taxes or the introduction of tradable permits.

Planning

As in the case of the expansion at Heathrow, cost benefit analysis can be used to try to resolve the competing claims of different stakeholders. It can provide a more rational way of resolving controversial issues. It also provides government bodies such as the National Health Service and the Department of Environment with a means of deciding which investments in the public sector should be selected and which rejected.

Research task

1 Assess the contribution that cost benefit analysis can make to rationing scarce resources in relation to improvements in the rail network.
2 Cost benefit analysis is a good topic for further research. The principles are relatively easy to understand and there is plenty of scope for primary and secondary research. You might start by picking a market in which you consider there are significant positive or negative externalities. You would need to try to put a monetary value on such externalities, and suggest possible government intervention strategies. Develop your skills of evaluation by considering the strengths and weaknesses of the technique, the data that you collect and any analysis undertaken. Do not rely on one source for your information and do not get public and private costs and benefits muddled up.

Hot potato

What value would you put on the lives of an 18-year-old male compared with an 18-year-old female?

Summary

Cost benefit analysis is a particularly valuable tool in helping improve the quality of decision making both by publicly- and privately-funded projects. However, the whole planning process for building major infrastructure products is very slow and many fall behind deadlines and run over budget. Currently plans for a new cross London rail link, as well as improvements to the link with the Channel tunnel, are well behind schedule.

Quick check	
List three advantages and three problems associated with cost benefit analysis as applied to transport markets.	

Railways

Congestion occurs at some stations at pinch points in the system and when faults occur. The remedies are simple but expensive in terms of improving maintenance and upgrading both track and rolling stock. The Strategic Rail Authority (SRA) has taken over overall planning and scheduling of services and has limited the freedom of the operating companies to run trains whenever they like on routes of their choosing. This has resulted in reducing the frequency of some services. The issue is whether or not the government has committed sufficient funding to repair the defects caused by years of under-investment in the rail network,

Airways

There are problems with congestion in the air and on the ground. One of the government's private/public partnership agreements was for the installation of a new, more powerful air traffic control system which would allow more effective use of air space and improved safety standards. This is late, still not fully functional and over budget.

The construction of new airports is a prolonged and difficult process as few people welcome such developments near where they live. It took ten years to agree the new Heathrow terminal which is currently being built, and proposals for expansion at Gatwick, Stansted, Rugby and other regional centres face vigorous opposition.

Roads

As noted earlier, there has been a continued increase in the demand for road space. In 1998, traffic levels were 455 billion vehicle kilometres and are projected to rise to 524 billion vehicle kilometres by 2006. As a result, the speed at which vehicles travel is declining. For example, in 1995, motor vehicles travelled at an average of 63 miles per hour. By 1998 this was down to 56 miles per hour. In addition to slowing traffic flow, congestion tends to occur at particular pinch points in the road network. Thus, users of the M6 north of Birmingham and the M25 between the junctions for the M1 and M4 are often involved in lengthy traffic jams as are users of the main roads into and out of most major cities.

Congestion is not just an irritant to the traveller; it poses considerable negative private and social costs to the UK economy. A RAC report published in 2000 put the total cost of congestion in the UK at £23 billion a year. This total cost is composed of a number of factors.
- Higher transport costs: more is spent on fuel and time getting to destinations. Time lost has an opportunity cost.
- When the number of journeys on a particular road reaches a certain level, traffic is slowed down and negative externalities occur.

Transport congestion
4.32

Synoptic link

Transport congestion is a direct result of the changing patterns of transport use identified in Section 4.16. You will have dealt with underlying theoretical concepts when looking at different forms of government intervention in your AS course. This section is devoted to a more detailed consideration of this major transport problem and it will help you evaluate the likely effectiveness of economic measures to reduce congestion. Congestion in the UK applies to:
- railways
- airspace/airports
- roads.

There are different policy options for each mode of travel.

- Higher costs to transport firms, for example haulage firms, bus and coach companies. The increased time it takes to complete a journey reduces the productivity of vehicles. They will carry a lower volume of goods or passengers per hour.
- Higher costs to other firms: firms which use haulage companies or use their own vehicles to transport their goods will experience higher costs which they are likely to pass on, at least in part, to consumers in the form of higher prices. This reduces international price competitiveness.
- Stress-related illnesses which, as with accidents, reduce output and increase the demand on health service resources.
- Pollution: the amount of air pollution is greater when vehicles are stuck in traffic jams.

Policy approaches

Congestion arises because the demand for road space has grown much more rapidly than the supply. The government can respond to this problem in a number of ways. It can increase the supply of road space by, for example, building more roads, widening existing ones or freeing up space on roads by discouraging on-road parking through parking charges and yellow and red lines. In practise the road-build option is limited both by finance and by the conflicts that it presents with other objectives of government policy such as preservation of the countryside. Moreover, as has already been noted, such a policy could be counter-productive as increasing the supply of road space tends, by initially speeding up the flow of traffic, to generate higher demand and creates wider environmental problems. Congestion also does not seem to be self-correcting. The market for road space fails, or could be said to be missing, as there is no mechanism to ensure that equilibrium between demand and supply is reached.

As supply policies appear not to work, the UK Government has considered a number of policy options.
- Charging people to park at work. The intention is to discourage people from taking their cars to work. This is a measure that is used in California in the USA. The State runs a 'parking cash out' scheme. Employers charge a market price to any of their employees who use the car parking they provide and pay every employee an amount that, after tax, is equal to the charge.
- Providing park-and-ride schemes, which are designed to reduce congestion in city centres.
- Encouraging the use of public transport. One way is by making public transport cheaper by means of subsidies. However, it is thought that a more effective way of raising the attractiveness of public transport is to increase the quality of the service.
- Taxing car ownership and petrol. This raises the entry price on the road system and probably does reduce demand for road space. The tax on

petrol use does have the advantage of taxing heavy vehicles and fuel-inefficient firms more, thereby reducing pollution. However, the effect may not be very significant since, as mentioned earlier, demand for car use is relatively price inelastic and it does not discriminate between when and where people use their cars. So the effect on congestion is thought to be small.

Road pricing

This is a measure that is advocated by a number of economists and is being increasing considered as the only long-term solution as it directly addresses the fundamental problem of the negative externalities caused by vehicle use. The private costs of passenger and freight transport are less than the cost to society (social cost) because of the external costs they create, such as pollution and congestion, which makes the quantity of road space used greater than the socially optimum level. Drivers gain at the expense of non-drivers. Road pricing is said to be a market solution as it is based on working through the price mechanism and making that system work more efficiently. This is because the prices charged are, in theory, based on the negative externalities generated by use of particular roads at particular times. However, the gap between theoretically appropriate solutions and their effective use is large. It requires:

- calculation of the negative externalities
- accurate measures of the price elasticity of demand for road space
- measuring the use of road space by individual vehicles
- charging the appropriate fee
- collecting the fee.

The simplest form of road pricing used in many countries is the collection of a toll. This will only work on roads on which non-payers can be excluded. There must be limited entry and exit points, such as motorways and tunnels. There is also the risk that tolls merely shift the problem of congestion by encouraging drivers to use alternative routes. Thus tolls are changed only on east to west traffic on the Severn Bridge leading to increased westbound traffic via Gloucester and Ross. Although simple and effective to operate, it would be difficult to use this method in urban areas in which the negative externalities of road use are probably greatest.

Alternatively electronic equipment can be used to monitor the movement of vehicles, which can be identified and charged according to their use of particular roads at particular times. The revenue, or at least some of it, received from road pricing could be used to fund improvements in the quality of public transport. It now seems inevitable that the long-term solution to road pricing will involve the creation of systems to charge road users according to their actual usage of roads.

The Singapore experiment

One of the first tests of the imposition of a road-pricing scheme was in Singapore which has been in use for 30 years. The scheme involves:

- electronic road pricing, whereby those driving into town and city centres pay a large fee
- a quota and auctioning system, whereby people have to pay a large amount for the right to buy a certificate of entitlement which gives them the right to own a car
- a high rate of taxation on fuel
- the provision of a good alternative form of public transport in the form of a subsidised, high-quality transit system.

Central London

In February 2003, Mayor Ken Livingston introduced a road-pricing scheme to central London, modelled on the example of Singapore. Those using roads in central London in the daytime have to pay a £5 fee. Cameras are used to record cars entering and leaving central London and a computer system checks that the owners have paid the fee. For those who do not, fines are automatically generated.

There was considerable opposition to the scheme but it appears to have worked in cutting congestion at peak times. Initial reports indicate that:

- road use has been significantly cut
- tubes are the preferred substitute to the newly improved bus fleet
- journey times have been cut
- enforcement has been reasonably successful
- as the fall in road use has been greater than expected, revenue predictions have not been met limiting the amount available for investment in better public transport.

Finally

In June 2003, the government announced that it was considering a national scheme to tag and charge cars according to their use of particular roads and that they were considering abandoning other forms of car taxation – a truly economic solution.

Work and leisure

Activity 1

(a) Explain why demand for labour is a derived demand.
(b) What determines the elasticity of demand for a particular group of workers?

Activity 2

(a) Explain what is meant by marginal revenue productivity.
(b) Identify two possible causes of a rise in the MRP of plumbers.

Activity 3

(a) Explain the connection between elasticity of supply and economic rent.
(b) Discuss whether doctors or professional footballers are likely to earn more economic rent.

Activity 4

(a) Why is there a shortage of nurses?
(b) Discuss three ways the government could increase the recruitment of nurses.

Activity 5

(a) Has the introduction of the National Minimum Wage (NMW) reduced income inequality in the UK?
(b) Discuss two other measures the UK government employs to reduce income inequality.

Activity 6

(a) What has enabled low cost airlines to enter the market for passenger air travel?
(b) What effect has the entry of low cost airlines into the market had on the behaviour and efficiency of established firms in the market?

Transport economics

Activity 1

(a) What factors influence demand for transport?
(b) Compare the relative merits of road and rail passenger travel.

Activity 2

(a) Why has demand for bus travel fallen in recent years?

(b) Identify three policies a government could employ to increase the number of bus journeys.

Activity 3

(a) What factors do firms take into account when choosing which mode of freight transport to use?

(b) Should the UK government permit heavier goods vehicles to be driven on UK roads?

Activity 4

(a) Explain what is meant by deregulation in transport.

(b) Has deregulation in the airline industry increased economic efficiency?

Activity 5

(a) How would a cost-benefit analysis on a major new airport be carried out?

(b) Should a new London airport be built?

Activity 6

(a) What is meant by a 'natural monopoly'?

(b) Should the railways be re-nationalised?

Q1 Answer the following question.

Women graduates still suffer pay gap

Women graduates are paid 15 per cent less than their male counterparts at the start of their working lives and more than 30 per cent less by the time they reach their fifties, a survey reveals today.

The widening gap in pay was condemned by the Equal Opportunities Commission (EOC), which said employers were still ignoring equal pay legislation and recruiting women 'on the cheap'.

Research for the EOC shows that male college-leavers earn an average of £16,738 by the age of 24, compared with an average salary of £14,592 for female graduates.

At 37, men with degrees can expect to earn £32,555, compared with an average salary of £23,630 for women.

By their fifties, the average male graduate can expect to earn £38,153, which is £11,604 more a year than his female counterpart.

Julie Mellor, chairwomen of the EOC, warned that employers with a complacent attitude were in danger of losing the best recruits.

More than 30 years after the Equal Pay Act of 1970, there is still an 18 per cent pay gap between male and female earnings. To tackle the divide, the EOC has urged big employers to carry out pay reviews so disparities over pay scales, promotion prospects and bonuses can be put right.

Source: 'Women graduates still suffer pay gap' by Lorna Duckworth, *The Independent*, 8/3/02, Page 10.

1 (a) (i) Define discrimination.   (2)

     (ii) Identify, from the passage, three forms of labour market discrimination.   (3)

 (b) (i) Calculate the pay differential between male and female graduates aged 37.   (2)

     (ii) Explain why graduates are paid more than non-graduates.   (3)

 (c) Explain why employers who discriminate are likely to be at a disadvantage compared with those who do not.   (4)

 (d) Discuss whether the pay gap between male and female employees is likely to widen or narrow in the next ten years.   (6)

Select one of the following essay questions:

2 (a) Explain what factors influence the occupational and geographical mobility of labour.   (10)

 (b) Discuss to what extent unemployment is caused by labour market failure.   (15)

3 (a) Explain why trade union membership in the UK declined from 1993 to 2003.   (10)

 (b) Discuss the effect trade unions have on the efficiency of labour markets.   (15)

4 (a) Explain the possible effects on an economy of hosting the Olympic Games. (10)

(b) Discuss whether some public funding should be switched from subsidising ballet and theatre productions to subsidising the building of major sports arenas. (15)

Transport economics

Q1 Answer the following question.

Motorways in tunnels 'will ease congestion'

A thousand miles of new motorways and dual carriage-ways will be needed over the next 30 years to cope with rising traffic levels, a study has found.

The new roads would fill 25 square miles of countryside and require road-building on the scale of the 1970s expansion of the motorways.

A quarter of the total length would need to be built in tunnels to preserve the most environmentally sensitive areas. The RAC commissioned the report from Halcrow consultants which found that traffic, on present trends, would increase by 46 per cent by 2031.

A separate study by Traffic-master, the congestion-monitoring company, found that car journey times had increased by 16.5 per cent on a sample of key routes since 1998.

Table 1 Increase in journey times across the country

Journey	1998 Time	2002 Time
London to Leeds	2 hours 43 mins	3 hours 6 mins
Birmingham to Bristol	1 hour 30 mins	1 hour 42 mins
Manchester to Liverpool	28 mins	33 mins
Oxford to Southampton	1 hour 4 mins	1 hour 14 mins
Cambridge to Ipswich	47 mins	56 mins

The roads proposed in the RAC report would cost £70 billion and require the government to increase its annual spending on new roads by 50 per cent to £2.4 billion. The report states that 500 miles of new motorways and another 500 miles of trunk roads will be needed to prevent congestion from spreading across the country. In addition, 800 miles of existing motorways and trunk roads would need to be widened.

The proposals go far beyond the government's ten year transport plan, which includes 40 major new roads and 360 miles of widening.

An RAC spokesman denied that it was withdrawing its support for tolls, but added that they could only ever be one part of the solution to congestion.

New roads were urgently needed to accommodate the explosion in car ownership, with 24 million cars registered last year, a rise of 700,000 on the previous year.

Source: 'Motorways in tunnels 'will ease congestion' by Ben Webster, *The Times*, 26/11/02, page 14.

(a) (i) Define congestion. (2)
(ii) From the table, identify which route has experienced the
greatest increase in congestion. Explain your answer. (2)
(b) (i) Explain two positive externalities that could arise from
building more roads. (4)
(ii) Identify two ways that extra government spending on roads
could be financed. (2)
(c) (i) Describe two causes of the increase in car ownership. (4)
(ii) Comment on the possible effectiveness of two measures
designed to reduce congestion that are mentioned in the extract. (6)

Select one of the following essay questions:

2 (a) Explain the external costs caused by traffic congestion. (10)
(b) Discuss how you would assess whether the introduction of road
pricing has proved to be successful. (15)

3 (a) Explain the characteristics of a contestable market. (10)
(b) Discuss the extent to which the market for bus travel is a
contestable market. (15)

4 (a) Explain what is meant by a sustainable transport policy. (10)
(b) Discuss the extent to which the government's transport policy
is a sustainable one. (15)

Exam guidance

You need to allocate your time carefully on this paper. You should devote approximately 45 minutes to answering the data response question and the same amount of time to answering the essay question.

Most candidates choose to tackle the data response question first. Remember that the data response question parts are arranged in a logical order and, to a large extent, in an increasing skill order. This means that while you can answer the question parts in any order, it is best to answer them in the order they are asked. The penultimate question part requires you to analyse and the last question part to evaluate. Deducting the time it will take you to read the data and the question parts, this will give you about two minutes per mark. This means that you should, for example, spend approximately twelve minutes on the last question part.

Your choice of essay question is important. Make sure you can answer both question part (a) and question part (b) well. Before starting to write your answer, think through the questions carefully and make a brief plan. The second question part requires most thought. In both cases you should write a sentence or two answering the question directly. Then you should provide analysis and evaluation to support your opening statements.

Economics of work and leisure

Data response paper

1   (a) (i) A straightforward question, testing knowledge and understanding. Remember discrimination is treating one group differently from other groups.
    (ii) This part of the question tests application. The information needed to answer it comes from the last sentence of the passage. This indicates that women suffer labour market discrimination in the form of lower pay, lower bonuses and less chance of gaining promotion.

   (b) (i) There is usually one question part on the paper requiring you to undertake a calculation. In this case the difference in pay is £8,925 or 37.77%.
    (ii) To gain full marks here you need to analyse. It would be useful to draw diagrams showing the markets for graduates and non-graduates. These should reflect the different levels, and elasticities, of demand and supply. In your written explanation of the level of demand do not forget to cover differences in marginal revenue productivity.

   (c) This question part also requires you to analyse. You need to consider how engaging in discrimination is likely to affect an employer's cost of production, her output, the price she charges, her revenue and profits. Again it would be useful to draw a diagram to aid your analysis.

(d) Most economists think that the pay gap will narrow. You should apply demand and supply analysis and consider other influences on pay in your discussion. You need to discuss the extent to which the pay gap is likely to close.

Essay questions

2 (a) Analyse the factors, making sure you explain why and how these influence mobility. Do not forget to consider the influence of government policy.

(b) This is quite a demanding question. You need to assess how significant labour market failure is in causing unemployment and, by implication, the extent to which unemployment is the result of a failure of government policy.

3 (a) A straightforward first part. Analyse the causes, commenting on their significance.

(b) You should analyse both reasons why trade unions may increase the efficiency of labour markets and why they may not. Then you need to make an overall assessment based on your analysis.

4 (a) Analyse the possible effects on the balance of payments, unemployment, real GDP and inflation. It would be useful to consider both the short-run and long-run effects.

(b) An interesting question part. Discuss the arguments for and against including issues such as equity, information failure and externalities. Again, come to an overall conclusion supported by analysis.

Transport economics

Data response question

1 (a) (i) A relatively easy introductory question part. Congestion occurs when journeys take longer than expected.

(ii) A2 data response question papers often have an early question part which requires you to undertake a basic calculation. Here you can calculate the greatest increase in terms of the actual rise in journey time or the percentage rise. The greatest increase in minutes has occurred on the route from London to Leeds (23 minutes). In percentage terms it is the route from Manchester to Liverpool (17.86%).

(b) (i) Explain how the building of more roads may give rise to two beneficial effects on third parties.

(ii) Here you just have to state two ways e.g. tolls and road pricing via smart cards.

(c) (i) A straightforward question. Identify two causes and describe how they influence car ownership. For example, cars have positive income elasticity of demand and rising incomes have resulted in more households having a car and more households having more than one car.

(ii) Here you need to evaluate two measures. Assess the relative advantages and disadvantages of building new roads and new tolls.

Essay questions

2 (a) Explain what is meant by external costs. Analyse those, including pollution, blight and damage to buildings, caused by traffic congestion. It would be useful to include a diagram.

(b) Consider the objectives of road pricing. Then evaluate the advantages and limitations of its possible success. Mention that the overall assessment will depend on the relative social benefits and social costs.

3 (a) Analyse the key features of a contestable market, bringing out the benefits to consumers particularly in terms of efficiency.

(b) You need to assess the ways in which the market for bus travel matches the characteristics, behaviour and performance expected in a contestable market and the ways in which it does not. Having undertaken this analysis, you need to reach an overall conclusion on the extent to which it is a contestable market.

4 (a) Here you need to explain what features a government transport policy should possess for it be sustainable, You should consider the likely level of future transport needs, the most appropriate modes and the appropriate policies.

(b) Assess whether the government's transport policies are likely to meet not only the current population's transport needs but also future population's needs. Evaluate the balance between the different modes of transport, infrastructure needs and other policies which have an impact on transport demand e.g. the siting of new schools.

PART 5/A2

The UK economy and economic development

The UK economy and economic development – an overview

Introduction

You will study one of these two options. Both build on your AS knowledge and understanding, particularly that gained from your study of the National and International Economy module.

Both modules require you to assess macroeconomic performance, the influences on macroeconomic performance, the key issues facing economies and economic policies. In both cases you will explore some topics, including measures of living standards and comparative advantage, and learn new concepts and theories – see spider diagrams.

Economics of development

The economic development option is often selected by those students who are also studying A2 geography. This can provide useful background information but it must remembered that it is an economics examination. If you are also a geography student you must make sure that you are answering from an economic perspective.

Economic development is a controversial and vital area of economic study. The challenge is not just that economists can differ radically in their views but that it addresses issues vital to the majority of people alive today. In 2003 it was estimated that:

■ 840 million people in the world are malnourished
■ hunger kills six million children a year
■ 36 million people in sub-Saharan Africa are living with AIDS.

The UK economy

The risk with this module is that you may think that the knowledge and understanding you gained on the AS module The National and International Economy is sufficient. It is not. You must explore the topics in more depth, master new concepts and theories and develop your analytical and evaluative skills.

It is, nevertheless, an important and fascinating area of study. You will explore some of the key issues facing the economy in which you live. These include:

■ are living standards improving
■ is there still a conflict between reducing unemployment and inflation
■ is the value of the pound too high?

The examination

As with the microeconomic papers these modules are assessed in a $1\frac{1}{2}$ hour paper. The examination counts for 15 per cent of the total A level marks. It consists of a data response question and one structured essay question chosen from three.

Maximising your grade

You can do well in this module if you:

- keep up-to-date
- appreciate the links between economies
- apply relevant economic concepts and theories in analysing macroeconomic issues
- make judgements about the causes, consequences and remedies to economic problems
- write clearly.

You need to know how to interpret trends in data and to assess information critically and to decide on appropriate economic problems.

You must select the essay question carefully. Make sure that you can do well on both parts of the question. As with the microeconomic questions, the first part will require you to analyse and the second part to both analyse and evaluate. Answer the question directly, supporting your answer with relevant economic theory, awareness of recent events and well-supported evaluative comments.

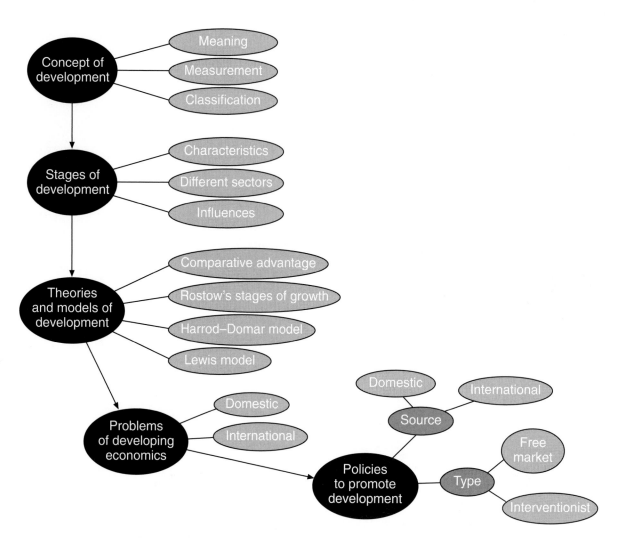

Economics of development

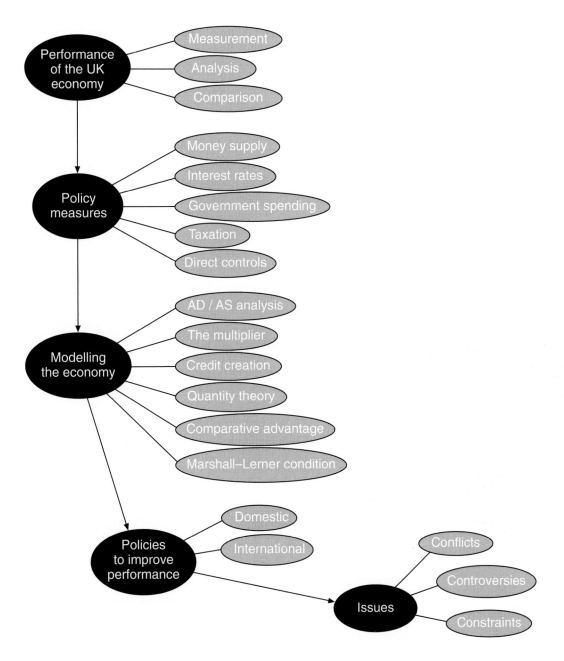

The UK economy

Measurement and analysis of economic performance

5.1

Synoptic link

In the AS course you covered the key indicators of economic performance. Before starting this section it would be useful to refresh your understanding of AS Sections 3.3, 3.4, 3.5 and 3.6.

Introduction

A key role of economists is to measure and analyse economic performance. In assessing economic performance, it is possible to examine a range of key indicators. Care, though, has to be taken in interpreting economic data.

Key indicators

Among the key indicators of macroeconomic performance are the economic growth rate, the inflation rate, the unemployment rate and the balance of payments position. A sign of a healthy economy is a stable, sustainable economic growth rate, which matches a good trend growth rate. A stable economic growth rate is one which is steady and not fluctuating. A sustainable one is one that can be achieved without threatening future generations' ability to enjoy higher output. The trend growth rate is the increase in productive capacity. If the economic growth rate is higher than this (i.e. actual output is greater than potential output) there is an output gap and it will not be possible to continue to grow at this rate. If the economic growth rate is below the trend growth rate there will again be an output gap, this time one that reflects the fact that some resources are not being used – the economy is operating inside its production possibility frontier and below full capacity.

Governments also aim for what they call price stability. This actually refers to a low and stable inflation rate. In the UK, the government is intending to set the Bank of England the target of achieving an inflation rate of 2 per cent as measured by HICP. It is thought that this rate will avoid most of the significant costs of inflation including loss of international price competitiveness.

The lowest rate of unemployment a government can achieve is described as full employment. This is thought to be an unemployment rate of 3 per cent. There will always be some unemployment of a frictional nature.

Governments usually aim for a current account balance in the long run although they will be less concerned about any deficits which are likely to be self correcting, for example a deficit arising from the import of raw materials that will be converted into finished products, some of which can be exported. They may also not be too concerned if a current account deficit is covered by an inflow of FDI.

There are also other indicators of the macroeconomic performance of an economy, most of which tend to influence the best-known indicators. These include, for instance, productivity and net investment. A high rate of productivity growth would indicate an improving economic performance as it will cause a reduction in average costs, thereby reducing inflationary pressure and increasing international competitiveness. Net investment (extra capital goods) would indicate that the economy is expanding and should be experiencing rising productivity and falling average costs.

Trends and comparison

In analysing a country's economic performance, it is important to consider trends over time and to make international comparisons. The economy's performance can also be measured against the government's objectives. An unemployment rate of 6 per cent, for instance, which has fallen consistently from 10 per cent in recent years indicates a better current economic performance than a 6 per cent rate which has risen from 3 per cent over the same period.

An economic growth rate of 1 per cent would be low in historical terms for the UK. However, if this is above that of other industrialised economies, some of which may be experiencing a recession, it may indicate that the UK is coping better with a world economic downturn than most.

The current UK government is seeking, among a range of objectives, to raise productivity and to achieve a low and stable inflation rate. Falling productivity and a high and fluctuating inflation rate would indicate that the government is not achieving its objectives. Economists would seek to analyse why the government has been unsuccessful. Among the factors they would consider would be the appropriateness of the economic policies pursued and whether the economy has been thrown off course by external shocks.

Interpreting data

In comparing the UK's and US's economic performance (Table 1 and Table 2, page 296) a number of points can be made. One is that while the USA has a higher average economic growth rate than the UK, 2.6 per cent compared to 2.3 per cent, the UK has a more stable economic growth rate. In 2001, the US economy came very close to experiencing a recession. Neither government is likely to have been satisfied with its economic growth performance. The UK government would have been concerned that its economic growth rate was below its trend economic growth rate in four of the five years, although of course during this period there was a global downturn. The US government would have been worried that its economic growth rate had fluctuated from a high 4.1 per cent to a low of 0.2 per cent.

The 2003 figure for not only the economic growth rate, but also for inflation, unemployment and the current account balance, has to be treated with caution. This is because the figure is a forecasted one. Economists seek to make their forecasts as accurate as possible but due to unforeseen events or shortcomings of the economic model used, the actual figure may have differed from the forecasted one.

The data indicates that the UK experienced a lower inflation rate than the US during this period. However, the US economy actually appears to have performed better in terms of inflation. This is because the UK's figures are very low. They suggest that the UK was coming close to experiencing deflation, with the risk that output could fall as consumers and producers postpone some of their purchases in anticipation of lower prices in the future.

Table 1: UK's economic performance 1999-2003

| | Economic growth rate | Inflation rate | Unemployment rate | Current balance | | % change in productivity |
				$bn	% of GDP	
1999	2.4	1.6	4.1	-32	-2.2	0.9
2000	3.1	0.7	3.6	-29	-2.0	1.7
2001	2.1	0.9	3.2	-18	-1.3	1.3
2002	1.8	0.9	3.1	-13	-0.8	1.6
2003	2.2	1.8	3.2	N/A	-1.2	N/A

Table 2: US economic performance 1999-2003

| | Economic growth rate | Inflation rate | Unemployment rate | Current balance | | % change in productivity |
				$bn	% of GDP	
1999	4.1	1.6	4.2	-293	-3.2	2.5
2000	3.7	2.6	4.0	-410	-4.2	1.3
2001	0.2	2.0	4.8	-393	-3.9	0.4
2002	2.5	1.4	5.8	-503	-4.8	2.8
2003	2.5	2.0	5.7	N/A	-4.8	N/A

Again, though, caution has to be applied in interpreting the inflation figures. This is because the tables do not show what measure of inflation was used. The strength of any comparison would be weakened if the inflation figures for the two countries are based on different measures. In fact, both sets of figures are based on a measure known as the private consumption deflator, an index of consumer prices.

The same caution has to be applied when considering the unemployment data as different measures might have been used. However, they are, again, the same measure, a standardised measure of unemployment. In this case, the UK appears to have a better performance than the USA. In every year it had a lower unemployment rate than the US. It starts off with a similar unemployment rate, a difference of only 0.1 per cent points, but ends up with a forecasted unemployment rate of 2.5 per cent points lower. No clear trade off is shown by the inflation and unemployment figures.

It is much more revealing to compare unemployment rates than figures showing the number of people unemployed in each country. This is because, even if the US had a much better unemployment record than the

Research task

Research the trends in the UK's economic performance over the last decade.

UK, it would have a higher number of people unemployed as it is a much larger economy.

For the same reason, when comparing the current account performance of the two countries, it is more appropriate to use the current balance expressed as a percentage of GDP than the total figure. On this basis, the UK did have a lower current account deficit than the US. Both countries had a deficit throughout the period. The UK's deficit is lower at the end of the period than at the start while the US's is larger. Of course, without more information, we do not know what has caused the deficit.

The US has a higher rate of productivity growth in each year except 2001. The UK's figures are relatively low and disappointing. The tables do not show what the source of the data is. It has actually been taken from the National Institute Economic Review, a very reliable source.

The UK's recent economic performance

Over the decade 1993-2003, the UK's economic performance has been relatively good. In contrast with the 1980s and 1970s, our economic growth rate has been higher and more stable than most industrialised countries, with the exception of the USA. Inflation has been low and stable, averaging 2.5 per cent over the last ten years and unemployment has fallen virtually to the full employment level.

Some economists have attributed this improved performance to the supply-side reforms of the 1980s, including tax cuts which have increased incentives, and the improved the macroeconomic policy framework of the last ten years. This improved framework includes an independent Bank of England operating with an inflation target and fiscal rules that limit government borrowing.

However, concerns still exist about the UK's slow growth in productivity and internationally relatively low levels of net investment.

Quick check

1 What are the key indicators of economic performance?
2 What is the government's aim for inflation?
3 What constitutes a good economic performance?
4 In assessing the relative economic performance of two countries, which is the more appropriate measure, the unemployment rate or the numbers unemployed?

Synoptic link

This section builds on the understanding you gained in AS Section 3.3 on economic growth.

Thinking like an economist

Explain how increases in healthcare may contribute to economic growth.

Introduction

It is not easy to measure living standards as it is difficult to assess what constitutes a good quality of life. One of the best-known indicators of living standards of residents of different countries is real GDP but there is also a range of other indicators.

Living standards and real GDP

Increases in real GDP are usually associated with increases in living standards. When output rises there are more goods and services for people to enjoy. Economic growth also tends to be associated with reduced levels of absolute poverty, reduced water pollution, improved education and increases in life expectancy. In turn, improvements in health, education and environmental standards can contribute to economic growth.

For the 2.4 billion people who live on less than $2 a day, it is fairly clear that a rise in incomes is needed to improve their lives. In many industrialised countries, however, the quality of people's lives does not always seem to rise in line with real GDP. This is for a number of reasons including that high living standards require more than money.

Changes in real GDP and living standards

There are a number of reasons why an increase in real GDP may not raise living standards. One problem of interpretation that economists can eliminate is that a rise in output may be exceeded by a rise in population. If there is, for example, 4 per cent more output and 7 per cent more people to share the output between, on average each person will be worse off. So what economists often assess is real GDP per head (or per capita). This is found by dividing real GDP by population.

However, there are other problems involved in comparing a country's real GDP over time and between countries. One is the existence of the unofficial (or hidden) economy. This term covers undeclared economic activity. The output of a country is likely to be higher than its official real GDP figure suggests. Some people selling goods and services may not include all the money they have earned on tax returns, and those engaged in illegal activities such as selling non-prescribed drugs, will not be declaring any of their income from such activities. The size of the unofficial economy is influenced by social attitudes to tax evasion, penalties involved, the risk of being caught out, tax rates and the range of activities that are declared illegal. For example, in a country with high marginal tax rates the size of the unofficial economy may be high.

It is also not just the size of the real GDP and its increase which are significant. What is also important in deciding how the level and changes in real GDP affect people's living standards is the composition of real GDP. If more is produced but the extra output consists of capital goods, people will not immediately feel better off although they will in the long run. If the rise in real GDP has been accounted for by increasing the police service to match rising crime people may actually feel worse off.

A rise in real GDP may not benefit much of the population if income is very unevenly distributed. Economists use a variety of methods to measure the distribution of income and wealth including deciles, quintiles, Lorenz curves, and the Gini coefficient (see Work and leisure, Section 4.14). Figure 1 shows the degree of income inequality in the UK in 1999–2000.

Higher output may also result in people feeling the quality of their lives has not improved if they are working longer hours or working under worse conditions. These are factors that the official figures do not take into account.

The official figures also do not include positive and negative externalities. So, for example, if pollution rises, real GDP does not fall even though people will experience a lower quality of life. Indeed if measures have to be taken to cope with the higher pollution such as extra cleaning, real GDP will rise.

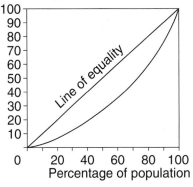

Figure 1: UK income distribution 1999-2000

Quality of life indicators

In 1998, the Labour Government introduced a series of thirteen new headline main indicators, covering 120 separate categories. These allow the government's performance to be judged not only by economic growth rates but also by the effect of policies on the environment and social welfare.

The thirteen indicators are:
- economic growth
- social investment, for example investment in buses, hospitals and schools
- employment
- health including life expectancy
- education and training
- housing quality
- climate change
- air pollution
- transport
- water quality
- wildlife
- land use
- waste.

Measurable Economic Welfare (MEW)

MEW starts with real GDP figures but then adjusts them by adding a value for leisure, positive externalities and other items which are currently not included but which make a positive contribution to people's well-being. It deducts regrettables such as defence spending, police services and other items which are included but which may not contribute to the quality of people's lives. It also reduces GDP figures to take account of negative externalities.

Human Development Index

This is a measure of the quality of people's lives, in the form of human development, first published by the United Nations in 1990. It takes into account longevity, knowledge and 'a decent standard of living' and is measured by life expectancy, educational achievement and real, per capita GDP.

Table 1: The 2000 HDI top twenty rankings

1	Norway
2	Sweden
3	Canada
4	Belgium
5	Australia
6	United States
7	Iceland
8	Netherlands
9	Japan
10	Finland
11	Switzerland
12	France
13	United Kingdom
14	Denmark
15	Austria
16	Luxembourg
17	Germany
18	Ireland
19	New Zealand
20	Italy

The Human Poverty Index

This measures how progress is distributed in a country and takes into account the proportion of people who are left behind; the extent of deprivation.

HPI-1

This measures poverty in developing countries. It takes into account:
- the percentage of people expected to die before the age of 40
- the percentage of adults who are illiterate
- the percentage of people without access to health services and safe water
- the percentage of underweight children under 5.

Table 2: HPI-1: lowest ten countries 1999 (starting with the lowest)

1	Sierra Leone
2	Niger
3	Burundi
4	Burkina Faso
5	Ethiopia
6	Mozambique
7	Guinea-Bissau
8	Chad
9	Central African Republic
10	Mali

HPI-2

This measures poverty in rich, industrial countries and accepts that human deprivation varies with the social and economic conditions of the country. It takes into account:
- the percentage of people likely to die before the age of 60
- the percentage of people whose ability to read and write is far from adequate
- the percentage of people with disposable income of less than 50 per cent of the median
- the percentage of long-term unemployed (twelve months or more).

Life survey indicators

Surveys are now undertaken to assess what proportion of people are satisfied with life. In a survey of the EU fifteen conducted in 2003, the UK came sixth. There was some correlation between happiness and income levels as Denmark and Sweden, two of the riches countries, came top while Portugal and Greece, the poorest two, were at the bottom. It was, however, not a perfect fit with the relatively rich countries of France and Germany coming quite low down. What has also been found is that experiencing a divorce, feeling in poor health, lacking job security and fearing crime are significant factors in reducing the quality of some people's lives.

Quick check

1 Identify two reasons why an increase in real GDP per head may not result in an increase in most people's living standards.
2 Distinguish between GDP and HPI.
3 What effect are mobile phones having on the quality of people's lives?
4 Explain the possible effect an increase in car production will have on real GDP and living standards.

Puzzler

UK citizens are richer today than ten years ago, but are they happier?

Introduction

Interest rates play a significant role in the economy. They influence consumption, investment and production decisions and are used by the monetary authorities to influence economic activity. At any one time there is a whole range of interest rates. Economists frequently talk about the rate of interest as interest rates tend to move in the same direction. There are two main theories that seek to explain how the rate of interest is determined.

The role of interest rates

The rate of interest is a reward for forgoing current liquidity and so consumption. It encourages those people and firms that have more money than they currently want to use, to lend it to those who want to borrow. It directs money to where it is most demanded, as indicated by the offer of a higher rate of interest.

Different interest rates

Among the vast range of interest rates are the rate of interest paid on a National Savings Account, the rate of interest charged on a mortgage loan, the rate of interest paid to someone with a building society deposit account and the rate of interest charged by a finance company.

Banks and other financial institutions act as financial intermediaries, transferring money from those with excess funds to those in need of funds. They make a profit by charging borrowers a higher rate of interest than they pay to savers.

The rate of interest paid to lenders is influenced by two key factors. One is the perceived level of risk. For example, the rate of interest charged on a loan to the government or a well-known, reliable firm with a good track record is likely to be lower than charged on a loan to a newly-established firm. The other key influence is the length of time of the loan. Generally, interest rates are lower on short-term loans than on long-term loans. This is because long-term loans involve more risk and more sacrifice.

Determination of interest rates

There are two main theories that explain how interest rates are determined. These are the **loanable funds theory** and the **liquidity preference theory**. Both focus on the interaction of demand and supply, but they differ in terms of what the demand and supply is of that determines the rate of interest.

Synoptic link

The influence of interest rates on consumption and investment was touched on in AS Section 3.8 and its role as a monetary policy instrument was discussed in AS Section 3.15.

Definitions

Loanable funds theory: the view that the rate of interest is determined by the demand and supply of loanable funds.
Liquidity preference theory: the view that the rate of interest is determined by the demand and supply of money.

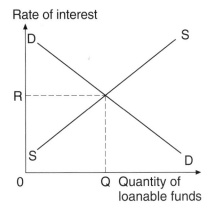

Rate of interest

Figure 1: The determination of the rate of interest according to the loanable funds theory

Thinking like an economist

Analyse the likely effect a rise in saving would have on aggregate demand, output and employment.

Loanable funds theory

The loanable funds theory states that interest rates are determined by the demand for loanable funds and the supply of loanable funds as shown in Figure 1.

The demand for loanable funds comes from a number of sources including firms wishing to invest. Firms are likely to want to invest if they think that the rate of return from capital (referred to as the marginal efficiency of capital or the marginal efficiency of investment) exceeds the rate of interest. The supply of loanable funds comes from saving.

The loanable funds theory suggests that a rise in the rate of interest will cause an extension in the supply of loanable funds and a contraction in the demand for loanable funds. A higher rate of interest will increase the reward for saving but will also increase the price of borrowing and raise the opportunity cost of investment. The theory also suggests that the rate of interest will fall if savings increase or investment decreases. This led its supporters to advocate a rise in savings during the depression of the 1920s and 1930s. The thinking was that more savings would increase the supply of loanable funds, lower the rate of interest and encourage investment.

Keynes argued that the economists were following an incorrect theory and that by encouraging saving, and thereby discouraging spending, they made the depression worse. He developed the liquidity preference theory.

The liquidity preference theory

In contrast to the loanable funds theory, the liquidity preference theory argues that the rate of interest is determined by the demand and supply of money. The demand to hold wealth in a money form (notes, coins, current (sight) bank and building society accounts) he called liquidity preference. The demand, he claimed, comes from three motives. The first two motives are largely interest inelastic. These are the transactions and precautionary motives. Households and firms keep money in order to make purchases (transactions motive) and keep some extra money in order to meet unexpected expenses and to take advantage of unexpected bargains (precautionary motive). The third motive for holding money, the speculative motive, is one that is interest elastic and applies mostly to those who deal in financial markets. These people will hold money when the price of bonds is high (and so the rate of interest is low) and expected to fall. This is because buying bonds now may result in a financial loss and because the opportunity cost of holding money is low.

The supply of money is largely determined by the central bank and can be assumed to perfectly inelastic in the short run. A decrease in the rate of interest may be caused by an increase in the money supply or a decrease in the demand for money. Figure 2 shows the money supply increasing from M to M1, which causes the rate of interest to fall from R to R1.

When the rate of interest reaches very low levels, there is a risk that the economy may experience a **liquidity trap**. This is a situation where it becomes very difficult to lower the rate of interest. This is because any increase in the money supply will be held. Speculators, seeing that interest rates are low (and the price of government bonds is high), will not want to buy bonds now as they will expect the price of bonds to fall in the future. So they hold any extra money and demand for money becomes perfectly elastic. Any increase in the money supply will now have no effect on the rate of interest. Figure 3 shows that a rise in the money supply leaves the rate of interest at R.

Quick check

1   Why do short-term interest rates tend to be lower than long-term interest rates?
2   According to the loanable funds theory, what determines the rate of interest?
3   What are the three motives for holding wealth in a liquid form?
4   What effect is an increase in the money supply likely to have on the rate of interest?

Puzzler

Why do you think Japan experienced a liquidity trap in the early 2000s?

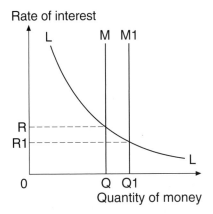

Figure 2: The effect of an increase in the money supply

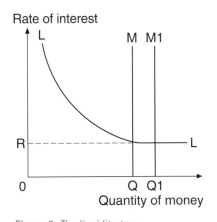

Figure 3: The liquidity trap

Thinking like an economist

Analyse the likely effect of lower cost, more comprehensive insurance on the precautionary motive, liquidity preference and the rate of interest.

Determination of exchange rates

Synoptic link

This section draws on the knowledge you gained in AS Section 3.15. Before starting this section, check your understanding of interest rate and exchange rate changes.

Introduction

The exchange rate is the price of a currency in terms of another currency or currencies. For example, the sterling effective exchange rate is the value of the pound in terms of a weighted basket of currencies, weighted according to their importance in the UK's pattern of trade.

A country or area may operate a freely floating exchange rate system or its government may intervene to influence or fix the exchange rate. These different exchange rate systems have both advantages and disadvantages.

Determination of exchange rates

A fixed rate is one that is determined by the government. It is likely to set the exchange rate at a value that it thinks is close to its long-run equilibrium level since it will be difficult to sustain any other level. If market forces do threaten to move from its set rate, the government will intervene. For example, if demand for the currency is falling, the government will either demand some of the currency itself (paying in foreign currencies) and/or will seek to generate private sector demand by raising the domestic rate of interest.

A floating exchange rate is one that is determined by the market forces of demand and supply. If demand for the currency rises this will raise the exchange rate whereas if the supply of the currency increases, the exchange rate will fall in value.

A managed exchange rate is effectively a combination of a floating and fixed exchange rate. The exchange rate is largely allowed to be determined by market forces but the government will intervene to affect its value if it thinks the rate is in danger of falling too low, rising too high or is fluctuating too much. In the UK's case, the Bank of England will make use of its exchange equalisation account if it is considered necessary to influence the value of the pound sterling. This is the account in which the Bank of England keeps its foreign currency reserves.

Factors affecting exchange rates

A number of factors influence the value of a floating exchange rate and put upward or downward pressure on a fixed and managed exchange rate.

The demand for pounds is likely to be high and the supply is likely to be low if UK products are internationally competitive. If UK goods and services are of a good quality and are price competitive, foreigners demand for pounds will be high and the supply of pounds will be low as demand for imports will be relatively low. Among the key factors that influence international competitiveness are labour productivity, investment and relative inflation rates.

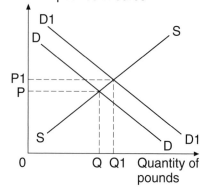

Figure 1: The effect of an increase in demand for pounds

The exchange rate is also influenced by incomes at home and abroad. If, for instance, incomes are rising abroad then foreigners are likely to buy more UK exports. This will increase demand for pounds and cause a rise in the value of the pound as shown in Figure 1.

Rising incomes at home may put downward pressure on the value of the pound. This is because UK's citizens tend to spend a higher proportion of their income on imports as their incomes rise and because firms tend to divert some of their products from the export market to the now more buoyant home market.

A rise in UK interest rates, perhaps implemented to reduce inflationary pressure, will be likely to increase demand for pounds. Foreigners will want to buy pounds in order to undertake short-term financial investment in the UK. **Hot money flows** are influenced not only by interest rate changes but also by expectations about the state of the economy, future interest rate changes and future exchange rate levels. Speculation now accounts for a high proportion of foreign exchange dealings and can have a significant influence on the value of a currency at any one time.

Speculators buy and sell currency, hoping to make a profit from movements in interest rates and exchange rates. Speculation can have a stabilising or a destabilising effect on exchange rates. If speculators respond to a falling exchange rate by selling some of their holdings of the currency, this will drive the rate down even further. However, if they think the rate will soon start to rise they will purchase the currency now thereby preventing a large fall. Speculation is something of a self-fulfilling principle – by their action speculators bring about what they expect to happen.

Pounds are also bought and sold by those wishing to undertake foreign direct investment. For instance, a Japanese firm will buy pounds if it wants to buy a UK car company. Foreign direct investment in the UK will be attracted by a strong UK economic performance, a flexible labour force and favourable government policies including regional development grants open to incoming foreign firms.

Advantages and disadvantages of a fixed exchange rate

The main advantage claimed for a fixed exchange rate is the certainty it provides to traders, investors and consumers. A firm buying raw materials from abroad will know how much it will have to pay in terms of foreign currency; a firm selling products abroad will know how much it will receive in terms of its own currency; investors will know the cost of and expected return from their investment; and consumers going on holiday abroad will know how much they will have to pay.

Another advantage claimed is that a fixed exchange rate imposes discipline on government policy. For example, if the country is experiencing inflation

Thinking like an economist

What effect is a favourable report on the future prospects of the UK economy by an international organisation likely to have on the value of the pound?

a government could not rely on the exchange rate falling to restore its international competitiveness, it would have to tackle the causes of the inflation.

To maintain the **parity**, however, other policy objectives may have to be sacrificed. For instance, if the exchange rate is under downward pressure, the government may raise its interest rate, which could slow down economic growth and cause a rise in unemployment.

There is also no guarantee that the parity set will be at the long-run equilibrium level. If it is set too high, this will put its firms at a competitive disadvantage since exports will be relatively high in price while its imports will be relatively low in price. In this case, the rate would not be sustainable and the value of the currency would have to be reduced. In addition, reserves of foreign currency have to be kept in case the central bank has to intervene to increase demand for the currency. This involves an opportunity cost – the foreign currency could be put to alternative uses.

Advantages and disadvantages of a floating exchange rate

Operating a floating exchange rate means that the exchange rate no longer becomes a policy objective. The government does not have to sacrifice other objectives and does not have to keep foreign currency to maintain it. Also, in theory, a floating exchange rate should move automatically to ensure a balance of payments equilibrium. For example, if demand for the country's exports fall, demand for the currency will fall and supply will rise. This will cause the exchange rate of fall, making exports cheaper and imports more expensive.

In practice, however, the exchange rate position is influenced not just by demand for exports and imports. A country may have a deficit on the current account of its balance of payments but speculation may actually lead to a rise in the exchange rate.

A floating exchange rate can create uncertainty, with traders and investors being unsure how much the currency will be worth in the future. Some may seek to offset this uncertainty by agreeing a price in advance but this involves a cost. The degree of uncertainty will be influenced by the extent of fluctuations in the currency.

Quick check

1 Identify three factors that could cause a fall in a country's exchange rate.
2 Distinguish between a fixed and a floating exchange rate.
3 Explain why operating a fixed exchange rate involves an opportunity cost.
4 Why may a floating exchange rate create uncertainty?

Introduction

Taxes have a significant impact on households, firms and the economy as a whole. In assessing this impact, it is important to consider the types of taxes imposed, the qualities of a good tax and the relative merits of direct and indirect taxes.

Types of taxes

Most tax revenue in the UK comes from income tax, followed by value added tax (VAT). Income tax is a direct and progressive tax – as income rises both the amount and the percentage that a person pays in tax rises. VAT is an indirect and largely regressive tax. It is imposed on the sale of goods and services at different rates. The standard rate is 17.5 per cent but a few items, including sanitary protection, are taxed at 5 per cent. Some products such as most foods, children's clothing, prescription medicines, books and newspapers are zero-rated. This means that the firms selling the products cannot charge VAT but can reclaim any VAT paid on their inputs. Others, including education, finance and health services, are VAT exempt. In this case the firms do not charge VAT but cannot claim back any VAT they have paid.

Other taxes include excise duty, capital gains tax and inheritance tax. Excise duty is an indirect tax imposed on specific products. The main products it is imposed on are alcohol, petrol and tobacco. The rate varies depending on the product. Capital gains tax is a tax on the increase in the value (difference between purchase and selling price) on items such as shares, second homes and paintings. A large number of assets are exempt, including agricultural property, private motor cars and winnings from gambling. Inheritance tax is a tax on transfers of wealth above a certain amount.

Qualities of a good tax

Four qualities of a good tax were identified by Adam Smith, author of the *Wealth of Nations* published in 1776. He argued that a good tax should be equitable, certain, convenient and economical.

Equitable: This means that the amount of tax that a person or firm pays should be fair. Economists now discuss horizontal and vertical equity. Horizontal equity occurs when people or firms with the same income and financial circumstances pay the same amount of tax. Vertical equity occurs when the amount that people and firms pay is based on their ability to pay, so that people with high incomes pay more than those with low incomes. Some economists argue that taxes should be based not on the **ability to pay** principle but on the **benefit principle**. This latter suggests that people should pay taxes related to the benefit they receive from public expenditure. It would be relatively easy to apply this principle in connection with services that can be provided privately and which do not have significant

Synoptic link

This section draws on the knowledge and understanding you gained in AS Section 3.14.

Research task

Check details on the most recent budget to discover which tax rates have changed and why.

Definitions

Ability to pay principle: the rule that people with higher incomes should pay more in tax.
Benefit principle: the rule that the amount people pay in tax should be related to the benefit they derive from public expenditure.

externalities. It is more difficult to apply when it is hard to estimate who benefits and to what extent they benefit.

Certain: This means that it should be clear to people and firms how much tax they will have to pay.

Convenient: The tax should be easy for taxpayers to pay and for the government to collect.

Economical: An economical tax is one that, relative to the revenue raised, is cheap for people or firms to pay and for the government to collect.

Since Adam Smith's time economists have added two additional criteria – flexible and efficient.

Flexible: This means that it must be possible for the tax to be changed relatively quickly in the light of changing market conditions.

Efficient: An efficient tax is one that increases efficiency in markets. An example of an efficient tax is a Pigouvian tax (see Section 5.6).

Direct and indirect taxes

In the last two decades there has been a shift in the UK and other European Union (EU) countries from reliance on direct to indirect taxes. Income tax and corporation tax rates have been cut while VAT rates and excise duty have been raised. The main arguments for such a move are to reduce disincentive effects, reduce tax evasion and increase flexibility of fiscal policy. Some economists argue that high levels of income tax and corporation tax can act as a disincentive to effort and enterprise and entry into the labour force. If income tax rates are high, some workers may decide not to work overtime, some may decline promotion, some of the unemployed may decide they are better off on benefits and some economically inactive people may be discouraged from becoming economically active. The Laffer Curve suggests that a cut in higher tax rates may result in higher tax revenue on the grounds that incentives will increase and tax evasion will fall. High levels of corporation tax may discourage investment as it will reduce the funds available and the returns from investment.

Some economists, however, claim that the key influence on investment is changes in real GDP, that high income tax rates may encourage some people to work longer hours and take promotion in order to obtain what they regard as a reasonable level of disposable income, and that, even with high income tax rates, benefits may still be significantly below the disposable income that can be gained from paid employment.

Indirect taxes do tend to be easier to adjust than direct taxes and they are more difficult to evade as they are included in the price of products, although there is some evasion via the hidden economy.

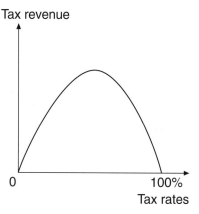

Exam hint

When considering the impact of taxation on fairness (equity), make sure you discuss both the ability to pay and the benefit principles.

Figure 1: The Laffer Curve

Both indirect and direct taxes help to regulate the economy as they both act as automatic stabilisers. Tax revenue from both sources rises during an economic boom and falls during a downturn, thus dampening down fluctuations in real GDP. However, direct taxes and indirect taxes have a different impact on the distribution of income. Direct taxes tend to be progressive and so redistribute income from the rich to the poor. Indirect taxes are largely regressive as they take a higher percentage from the income of the poor than of the rich. This is thought by some to be the main disadvantage of indirect taxes.

Hypothecated taxes

A **hypothecated tax** is one that is raised, or raised in part, for a specific purpose. So the revenue, or some of the revenue, is 'ring fenced'. In November 1999, the Chancellor of the Exchequer, Gordon Brown, announced that some of the revenue raised from tobacco duty would be earmarked for the National Health Service to spend directly on fighting smoking-related diseases. It was the first time that he had specifically earmarked revenue for public spending, although later that month he also said that any further increases in petrol and diesel duties will be devoted to spending on transport.

Benefits of hypothecation:
- gives consumers some choice
- can give some idea of how much people are prepared to pay for a particular service
- can be used to take money from those creating negative externalities and used to compensate those who suffer from the negative externalities.

Hypothecation, however, reduces the Chancellor's flexibility in changing tax revenue and government spending to influence economic activity. The revenue earned is also itself subject to changes in economic activity. It is debatable whether many people would want spending on the NHS to fall during a recession, for example. There is also the question of financing categories of government spending which are less popular than education and health and, if adopted on a large scale, the technical problems of aggregating individual preferences.

Definition

Hypothecated tax: a tax raised for a specific purpose.

Quick check

1. What effect would a shift from direct to indirect taxes be likely to have on the distribution of income?
2. What are the advantages and disadvantages of hypothecated taxes?
3. What are the qualities of a good tax?
4. Is income tax based on the ability to pay principle or the benefit principle?

Thinking like an economist

Analyse the arguments for and against cutting tax on wine.

Public expenditure

Synoptic link

This section again draws on the knowledge and understanding you gained in AS Section 3.14. Before starting this section, check your understanding of public expenditure (government spending).

Definition

Transfer payments: money transferred from one person or group to another not in return for any good or service.

Introduction

Changes in the level and distribution of public expenditure can have a significant impact on households, firms and the economy as a whole. Public expenditure compared with tax revenue gives the government's budget balance.

Forms of public expenditure

Public expenditure can also be referred to as government spending. It includes spending by both central and local government and public corporations. It can be divided into:

- capital expenditure – on hospitals, schools and roads etc.
- current spending – on the running of public services and includes teachers' pay and the purchase of medicines to be used in the NHS
- **transfer payments** – money transferred from tax payers to recipients of benefits, for example pensioners and the unemployed
- debt interest payments – payments made to the holders of government debt, for example holders of National Savings Certificates.

Capital and current expenditure are sometimes referred to as real or exhaustive expenditure as they make use of resources directly. When the government builds a new school it is paying for the use of the land, materials and other resources. On the other hand, transfer payments and debt interest are non-exhaustive forms of expenditure. In their case, the government is not buying the use of resources but enabling others to do so and it is the recipients of the benefits and interest that will determine the use of resources.

Forms of government spending

The four most important areas of government spending are social security payments, health, education and debt interest. The amount and proportion spent on different items is influenced by a number of factors. For example, spending on social security, while influenced by benefit rates, is much more significantly affected by economic activity. It rises during periods of increasing unemployment and falls during periods of falling unemployment.

Expenditure on health and education is affected by government priorities, government policies (for example the replacement of student grants with loans) and changes in the age composition of the population among other factors. The UK's ageing population is putting upward pressure on government spending.

Debt interest payments are affected by the level of government debt and the rate of interest. Spending on other categories is influenced by a number of factors. For instance, spending on defence rose in 2003 due to the Second Gulf War.

The Labour government has introduced a comprehensive spending review that decides on the amount that departments can spend over the next three years.

The effect of higher public expenditure financed by borrowing

It is generally thought that higher government spending will lead to a multiple increase in aggregate demand. New classical economists, however, argue that an increase in government spending financed by borrowing will not always cause aggregate demand and economic activity to increase. This is because they believe it can lead to crowding out. This means that the extra government spending does not add to total expenditure, it merely replaces some private sector spending. The thinking is that the higher borrowing used to finance the increased spending pushes up demand for scarce funds and thereby raises the rate of interest. The higher rate of interest discourages private sector consumption and investment. It may also cause a rise in the rate of exchange rate that will further reduce demand for the country's output.

Keynesians, however, argue that increased government spending can cause a rise in private sector spending – crowding in. They believe that higher government spending will encourage firms to increase their output, either because the government is buying directly from them or because the recipients of benefits will buy more from them. The higher incomes that arise will result in increased savings that can finance the borrowing.

The effect of higher public expenditure financed by higher taxation

It might be expected that higher government spending financed by taxation would have a neutral effect on aggregate demand. In practice this is rarely the case. This is because the recipients of government spending often spend a relatively high proportion of their disposable income, while taxpayers, especially high tax payers, tend to spend a lower proportion of their income. So higher public expenditure will tend to increase aggregate demand. If the economy is initially operating below its full capacity output, higher aggregate demand should raise output and employment. It may also have an inflationary impact if output rises close to full capacity.

Changes in the distribution of public expenditure

Even if the level of public expenditure does not change, the government can use its spending to influence economic activity and affect the distribution of income. Increased government spending on unemployment benefits and assistance to areas of high unemployment and decreased compensatory spending on higher education and on government offices based in

Thinking like an economist

Education and healthcare have positive income elasticity of demand. Explain what this means and its significance for the government's budget position.

prosperous areas is likely to make income more evenly distributed. It is also likely to increase aggregate demand as the poor spend more of their income than the rich. Of course, reduced government spending on higher education may have an adverse effect on aggregate supply and the economy's long-term economic prospects.

Some government benefits are what are known as universal benefits while others are means tested. Universal benefits are paid to everyone in a certain category, for example the basic state pension is paid to all those of retirement age. These benefits have the advantage that they are cheap to administer and they avoid the problem of poor take-up as there is no stigma attached to receiving them and complicated forms to do not have to be completed by the recipients. They can, however, be expensive and some who receive them do not really need them. In contrast, means-tested benefits are targeted to particular individuals. They are income related and are only paid to those who are considered to be in need of assistance, for example working families tax credit (WFTC). These can be relatively cheap in total but they are expensive to administer, often have a low take up and are frequently disliked by the recipients.

Fiscal policy and living standards

Changes in fiscal policy can alter the country's living standards by altering real GDP per capita. If the economy is operating below full capacity, an expansionary fiscal policy will be likely to raise real GDP per capita. Figure 1 shows the effect of an increase in government spending. The higher government spending raises aggregate demand, which in turn results in a rise in real GDP.

A cut in income tax, which raises disposable income and so consumption would also raise aggregate demand and GDP. Fiscal policy measures can also affect the extra items that are included in the composite measures of MEW and HDI. For example, taxes on polluting firms may reduce pollution and government spending on public transport may reduce congestion – both of which would improve MEW. Government spending on education and healthcare would raise real GDP. It would also increase living standards and the HDI if it results in improved education and increased life expectancy.

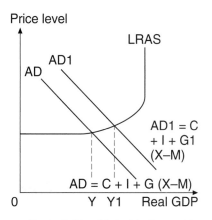

Figure 1: The effect of an increase in government spending

Hot potato

What effect would a reduction in child benefit and an increase in child tax credit have on the distribution of income?

Quick Check

1   Is government spending on road maintenance an example of exhaustive or non exhaustive government spending?
2   What factors influence government spending on education?
3   What effect would a cut in government spending and a cut in income tax have on aggregate demand?
4   When is a rise in government spending likely to be inflationary?

Introduction

The budget is presented annually by the Chancellor of the Exchequer, usually in March. To calculate the country's budget position, tax revenue and government spending are compared. A budget surplus arises when tax revenue exceeds government spending and a budget deficit occurs when government expenditure exceeds tax revenue. A budget deficit will increase demand in the economy as the government is injecting more spending into the economy than it is withdrawing from it.

The effect of a cut in income tax rates on the budget position

A cut in income tax rates will initially reduce government tax revenue. This will move an existing budget balance into deficit, an existing deficit to a larger deficit and a budget surplus to a smaller surplus, balance or deficit.

In the longer term, however, a cut in income tax may, for example, reduce a budget deficit. This is because it is likely to increase government tax revenue and reduce government spending on benefits. A cut in income tax will increase disposable income and the incentive to work. Higher disposable income is likely to raise consumption and so indirect tax revenue. The higher consumption and greater incentive is likely to result in a rise in output and employment and so higher direct tax revenue. Government spending on jobseekers' allowance, housing benefits and other benefits is likely to fall as employment and incomes rise.

Fiscal stance

Fiscal policy can have a significant impact on aggregate demand. Fiscal stance refers to whether the government is seeking to raise or lower aggregate demand through its fiscal policy measures. Discretionary fiscal policy covers fiscal policy measures that are used to influence aggregate demand – active demand management. A **reflationary** or expansionary policy is one that is increasing demand, whereas a **deflationary** or contractionary fiscal policy aims to reduce aggregate demand. It is, however, harder to assess a government's fiscal stance than might initially appear to be the case. A government may be trying to raise aggregate demand but may end up with a budget surplus. This is because the budget position is influenced not only by government policy but also by changes in the level of economic activity.

Figure 1 (see page 316) shows how tax revenue rises and government expenditure falls as real GDP rises. At income level X there is a cyclical deficit, at income level Y there is a balanced budget and at income level Z there is a cyclical surplus.

Synoptic link

This section draws on the knowledge and understanding of fiscal policy, the budget and aggregate demand you gained in Sections 3.14. 3.17 and 3.19, and in the previous A2 sections.

Definitions

Reflationary fiscal policy: increases in public expenditure and cuts in taxation designed to increase aggregate demand.

Deflationary fiscal policy: decreases in public expenditure and increases in taxation designed to decrease aggregate demand.

Tax revenue and government expenditure

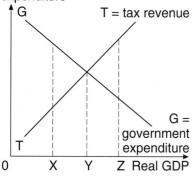

Figure 1: The effect of changes in economic activity on tax revenue and government spending

Budget position

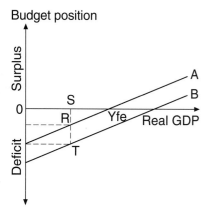

Figure 2: The full employment budget

A number of forms of government expenditure and taxation adjust automatically with economic activity to dampen down the fluctuations. These are referred to as automatic stabilisers. For example, spending on job seekers' allowance falls when economic activity picks up. Of course, some forms of government expenditure and taxation are not automatic stabilisers. For example, spending on child benefit is not linked to the economic cycle.

Full employment budget position

To try to assess how a budget's position is influenced by cyclical fluctuations, economists sometimes make use of the full employment budget concept. This plots the budget position that would occur taking into account only cyclical factors achieving a balanced position at full employment. This is shown in Figure 2 by line A. Then the government's actual budget position is plotted on line B. If GDP is at S, there is budget deficit of ST. Of this SR is the cyclical deficit component and RT is the structural deficit. A structural deficit arises from government policy on taxation and spending and is the result of government spending being too high relative to tax revenue over the whole economic cycle.

Reflationary and deflationary fiscal policy

A government may implement a reflationary fiscal policy by increasing public expenditure and cutting taxation during a recession. If the economy is overheating, the government may implement deflationary fiscal policy by reducing its level of spending and/or raising taxes. This, however, may not be that easy as households and firms get used to higher levels of government spending and do not like tax rises.

Seeking to influence the level of aggregate demand in the economy is sometimes referred to as demand management. Governments do this to create greater stability. They try to act counter-cyclically, injecting extra demand when private sector demand is thought to be too low and reducing its own demand when private sector demand is thought to be too high. In the past governments frequently engaged in fine-tuning. This involved short-term changes in government spending and/or taxation with the aim of achieving a precise level of aggregate demand. Governments, however, now accept that fiscal policy cannot be used so precisely. They may be said to engage in coarse-tuning. This involves less frequent changes in policy designed to move the economy in the right direction.

The Public Sector Net Borrowing

The Public Sector Net Borrowing (PSNB) is the amount a government needs to raise to cover a shortfall between its spending and its revenue. The main determinant of the PSNB position is the government's budget position. If the government has a budget deficit, with government expenditure exceeding tax revenue, there will be a positive PSNB. A negative PSNB means that revenue exceeds expenditure. This enables a government to repay past debt.

The funding of a PSNB

A PSNB can be funded from four main sources. The most commonly used source, usually accounting for at least 80 per cent of any PSNB, is borrowing from the non-bank private sector. The government, through the Bank of England, sells government bonds, national insurance certificates and other securities to insurance companies, other companies and the general public.

Another source is the banking sector. The government can sell government bonds and treasury bills to commercial banks and merchant banks. The government can always borrow from the Bank of England. In return for government securities, the Bank of England will provide the government with money to spend.

The least frequently used source of finance is borrowing from abroad with government securities being sold to foreign companies, banks and households.

The PSNB and the money supply

If a PSNB is financed by selling government bonds to the non-bank private sector, it will have no effect on the money supply. The government will be using existing money, which will be transferred from, for example, insurance companies to government departments. However, if it is financed by borrowing from the banking sector or from abroad, it will increase the money supply. Borrowing from the Bank of England is sometimes referred to as resorting to the printing press. The government will sell securities to the Bank of England. In return, its account held at the Bank of England will be credited, enabling it to spend more. Some of the money received will be paid into commercial banks enabling them to lend more and increase the money supply.

If the government borrows from the commercial banks it will, via the Bank of England, sell treasury bills. To pay for these the commercial banks will draw on their balances at the Bank of England. So the initial effect will be to replace one liquid asset, balances at the Bank of England, with another liquid asset, treasury bills. However, within a short space of time the recipients of government spending will pay some of the money they have received into banks. So the commercial banks will receive more deposits. This will increase their ability to lend and this may have a significant impact on the money supply.

Borrowing from abroad will again increase the money supply. The government may borrow sterling which was held abroad. If it borrows foreign currency this will be converted into sterling.

Definition

Public Sector Net Borrowing (PSNB): excess of public expenditure over revenue.

Exam hint

Be careful not to confuse a budget deficit and a balance of payments deficit.

However, in practice as noted above most government borrowing is usually financed by selling government securities to the non-bank private sector and so does not add to the money supply.

EU policy and member governments' budget positions

The EU influences member budget positions in a number of ways. The fundamental way is that all member countries are expected to avoid 'excessive' budget deficits.

The Stability and Growth Pact states that the medium-term objective for the budget positions of countries in the single currency should be close to balance or in surplus. Countries are allowed to react to normal cyclical fluctuations but are required to keep to the budget deficit limit of 3 per cent of GDP, except in exceptional circumstances.

Quick check

1   Distinguish between exhaustive and non-exhaustive government spending.
2   Identify three possible reasons why the government may increase its spending on health.
3   Why might higher government spending not increase aggregate demand?
4   Is housing benefit a universal or a means-tested benefit?
5   Explain two reasons why a government's budget position may move from a deficit into a surplus.
6   What is meant by crowding out?
7   Distinguish between a structural and a cyclical deficit.
8   Explain the relationship between the PSNB and the economic cycle.

Introduction

A government may use a range of methods of controlling the performance of the UK economy through direct controls such as minimum wages, import tariffs and quotas, retraining and relocation of labour, limits on public sector wage rises and discrimination legislation.

Minimum wages

The UK government introduced a National Minimum Wage (NMW) in 1997 (see Work and leisure, Section 4.12). Sixteen- and seventeen-year-olds were excluded to avoid them being priced out of the employment market. In July 2003, however, the government announced that it was planning to extend the law to this group in October 2004. The coverage of this law, which places a lower limit on hourly pay, will include sixteen- and seventeen-year-olds who have weekend or evening jobs, even if they are in full-time education.

Before the introduction of the NMW, fears were expressed that it would result in job losses. In practice this did not occur, and in July 2003, the government estimated that 1.3m people had benefited from its introduction.

Import tariffs and quotas

The UK government cannot impose import restrictions on its EU partners. Its ability to impose such restrictions on non-EU members is limited by its membership of the WTO. The UK government, though, may gain approval from the WTO to impose tariffs or quotas on products that are being 'dumped' in the UK or are coming from countries that employ child or slave labour. The UK has also participated in EU trade wars against the USA. Such trade wars tend to slow down economic growth in both areas as they distort comparative advantage.

Retraining of labour

The UK government has recognised that the demand for high-skilled workers is rising relative to low-skilled workers. This shift in demand is coming from the development of computer technology and information technology and increased competition from developing countries. Advances in computer technology are automating a range of operations undertaken by low-skilled workers and improvements in productivity in developing countries are reducing the need for low-skilled workers. At the same time, developments in information technology and the shift in comparative advantage are increasing demand for workers with high levels of IT, communication and social skills.

Direct controls
5.8

Synoptic link

There are a number of AS and A2 sections it would be useful to read over before starting this section. These are AS Sections 3.25 and 3.26 and A2 Sections 4.9, 4.12, and 4.15.

Thinking like an economist

Explain why extending the coverage of the NMW may actually reduce firms' labour costs.

The government takes a direct role in providing and promoting retraining of workers to meet this changing situation because it believes that if left to market forces there will be insufficient training provided. This labour market failure arises due to a lack of information and the existence of positive externalities (see Work and leisure, Section 4.9).

Relocation of labour

In a bid to reduce regional unemployment a government may encourage unemployed workers to move from depressed regions with high unemployment to more prosperous regions with job vacancies. It may seek to do this by providing information, relocation grants and subsidised housing. Such an approach is not without problems. Some of the unemployed may find it difficult to move because of social ties. Those who do move may cause the area from which they have departed to become more depressed. The exit of people from an area creates a downward multiplier effect with falling demand that may result in higher unemployment. The areas to which the people move may also experience problems since their entry will put increase pressure on the areas' social capital.

Limits on public sector wage rises

A government may place limits on public sector wage rises if it is concerned about the level of government spending or about the risk of cost-push inflation. Public sector wages account for a large part of government current spending and so increases in public sector pay can have a significant impact on the government's budget position. The government's golden rule involves not borrowing to finance current spending, over the economic cycle.

A rise in the wages of public sector workers may encourage workers in the private sector to press for pay rises. Higher wages, not matched by equal increases in productivity, will reduce profits and encourage firms to pass on at least some of the cost in the form of higher prices. In turn, the higher prices will be likely to stimulate workers to press for even higher money wages in order to maintain their real wages. A wage-price spiral may be set in motion with prices continuing to rise. In the UK changes in wages are a significant factor since they account for approximately two-thirds of total costs. Placing limits on public sector wage rises may, however, make it difficult for the public sector to recruit labour and may create discontent among existing public sector workers.

Discrimination legislation

The government is planning to outlaw age discrimination in the labour market in October 2006. This will bring the UK into line with European

Thinking like an economist

1 Why might government failure occur in the case of government provision of training?
2 Analyse the possible effect on wages in a depressed region of some of its unemployed people moving to another area.

Hot potato

Should a limit be placed on the wage rises granted to maths teachers?

directives. It will become unlawful for firms to discriminate on the grounds of age in job advertisements. Also outlawed will be unjustified age discrimination in promotion and training opportunities and in the provision of health and pension benefits. Workers over 65 will be able to claim unfair dismissal or demand full redundancy.

Quick check

1 Who is covered by the National Minimum Wage?
2 Why are the employment prospects for an adult with only basic skills more bleak now than twenty years ago?
3 What social ties may prevent workers moving from one area to another?
4 Why might the government want to limit public sector wage rises?

The multiplier and fiscal policy

Synoptic link

It would be useful to review AS Section 3.12 before commencing this section.

Introduction

In assessing the expected impact that fiscal policy measures will have on the economy, economists make use of the concept of the multiplier. This is also sometimes known as the national income multiplier. The multiplier combined with the accelerator explains why there can be considerable fluctuations in national income.

The multiplier

The multiplier effect occurs when there is a change in an injection or leakage (withdrawal). The multiplier figure shows the relationship between an initial change in aggregate demand and the final change in national income (real GDP). For example, the government may increase its spending by raising child benefit. Parents, receiving more money, will spend some of the extra. The shopkeepers who benefit from the rise in spending will, in turn, spend some of the extra revenue they receive. Income will continue to rise until it reaches a new equilibrium where again injections will equal leakages. Figure 1 shows aggregate demand rising in stages. The initial increase in AD from AD to AD1 causes a greater final increase in real GDP from Y to Y5. Each increase in aggregate demand is smaller as each time income rises, more spending leaks out of the system.

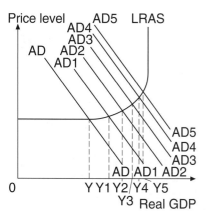

Figure 1

The size of the multiplier

The size of the multiplier can be calculated after the initial injection has taken effect by calculating final change in real GDP divided by the initial change in aggregate demand. For instance, if a rise in investment of £10bn leads to a final rise in real GDP of £25bn, the multiplier is 2.5.

The multiplier can also be estimated in advance by considering what proportion of extra income will be spent in the economy and what proportion leaks out, i.e.

$$\frac{1}{1 - \text{proportion of extra income that is spent on domestic products (consumed)}}$$

$$= \frac{1}{\text{marginal propensity to withdraw}}$$

The higher the tendency for income to leak out of the circular flow, the smaller the size of the multiplier. There are three leakages, the **marginal propensity to save (mps)**, the **marginal rate of tax (mrt)** and the **marginal propensity to import (mpm)**. If mps is 0.1, mrt is 0.1 and mpm is 0.2, the size of the multiplier is:

$$\frac{1}{0.1 + 0.1 + 0.2} = \frac{1}{0.4} = 2.5$$

Research task

What factors influence the amount people save?

Changes in the size of the multiplier

A rise in a leakage (withdrawal) means that less spending will be passed round the economy and so the size of the multiplier will fall. For example, if the size of the **mps** rises from the 0.1 in the example above to 0.2, and is not offset by a fall in **mrt** or **mpm**, the multiplier will fall to:

$$\frac{1}{0.2 + 0.1 + 0.2} = 2$$

Now with less income being passed on in the circular flow, any injection of spending will result in a smaller rise in real GDP. For example, a rise in investment of £10bn will now cause real GDP to increase by only £20bn.

In contrast, a fall in a withdrawal means that more spending will be passed round the economy and so the size of the multiplier will rise. Reductions in direct tax rates, for example, increase disposable income permitting more spending to occur.

The impact of fiscal policy

The larger the size of the multiplier, the more impact any changes in government spending and taxation will have on the economy. For example, if a government raises its spending by £50bn and the multiplier is 2, real GDP will rise by £100bn; but if the multiplier is 5 it will rise by £250bn. With a large multiplier, a government can move aggregate demand towards the full employment level by changing its fiscal policy measures by a relatively small amount.

If a government overestimates the size of the multiplier it may inject too much spending into the economy and cause the economy to overheat., whereas if it underestimates its size it may inject too little. Keynesians believe that it is possible to calculate the size of the multiplier reasonably accurately while new classical economists do not think it is. So the latter group believe it is difficult for a government to assess, in advance, the effect that changes in government spending and taxation will have.

Changes in fiscal policy and the size of the multiplier

Changes in fiscal policy can influence the size of the multiplier by altering any or all of the leakages. For example, an extension of tax free saving schemes or a reduction in the tax on saving would be likely to increase the marginal propensity to save and so reduce the size of the multiplier. An increase in income tax rates will directly raise the mrt and so reduce the size of the multiplier. A decrease in tariffs would be likely to increase spending on imports and so increase the marginal propensity to import. A higher mpm would in turn reduce the size of the multiplier.

Thinking like an economist

Analyse the likely effect of a fall in the value of the US$ on the UK's MPM and the size of its multiplier.

Definitions

Marginal propensity to save (mps): the proportion of extra income saved.

Marginal rate of tax (mrt): the proportion of extra income taken 1in tax.

Marginal propensity to import (mpm): the proportion of extra income spent on imports.

Redistributive fiscal policy may also alter the size of the multiplier. Taxes and government spending may be changed to redistribute income from the rich to the poor to a greater extent. Such a policy is likely to increase the size of the multiplier. This is because the poor have a lower mps than the rich.

Government spending changes may also indirectly change the size of the multiplier. If an injection of extra government spending increases real GDP, this is likely to reduce the size of the multiplier. This is for two reasons. One is that, as income rises, the **marginal propensity to consume** tends to fall while the marginal propensity to save tends to rise; as people become richer they can afford to save a higher proportion of their income. The other reason is that as income rises, UK citizens tend to spend a higher proportion of their income on imports and so the mpm tends to rise.

The accelerator effect

Both the multiplier and the accelerator effects are concerned with changes in injections and changes in real GDP. However, while the multiplier is concerned with how a change in an injection such as investment results in a greater final change in real GDP, the accelerator effect is concerned with how a change in real GDP affects investment.

The accelerator theory states that the level of investment depends on the rate of change of real GDP. It also states that demand for capital goods fluctuates more than the demand for consumer goods. The accelerator effect arises because when there is no change in real GDP the only investment needed is replacement investment (depreciation). However, if income and consumption rise there will need to be extra investment (net or induced) investment in order to expand capacity. For instance, if a firm initially has 10 machines making 1000 units, it may buy one replacement machine a year. If demand rises to 1400 (an increase in consumer demand of 40 per cent), the firm's demand for machines will rise to five (one replacement and four to expand capacity). This means that demand for machines has risen by 400 per cent.

The multiplier and accelerator effects interact to cause greater fluctuations in real GDP. A rise in investment will cause a multiple increase in real GDP, which in turn will cause a larger rise in investment. Real GDP will continue to rise until full capacity is reached or until real GDP starts to rise more slowly, thereby causing a fall in investment.

The usefulness of the accelerator theory

The accelerator theory is useful in explaining net investment. It concentrates on the main influence on investment which is changes in demand for consumer goods. Firms will investment when the expected yield exceeds the cost of investment. If demand is increasing, firms will expect to sell more goods and so receive a greater return.

Definitions

Marginal propensity to consume: the proportion of extra income consumed.
Accelerator theory: the view that net investment is determined by the rate of change in real GDP.

Hot potato

Why is a rise in government spending on transport infrastructure likely to have a greater multiplier effect than a cut in income tax?

However, the accelerator theory does not provide a complete explanation of the behaviour of net investment. Demand for consumer goods may rise without a greater percentage rise in demand for capital goods. Indeed there may be no change in investment. Firms will not invest to expand capacity if they do not believe that the increase in demand for consumer goods will last. Expectations are a significant influence on investment. Keynes referred to them as 'animal spirits'. If firms are pessimistic about the future they may not even replace machines as they wear out.

Firms may also not buy new capital goods if they have spare capacity. They will be able to respond to the rise in demand by making use of previously unused or underused capital. So spare capacity in consumer goods may result in no change or a smaller change in demand for capital goods. In contrast, it may be an absence of spare capacity in the capital goods industry which may prevent firms from being able to purchase more capital equipment. The consumer goods industries may want to buy more equipment but the capital goods industries may not have the resources to produce them.

Changes in technology may also mean that an increase in demand for consumer goods may bring about a smaller percentage increase in demand for capital goods. A new machine, embodying advanced technology, will be able to produce more goods than the machine or machines it replaces. Other influences on investment may change. So, for example, changes in investment may be the result of changes in the cost of machinery, corporation tax or government subsidies.

Quick check

1 What does it mean if the size of the multiplier is 3?
2 What effect would a fall in mpm have on the size of the multiplier?
3 If mps is 0.1, mrt is 0.05 and mpm is 0.05, what is the multiplier?
4 Explain two ways in which the government could raise the size of the multiplier.

Puzzler

In the late 1990s, Japan had a mps greater than one. What does this mean and what are the implications for the ability of fiscal policy to reflate the economy?

Monetarism and the Quantity theory

Synoptic link

This section builds on AS sections dealing with inflation (Section 3.5) and changes in aggregate demand and aggregate supply (Section 3.11) . Before you go any further, make sure you know about the causes of inflation and the effects of changes in aggregate demand and aggregate supply in both the short run and long run.

Exam hint

A useful quote to include when discussing monetarist explanations of inflation is:
'Inflation is always and everywhere a monetary phenomenon.'
Milton Friedman

Introduction

Monetarists believe that inflation is caused by excessive increases in the money supply. They believe such increases will spark off a series of increases in aggregate demand and decreases in short run aggregate supply, both of which push up the price level. In this section you will examine the monetarist model of the inflationary process, the theory they use to support their view and the contrasting view of Keynesians.

Monetarist model of the inflationary process

Monetarists argue that the cause of inflation is the money supply growing faster than output. They argue that if the supply of money increases faster than the demand for money, the value of money will fall and inflation will occur. They think that an excessive growth of the money supply will cause people to use some of the extra money to buy goods and services. This higher consumption will increase aggregate demand, shifting the AD curve to the right. In the short run, the higher demand will lead to an increase in output and the economy will move to point b on the short run aggregate supply curve as shown on Figure 1.

The increased demand for resources will, however, bid up their prices and so increase costs of production. So the SRAS curve shifts to the left. The economy moves to point c as workers and firms adjust to the rise in costs and prices. Output and employment return to their previous levels and aggregate demand again equals aggregate supply. The price level, however, has risen. Firms and workers will now expect the price level to continue to rise and so will act in a way which continues to push up the price level.

Transmission mechanism

The monetary **transmission mechanism** is the process by which changes in the money supply work through the economy. Changes in the money supply may affect output, employment, the price level and even the balance of payments. Monetarists and Keynesians have different views on the impact of changes in the money supply as discussed below.

The Fisher equation

In discussing the effects of a change in the money supply, monetarists refer to the **Fisher equation**, also sometimes called the equation of exchange. The equation is $MV = PY$ (or $MV = PT$) where M is the money supply, V the **velocity of circulation** (i.e. the number of times money changes hands in a given period of time), P is the price level and Y the level of output. T stands for transactions and is equivalent to output. As it stands the equation is a truism. One side represents total expenditure and the other is the value of goods sold so, by definition, they must be equal.

The Quantity theory

To provide an explanation of their view of the monetary transmission mechanism, monetarists developed the Fisher equation into a theory. This theory is called the **Quantity theory** of money (so-called because of the emphasis it places on the quantity of money in the economy).

To convert the equation into the Quantity theory, monetarists assume that V and Y are constant. They argue that, in the long run, output will be at the productive capacity level (full employment) and that V is largely stable. So they think a change in M will have a direct and proportional effect on P. For instance, initially M may be £50bn, V 6, P £10 and Y £30bn. Then if M increases by 50 per cent to £75bn and V and Y are unchanged, P will also increase by 50 per cent to £15. Now £75bn x 6 = £15 x £30bn.

The Keynesian view on the Quantity theory

Keynesians do not believe that the equation MV = PY can be converted into a theory. This is because they think V and T can be influenced by changes in M and so cannot be assumed to be constant. An increase in M may be accompanied by a fall in V and/or a rise in Y and have little effect on P. For example M may be £80bn, V 5, P £4 and Y £100bn. If M increases to £100bn and this increase in the money supply is accompanied by an increase in output to £125bn, P will remain at £4.

The Keynesian transmission mechanism

The Keynesian **transmission mechanism** explains how an increase in M may result in a change in either P or Y or a combination of the two. According to Keynesians, an increase in the money supply will initially affect mainly those dealing in financial markets. These people will buy more financial assets including government bonds. The increase in demand for bonds will raise the price of bonds and lower the rate of interest. A fall in the rate of interest is likely to generate increases in consumption and investment. It may also result in a rise in net exports if it leads to a fall in the exchange rate. The effect of higher aggregate demand will depend on whether the economy is

## Definitions 	❝❞

Fisher equation: an equation that shows the relationship between the money supply, the velocity of circulation, the price level and output (MV = PY).

Quantity theory: the view that a change in the quantity of money causes a direct and proportionate change in the price level.

Transmission mechanism: the process by which changes in the money supply influence the economy.

Velocity of circulation: also sometimes called the income velocity of circulation, it is the number of times money changes hands in a given time period. Calculating the velocity of circulation: If a £1000bn of products have been traded using a money supply of £200bn it means that, on average, each three must have changed hands five times (V = PY/M).

Irving Fisher (1867–1947) was an American economist who developed the equation of exchange.

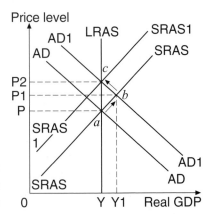

Figure 1: The effect on an increase in the money supply

Hot potato

Why do you think that the velocity of circulation increases during the Christmas period? What effect do you think an increase in the velocity of circulation will have on the economy?

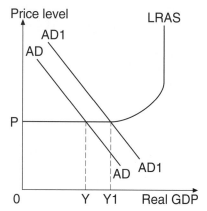

Price level

AD1
AD
LRAS

P

AD
AD1

0   Y Y1   Real GDP

Figure 2: An increase in aggregate demand having no effect on the price level

Exam hint

It is important to remember that the price of government bonds and the rate of interest are inversely related. For example, a government bond issued for £1000 may pay £10 interest (i.e. 10 per cent). If the price of the bond rose to £2000 the £100 interest would now be 5 per cent.

initially operating with spare capacity and the extent to which productive capacity rises with higher investment. It is possible that output may increase but the price level may remain unchanged as shown in Figure 2.

Line of causality

Monetarists argue that it is increases in the money supply which cause inflation. Keynesians accept that inflation is a monetary phenomenon in the sense that it will be accompanied by a rise in the money supply. However, they argue that it is a rise in the price level that leads to a rise in the money supply and not the other way round. If the price level is rising, firms and households will demand more money in order to cover higher costs and prices. The rise in bank lending will increase the money supply.

Quick check

1   If M is £20bn, V is 5, Y is £40bn, what is P?
2   What does monetarist theory suggest about V and T?
3   Why might an increase in M have no effect on P?
4   Assume M is £0bn, V is 4, P is £2 and Y is £60bn. If M increases to £45bn, what will happen to P according to the monetarists?

Introduction

Credit creation refers to commercial (high street) banks' ability to create bank loans. Bankers refer to bank loans as bank advances. When a bank lends money it opens up an account for the borrower. These accounts (which can also be called deposits) are included in the main measures of the money supply. Indeed the main form of money in the UK is bank deposits. Commercial banks are in a powerful position to influence the size of the money supply but their power is not limitless.

The credit creation multiplier

The credit creation multiplier indicates how many times greater the expansion in bank deposits (money supply) can be as a result of an increase in cash deposits. Banks make most of their profit by lending to customers. They have to balance profitability, though, with liquidity. They have to be sure that they can meet their deposit holders' demand for cash. To do this they keep a certain proportion of their assets in a liquid form, i.e. in the form of cash and in the form of assets that can be turned into cash quickly and without loss.

The size of the credit creation multiplier is influenced crucially by the size of the **liquidity ratio** (which can also referred to as the cash or reserve asset ratio) it keeps. The credit creation multiplier can found by dividing 100 by the liquidity ratio. If a bank keeps a liquidity ratio of 10 per cent, for instance, it means that the credit creation multiplier will be 100/10 = 10. Whereas if it keeps a ratio of 5 per cent, its credit creation multiplier will be 20 (100/5). The amount of loans (money) which is created is found by the total rise in deposits minus the original deposit.

The liquidity ratio and bank loans

The liquidity ratio may be set down by the central bank. This is not the case in the UK – banks are just required to keep a prudent ratio. What influences the ratio a bank chooses to keep is mainly what percentage of deposits it thinks its customers will take out in the form of cash. For instance, if a bank finds that its customers are taking out less cash perhaps because they are making more use of credit cards and other forms of non-cash payments, it may reduce its liquidity ratio. If a bank does lower its ratio from say 10 per cent to 8 per cent, its credit creation multiplier will become 100/8 = 12.5. Now a cash deposit of £100 will enable the bank to increase loans and so the money supply by £1250 (change in total deposits) - £100 (the initial deposit) = £1150.

Other influences on the ability of banks to create credit

In practice, banks have to follow similar lending policies. If only one bank increases its lending, it will get into debt with the other banks as its

Synoptic link

A2 Section 5.7 touched on the causes of changes in the money supply.

Definitions

Credit creation: the ability of banks to create loans (money) by a multiple of any increase in cash deposits.
Liquidity ratio: the proportion of liquid assets to bank deposits.

customers make payments to customers of other banks. The expansionary bank will have to settle these payments by drawing on its account held at the Bank of England. This account (called balances at the Bank of England) counts as a liquid asset and a reduction in its value will force the bank to cut back its loans.

Banks may also have the ability to lend but there may a lack of suitable creditworthy borrowers. Households and firms may also not want to borrow. This is particularly likely to be the case if the economy is heading towards a recession.

Increases in the money supply

The money supply may increase as a result of credit creation, an increase in the monetary base and an increase in the net flow of money into the country. These reasons are inter-linked.

As noted above, credit creation is a major cause of increases in the money supply. If banks attract more deposits, or if currently they are not lending as much as their deposits and liquidity ratio permits, they will have the potential to lend more. The Bank of England could also increase the money supply by financing the government's budget deficit by printing more bank notes or by borrowing from the banking sector. An increase in bank notes and an increase in banks' balances at the Bank of England will raise the money supply as measured by MO. The Bank of England could also raise the money supply by buying government bonds – expansionary open market operations. A rise in the monetary base is likely to led to a rise in cash deposits and hence bank loans.

If the economy moves into a current account surplus more money will be entering the country. When this is converted into pounds, and if it is not offset by other movements or by sales of government bonds, it will add to the domestic money supply.

The effect of an increase in the money supply on economic performance

There are different views on the effect that an increase in the money supply will have on a country's economic performance. Monetarists argue that an increase in the money supply, which is greater than the increase in real GDP, will lead to inflation. They use the Quantity theory in support of their view that an increase in the money supply will cause a direct and proportionate increase in the price level.

If an increase in the money supply does result in inflation, this may have an adverse effect on economic performance. Inflation can impose a number of costs on the economy. These include, for instance, menu costs and the arbitrary redistribution of income. If the inflation rate rises above that of the country's competitors, the country's products will become less price competitive. This will reduce exports and increase imports and so will worsen the current account of the balance of payments. The lower aggregate demand will also be likely to increase unemployment and reduce the economic growth rate.

Keynesians, however, argue that the effects of an increase in the money supply depend on the initial state of the economy and how economic agents respond. An increase in the money supply, they claim will cause the rate of interest to fall. A lower interest rate may stimulate consumption and investment and may increase net exports. People may spend more as a lower rate of interest reduces the return from saving, decreases the cost of borrowing and increases the amount people with mortgages have to spend. Investment is likely to rise as the cost of borrowing decreases (both the direct cost and the opportunity cost) and as it would be expected that consumption would rise. In practice, though, investment can be relatively interest inelastic especially if entrepreneurs are pessimistic about the future. Net exports may increase as a lower interest rate will reduce the exchange rate if foreigners are discouraged from buying pounds to put into UK financial institutions. A rise in export revenue and a fall in import expenditure will improve the current account of the balance of payments.

Consumption, investment and net exports are all components of aggregate demand. An increase in aggregate demand will increase output and employment if the economy is producing below its full capacity level as shown in Figure 1.

Of course, there is a risk that if aggregate demand rises to the point where the economy is at or close to full employment, inflation may occur as shown in Figure 2.

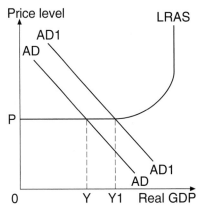

Figure 1: The effect of an increase in aggregate demand in an economy with spare capacity

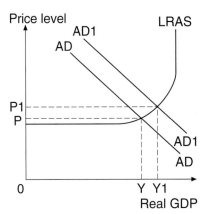

Figure 2: The effect of an increase in aggregate demand in an economy approaching full employment

Quick check

1 How do banks create credit?
2 If a bank keeps a liquidity ratio of 20 per cent, what is the size of its credit creation multiplier?
3 Why may a bank lend less than its liquidity ratio permits?
4 What does 'investment being interest inelastic' mean?

Thinking like an economist

Using aggregate demand and aggregate analysis, discuss the effect of a decrease in the money supply.

5.12 International trade (I)

Introduction

A small part of current day international trade can be explained by what economists refer to as absolute advantage. Most international trade, however, is based on comparative advantage.

Absolute advantage

A country is said to have an **absolute advantage** in producing a product when it is better at producing it than other countries. More technically, it means that it can produce more of the product from each unit of resource than other countries – it has a greater productivity.

Table 1 is based on the assumption that there are ten workers in the USA and ten workers in Malaysia. Initially each country divides its workers equally between car and rubber production. It is further assumed that each worker in the USA can make either 6 cars or 10 units of rubber and each worker in Malaysia can make either 2 cars or 60 units of rubber. The table shows that the USA has the absolute advantage in the production of cars as it can make three times as many cars per worker as Malaysia; Malaysia has the absolute advantage in rubber production as it can make six times as much rubber per worker as the USA.

In this case, it is clear that the USA should specialise in the production of cars and Malaysia in the production of rubber. Both countries would gain as a result of specialisation and trade. In our simplified example, if the USA now specialised in cars and Malaysia in rubber, output would rise to the levels shown in Table 2. The USA could export 20 cars to Malaysia in return for 200 rubber units and both countries would be better off in comparison with the situation before specialisation and trade.

Comparative advantage

Although absolute advantage explains a small amount of current international trade, most is now based on **comparative advantage**. A large proportion of the UK's trade, for example, is with countries producing products that country is either making or could make in fairly similar

Synoptic link

Review AS Section 3.24 before commencing this section.

Table 1: The position before specialisation and trade

| | Output | |
	Cars	Rubber
USA	30	50
Malaysia	10	300
Total	40	350

Definitions

Absolute advantage: the ability to produce output using fewer resources than other regions or countries.

Comparative advantage: relative efficiency – the ability to produce a product at a lower opportunity cost than other regions or countries.

Table 2: The position after specialisation

| | Output | |
	Cars	Rubber
USA	60	–
Malaysia	–	600
Total	60	600

Table 3: The position after specialisation and trade

| | Consumption | |
	Cars	Rubber
USA	40	200
Malaysia	20	400
Total	60	600

quantities per worker. Comparative advantage, as its name suggests, is concerned with relative efficiency. A country is said to have a comparative advantage in a product when it is even better at making that product or not so bad at making the product. This can also be expressed in terms of opportunity cost – a country has a comparative advantage if it can produce it at a lower opportunity cost than another country.

The principle or theory of comparative advantage states that both of two countries will benefit from specialisation and trade even if one country is more efficient at making both products as long as there is a difference in its relative efficiencies.

Table 4 again assumes there are ten workers in the USA and in Malaysia and that the workers are divided equally between the two products. In the USA each worker can make either 6 cars or 120 toys. In Malaysia each worker can make either 2 cars or 80 toys.

The USA has the absolute advantage in the production of both of the goods. Its comparative advantage, however, lies in the production of cars. It can produce three times as many cars as Malaysia but only one and a half times as many toys. The opportunity cost of one car in America is lower than in Malaysia, 20 toys as opposed to 40 toys.

Malaysia's comparative advantage is in toys. It can produce two-thirds as many toys as the United States, but only one-third as many cars and it has a lower opportunity cost in the production of toys.

Table 5 shows the situation if the United States concentrates mainly on car production, devoting eight workers to car production and two to toy production and Malaysia specialises completely in toy production.

Specialisation has caused total output to rise. Countries will benefit from trade if the exchange rate lies between their respective opportunity cost ratios. If it is not, one of the countries would gain more of a particular product by switching its own resources. For example, if the USA wanted more toys and it could only exchange one car for ten toys through international trade, it would be better moving workers from car to toy production. However. if the exchange rate does lie between the opportunity cost ratios, both countries can gain. Table 6 shows the position if the exchange rate is one car for thirty toys and the USA exports thirteen cars.

Table 4: The position before specialisation and trade

| | Output | |
	Cars	Toys
USA	30	600
Malaysia	10	400
Total	40	1000

Table 5: The position after specialisation

| | Output | |
	Cars	Toys
USA	48	240
Malaysia	–	800
Total	48	1040

Table 6: The position after specialisation and trade

| | Consumption | |
	Cars	Toys
USA	35	630
Malaysia	13	410
Total	48	1040

Table 7

| | Output per worker | |
	TVs	Vacuum cleaners
Germany	4	20
Greece	3	6

Thinking like an economist

Look at Table 7 and answer the questions that follow.
1 Which country has the absolute advantage in the production of both goods?
2 What is the opportunity cost ratio of one TV in Germany and in Greece?
3 Which country has the comparative advantage in TV production?

Limitations of the principle of comparative advantage

While the principle of comparative advantage highlights the importance of differences in relative productivity, it does have its limitations in explaining the pattern of international trade which actually occurs. It is often expressed, as here, in terms of a few countries and a few products. Of course in the real world, as there are many countries, many products and as situations are always changing, it is more difficult to work out where comparative advantages lie.

The principle ignores transport costs that may outweigh any comparative advantage, particularly in terms of heavy products. However, as noted earlier, one feature of globalisation is reduced transport costs. The principle also assumes constant opportunity cost ratios and productivity as resources are shifted. So that, in our example shown in Table 5 when Malaya doubled the number of workers producing toys, the output of toys doubled. However, in practice the workers most suited to toy production are likely to be employed first so that when more are employed these are likely to be less productive. This would mean that the opportunity cost of increasing toys would rise and so the returns from specialisation would be reduced.

The benefits of specialisation and trade are also reduced in the real world by the existence of import restrictions and, for some countries, by differences in bargaining power. A country may have a comparative advantage in a particular product but may have difficulties exporting it because other countries impose tariffs, quotas or other trade restrictions on it. Developing countries may also find that exchange rates are set in a way which disadvantages them.

In addition, a country may not specialise to the extent that the principle suggests because it may wish to keep a more diversified industrial structure in order to reduce the risks arising from sudden shifts in demand and supply. There are a number of other reasons why a country may seek to maintain industries in which it does not currently have a comparative advantage, including strategic industries and new industries.

Quick check

1 Distinguish between absolute and comparative advantage.
2 Why might a country have a low cost of employing labour per unit hour but still have high unit wage costs?
3 What causes comparative advantage to change?
4 What are the advantages of having a comparative advantage in knowledge-based industries?

Introduction

In the previous Part of International trade, the nature of comparative advantage was examined. In this Part, changes in comparative advantage are discussed. The benefits and costs of international trade are also considered.

Changes in comparative advantage

The products in which countries have a comparative advantages are changing. Developing countries are becoming more efficient at producing manufactured goods. Their comparative advantage at the moment is mainly in manufacturing industries which make use of low-skilled labour. They have a large supply of low-skilled workers and so their wage rates are lower. In the past this did not result in a comparative advantage since although wages were low, so was productivity and as a result unit wage costs were high. However, now with rises in productivity, particularly in NICs (newly industrialised countries), unit wage costs have been falling. Some commentators have expressed the concern that this will result in a rise in unemployment and a fall in wages in industrialised countries. Their fear is that multinational companies will locate more of their processes in developing countries and that developing countries' firms will gain a larger share of the market for manufactured goods.

This, however, is only part of the picture. What is happening is not so much that industrialised countries are facing a fall in demand for their output but a shift in demand from some products towards other products resulting from changes in relative efficiencies. Resources will have to shift to reflect these changes and this process is already under way. Average wages are not falling in most industrialised countries but the wages of unskilled workers are falling relative to skilled workers. Industries producing goods and services requiring high-skilled labour are experiencing rises in demand while some relying on low-skilled labour are facing lower demand. In the case of the UK, some processes are being relocated to lower production cost countries but at the same time foreign direct investment is being attracted by the high-skilled labour force of the country. So while jobs requiring low skill levels are declining, jobs requiring high skill levels are increasing. To ease the shift in resources, educational and vocational qualifications need to rise.

Of course, the situation is always changing and economies and their citizens have to be adaptable. Currently the UK has a comparative advantage in, for example, oil, financial services, business services and scientific instruments, but in a few years time, with skill levels rising throughout the world and patterns of demand and supply changing, this may alter.

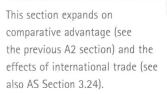

International trade (II)

Synoptic link

This section expands on comparative advantage (see the previous A2 section) and the effects of international trade (see also AS Section 3.24).

Hot potato

Why did James Dyson relocate his vacuum-manufacturing firm from Swindon to Malaysia?

Benefits and costs of international trade

If countries specialise and trade, total output should be greater than otherwise. The resulting rise in living standards is the main benefit claimed for free international trade. Consumers can benefit from the lower prices and higher quality that result from the higher level of competition that arises from countries trading internationally. They also enjoy a greater variety of products, including a few not made in their own countries.

Although firms will face greater competition in their domestic markets, they will also have access to larger markets in which to sell their products (enabling them to take greater advantage of economies of scale) and from which to buy raw materials.

However, despite all these advantages and increasing trade liberalisation, restrictions on exports and more particularly imports still exist. This is explained, for example, by governments being concerned that certain undesirable products may be imported, that the continued existence of new and strategic industries may be threatened and other countries may not engage in fair competition.

International trade faces countries with challenges. Competition from other countries and access to their markets results in some industries contracting and some expanding. This requires the shifting of resources which can be unsettling and may be difficult to achieve due to, for example, occupational immobility of labour.

Thinking like an economist

Explain three benefits a UK insurance company could gain from engaging in international trade.

Quick check

1 Why is productivity rising in NICs?
2 Why does the UK no longer have a comparative advantage in textiles?
3 What is the main benefit of international trade?
5 Which firms benefit from international trade?

Introduction

As discussed in Section 5.4, countries can operate **fixed** or **floating** exchange rates. In the first case, the exchange rate is largely a policy target. In both cases, the exchange rates are influenced by changes in government policy. Changes in the exchange rate can also have a significant impact on the country's inflation rate, unemployment and the balance of payments.

Target

If a government operates a fixed exchange rate, the exchange rate is likely to become a policy target or objective. A fixed exchange rate is one where the price of the currency is pegged against other currencies (for example £1 = \$1.5). If the price comes under threat by market forces, the central bank, acting on behalf of the government, will step in to maintain the value by either buying or selling the currency and/or changing its interest rate. For example, Figure 1 shows an exchange rate set at £1 = ¥5. If, due to an increase in the supply of the country's currency, the exchange rate comes under threat, the government would intervene by buying its currency and/or increasing its interest rate. Figure 2 shows the effects of these events.

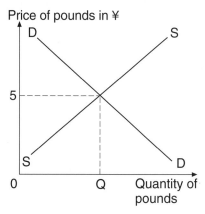

Figure 1: The exchange rate

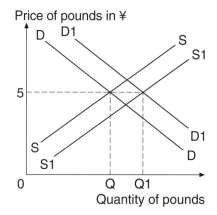

Figure 2: Preventing a fall in the value of the pound

A government may also, on occasions, try to influence the value of a floating exchange rate if it thinks it is rising too high (to a level which is not sustainable and which is harmful for the economy), falling too low or is too unstable. In this case, it is effectively changing the exchange rate from a floating to a managed exchange rate.

If a government aims to maintain an exchange rate at a certain value it may have to sacrifice other policy objectives to achieve this. As noted above, a government may have to raise the interest rate and such a measure may reduce output growth and raise unemployment at least in the short run.

Synoptic link

This section builds on AS Sections 3.15 and 3.22 and A2 Section 5.4. Before you start this section, check your understanding of the exchange rate and exchange rate adjustment.

Definitions

Fixed exchange rate: an exchange rate fixed against other currencies that is maintained by the government.

Floating exchange rate: an exchange rate determined by market forces.

Thinking like an economist

What action would a central bank take to reduce the exchange rate?

Instrument

A government may change the value of a fixed exchange rate from one price to another or it may seek to influence the value of a floating exchange rate. In this case, the exchange rate becomes a policy instrument (tool or measure). For example, a government may undertake a **devaluation** of its fixed exchange rate or encourage a **depreciation** in a floating exchange rate in order to improve the current account of the balance of payments, raise output and/or increase employment.

Effects of exchange rate movements

The first effect of a change in the exchange rate is a change in the price of exports and imports. A rise in the exchange rate will raise the price of the country's exports in terms of foreign currencies and reduce the price of imports in terms of the domestic currency. This will put downward pressure on inflation. This is because the price of imported raw materials will fall, thereby reducing the cost of production and the price of imported finished products that count in the calculation of the country's inflation rate. In addition, domestic firms, facing cheaper imported rival products at home and facing the prospect of their products becoming more expensive abroad, will be under pressure to cut their costs in order to keep their prices low.

A rise in the exchange rate will improve the **terms of trade**. The sale of each export would enable more imports to be purchased. However, the change in prices will affect demand. If demand for exports is elastic, the revenue earned from selling exports will fall, thereby reducing the overall purchasing power of the country. Elastic demand for exports and imports will also mean that a fall in the value of currency will result in a deterioration of the balance of payments.

Higher priced exports and cheaper imports by reducing net exports will lower aggregate demand. A fall in aggregate demand is likely to reduce the rate of economic growth and increase unemployment. A higher exchange rate may indeed reduce aggregate demand so much that it results in a reduction in the industrial base of the country. Some firms may not be able to compete at home and/or abroad as a result of the higher exchange rate and some may go out of business.

Frequent changes in the exchange rate can have harmful effects on the economy. Firms will be uncertain how much they will have to pay for imported raw materials and how much they will earn from exporting. This uncertainty is likely to reduce investment and so economic growth.

A fall in the exchange rate and the balance of payments

A fall in the UK's exchange rate will lower the price of UK exports, in terms of foreign currency, and raise the price of imports, in terms of pounds. The effect that such price changes have on the balance of payments will depend principally on the price elasticity of demand for exports and imports. If demand for exports is inelastic, a fall in price will result in a greater percentage rise in demand and so a rise in export revenue. Elastic demand for imports will cause a greater percentage fall in demand and a decrease in import expenditure. The **Marshall–Lerner condition** states that for a fall in the exchange rate to improve the current account of the balance of payments, the price elasticity of demand for exports and imports must be greater than one.

However, it takes time for consumers and firms to recognise that prices have changed and for contracts to be changed. In the short run, therefore, demand for exports and imports tends to be inelastic. This tendency for a depreciation in the exchange rate to make the current account position worse before it improves is referred to as the **J-curve effect**. Figure 3 shows the current account deficit getting larger before it moves into surplus.

As well as price elasticity of demand, there are a number of other factors that can influence the effect of a depreciation on the current account position. These include whether other economies alter their exchange rates, whether trade restrictions abroad make it difficult to raise exports and whether foreigners' ability to buy UK products is being adversely affected by falling foreign incomes.

If the depreciation does raise net exports, aggregate demand will increase. The effect that an increase in aggregate demand has on the economy depends on the current state of the economy and whether long-run aggregate supply is increasing in line with the rise in aggregate demand. If, for example, net exports increase when the economy has spare capacity, output and employment will rise. If, however, aggregate demand increases when the economy is close to full capacity and is not matched by an increase in LRAS, inflation will occur.

The relationship between the interest rate and the exchange rate

A country's interest rate and its exchange rate are closely linked. If the rate of interest is increased, it is likely that the exchange rate will also rise. This is because a higher interest rate usually results in an increase in demand and a fall in the supply of the country's currency. More foreigners will want to buy pounds to place into UK financial institutions to take advantage of the higher returns. Fewer UK citizens will sell pounds to buy foreign currencies to place into foreign financial institutions – they will switch their financial investment to the UK.

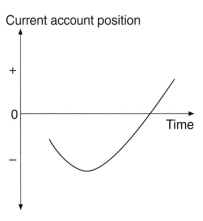

Figure 3: The J-curve effect

Definitions

The J-curve effect: the tendency for a fall in the exchange rate to make the trade position worse before it gets better.

The Marshall–Lerner condition: the view that for a fall in the exchange rate to be successful in improving the balance of payments, the combined elasticities of demand for exports and imports must be greater than one.

A country's exchange rate can be affected indirectly by changes in other countries' and areas' interest rates. For instance, if the European Central Bank and the Federal Reserve Bank of the USA raise their interest rates, the Bank of England is likely to follow suit. This is because the UK government and the Bank of England try to avoid destabilising changes in financial flows into and out of the country. Again a higher interest rate is likely to result in a rise in the exchange rate. However, the effect is actually influenced by changes in relative interest rates. If the UK's interest rate rises in line with that of the EU and the USA, the relative interest rate has not changed and the exchange rate may not be affected.

Changes in the exchange rate can also influence the rate of interest. A central bank, for instance, may cut its interest rate if it thinks that the country's exchange rate is rising too much. It may be concerned that the higher exchange rate is putting too much pressure on exporting firms and those firms which compete with imported products.

Research task

Using recent newspaper articles, decide whether the value of the pound sterling is currently thought to be too high, too low or about right.

Quick check

1 Explain why the government may seek to reduce the exchange rate.
2 Why is an increase in the rate of interest likely to raise the exchange rate?
3 What effect is an unstable exchange rate likely to have on employment?
4 Explain the likely effect on the government's four main macroeconomic objectives of a rise in the exchange rate.

Introduction

In recent years there has been a shift away from relying on fiscal policy to influence aggregate demand in the short run to greater reliance on interest rate changes. This is one of the monetary policy tools. The other two are changes in the money supply and changes in the exchange rate. The prime aim of monetary policy has been to try to achieve price stability. However it is also used to achieve the other main government objectives, i.e. full employment, economic growth and balance of payments equilibrium.

Changes in the money supply

Measures of the money supply became prominent when the Conservative government started to target the growth of the money supply. Measures are still produced today and, while they are not given the prominence they once were, they are still taken into account by the Monetary Policy Committee (see below). The two main measures of the money supply are M0 and M4. M0 includes notes, coins and high street banks accounts at the Bank of England. M4 covers the items in M0 and bank and building society deposits (accounts).

The amount of money in existence is heavily influenced by the lending policies of the high street banks. When banks lend they open up deposits for the borrowers. As these deposits can be spent they are money and are included in the M4 measure of the money supply.

Measures to reduce the growth of the money supply

The Bank of England, acting on behalf of the government, can seek to reduce the growth of the money supply either by reducing the ability of the banks to lend and/or by reducing demand for loans. There are a number of policy measures they can implement to achieve this.

- Open market operations: This involves buying and selling government bonds. If the Bank of England is seeking to restrict bank lending it will sell government bonds. The intention is to use up some of the banks' liquid assets and thereby reduce their ability to lend.
- Funding: This involves converting government debt from short term to long term with the intention of reducing the value of liquid assets that banks can get hold of.
- Moral persuasion: This involves the Bank of England asking banks to lend less.
- Interest rates: Raising interest rates works on the demand for loans by increasing the price of the loans. This is thought to be the most effective way to control bank lending and is the main way in which the authorities seek to control the growth of bank deposits.

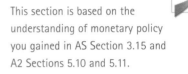

Monetary policy 5.15

Synoptic link

This section is based on the understanding of monetary policy you gained in AS Section 3.15 and A2 Sections 5.10 and 5.11.

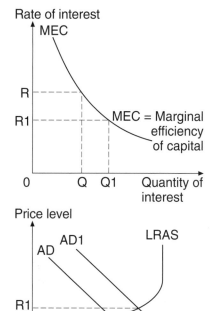

Figure 1: The monetary transmission mechanism

Research task

By assessing relative data, decide whether the MPC should lower, raise or leave interest rates unchanged this month.

The monetary transmission mechanism

As noted in Section 5.10, the monetary transmission mechanism is the process by which changes in the money supply come to affect output, employment, inflation and the balance of payments. For example, an increase in the money supply will mean that people will have more money to spend on financial assets. This will raise the price of financial assets and reduce the rate of interest. A rise in the price of financial assets results in a fall in the rate of interest. Lower interest rates stimulate consumption and investment. They also tend to reduce demand for the currency, thereby lowering its value and increasing demand for exports and lowering demand for imports. So three components of aggregate demand are likely to rise. The effect of the shift to the right of the AD curve will depend on at what level of output the economy was initially operating. If, for example, the economy was operating close to full employment the effect is likely to be to raise both output and the price level. The monetary transmission mechanism is illustrated in Figure 1.

The role of the Monetary Policy Committee

The MPC sets the rate of interest with the prime objective of achieving the government's target rate of inflation. Subject to meeting that objective, it has been instructed to support the economic policy of the government, including its objectives for employment and economic growth. The MPC consists of five members drawn from employees of the Bank of England, including the Governor of the Bank of England, and four economists nominated by the Chancellor of the Exchequer. It meets monthly to review evidence on the performance of the economy and indicators of changes in inflationary pressure. This information includes figures on the current and predicted growth of the money supply, the exchange rate, wage rates, employment, productivity, retail sales and surveys of business and consumer confidence. If the MPC believes that the information points to the risk that inflation will rise above the target it will raise interest rates.

The independence of the Bank of England

The government gave the Bank of England operational independence to set interest rates in May 1997. In January 2000, the newly appointed shadow chancellor, Michael Portillo, stated that the Conservative Party accepted that the Bank of England should remain independent so now there is agreement between the two main political parties on the issue.

The arguments for permitting the Bank of England to decide on the appropriate level of interest rates are that:
- it has considerable experience in financial markets
- it is more likely to take a longer-term perspective

- it will not be tempted to lower interest rates just prior to an election to win popularity
- doing so allows the government to concentrate on other policy measures.

However, some argue that the Bank of England is too concerned with price stability and is sometimes prepared to sacrifice jobs to pay for it. The independence of the members has also been questioned as the Governor of the Bank of England and the four economists are appointed by the Chancellor of the Exchequer.

Monetary policy stance

A tight (or restrictionist) monetary policy approach is one which aims to reduce aggregate demand, or at least the growth of aggregate demand, usually in a bid to lower inflation or improve the balance of payments position. In contrast, an expansionary monetary policy approach (loosening monetary policy) is one which encourages a growth in aggregate demand. So reducing the rate of interest would be regarded as an expansionary approach.

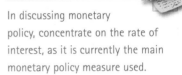

Exam hint

In discussing monetary policy, concentrate on the rate of interest, as it is currently the main monetary policy measure used.

Quick check

1 Distinguish between narrow and broad money.
2 Explain two ways the Bank of England could seek to reduce the money supply.
3 Why may profitability and liquidity conflict for a bank?
4 Explain three factors that could cause the MPC to consider raising interest rates.

5.16

Changes in fiscal, monetary and supply-side policies

Synoptic link

This section builds on the AS sections on fiscal and monetary policy, Sections 3.14–3.16 and A2 Sections 5.5–5.7, 5.9 and 5.15.

Thinking like an economist

Explain why tax harmonisation may increase economic efficiency.

Introduction

In recent years there have been a number of changes in the operation of UK fiscal, monetary and supply-side policies caused in part by experience and in part by the government's desire to achieve greater stability.

The current government's fiscal policy

The government has stated that its aims for fiscal policy are to raise sufficient revenue to pay for the services which its policies require, to pay necessary interest on national debt while keeping the burden of taxation as low as possible, to promote fairness and to encourage work, saving and investment.

It has also sought to increase stability in fiscal policy by introducing the comprehensive spending review and fiscal policy rules. The first rule is called the golden rule. This is a commitment that, over the economic cycle, the government will only borrow to finance capital spending. The second is the public debt rule. This is the requirement to keep public sector debt at 40 per cent over the period of the economic cycle. The motives behind promoting stability of government policy is to make it easier for government departments, firms and consumers to plan.

Fiscal policy and the EU

If the government decides to enter the single currency it would have to accept a limit on any budget deficit to 3 per cent of its GDP. This could be difficult especially during a downturn in the economy.

UK fiscal policy is already being influenced by its membership of the EU. Under the Conservatives, the UK entered into an agreement linking its VAT rates to those in the EU. There are calls for greater tax harmonisation (i.e. the standardisation of tax rates) within the EU. The main argument behind such a move is that for an area to operate as a single market similar, if not the same, rates of taxes must operate in the different member countries. Without such a standardisation, countries can gain a comparative advantage in product, labour and capital markets by operating lower rates of taxation. For example, workers may be tempted to work in countries with low income tax rates, consumers to buy in countries with low excise duty and firms to locate in countries with low corporation tax. Probably the best-known evidence of the effects of differences in tax rates are the 'booze cruises' – UK citizens travelling to France where tax rates are lower to stock up on alcohol and cigarettes.

Changes in monetary policy

When the Conservatives came to power in 1979, their main priority was to reduce inflation. As they believed that inflation was caused by excessive growth of the money supply, they sought to reduce the growth of the money supply. They found this very difficult to achieve and statistical evidence for the period suggested that there was not a clear link between the growth of the money supply and inflation. So, in 1990, the emphasis of monetary policy switched to the exchange rate.

In 1990, the UK joined the ERM (the Exchange Rate Mechanism). This was a pegged exchange rate system in which currencies could vary only by a small amount relative to the other member currencies. The UK went in at a high exchange rate in the belief that this would put downward pressure on domestic inflation. The rate, however, was not sustainable and the UK left the ERM in 1992. It then decided to target inflation and to use the rate of interest to influence its level. (It is thought that setting an inflation target may itself reduce inflationary pressure by persuading firms and consumers that the government is taking a determined approach to keeping inflation low.) This is still the approach of the government, although the operational determination of the rate of interest has been given to the Bank of England.

Monetary policy and the EU

Entry into the European single currency means that a country loses autonomy over its monetary policy since the euro area operates one exchange rate and one interest rate. The European Central Bank (ECB) sets the interest rate and can influence the exchange rate. Some commentators have expressed concern that the interest rate policy pursued by the ECB and the value of the euro may not benefit the UK. This, however, it could be argued is one of the reasons why it is important for a country's economy to converge with that of the eurozone before it considers membership.

Even outside the eurozone the UK's monetary policy is influenced by the ECB's actions. If, for example, the euro falls in value relative to the pound sterling, the UK's price competitiveness against its main trading partners declines. In addition, if the UK's interest rate falls below that of the ECB's, money may flow out of UK financial institutions into those of the eurozone which would put downward pressure on the value of the pound.

Fiscal and monetary policy

In recent years the main use of macroeconomic policy has been to control the rate of inflation. The main policy instrument used has been the monetary policy instrument of the rate of interest. What are often perceived as fiscal policy measures have actually been used as supply-side measures to increase the trend rate of economic growth. For instance, lower rates of income tax have been cut to increase the gap between paid employment and unemployment and so to increase the incentive to work.

Hot potato

Why has the government chosen to use the rate of interest as the main measure to influence aggregate demand in the short run?

Supply-side policies

Over the last three decades increasing emphasis has been placed on the use of supply-side policies by both Conservative and Labour governments. These policies have met with some, but not total, success in recent years. It could be argued that by increasing productive capacity, measures such as privatisation, deregulation, and reform of trade unions have reduced inflationary pressure and so have contributed positively to international competitiveness. Privatisation and deregulation have increased competitive pressure in a number of markets, including telecommunications and air transport – providing both a carrot (potentially higher profits) and a stick (the risk of going bankrupt) for firms to achieve productive and allocative efficiency.

Supply-side policies, however, have not yet significantly increased UK productivity. Higher productivity would lower the unit (average) cost of production and so make the UK more internationally price competitive. A number of supply-side policies have been implemented to raise labour productivity, for example increased spending on education, and to increase net investment, for example cuts in corporation tax. Of course, it can take some time for these measures to take effect and the UK government is still in the process of, for instance, reforming higher education in a bid to ensure that at least 50 per cent of young people go to university.

The UK's international competitiveness has also been affected by other policy measures, most notably the monetary policy measure of interest rate changes. The Monetary Policy Committee (MPC) has been largely successful in keeping inflation low, meeting the government's target, but some argue that it has kept interest rates too high which has raised the value of the pound and so offset the positive effect on UK price competitiveness of low inflation.

> ### Quick check
>
> 1 What are the advantages of a stable fiscal policy?
> 2 Explain the government's rules for fiscal policy.
> 3 Why might an exchange rate be unsustainable?
> 4 Why did targets for the money supply prove ineffective in reducing inflation?

Introduction

In practice there are a number of reasons why government policy measures may not be as effective as expected. There is also the possibility, particularly in the short run, that there may be conflicts between policy objectives.

Views on government policy

Keynesians believe that markets do not work efficiently. They think that market failure is a real problem. They also think that governments have the appropriate knowledge, skills and tools to intervene and improve the performance of the economy. In contrast, new classical economists argue that markets work efficiently and that there is a real risk that government intervention will make the situation worse. They believe that governments should remove some past policies, laws and regulations which are hampering the smooth working of free market forces, should keep tax low and should concentrate on creating a low inflationary climate which will provide the basis for achieving the other three macroeconomic objectives.

Government failure

Government failure occurs when government intervention, instead of improving the performance of markets, makes it worse. As noted above, new classical economists believe that government failure is a more significant problem than Keynesians do. There are a number of possible causes of government failure.

Poor quality of information

If a government lacks information or has inaccurate information it may make the wrong policy decisions. For example, if the Bank of England wrongly believes that aggregate demand will rise too rapidly in the future it may raise interest rates now. If the economy is actually on the brink of a recession this will reinforce the downturn in demand.

The government employs a high number of economists who supply it with analysis and advice. The government also receives advice from other economists working in academia, the media and industry. Some of these economists now use very sophisticated models but the accuracy of these models is influenced by the information and theories fed into them and how the predictions are interpreted.

Economic theory

The policies adopted are influenced by the economic theories followed by politicians and their economic advisors. However there are disagreements as to which are the appropriate theories to follow.

Policy conflicts

5.17

Synoptic link

This section builds on the knowledge and understanding you gained in the AS Sections on fiscal policy, monetary policy, supply-side policies, policies to reduce unemployment, inflation, promote economic growth and improve the balance of payments.

Hot potato

What effect would a decision by the MPC to lower interest rates have at a time when the economy is just beginning to enter a downturn?

Time lags

By the time some government policies take effect, the situation which caused them to be implemented has changed. For example, a government may cut income tax to increase consumer spending but by the time the tax rates are changed the economy may be entering a boom period. There are three main time lags involved with government policy.

- Recognition lag: This refers to the time it takes for a government to recognise there is a problem.
- Implementation lag: It can take time for a government to decide on the appropriate policy measure and implement it.
- Behavioural lag: This is the time it takes for people and firms to change their behaviour in the light of government policies. For example, a government may cut income tax but people may take time to adjust their spending.

Unexpected responses

Economics is a social science, it deals with people, and people and the firms they run do not always react in the way the government expects or wants. For example, in 1998 the Japanese government cut interest rates and income tax hoping to stimulate a rise in aggregate demand. However, this failed to materialise because consumers and firms were pessimistic about the future and so actually saved more.

Economists have also noted that targeting can itself alter the behaviour of what is being targeted. This phenomenon was identified in **Goodhart's law**. This states that any measure of the money supply behaves differently when it is targeted.

Complexity

The world is a complex, increasingly integrated and constantly changing place. Economic growth of a country can be knocked off trend by sudden and unexpected events abroad. For example, a recession in the USA, one of the UK's main trading partners, will reduce UK aggregate demand and so may reduce the UK's economic growth rate and increase its unemployment rate. The UK economy is also significantly affected by the economic performance of the rest of the EU. This is because the EU is the main destination of UK exports and the main source of UK imports. In addition, changes in EU policy, such as reform of the CAP, impact on the UK economy.

Conflicts of objectives

Policy instruments simultaneously affect a number of objectives. So a rise in income tax designed to reduce inflation may also raise unemployment. However, it is interesting to note here that new classical economists argue that policy objectives do not need to conflict. They think that if the government keeps inflation low, largely by avoiding the temptation for itself to increase aggregate demand, the other three objectives will be achieved.

There is increasing agreement that supply-side policies can, in the long run, help a government achieve all of its major objectives. The new economic paradigm also holds out the promise of increasing the ease with which all four major objectives can be achieved simultaneously.

Government self-interest

The recommendations and decisions made by politicians and civil servants may be influenced by their own self-interest. For example, a government may receive advice from economists that now would not be an appropriate time to cut income tax. However, if it is approaching a general election, it may go ahead with such a change. After the election, if its pre-election policy measures have resulted in inflation and balance of payments difficulties, it may introduce measures to reduce aggregate demand.

Rigidities

As noted above, while market conditions are constantly changing it is difficult to change some aspects of government policy. For example, laws take time to change. Some forms of public expenditure are difficult to change. Once a government has started to build a hospital, it is difficult and costly to stop.

If governments are reluctant to admit their mistakes they may continue to spend money on a project which does not have long-term viability. However, where consumers and firms need to make long-term plans, frequent and large changes in government policies can cause problems. For example, a decision to remove grants to firms which have located in a depressed region three years after they were first announced may put the viability of their firms in question. A doubling of the rate of interest would also cause major problems for those with mortgages.

Policy constraints

Membership of international organisations and increasing globalisation limit the autonomy of national government policy. The UK government cannot impose tariffs on EU members and its rate of interest cannot be significantly out of line with that of the EU and the USA.

Thinking like an economist

Analyse the effect on the UK economy of a cut in the rate of interest by the European Central Bank.

Quick check

1   Why may the objectives of low inflation and low unemployment conflict?
2   Explain three constraints on government policy.
3   Explain how supply-side policies can strengthen the long-term performance of the economy.
4   Why are income tax rates unlikely to go up just before a general election?

Phillips curves

5.18

Introduction

Phillips curves are used by economists to analyse the relationships between unemployment and inflation and to assess the impact of changes in government policy on inflation and unemployment. In this Section you will assess different views on the likely shape of the Phillips curve. You will also develop the ability to plot Phillips curves to assess current relationships between unemployment and inflation in the UK and other economies.

The origin of the short-run Phillips curve

The Phillips curve is named after Bill Phillips, a New Zealander, who started his working life as an engineer. After the Second World War, he came to study sociology at the London School of Economics (LSE). During his course he became interested in economics and, in particular, in studying the effect of changes in unemployment rates on money wages. He stayed on at the LSE and studied unemployment rates and wages increases during the period 1861 to 1957. He found an inverse, non-linear, relationship between unemployment rates and wage increases. This means that as unemployment falls, rises in money wages increase but not at a proportionate rate – they accelerate. When unemployment falls to low levels, money wages rise rapidly, whereas when unemployment rises to high levels, workers resist cuts in money wages.

Development of the short-run Phillips curve

The Phillips curve was developed by two US economists, Paul Samuelson and Robert Solow in 1960, with changes in money wages being taken as an indicator of inflation to show the expected relationship between unemployment and inflation. Figure 1 shows the inverse relationship between unemployment and inflation.

When demand for labour rises, unemployment is likely to fall. The increased competition for workers is likely to bid up wage rates. Higher pay for workers can increase the price level via increased costs of production and higher aggregate demand as the workers spend their wages.

Economists had drawn up Phillips curves for most countries by the mid-1960s. In this period, the short-run Phillips curve was interpreted by economists and politicians to suggest that policy makers could trade off inflation and unemployment to reach a desired combination. For example, a reduction in unemployment from, say, 6 per cent to 4 per cent might have to be 'bought' at the price of a rise in inflation from, for example, 3 per cent to 5 per cent.

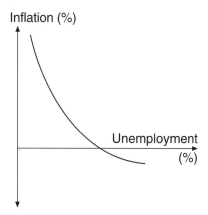

Figure 1: The short-run Phillips curve

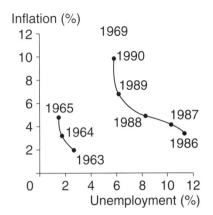

Figure 2: Phillips curve for the USA in the 1960s

Figure 3: The rightward shift of the short-run Phillips curve in the UK in the 1980s

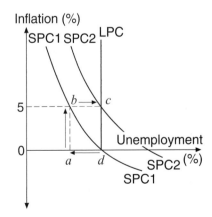

Figure 4: Milton Friedman

Changes in the relationship between unemployment and inflation

In the late 1960s and the 1970s, the Phillips curve came in for criticism. Some economists argued that the relationship it predicted still existed but that the curve had shifted to the right, indicating that a higher level of unemployment would be combined with any level of inflation. They suggested that in the 1970s workers had got used to higher levels of unemployment and so did not modify wage claims to the same extent when unemployment rose (see Figure 3).

The long-run Phillips curve

Milton Friedman (Figure 4), the most famous **monetarist** economist, went further. He questioned the accuracy, in the long run, of the traditional Phillips curve in predicting the effect of changes in aggregate demand on the level of unemployment and inflation. He argued that, while a **Phillips curve** relationship may exist in the short run between unemployment and inflation, in the long run changes in aggregate demand would influence inflation but leave output and unemployment unaffected. **The long-run Phillips curve** he developed is also sometimes referred to as the expectations-augmented Phillips curve.

Explanation of the long-run Phillips Curve

Figure 5 shows the economy initially operating on the short-run Phillips curve (SPC1) with 0 per cent inflation and 6 per cent unemployment. An increase in aggregate demand may, in the short run, encourage firms to expand their output and take on more workers. Unemployment falls and the economy is at point *a*. However, the rise in demand for goods and services and the resources to produce them will result in inflation. The economy now moves to point *b*. When producers and workers realise that inflation has

Definitions

Monetarists: a group of economists who believe that increases in the money supply in excess of increases in output will cause inflation.

Long-run Phillips curve: a curve that indicates there is no long-run trade off between unemployment and inflation.

Figure 5: The long-run Phillips curve

eroded their real profits and wage levels they adjust their behaviour. This, combined with some workers leaving their jobs because of the fall in real wages, causes unemployment to return to the NAIRU level (see Section 5.19). The economy now moves to point c on the long run Phillips curve (LPC) where there is no trade-off between unemployment and inflation. However, the economy is also on a higher level short-run Phillips curve since now expectations of inflation have been built into the system. Producers and workers have experienced 5 per cent inflation and so will base their future prices and wage claims on the assumption that the price level will continue to rise. Any future increase in aggregate demand, not accompanied by an increase in long-run aggregate supply, will result in an acceleration in inflation.

Policy implications of the long-run Phillips curve

The long-run Phillips curve implies that there is no trade off between unemployment and inflation in the long run and that governments are powerless to reduce unemployment by implementing expansionary fiscal and monetary policy. The view that government attempts to reduce unemployment by increasing aggregate demand would not succeed in lowering unemployment but would increase inflation was expressed by James Callaghan, the Labour Prime Minister, in a speech to the Labour Party Conference in 1976.

> 'It used to be thought that a nation could just spend its way out of recession and increase employment by cutting taxes and boosting government spending. I tell you in all candour that that option no longer exists. In so far as it existed in the past, it had always led to a bigger dose of inflation followed by a higher level of unemployment.'

The Conservative government, which came to power in 1979, subscribed to this view and the Conservative administrations of the 1980s and 1990s did not attempt to reduce unemployment by increasing aggregate demand.

The relationship between Phillips curves and aggregate demand and aggregate supply

The long-run Phillips curve is related to the long-run aggregate supply curve. An increase in aggregate demand, caused by, for example, a rise in government spending will, in the short run, increase real GDP and raise the price level. In the long run, there will be a decrease in short-run aggregate supply due to the rise in production costs that occur when output is produced beyond the productive potential level. Figure 6 shows, using both an aggregate demand and aggregate supply curve and Phillips curves, how an increase in aggregate demand results in higher inflation but unchanged unemployment in the long run.

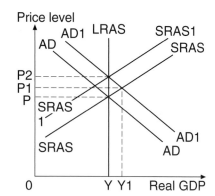

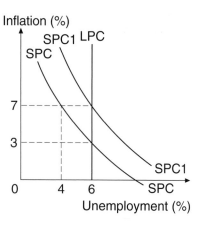

Figure 6: The effect of an increase in aggregate demand on inflation and unemployment

The recent relationship between unemployment and inflation

The late 1990s and early 2000s witnessed falls in both the unemployment rate and the inflation rate in the UK, USA and a number of European countries. Economic relationships appear to have changed in this period. Falling unemployment was not putting upward pressure on the inflation rate. There were a number of reasons advanced to explain why inflationary pressure may have fallen. These included changes in labour markets (for example reduced trade union power and increased labour market flexibility), advances in technology (which reduce unit costs) and increased competition from abroad (forcing firms to keep down rises in prices).

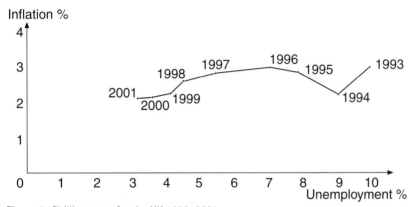

Figure 7: Phillips curve for the UK 1993–2001

Figure 7 shows an almost horizontal Phillips curve for the UK for the period 1993 to 2001. As the economy approached full employment, inflation remained low. A horizontal Phillips curve is an ideal situation for a government as it means that it can achieve both low unemployment and low inflation – there is no policy conflict.

Quick check

1 Why might a fall in unemployment cause an increase in inflation?
2 In what sense does the short-run Phillips curve indicate a policy conflict?
3 Why in the long run may there be no trade off between unemployment and inflation?
4 What could cause the long-run Phillips curve to shift to the left?

Thinking like an economist

Plot a Phillips curve for the UK from 2000 onwards and analyse the relationship you have found.

The natural rate of unemployment hypothesis

Synoptic link

This section builds on AS sections 3.4, 3.16 and 3.17. Before starting this section, check your understanding of the causes of unemployment, supply-side policies and policies to reduce unemployment.

Definition

NAIRU (the non-accelerating inflation rate of unemployment): the level of unemployment which exists when the labour market is in equilibrium.

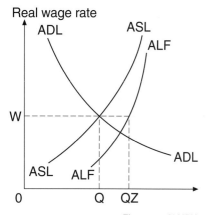

Figure 1: NAIRU

Introduction

NAIRU (the non-accelerating inflation rate of unemployment) is the level of unemployment which exists when the aggregate demand for labour is equal to the aggregate supply of labour at the going wage rate. This is why it is also sometimes referred to as equilibrium unemployment. As the name NAIRU suggests, it is consistent with the level of unemployment at which there is no upward pressure on the wage rate and inflation. If unemployment falls below this level, perhaps because a government raises aggregate demand in a bid to reduce unemployment, the rate of inflation increases. In contrast, if unemployment rises above NAIRU, this time perhaps because the government is seeking to reduce inflation, the wage rate and inflation will fall.

The nature of NAIRU

NAIRU consists of voluntary, frictional and structural unemployment. These are the people who are out of work because they are unaware of vacancies, unsuited to take up the vacancies or are unwilling to take up the vacancies. Some economists argue that all these are voluntarily unemployed because they could put more effort into finding out about job vacancies, could be more prepared to move to find employment and be more prepared to accept, for a period of time at least, a lower-paid job than they ideally would like.

NAIRU can be illustrated on a diagram that shows the aggregate labour force (ALF) but separates out from the labour force those prepared to work at the going wage rate (the aggregate supply of labour, ASL). The gap between the aggregate labour force and the aggregate supply of labour consists of NAIRU. The gap between ASL and ALF narrows as the wage rate rises as more of the labour force is prepared to work at the higher the wage rate.

Figure 1 shows the labour market is in equilibrium at q. However, there are still unemployed workers, Q-QZ, consisting of those not willing to work at the going wage rate.

Views on NAIRU

NAIRU was originally referred to as the natural rate of unemployment and was almost exclusively associated with new classical economists. This group believes that the real wage rate adjusts quickly and smoothly to changes in labour market conditions so that any unemployment which occurs must be of an equilibrium level. It is now more frequently referred to as NAIRU, in part because the term 'natural' implies that a certain level of unemployment should exist and also because it emphasises the connection with inflationary pressure.

Keynesians also argue that while during a recession the main cause of unemployment is a lack of aggregate demand, at any time unemployment can include both equilibrium and disequilibrium forms as illustrated in Figure 2.

Keynesians, however, believe that real wages do not adjust smoothly to changes in labour market conditions to eliminate disequilibrium unemployment. They also argue that those experiencing frictional and structural unemployment may be experiencing real difficulties in gaining employment. For example, the longer someone is unemployed, the more problem they may find in gaining a job because their skills have become out-of-date and perhaps because they have lost the habit of working and some of their confidence. This tendency for unemployment to generate longer-term unemployment and to push up NAIRU is called **hysteresis**.

Factors affecting the NAIRU rate

A number of factors are thought to affect the rate of unemployment which is consistent with stable inflation.

- **Hysteresis**, as discussed above: This can be influenced by government policy. If a government, seeking to reduce inflation, reduces aggregate demand and causes a rise in unemployment, the level of unemployment may not return to the former NAIRU rate because of hysteresis.
- Educational standards, training and skills of the labour force: The higher the quality and quantity of education, training and skills, the more occupationally mobile workers are likely to be and the easier they are likely to find it move from one job to another.
- Unemployment benefits: New classical economists argue that if there is only a small gap between wages and job seekers' allowance, there will be little incentive for the unemployed to seek work. So they favour widening this gap, which is called the **replacement ratio**, and tightening up the eligibility criteria for receiving benefit.
- Flexibility of labour: The more flexible labour is in terms of the hours worked, the length of employment contract, the type of tasks undertaken and location, the lower NAIRU is likely to be.
- Trade unions: New classical economists argue that trade unions can increase NAIRU by engaging in restrictive practices.
- Income tax rates: Lower income tax rates increase the return from working.
- Labour market regulations: New classical economists argue that the more government controls there are on the employment of workers, the higher NAIRU will be. This is why they opposed the signing of the Social Chapter of the EU which, for example, puts a limit on the number of working hours per week and gives male workers paternity rights.

Policies to reduce NAIRU

As noted above, new classical economists favour measures which increase the flexibility of labour markets, make work more attractive relative to unemployment by cutting income tax rates and job seekers' allowance, remove labour market regulations except for 'essential' health and safety rules and reduce trade union power.

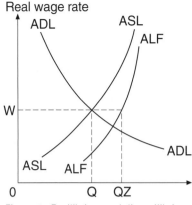

Figure 2: Equilibrium and disequilibrium unemployment

Definitions

Hysteresis: the view that unemployment generates unemployment.
Replacement ratio: the relationship between unemployment benefit and income from employment.

Thinking like an economist

Discuss whether a fall in wages will reduce or increase unemployment.

In contrast, Keynesian economists favour more interventionist policies, including increased government spending on education and training and regional policies. The latter seek to reduce regional unemployment largely by moving work to workers. This policy approach is based on the view that social ties can make labour immobile, that firms do not always seek the optimum location sites and moving people out of areas of high unemployment can depress them further and waste social capital.

Recent labour governments have sought to reduce NAIRU by using interventionist and, to a greater extent, free market supply-side policies. These policies have included:

- raising spending on education and setting higher performance standards
- widening the gap between the amount that low-paid workers receive and the amount that the unemployed receive. To date, it has done this by cutting income tax rates, introducing the working families tax credit and introducing the minimum wage. Cutting income tax rates raises workers' disposable income. The working families' tax credit is a top-up payment given to the low paid. Once in work it is anticipated that most of the recipients will move into higher-paid jobs and so no longer require the subsidy. The introduction of the national minimum wage has raised the pay of the very low paid – although this is a measure opposed by many new classical economists who argue that it creates a labour market imperfection.
- introducing the New Deal. The intention is to reduce hysteresis by developing the skills and work experience of the unemployed. Initially it was targeted at those aged between 18 and 24 and then extended to most unemployed adults. Under the scheme the unemployed have to take up the offer of a job subsidised by the government, a place on an educational or training course or on the government's environmental task force.
- introducing compulsory job advice interviews for those receiving benefits, including those receiving income support and housing benefit. For example, lone parents are made aware of how they might be able to combine working with bringing up their children, including undertaking part-time employment. Again the intention is to maintain the habit of work and keep skills up to date.

Hot potato

It is claimed that the UK's NAIRU is now lower than it was in the 1990s while Germany's NAIRU rate is higher. What may explain this?

Quick check

1   What is the difference between the aggregate supply of labour and the aggregate labour force?
2   Who are unemployed at NAIRU?
3   Explain three factors that could result in an increase in NAIRU.
4   Explain why advances in technology may reduce NAIRU.

Introduction

The UK is operating in a global economy. Advances in technology and reductions in transport costs are enabling UK consumers to access markets throughout the world. UK firms are selling their products throughout the world and locating separate parts of their production processes in a range of countries. However as the demonstrations which regularly occur at meetings of the World Trade Organisation and other international organisations show, some people are concerned about the effects of globalisation.

The meaning of globalisation

Globalisation is the development of the world into one market place. National barriers are being broken down in terms of where firms make their products and in terms of where people buy their goods and services. Countries have always traded with each other but now the scale of the movement of goods and services, ideas and capital investment between countries is increasing rapidly. The production processes and patterns of consumption are becoming more and more integrated. Consumers in, for example, China, France and Nigeria buy more and more of the same products, for example Manchester United shirts and Coca-Cola. Parts of products, including cars and toys, are being assembled in a number of industrial and developing countries.

Features of globalisation

Globalisation is manifesting itself in the following main forms:
- the rapid increase in international trade. This is growing faster than world output.
- an increase in foreign direct investment which is the movement of physical capital between countries.

Other periods, for example the end of the nineteenth and start of the twentieth centuries, have witnessed rapid increases in international trade and international capital movements, but now these are also accompanied by:
- the growth of multinational companies (MNCs) which are increasingly thinking and operating globally, not only owning plants in different countries, but also engaging in the fragmentation of production. This involves MNCs spreading different stages of production around the world, sometimes using their own plants and sometimes a combination of their own plants and other firms' plants. So when the managers of these MNCs plan their production processes they do not just consider producing a product in one location. Instead they think transnationally – they consider assembling parts in a range of countries and they use a decentralised management structure.
- an increase in the number of countries producing manufactured goods
- for export.

Synoptic link

This section is linked to AS Sections 3.23 and 3.24, and A2 Sections 5.12 and 5.13. It would also be useful to look at A2 Section 5.30.

Thinking like an economist

Analyse the effects that globalisation is likely to bring about in demand for labour in industrialised countries and in developing countries.

Causes of globalisation

Globalisation is occurring due to:

- improved communication: Advances in information technology are increasing the ease with which consumers can find out about and buy products from other countries and the ease with which producers can co-ordinate production throughout the world. For example, consumers in the UK now regularly order CDs, books and other items from the USA and other countries over the Internet. Managers of UK MNCs keep in touch with their staff in other countries using a range of information technology including e-mail and teleconferencing.
- reduced transport costs: Over time with the development of containerisation and increasing use of larger ships and planes, transport costs have been falling.
- trade liberalisation: Since the Second World War the barriers to the free movement of goods and services and capital have been reducing.
- increased competition in manufactured goods: This is coming from developing countries, particularly from the newly industrialised countries (NICs) of South East Asia such as South Korea and Singapore.
- rise in skill levels throughout the world: This is enabling multinational companies to assemble parts not only in industrial countries but also in developing countries.

Consequences of globalisation

Globalisation is having a number of significant effects including:

- changing the nature of international trade: An increasingly higher percentage of international trade consists of the exchange of similar products from the same industries (for example, different makes of computers from China to the USA and from the USA to China) and a smaller percentage consists of different products from different industries (for example, textiles from India to France and cars from France to India). At the start of the twentieth century, manufactured goods were being exported from Europe and the USA to developing countries in return for raw materials, Now at the start of the twenty-first century, Europe and the USA are still exporting manufactured goods to developing countries but now in return for manufactured goods.
- causing more and more firms to think globally: As already noted, advances in technology and transport are enabling firms to target consumers throughout the world and to operate in a range of countries.
- increasing foreign direct investment: This is linked to the point above. Multinational companies are seeking out the lowest cost countries in which to locate production and parts of the production process. Indeed some are now being referred to as transnationals as they have substantial operations in a large number of countries and have a decentralised management structure.

- increasing the susceptibility of countries to external shocks: The increased integration of economies means that problems in one part of the world quickly spread to other countries. This was seen during the East Asian Crisis of 1997-1999. The difficulties faced by financial institutions in Japan, Thailand, Indonesia and other East Asian countries resulted in slowed world growth, and reduced aggregate demand in the West and caused problems for US and European firms and banks with links to the Far East.

- affecting government policy: A global market increases the pressure on economies to be economically efficient. The UK government is seeking to raise the economy's long-term performance by using supply-side policies. It is also using regional policy to help those areas and their workers who have been hit by increased competition from abroad.

- increasing the role of international organisations in overseeing world trade, including the World Trade Organisation (WTO) and the International Monetary Fund (IMF). The WTO was formed in 1995, replacing GATT. It seeks to reduce tariffs and other restrictions on international trade and provides a means by which countries can settle their trade disputes. (The WTO is discussed in more detail in Section 5.26.) The IMF was established in 1947 with the main aim of encouraging world trade. It acts as international bank offering assistance to countries in financial difficulties.

- changing countries' comparative advantage: The rise in the level of competition coming particularly from the newly industrialised countries is causing a shift in resources in Europe and the USA.

- reducing price differences between countries: A market is said to be completely integrated when identical products sell at the same price in different countries.

Quick check

1   What is causing globalisation to occur?
2   Explain two possible advantages and disadvantages of globalisation for consumers.
3   What is meant by 'firms thinking transnationally'?
4   What factors could slow down globalisation?

Puzzler

Will globalisation lead to greater prosperity or greater inequality?

International competitiveness, multinational companies and foreign direct investment

Synoptic link

This section is linked to Section 5.20 and has connections with balance of payments performance (see AS Sections 3.6 and 3.20).

Thinking like an economist

What is the connection between FDI and the current account position?

Introduction

The UK is a main recipient of inward foreign direct investment in the European Union, although its share has fallen since 1999. The presence of foreign multinational companies in the country can bring a number of advantages including the introduction of new technology. Such advantages should help to raise the country's international competitiveness.

Foreign direct investment

UK multinational companies invest abroad and foreign multinational companies invest in the UK. This investment includes the establishment of new plants, the expansion of existing plants and the purchase of existing plants and firms.

Multinational companies seek the highest return on their capital. So the amount of foreign direct investment attracted by a country is influenced by the productivity and flexibility of its workers, its tax rates, the stability of its economic policies, its rate of economic growth, the size of its market and the perception of its future economic prospects. The UK is currently an attractive location for FDI because of:

- government grants especially for multinationals setting up in the poorer regions of the UK
- its flexible labour force
- its time zone advantage in financial services
- its membership of the EU: Setting up in the UK gives, for example, a Japanese or US multinational company access to the EU market without having to pay the common external tariff. Some economists, however, believe that if the UK continues to stay out of the single currency, FDI may be reduced.
- the use of the English language: This is the main language of the Internet and is frequently used in international business. In addition, it is obviously spoken by Americans and is the most popular foreign language learnt by the Japanese and South Koreans.

The effects of foreign direct investment

These include:

- an initial inflow of investment which will appear as a credit item in the financial account. However, in the longer run money will flow out of the country in the form of investment income (profit, interest and dividends) which will appear in the current account. The goods and services that the multinational company sells abroad will count in the country's exports. The net effect on imports is rather more uncertain. Some goods and services which had previously been bought abroad from the MNCs may now be purchased from their plants in the home country. However the MNC may purchase some of their raw materials and services from their home countries.

- MNC may cause a rise in employment. This is one of the key reasons that governments give grants to MNCs to set up in their country. They hope that the MNCs will increase employment directly by taking on workers and indirectly by increasing economic activity and demand in the area in which they are based. However, some of those employed by the MNCs, particularly in top management posts, may be bought over from the home country. Even more significantly, if the competition from MNCs leads to domestic firms going out of business, they will not be creating employment, merely replacing jobs.
- MNCs, especially in developing countries, can help to spread knowledge and understanding of recent technological advances. A high proportion of MNCs are high tech, capital intensive firms.
- MNCs can bring in new ideas of management techniques. The establishment of Japanese and South Korean MNCs in a range of countries has resulted in their host countries reviewing their management styles.
- MNCs' output counts in the home country's GDP and in many cases their contribution to output and growth is significant.
- MNCs tend to have high labour productivity. This is mainly because of high capital/labour ratios. This may encourage domestically owned firms to raise their productivity levels and may reduce inflationary tendencies.
- a rise in tax revenue may occur but some MNCs try to reduce their tax payments by moving revenue around their plants in different countries in order to minimise their payments.
- pollution levels may rise. This is particularly the case in developing countries where MNCs may locate in order to get round tighter environmental regulations at home. MNCs may also be attracted by less strict labour market policies in terms of working hours, health and safety, minimum wages and lowest working age.

International competitiveness

International competitiveness can be defined as the ability of a country's firms to compete successfully in international markets and thereby permit the country to continue to grow. Sometimes referring to a country as being internationally competitive is taken to mean that it can produce products more cheaply than most other countries. However, it is more commonly taken by economists in a wider context to also include competitiveness in terms of quality and marketing.

Indicators of international competitiveness

In assessing how internationally competitive an economy is, economists examine a range of indicators including:
- growth rates: Competitive economies tend to grow faster than non-competitive ones because their products are in high world demand.

Thinking like an economist

1 What effect may the presence of MNCs in a country have on the country's employment?
2 Explain the connection between a country's international competitiveness and its economic growth rate.

Research task

Assess the impact that MNCs are having in your area.

- productivity levels: Higher productivity levels increase the country's productive capacity and allow long term growth to occur.
- unit labour costs: This is obviously linked to productivity levels. If output per worker rises more rapidly than wages and other labour costs, unit labour costs will fall.
- share of exports in world trade: It is becoming increasingly difficult for an industrial country to maintain its share of world trade in the face of increasing competition from a number of developing countries, particularly the NICs.
- balance of trade in goods and services: This is linked to the point above. A competitive country is not likely to have a large deficit on its trade in goods and services balance.
- investment as a proportion of GDP: Investment is seen as an important cause of economic growth.
- education and training: As with investment, these are thought to be very important indicators. A country with high quality education and training is likely to have a flexible, highly-skilled and highly-productive labour force.
- investment in research and development: High levels of expenditure on research and development are likely to develop and encourage the implementation of new technology.
- communications and infrastructure: Good communications and infrastructure will increase the efficiency of firms by lowering their costs and increasing their speed of response to changes in market conditions.
- industrial relations: Good industrial relations increase the quantity and quality of output.
- composite indicators: The Swiss-based International Institute for Management Development (IMD) each year publishes a global league table for international competitiveness. This ranks 46 countries on 259 criteria designed to measure factors providing a good business environment. These include economic performance, infrastructure, the role of government, management, the financial system and technological competence. Two-thirds of the criteria are based on statistical data and one-third comes from an opinion survey of more than 4000 business executives world-wide. The USA has, so far, always come top of the league table.

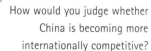

Hot potato

How would you judge whether China is becoming more internationally competitive?

Changes in international competitiveness

There are a number of key factors which may raise a country's international competitiveness. Two of the most important are:
- changes in the exchange rate: If the pound falls in value, the country's products will become relatively more competitive.
- changes in relative inflation rates: If the country's products rise in price less than their competitors' price levels, its products will again become more competitive.

UK's international competitiveness

The UK's position in the IMD league table fluctuates, but in recent years the trend has been upwards. On certain of the criteria used to measure competitiveness, the UK has been performing well in recent years. These include economic growth (where the trend economic growth rate has improved), a reduction in strikes and high levels of FDI. However, investment and productivity levels still remain below some of the UK's main competitors and the high value of the pound has been putting pressure on the price competitiveness of exporters.

Government measures to promote competitiveness

These include:

- maintaining price stability and general economic stability
- promoting FDI
- increasing the quality and quantity of education and training
- encouraging investment.

New classical economists also favour privatisation and deregulation as they believe that these measures increase the efficiency with which industries work.

Quick check

1 Why do governments seek to attract FDI?
2 Identify two disadvantages of capital inflows from MNCs.
3 What is meant by 'a country increasing its international competitiveness'?
4 In what ways might increased investment raise a country's international competitiveness?

5.22 What is development?

Synoptic link

This section is directly linked to work that you have done for AS on using GDP as a macroeconomic measure. If you cannot remember the arguments about the value and limitations of this measure check back to Part 3, Section 3.1 of AS. You will also use what you have learned about economic growth and government polices for AS and for A2. This is a good topic to help you see the various connections between different aspects of economics.

Research task

Evaluate the usefulness of national income statistics in helping measure economic development in different countries.

Development indicators

Historically there have been three different ways in which economic development has been defined. In the 1960s and 1970s, the United Nations focused upon positive changes in real GDP or GNP and set developing nations the target of hitting a 6 per cent growth rate per annum. It was assumed that the benefits of such growth would trickle down to benefit the mass of population of any given country. Most economists now realise that it was a mistake to equate economic development with economic growth. While it is true to argue that people will not become better off without economic growth, this is not a sufficient condition to ensure that the welfare of most people is improved. For example, a country may produce more goods and services but if these are very unevenly distributed and if they are produced at the cost of damage to the environment, it can be questionable whether economic development has occurred.

An alternative view of development became more widely accepted in the 1980s, which acknowledged the importance of economic growth but also included reference to the reduction of poverty, inequality and unemployment. Although the 'trickle down' approach was still considered valid by such organisations as the World Bank and the IMF, by the end of the 1990s there was broad acceptance of the wider definition of development.

Some economists use an even wider definition of development to focus on human rather than economic values such as empowerment, self-esteem and freedom. Meeting targets such as these often requires institutional and attitudinal change as well as a faster rate of economic growth. It is important for you to understand the strengths and weaknesses of using different measures in relationship to the needs of developing countries. These include:

- GDP
- infant mortality and life expectancy
- literacy rates
- proportion of the population employed in agriculture
- compound measures: the two best-known ones are the UN's human development index (HDI) and the human poverty index (HPI).

GDP

You should already be familiar with the problems of using GDP as a macroeconomic measure in a developed economy such as the UK. Even if real GDP per capita is used, this measure may fail to account for:

- the mix of goods produced
- inequalities in income
- the production of externalities
- the output of the social economy.

It can also be distorted by recording and accounting problems.

These factors also apply to countries with developing economies and in some cases are even more important. In a worse case scenario, it is possible to consider economic growth occurring in the context of gross inequalities of income, which results in the production of luxury goods rather than basics for survival. This growth could be unsustainable involving the once and for all consumption of non-renewable resources, whereas the mutual support offered by poorer groups and extended families would not be recognised. Finally if government and civil services are weak, it is likely that official statistics would be incomplete. This extreme scenario illustrates the shortcomings of relying on **GDP** as a measure of development.

GNI

GNI stands for gross national income and the measures that are used in this Section are those used by the World Bank. Although it is not possible to make judgements about development using this this data alone, the underlying significance of GNI per capita must never be underestimated. If per capita income figures are low, as is the case with Angola (Table 1), it follows that poverty, suffering and starvation will be major problems and that such countries are always going to be faced with massive problems in terms of fincancing development programmes.

Moreover it is important to consider the nature of the economic growth being experienced. For economic growth to take place the economic growth must be sustainable, i.e. achieved in a way which does not reduce future populations' ability to produce more. Some developing nations, particularly in Africa, have in the past achieved relatively high levels of growth but at the opportunity cost of using up non-renewable resouces.

Infant mortality and life expectancy

These two measures are commonally used to give a quick notion of the quality of life in different countries. This is illustrated in Table 2.

Table 2: Infant mortality and life expectancy for selected countries

Country	Infant mortality 2001 (per thousand live births)	Life expectancy 2001 (years)
Angola	154	46.6
Argentina	16	74.1
Belarus	17	68.1
Cuba	7	76.6
Switzerland	5	79.8
Syria	23	70.0
Thailand	24	69.0
UK	6	77.4

Source: *World Development Indicators Data Base*, April 2003, World Bank

Definition

GDP stands for Gross Domestic Product and this represents the value of the total output of a country.

Table 1: GNI per capital for selected countries

Country	GNI per capita in 2001 (US$)
Angola	500
Argentina	6940
Belarus	1290
Cuba	Unknown
Switzerland	38,330
Syria	1040
Thailand	1940
UK	25,120

Source: *World Development Indicators Data Base*, April 2003, World Bank

Infant mortality is regarded as a very useful measure as it acts as a proxy variable for many other factors – quality of health care, clean water, the diet of mothers and so on. The data for Angola confirms the serious difficulties faced by its people, whereas those for Cuba indicate the priority given to healthcare in an otherwise poor country.

Literacy rates

There are different ways in which this indicator can be measured. The World Bank currently includes measures of both males and females aged 15 and above who are illiterate. The data for the countries identified in Table 2 is shown in Table 3.

Table 3: Literacy rates for selected countries

Country	Total illiteracy (percentage of population aged 15 and above) 2001	Female illiteracy (percentage of population aged 15 and above) 2001
Angola	unknown	unknown
Argentina	3.1	3.1
Belarus	0.3	0.4
Cuba	3.2	3.3
Switzerland	unknown	unknown
Syria	24.7	38.4
Thailand	4.3	5.9
UK	unknown	unknown

Source: *World Development Indicators Data Base*, April 2003, World Bank

Sectorial analysis

Another measure that is used considers the importance of the agricultural sector in a given economy. The World Bank compares the proportion of GDP contributed by the agricultural, industrial and service sectors. The usefulness of this measure is based on the proposition that, as countries develop, the agricultural sector becomes relatively less imporant relative to the contributions of the industrial and service sectors. The data for the eight countries chosen is shown in Table 4.

Human Development Index (HDI)

An alternative and more comprehensive set of measures of economic development are those developed by the United Nations Development Programme which focuses on the human impact of various economic

Table 4: Proportion of GDP contributed by agricultural sector for selected countries

Country	Value added in agriculture (per cent of GDP), 2001
Angola	8.0
Argentina	4.8
Belarus	10.9
Cuba	6.7*
Switzerland	1.7
Syria	22.5
Thailand	10.2
UK	1.0

* 2000 data

Source: *World Development Indicators Data Base*, April 2003, World Bank

factors. It is assumed that development should focus on three aspects of human development:

- how long people might expect to live
- access to knowledge and learning
- standard of living.

The most recently available index is reproduced in Table 5. In the words of its authors, *'The concept of Human Development looks beyond per capita income, human resource development, and basic needs as a measure of human progress and also assesses such factors as human freedom, dignity and human agency, that is, the role of people in development. The HDR argues that development is ultimately a process of enlarging people's choices, not just raising national incomes.'* (UNDP July 2002)

This most recent UNDP report also highlights that over 50 countries have been faced with declines in their development. Two, Jamaica and Madagascar, are worse off than they were over 25 years ago, and many countries who were part of the old communist block, as well as most African countries, are becoming worse off.

Table 5: HDI for selected countries

Country	HDI rank
Jamaica	86
Madagascar	147
UK	13

Summary

There are a range of indicators which can be used to judge development in different countries. The World Bank uses measures which focus more on economic dimensions to development whereas the UN focuses more on social factors. Both organisations generate amazing amounts of data which are easily accessed. Whatever measures are used, these data shows that most of the least developed countires are to be found in Sub-Saharan Africa. These indicators also show that over 50 countries in the world are becoming worse off than they were in the past.

The following Sections will try to help you understand which factors are likely to aid economic development and which factors act as barriers. With growing instability in the world it could be argued that having a better understanding of global inequalities is one of the most important challenges for all of us.

Hot potato

The Gini Co-efficient for Zambia is 49.8 compared with 36.1 for the UK. What are the implications for the effects of positive economic growth in Zambia?

Weblink

The best portal for data on development is http://www.developmentgateway.org

---

Quick check

What global patterns can you find in the data about development contained in this Section?

Latin America

Synoptic link

This and the following two sections are each devoted to looking at development issues in three parts of the world. They all follow directly from the preceding sections on indicators of development. The three regions are:

- Latin America
- Asia
- Sub-Saharan Africa.

The development of each region is illustrated by maps and statistics and each of these three sections includes consideration of the factors which will have influenced development within the region. These involve a consideration of the inter-relationship between historic, political and economic factors.

Introduction

This Section focuses on Latin America, which includes countries at different stages of development. In terms of the UNDP, most Latin American countries fall into the middle group of countries: most have significant raw materials, levels of education for most people are not exceptionally low, but there also tends to be huge inequalities in the distribution of income and wealth, which have been a source of political instability for over 100 years. This instability has had a very negative effect on development.

Historical factors

Prior to colonisation by the Spanish and Portuguese from 1492 onwards, Latin America was a comparatively under-populated continent, which had supported extensive and complex civilisations such as the Mayans and Aztecs. There were also tribal societies living in what some would call subsistence economies which others would describe as self sustaining and stable. Considerable advances had been made in agriculture and the development of cures for disease and in understanding ecological systems. It would be a mistake to describe these various cultures as undeveloped.

The European invasions, which followed early voyages of discovery by Columbus, Vespucci and others, changed all this; most of the indigenous people of the West Indies and the more accessible coastal fringes of Latin America were exterminated. Those surviving fled to less accessible regions. The Spanish and Portuguese were primarily looking for wealth to take back to Europe; the Spanish were particularly successful in expropriating rich reserves of gold and silver which was shipped back to Europe to provide the financial basis for the expanding political and social power of the Spanish empire during the sixteenth century. The riches of countries like Peru and Columbia financed the growing power of Spain.

These early stages of colonisation involved the use of considerable military power to establish new colonies under the direct control of Spain and Portugal. British, French, Dutch and Swedish settlers also established small colonies, especially in the Caribbean, and tended to be in conflict with each other as well as with the Spanish.

In the late sixteenth and early seventeenth centuries, more direct colonisation took place. The richer and more productive lands were incorporated into large estates and ownership was taken up by Spanish families who were already wealthy. The tobacco and sugar industries flourished, creating more income for their owners which tended to flow back to Europe. Profits were boosted by the importation of slaves from West Africa especially to the West Indies and Brazil. In short, most of south America consisted of feudal economies supporting a small number of very wealthy Europeans and a large mass of slaves and peasants living in conditions of exploitation and extreme suffering.

In the latter part of the nineteenth century, there were relatively large migrations of Europeans, especially from Spain and Italy but also from Germany and other European countries, who helped form a small but growing middle class. Spain's economic and political power was by then declining, and from the 1820s onwards the inequalities arising from these still feudal societies led to a series of independence movements. This coincided with conflict between the USA and Spain, which led to independence in Cuba and an increasing US commercial and political interest in the continent. By the beginning of the twentieth century, most countries had achieved independence from Spain but were increasingly regarded by the US as part of its growing empire.

In the 1880s, countries such as Chile, Uruguay and Argentina had made reasonable progress in terms of early economic development. Chile was the world's largest producer of guano (bird droppings which were used as fertiliser) while other countries in the south of the continent produced wheat and beef for international markets. Some studies show that Argentina was roughly equal to the US in terms of its economic development at that time. It shared vast reserves of natural resources, enjoyed high levels of investment from Europe, had a growing agricultural sector and similar political and commercial institutions. Although less developed, other countries such as Uruguay, Chile, and Brazil had extensive natural resources and relatively small populations, seemingly set for take off according to Rostow's model. However, this has never really happened and Argentina, along with most other countries in South America, has achieved slow and erratic economic development.

In the twentieth century, further investment led to greater industrialisation but most countries were largely dependent on exports of primary products to the US and Europe. The economies of South American countries tended to follow the economic cycles of the countries to which they exported. Wars in Europe tended to promote greater development of import-substituting industries leading to an increase in living standards in South American countries, but no significant changes in the distribution of wealth and income.

There have been periods of economic growth – reaching 10 per cent per annum in the 1960s in Brazil – and some improvements in infrastructure, but most South American economies have also experienced hyper-inflation, social unrest, and many continue to be dependent upon the export of primary products. In the 1970s and 1980s, there were large movements of foreign capital into South America and many international financiers believed that long awaited take off of these economies was about to occur. This did not happen and many countries in Latin American have been left with very high levels of international debt, which can only be repaid at the expense of domestic investment. Over the last decade, many countries in Latin America have experienced falling growth rates, increased social unrest, and some have been ruled by brutal right-wing dictatorships.

Although there are differing views as to why a well-resourced continent should grow so erratically the following factors are significant.

Inequalities in wealth and income

These are greater than in most other parts of the world as is shown by Table 1.

Table 1: Gini Co-efficients for selected countries in Latin America (with comparisons). This is a measure of equality in the distribution of incomes. Zero would represent perfect equality and 100 percent perfect inequality.

Country	Gini Index score	World ranking
Slovakia	18.2	Most equal distribution of income
UK	36.1	
Costa Rica	47	
Chile	56.5	
Paraguay	59.1	
Brazil	60	
Sierra Leone	62.9	Least equal distribution of income

Source: UNCTAD 2001

These inequalities are partly attributable to great disparities in the distribution of wealth. As noted earlier, resources tend to be owned by a small minority of the population. This has meant that the benefits of periods of economic growth tend to be enjoyed by small elites and that their great wealth has reduced the incentive to invest in technologies which would increase productivity both in industry and agriculture.

Inequality means great wealth for the few and relative poverty for the many. This is readily apparent in most cities in Latin America, where the rich live side-by-side with the poor, and provides a breeding ground for both criminal and revolutionary activity. Rio de Janeiro is currently terrorised by rival drug gangs whose violence is such that normal daily activities are limited.

Undemocratic institutions

These economic inequalities create the conditions for civil unrest which has, in turn, been used by the armed forces to justify military coup resulting in the suspension of democratic processes and ruthless suppression of dissent.

In the last 50 years, every country in South America has experienced a period of military rule, while at other times totalitarian governments have been kept in power by the support of the military. It is now realised that persistent inequalities and lack of democratic institutions are major barriers to economic development.

Lawlessness and civil conflict have been exacerbated by the enormous potential profits to be made from the international trade in illegal drugs. In countries such as Columbia, these profits have been used to finance the arming of private armies largely beyond the control of governments. Other governments, for example in Bolivia, Panama and in the West Indies, have used drug money to stay in power.

One of the further outcomes of the persistence of conflict is that resources are diverted into military expenditure at the expense of investments which might lead to economic development.

Figure 2: A favela in Rio de Janeiro, Brazil

Lack of competitiveness

In the 1950s and 1960s, a number of South American countries applied the two-sector development model and invested heavily in the development of manufacturing, protecting their infant industries with tariffs and import controls. This created excessive short-term profits but little incentive to invest further. It has proved hard for these industries to compete in international markets, while at the same time investment in agricultural improvements are limited. For many South American countries, this has resulted in repeated balance of payment crises to which the response of governments was often to cut domestic demand leading to acute social problems as so many people were living at or below the poverty line.

Another economic problem with similar consequences and causes has been periods of rapid inflation, caused by falling exchange rates, excessive growth in the money supply and limited productivity gains. Deflationary policies have often caused further suffering and social unrest.

Foreign interference

As noted earlier, South American countries have been dominated firstly by Spain and more latterly by the US. Some economists have argued that it was in the interest of these dominant countries not to promote and support economic growth and to regard South American countries as important sources of raw materials.

The US has instituted a trade blockade on Cuba since the establishment of a left wing government in 1959. This has had direct repercussions on the ability of the Cuban government to trade with other countries. Similarly right-wing military governments tended to be supported by successive US governments, which have probably gone so far as to help in the overthrow

Hot potato

How far do you agree that the experience of South America shows that economic theories are of little use in understanding development issues?

It must be stressed that
looking at development on a
continent-wide basis, helps us make
some useful generalisations about
development in different regions but
also tends to hide significant
differences between neighbouring
countries, for example Uruguay
and Paraguay.

of a democratic government in Chile and to be involved in fighting revolutionary forces in Columbia, Venezuela and Ecuador, especially where activity has threatened to disrupt the activities of western multinationals producing oil.

More recently the US has had a strong influence on the policies of the World Bank and the IMF. In the 1990s, Argentina had been forced to open up its financial sector to foreign banks and when, in 2001 and 2002, the country was faced with a severe financial crisis, foreign-owned banks responded by cutting their lending to local businesses. This drove many to bankruptcy. These led to the collapse of some banks and the savings of many of the middle classes were lost.

Quick check

Why do you think that development in Latin America has been so slow?

Introduction

Economic development in many Asian countries is very different to that of many South American countries. Their experience of colonisation has been more varied, and some Asian economies have shown very high rates of economic growth over the last 30 years as shown in Figure 1. A significant number of Asian countries were part of the former USSR and they have shared many problems in moving from command-based to market-based economies. In terms of HDI rankings, there are proportionally as many Asian countries in the high category as there are in the low. As with Latin America, the majority of Asian countries fall into the middle category. Although there are exceptions, countries in Asia have generally made better development progress than those of Sub-Saharan Africa or Latin America. This Section follows that of the previous one by focusing on the interplay between historical, political and economic factors which go some way in helping understand economic development in the world's largest continent.

Historical factors

Asia contains a number of former civilisations which predate the capitalist developments in Europe. Indeed contact between Arab and other eastern cultures is seen to be one of the driving forces behind the establishment of economic growth and development in Europe. Venice's growth and expansion from around 1250 onwards was directly related to growing trade with countries to the east of Europe. Prior to this, Arab cultures were far more advanced in terms of mathematics and the sciences and these in turn were interlinked via trade with cultures further east.

There was a similar historical relationship between the Scandinavia countries and these trading links lasted for many years until challenged by more aggressive policies of colonisation, which started in the 1700s when the UK tried to develop closer ties with countries such as India. By this time Asia tended to be dominated by four counties: China, Japan, India and Russia. The latter was a feudal monarchy with relatively low levels of development but the other countries were highly developed in terms of technologies, urbanisation, state organisation and bureaucracy and internal trade. In this respect Asia was very different to both Latin America and Sub-Saharan Africa – both had previously supported advanced civilisations but these had had relatively less impact on what, to European eyes, were undeveloped primitive societies.

At the time that European navigators were exploring and charting Latin America, voyages of discovery first revealed to Europeans the full extent of Africa and then opened up new sea-bound trading routes to southern Asia. The routes first travelled around Africa and later, in the middle part of the seventeenth century, sailed westwards from central and South America. Although the Portuguese established early settlements in India, the British pursued more aggressive trade and colonial policies, by supporting a state-

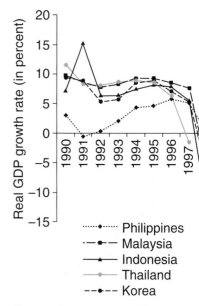

Figure 1 Comparative real GDP growth rates (selected Asian countries, 1990–98)

Hot potato

How far do you agree that the history of colonisation in Asia is all about access to raw materials and the monopoly power of the developed countries?

run monopoly – the British East India Company. The British were able to exploit differences between local rulers to establish increasing political influence. India became an important source of raw materials especially cotton, which was imported into the UK to be turned into clothing, and other cotton goods some of which we then exported back to India. In some ways southern Asia provided the impetus for the Industrial Revolution which occurred between 1750 and 1850 in England. Evidence of the power that the UK exercised is provided in her ability to forbid the manufacture of cotton goods in India in order to prevent competition for the newly established cotton industry in Lancashire.

In the latter part of the nineteenth century, there was much stronger competition between European countries and Russia to establish empires. The Russians pushed eastwards and southwards, the UK expanded from its bases in India, and also tended to dominate the Middle East. The French established colonies in Indo China, i.e. Vietnam, Laos and Cambodia. The Dutch took over much of what we now call Indonesia but both China and Japan were much stronger in resisting these colonial powers.

The UK and US forced China into the growing pattern of world trade by establishing their right to trade in opium within China and they were able to extend their power at the expense of a relatively weak Chinese political system. Japan remained largely closed to foreigners.

These emerging empires were challenged in the twentieth century, which was a century of conflict in different parts of Asia.

- In the late 1880s and early 1900s, Japan wanted to extend its influence and attacked Chinese- and Russian-controlled areas of north-west Asia.
- In 1919, the Communists took over what became the USSR and the country went through a period of civil war.
- From 1906 onwards, Jewish people were encouraged to emigrate to what was then known as Palestine, a British controlled part of the Arab world.
- The Second World War was escalated by the Japanese attack on Pearl Harbour in 1942 followed by the rapid military occupation of the bulk of South East Asia.
- There was a Communist revolution in China leading to their takeover of political power in 1949.
- 1954 Revolt and defence of the French in Indo China.
- The Vietnam War (1959-1975) was a war in which the Americans were defeated in their attempt to prevent independence and communist control in Vietnam.
- USSR occupies Afghanistan to be finally defeated in 1989.
- From 1990 onwards, the USSR collapsed.
- In 1992 the first Gulf War began.
- The second Gulf War occurred in 2003.

Although this list is not comprehensive, it indicates a very different recent history that has centred on conflicts between the US and Japan, the US and USSR, and now the US/UK and Arab peoples. The former colonial powers have been resisted strongly and had less impact on economic and social development than has been the case in other parts of the world.

The rest of this Section concentrates on those counties of South and East Asia which, in spite war and conflict, have tended to be the most successful in terms of their development: China, South Korea, Taiwan, Thailand, Singapore and Malaysia. In many ways the centre of world economic power has now shifted to South East Asia. The following factors have contributed to this relatively good economic record.

Research task

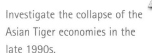

Investigate the collapse of the Asian Tiger economies in the late 1990s.

Great equality in wealth and income distribution

Although there are significant inequalities in income, these are less extreme than in other parts of the world. In their short period of occupation, the Japanese redistributed land and broke up the power of large landowners. The countries which have developed most rapidly have used their growing wealth to ensure that most people have access to good quality education and that attention is also focused on meeting the needs of the less well-off. Although these countries have faced periods of social unrest, these have not been on the scale or intensity of revolutionary and criminal activity in Latin America.

Table 1: Gini Co-efficients for selected countries in Asia (with comparisons). This is a measure of equality in the distribution of incomes.

Country	Gini Index score	World ranking
Slovakia	18.2	Most equal distribution of income in the world
Vietnam	36	
UK	36.1	
India	37.8	
China	40.3	
Thailand	41.4	
Sierra Leone	62.9	Least equal distribution of income in the world

Government intervention

Although there are variations, the governments of each of the South East Asian countries have taken a leading role in developing policies and structures that will lead to long-term economic growth. This is reflected in the importance that has been attached to investment in human capital through education, investment in high technology and information systems and careful control of imports and exports. There has been little hesitation about using the power of the state to ensure that there are few challenges to government and most of the growing countries in South East Asia have poor human rights records. The Chinese government appears to have controlled the transition to a highly competitive fast-growing economy, in which western influences have been accommodated, without seriously weakening the control of the communist government.

Competitiveness

The economies of these countries are also characterised by a very high savings ratio, which lends support to the linear stages theorists. This has provided a high proportion of investment funds without controls and influence from foreign investors. Productivity has also been relatively high giving these countries a clear competitive advantage in the production of a wide range of manufactured goods, and an increasing share of the financial services market. It has been very difficult for US and European economies to compete with these growing economies.

Foreign interference

Although countries in South East Asia have generally been able to have much more power in determining appropriate economic policies, their progress has been threatened by foreign interference. There have been long and acrimonious arguments between the US and China on the admission of the latter to the World Trade Organisation.

Although local savings ratios have been high, there have also been high levels of foreign lending and pressure from the IMF and World Bank to liberalise the economies of South East Asian countries. This has included pressures to open up capital markets. One of the results of this was the collapse in the exchange rates of countries like Thailand, South Korea and Indonesia in the late 1990s. Speculative forces forced exchange rates down leading to severe economic problems. The IMF urged further liberalisation and free market reforms, which led to civil unrest in Indonesia and a collapse of the Thai economy. Some countries such as Malaysia and South Korea resisted the imposition of free market solutions and they appear to be recovering more quickly from the crisis than those less powerful economies who had sever deflationary policies forced upon them.

> ### Quick check
>
> Why has China been the fastest growing economy over the last two decades?

Introduction

In the final of these three Sections on different world regions and their development, the focus is on Sub-Saharan Africa. Most countries in this region have suffered negative economic growth over the last two decades, In terms of the UN's HDI, the bottom 27 countries on their list of worst-off countries all come from this region, and the highest ranking country, South Africa, is ranked 107th in the world. These low or negative rates of development can partly be explained by looking at the inter-relationships between historical, political and economic factors.

History, politics and economics

Prior to exploration and settlement by Europeans, Sub-Saharan Africa was settled by tribal and pastoral groups, who had some contact with Arab traders from the north. Although there is evidence of past civilisations in countries such as Zimbabwe, comparatively little is known of their culture and impact. As noted earlier, from the mid-1400s, Portuguese sailors gradually sailed and mapped their way round Africa reaching the Cape of Good Hope in 1497. They gradually contined northwards, with Vasco de Gama eventually reaching India in 1498. Small trading centres were established around the coast but the central part of the continent was largely unexplored by Europeans. This pattern continued and expanded greatly in the eighteenth century as the demand for slaves to work in the Caribbean and southern states of the USA grew. Trade in slaves had long been a feature of complex relationships between Europeans and people from north and west Africa. A mixture of force and financial incentives was used to lure Africans into captivity to be transhipped westwards. It is estimated that between 12–24 million Africans were forcibly moved from their homelands. Those that survived the sea crossings were often brutally treated, families were broken up, and local customs and cultures were ignored. A similar trade, but on a much smaller scale, existed between Arab countries and East Africa.

From the middle of the eighteenth century, relatively small numbers of Dutch and Flemish settlers established farming communities in what we now know as South Africa. The colonisation of Sub-Saharan Africa happened only towards the end of the nineteenth century when what has been variously described as the 'scramble' or 'race' for Africa commenced. This was an outcome of intense rivalry between the newly-industrialised countries of Europe and the UK; Germany, France, Italy, Belgium and Portugal all rushed to conquer new territories. Each had different policies, but each of the countries in Sub-Saharan Africa was clearly ruled by a foreign power, supported by occupying armies of various sizes.

Part of the motivation for this rush to Africa was to 'civilize the dark continent', to bring Christianity to the black masses, but also to acquire rights to increasingly important finds of natural resources: diamonds from

Hot potato

The developed countries have a lot to answer for when it comes to understanding development issues – do you agree?

South Africa, rubber from the Congo, gold from Sierra Leone, copper from Northern Rhodesia. The colonising countries sought ways of making their colonies pay, which also meant the introduction of taxation which forced local Africans into work and membership of a cash-based economy that was previously less extensive. Some of the new rulers were particularly barbaric. Belgium rubber merchants forced local people in the Congo to go out into the jungle to collect rubber. The punishment for failing to harvest sufficient quantities was the removal of one arm. The response to further failures was equally barbaric, and many perished.

One of the outcomes of the First World War was the loss of the German colonies in south west Africa and Tanganyika (Tanzania). In the 1930s, Mussolini tried to capture Ethiopia, and in the late 1940s, the UK granted self-government to South Africa which became increasingly dominated by white racists of the Nationalist Party. In other parts of African there was a growth in independence movements which, in some countries such as Kenya, resorted to armed struggle.

In the 1960s, there was a rush by the largest colonial power, the UK, to give independence to its former colonies; this policy was followed by the French. The colonial powers moved out more quickly than they had moved in leaving behind poorly-educated populations, ill-trained civil servants and tribal rivalries which had been kept in check under colonial rule.

In southern Africa, white dominance was more deeply entrenched. South Africa embarked on policies euphemistically called 'separate development' which in reality condemned the bulk of the black population to low skill, low pay jobs and limited access to education. Black opposition was ruthlessly suppressed, and the South African government funded white settlers in Rhodesia (Zimbabwe) to remain in power and also supported anti-government movements in the newly independent countries of Angola and Mozambique. International pressure and armed resistance from the ANC led by Nelson Mandela eventually led to the overthrow of the white regime in 1994.

Over the last 20 years, Sub-Saharan countries has suffered disproportionately from both starvation, especially in 1985 in Ethiopia and Somalia, and civil war. Living standards have fallen and genocide in Rwanda, Burundi, Congo, Sierra Leone have all contributed to misery and suffering that cannot be described.

Why has this happened in Africa? The continent, although not all countries, is resource rich and some countries, such as Uganda and Cape Verde, have made progress, while the power and influence of South Africa is growing. However, this is not the norm. Economists and political scientists disagree as to the causes of the decline in living standards for most people in Sub-Saharan Africa but there is general agreement that the following factors have been important.

Poverty

Most Sub-Saharan countries are too poor to invest in human and physical capital. They inherited colonial infrastructures that we designed to facilitate the export of raw materials but not much more. Continuous under-investment has led to a decline in productive capacity and an inability in some cases to deal with natural disasters such as changing climatic conditions that reduce rainfall and make it less predictable.

One crop dependence

Many Sub-Saharan countries have historically been dependent upon exports of a single crop or raw material. Falling world prices for copper, coffee, and sisal have meant that countries such as Zambia, Ethiopia and Tanzania have been faced with dramatic cuts in their foreign earnings, forcing further cuts in investment and/or increasing reliance on foreign borrowing.

Bad governance

Governance is a term used to cover the effectiveness of all aspects of government and legal systems. Newly independent countries inherited European models of governance that have not been robust enough to survive without military intervention. Democratic institutions are not well established and a number of countries have been ruled by totalitarian despots with little regard for development. It is estimated that the late President Mobutu of Zaire (Congo) removed over £4 billion to foreign bank accounts in the 16 years he was in power. Moreover, dictators have spent a disproportionate amount of money on weapons and the break down of law and order in some countries such as Sierra Leone, Liberia and the Congo is fuelled by the easy availability of guns and other weaponry.

As noted earlier, poverty provides a breeding ground for instability and unlawful activity and this, coupled with weak governance, can lead to the breakdown of civil society as in Somalia and the Congo.

Foreign indifference and interference

Some of the worst episodes in recent African history, such as the genocide in Rwanda and the current wave of killings in Congo, could probably have been prevented by more vigorous intervention from the United Nations and former colonial powers.

In common with other developing nations, some in Sub-Saharan Africa have been subjected to inappropriate advice from the IMF and the World Bank. Their reliance on free market solutions has not been appropriate where markets do not necessarily exist and where the legal and financial structures and safeguards are lacking. The only way that really poor countries can repay foreign debt or invest in human and social capital, is by further decreasing living standards. Such strategies depress rather than encourage economic development.

Hot potato

Can economics aid development?

Table 1: Gini Co-efficients for selected countries in Sub-Saharan Africa.

Country	Gini Index score	World ranking
Slovakia	18.2	Most equal distribution of income in the world
Ghana	32.7	
UK	36.1	
Uganda	39.2	
Zimbabwe	56.8	
South Africa	59.3	
Sierra Leone	62.9	Least equal distribution of income in the world

Summary

The historical perspective presented in this and the two proceeding Sections is valuable in understanding the complexity and challenges of a process which is not really fully comprehended. Clearly history has left very different marks on the three regions investigated. Both Latin America and Sub-Saharan Africa have colonial pasts in which they were exploited for their raw materials and, in Africa's case, their labour. Many African countries lack basic facilities to prevent starvation, still less democratic and legal frameworks to support the effective working of markets. Both central planning in the ex-communist countries and the application of free market ideology in Latin America and Africa appear to have failed. Interestingly those countries in South East Asia which have developed the most have followed strategies in which there has been close collaboration between the private and pubic sectors, and have ignored conventional economic wisdom.

Quick check

Give the strongest three economic arguments as to why development has been so slow in Sub-Saharan Africa.

Weblink

You may have looked at this before, but access Bized's virtual economy of Zambia on www.bized.ac.uk

Introduction

All countries in the world operate within a global economy and those in the developing world are particularly dependent on the import and export of key commodities and products. This section highlights the importance of international trade both as a means of aiding and constraining development. The issues are highly topical as poorer countries are often in conflict with those from the developed world and the growing anti-globalisation movement shows that many in the world are concerned about the effects of globalisation.

Absolute and comparative advantage

The key theory in understanding why countries trade is that relating to absolute and comparative advantage (see Section 5.12).

Comparative advantage

Free international trade provides a number of potential benefits to both developed and developing countries. Most importantly, as the theory of comparative advantage demonstrates, free trade can lead to higher levels of output, leading to increased income and employment levels for all. However, it can also pose problems for countries, especially if they cannot trade on equal terms.

Trade barriers

In spite of the economic arguments for freer trade as an aid to development, both developed and developing countries use a range of techniques to protect their domestic markets. These include:

- quotas – actual limits on exports or imports of specified products
- exchange controls – especially in relation to 'hard' currencies
- embargoes – prohibitions often used for political reasons
- tariffs, i.e. import or export taxes.

The use of these measures is often supported by a range of arguments put forward by both developed and developing countries for imposing restrictions on free trade. These include arguments for raising revenue, protecting the whole industrial base of the country, protecting infant industries and dealing with balance of payments problems.

A further barrier to trade is that presented by Trade blocs such as the EU and ASEAN (the Association of South East Asian Nations) who encourage trade between members but often place barriers to trade with other countries.

Trade conflicts

Whereas the application of comparative and absolute cost theory provides a powerful case for freer trade which should benefit both developed and

Synoptic link

Read A2 Sections 5.12 and 5.13 for an explanation of absolute and comparative advantage before you start this section. This section takes the theory introduced in these units and applies it to issues relating to development strategies, which are explored more fully in A2 Sections 5.29 and 5.30.

Definition

Hard currencies are those currencies such as the dollar ($), pound (£) and euro (E), which are freely used for international trade. Many currencies of developing countries are acceptable as a means of payment for international trade.

developing countries, there are enormous conflicts between countries and trading blocks limiting agreements over freer trade. The EU and the USA are keen to open markets for their exporters but they are much more reluctant to open their own markets and many developing countries feel discriminated against.

The World Trade Organisation

The main body with a role overseeing world trade and promoting freer trade is the World Trade Organisation, which was formed in 1995 to replace the General Agreement on Tariffs and Trade (GATT). It seeks to reduce tariffs and other restrictions on international trade and provides a means by which countries can settle their trade disputes. The WTO, which currently has 136 member countries, seeks to promote trade liberalisation through a series of negotiations (which are often referred to as rounds). For example, the Uruguay Round achieved agreement to reduce trade barriers in textiles. Recently it admitted China as a new member after a number of years of discussion and conflict.

The role of the WTO has been criticised by developing countries which argue that industrial countries are favoured. For example, tariffs on tobacco have been reduced to 4 per cent while tariffs on tobacco products remain at 40 per cent. Developing countries argue that the differential has nothing to do with health concerns but is concerned with keeping industrial processing, where higher profits are made, in the west. They also claim that the WTO, by allowing industrial countries in certain circumstances to impose restrictions to prevent dumping, is often merely enabling them to protect jobs in sensitive industries that would prove politically unpopular to allow to decline.

Research task

Use CD-ROMs of newspapers, for example the *Times*, *Daily Telegraph* and *The Guardian*, or the Internet to research different views of the performance of the WTO and produce a brief summary of these.

Hot potato

Arguments about world trade show that the discipline of economics is of little value in understanding the trade flows between developing and developed countries.

Quick check ✔

How does comparative cost theory provide a rational for developing countries to remove barriers to international trade?

The previous section considered trade theory and its application to development. Additionally there is an extensive literature about development theories. OCR expect you to know about:

- linear stages (Rostow's model and Harrod Domar models)
- balanced growth theory
- Lewis's structural change model
- dependence theory
- new-classical theory.

Linear stages

These approaches tended to dominate thinking in the 1950s and 1960s which, in the developed world, was a period of fairly continuous economic growth, helped in Europe by the US which provided significant inputs of aid in the form of the 'Marshall Plan'.

Economists tended to think that development was a structured process which could be applied to all countries with a kick-start of high savings, investment or foreign aid.

Firstly two economists, Harrod and Domar, working independently, were credited with developing a simple model which focused on the savings ratio. They argued that economic development would follow once the savings ratio was high. This, they argued, would lead to high levels of investment that, in turn, would promote the growth in employment and income, leading to a virtuous cycle of development.

Harrod and Domar were important as their model highlighted one of the key constraints limiting development. Poor countries, it was argued, were likely to have high average propensities to consume and it follows that their savings' ratios would tend to be low. Such economies would be forced into a 'hand to mouth' economic system, unless radical steps were taken to increase savings. This could be forced, as in Stalin's USSR, or it could be provided by foreign direct investment.

A similar approach was taken in 1960 by an American economists, WW Rostow, when he published a book called 'The Stages of Growth: A Non-Communist Manifesto'. He argued that all economies passed through five different stages on their road to full economic development:

- traditional
- transitional
- takeoff
- drive to maturity
- high mass consumption.

Traditional economies were largely dependent upon subsistence, which was followed by a period of change usually in agriculture such that more food would be produced. Growing surpluses at this stage would, Rostow argued, lead to rapid expansion in investment. Higher investment would in turn promote greater growth while rising incomes would feed into increases in

Development theories 5.27

Synoptic link

There are direct links between the macroeconomics that you covered for AS and that for A2. Keynes' circular flow, Section 3.12, and treatments of aggregate demand and aggregate supply in Sections 3.8 and 3.9, along with Section 3.3 on economic growth are all relevant. Two models can be seen to be linked to Keynesian approaches to macroeconomics.

aggregate demand. Expanding investment, aggregate demand, employment opportunities and growing incomes would lead to the development of the infrastructure, human and physical capital associated with a mature economy, culminating in developing the final stage in which high levels of mass consumption would provide sustained demand for the outputs of a developed economy.

The crucial part of this model is 'take off'. The implication is that additional savings and/or investment could set off a chain reaction of development culminating in sustained economic development.

Balanced growth theory

These theories about development grew up when economists tried to account for relatively low levels of growth in poorer countries in east and south eastern Europe. They argued that small domestic markets limited the ability of newly established firms to benefit from the external economies of scale that would be expected in those countries with larger internal markets. They argued that if the growth of several major industries were stimulated at the same time, they would provide markets for each other's goods and contribute to the development of a better skilled workforce. In some ways this is another variant of Rostow's 'take off' stage.

Balanced growth theorists argued for state intervention to kick-start this mass industrialisation, but in many cases the scale of what was required was beyond the resources of poor countries. Nonetheless these theories were influential in determining strategies for development followed in a number of countries especially in South America.

Criticism of this theory led to the development of 'unbalanced' growth theory; if left to themselves, the growth and development of internal markets would automatically reveal missing or incomplete markets which would provide incentives for local investment to plug the gaps.

Structural change

This suggests that development can be increased by transferring workers from low productivity agriculture into the higher productivity manufacturing and service sectors. W. Arthur Lewis argued that in some developing countries, with a large number of underemployed people working in agriculture, some of the workers have zero marginal productivity. For instance, a small farm with three family members working on it might not experience an increase in output if an additional family member started work on the farm. If there are workers not contributing anything to agricultural output that could be moved into other sectors, then national output would increase. It follows that development would be prompted by additional investment in the urban manufacturing sector, and by facilitating the movement of workers from the rural to urban sectors. However, this presupposes there are job vacancies in the other sectors. In practice, in a number of developing countries the migration from rural to urban areas can cause problems. These include pollution, congestion and underused social capital in rural areas and a shortage of social capital in urban areas.

Dependence

In the 1970s, there was something of a backlash in response to the application of the linear and structuralist's models, which suggested that the causes of underdevelopment were to be found within developing countries. Various Marxists and neo-Marxists argued that underdevelopment was the result of external factors. Development did not take place because it was not in the interests of the leading economic powers. Indeed their comparative wealth and high levels of development were said to be partly the outcome of their exploitation of developing countries.

It was further argued that elite groups within developing countries often formed an alliance with interests from developed countries to ensure that inequalities and exploitation continued.

The most extreme policy implications of this approach to development are those that have been argued by various revolutionary groups that foreign influences have to be removed, local ruling elites need to be replaced, and land and wealth needs to be redistributed from the rich to the poor.

New-classical

In almost complete contrast to Marxist and neo-Marxist perspectives were those approaches to economics associated with the 1980s and 1990s, with the governments of President Regan in the US and Prime Minister Thatcher in the UK. New-classical economists used the arguments with which you will be familiar from other parts of your course. They believed that freely operating markets would ensure that development took place. They argued against any forms of government intervention in the form of subsidies to help the poor, or import controls to protect domestic employers.

Such policies were pursued with great energy in the 1990s by the World Bank, IMF and US Government. In many cases, aid was only given to countries on condition that market reforms, such a privatisation, freeing up capital markets and removing trade barriers were introduced. When these policies appeared to fail, the developing countries were often blamed for not making changes quickly enough, or for allowing corruption to go unchecked. New-classical economists appeared to fail to recognise that it has taken countries such as the UK hundreds of years to develop the legal checks and balances needed if markets are going to operate fairly and effectively.

Usefulness of theories of development

It is very hard to evaluate the usefulness of these different theoretical approaches to development. Some elements have been successful. Thus, high

Weblink

For access to thousands of indexed items on development issues, try www.newint.org – you can shop there too!

Research task

Who is Paulo Freire and why is his work important in understanding development?

savings ratios in many eastern Asian countries have contributed to relatively long periods of economic growth. The creation of more competitive markets in Poland has resulted in improvements in living standards for some elements of the population, and the redistribution of wealth from the rich to the poor in Cuba has lead to very high educational and health standards for all. However, as the data in the previous Section indicated, many countries have been going backwards. There is little doubt that the investments in heavy industry undertaken during communist rule in Russia and Eastern Europe did not lead to a sustained transformation of their economies, and that the free market changes introduced during the 1990s have actually led to a fall in living standards in these countries.

Development issues might be so complex that applying economic models is too limiting. Some developmental theorists adopt a more multidisciplinary approach while others advocate small incremental changes that cumulatively result in sustainable change.

Other factors

As this section has indicated, there are many links between economic and political change. Economic development is much harder to achieve in times of political instability. For about 40 years from 1945 onwards, the cold war between the US and the USSR provided a form of global stability. Conflicts occurred but much of the world was effectively divided between Russian and American spheres of influence. During this period, development appeared to have been relatively more successful. The end of the cold war appears to have created much greater instability. Many of the poorer African countries have been affected by civil war, and conflict has also been evident in the Middle East and near east. Perhaps the poor development record results from political instability rather than the failings of particular economic policies.

Quick check	
1 Which countries in the world have the highest savings ratios? Have they experienced high levels of economic growth?	
2 How would you sort out the relative merits of the different development theories outlined in this section?	

Back to basics

Although there maybe arguments as to what constitutes economic development and how this can best be measured, there is little dispute that if countries are to tackle the poverty and hunger associated with a lack of development, they have two options. Firstly, they can redistribute wealth from the wealthy minority to the mass of people. This could be described as a revolutionary approach to development and has occurred in the past in Russia, China and those countries which have had communist governments. Redistribution of wealth is not a painless or peaceful process but it can produce dramatic effects. According to the UN, Cuba is practically one of the leaders in terms of having reached the top of the list of those countries with a medium stage of human development. The average monthly income is around $20, but education, healthcare, and basic foodstuffs are available to everyone. This has been achieved by the redistribution of wealth but has not been without serious social problems. Over the last 40 years, better-off Cubans have left the country, many settling in Florida.

Although income inequalities are great in many developing countries, even if available wealth and income were shared equally, countries such as Angola, Sierra Leone and Niger all have per capita incomes of less than $500 a year which is not sufficient to ensure that hunger, disease and early death are not common place. Logically developing countries need to create more wealth in order to develop.

Five simple tools of analysis are useful in understanding the pre-requisites for economic growth:
- simple input/output analysis
- production possibilities frontiers
- circular flow
- AS/AD analysis
- market failure.

Input/output analysis

This should take you back to one of your first classes in economics. In order to produce wealth, four factors of production are required:
- land
- labour
- capital
- enterprise.

Lack of any of the above is likely to limit economic growth and the production of wealth. Most developing countries have access to different natural resources and almost all are characterised by large supplies of labour. However, if educational investment is low, labour is not likely to be productive. Almost without exception, developing countries lack capital. Levels of investment in infrastructure, health care, plant and machinery are all constrained by lack of finance. The availability of enterprise is more

Synoptic link

Your AS course should have helped you understand the economic processes which are needed for economic growth to occur. Economists use different tools to analyse growth and this can all be applied to the problems facing developing countries. Moreover, you will also be aware from your AS course of the significance of different forms of market failure and the benefits or otherwise of government intervention.
This section has been written to remind you of all these concepts which can be applied to economic development and are useful in understanding the effectiveness of different development strategies and the particular constraints which they have to overcome.

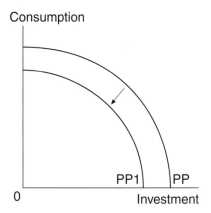

Consumption

0   PP1   PP   Investment

Figure 1: Production possibilities

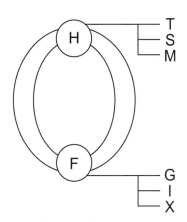

Figure 2: Circular flow model

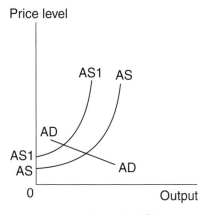

Price level

AS1   AS

AD

AS1
AS   AD

0   Output

Figure 3: AD/AS analysis

debatable. Survival in extreme and life-threatening conditions requires great enterprise, but not all cultures share the significance that is attached to personal material possessions and individual profit which is also associated with the notion of entrepreneurship.

Production possibilities

This is another concept which occurred right at the beginning of your course and which is really useful in understanding how hard it is for poor countries to develop. If a country is really poor, almost all its resources will be devoted to consumption. The opportunity cost of this is that less is available for investment. In many cases this is not likely to be sufficient to maintain the value of existing capital. In which case economic welfare as indicated by the production possibility frontier is likely to decline. This is illustrated in Figure 1 by the shift inwards of the production possibility frontier.

Circular flow

Introductory macroeconomics introduced you to the classic Keynesian circular flow model, which can be used to identify the conditions in which economic growth and the expansion of incomes are to occur. In case you have forgotten, if there are unused resources within an economy and if inflows of investment, export earnings and government spending exceed outflows of savings, spending on imports and taxation of economic growth will occur and the multiplier effect will increase the eventual impact of any stimulus. This model is illustrated in Figure 2.

Many developing countries are faced with low export earnings, high imports, low levels of government spending, investment, and in some cases high levels of taxation, all of which are unlikely to compensate for low levels of saving. This simple analysis points to the likely situation of negative economic growth and falling levels of income.

AD/AS analysis

This is another way of looking at low levels of economic growth. Both aggregate demand and aggregate supply in poor countries are likely to be relatively low. Inability to invest is likely to push AS to the left and reduce productive capacity. AD is also likely to be low but even modest levels can lead to potential inflation. This is illustrated in Figure 3.

Market failure

Markets can be said to fail if:

■ they produce socially unacceptable outcomes: thus, if incomes are very unequally distributed it is possible for a country to produce and import luxury goods to meet the demands of a wealthy elite, while at the same time fail to produce enough food or medical supplies to meet the needs of those without income to translate their needs into effective demand.

- externalities exist: externalities, both positive and negative, probably have a bigger impact on the working of markets in developing countries than they do in those countries which are considered more developed. Colonial powers and some transnational corporations have regarded the natural resources of some countries almost as free goods to be exploited and exported to developed countries with no consideration of the short- and long-term impact on local economies. Thus workers may be expected to work in conditions which would not be accepted in the developed countries, for example tin miners in Bolivia, child labour in Laos and asbestos workers in South America. Low levels of pay and poor health or even death impact on families and wider communities. Countries such as Brazil, and Indonesia are also responsible for massive deforestation which results in local and international negative externalities in terms of soil infertility and erosion and global warming. The most obvious positive externalities, which reliance on market-based solutions are unlikely to provide, are those which derive from improved access to education and healthcare. Healthier better-educated workers are likely to be more productive.

- monopoly power exists: industries in some small economies are easily dominated by firms with monopoly power, either publicly or privately owned. Although it is possible for dominant firms to produce at lower cost and in greater volume than would be the case if there were more competition, there is also the likelihood of higher prices, less choice and lower outputs.

- they are imperfect: in addition to monopoly power, market imperfections are likely to be significant in developing countries, especially the existence of asymmetric information, or imperfect knowledge which is especially likely to occur in major trading transactions.

Summary

None of the theories in this Section should be new to you, but using what you have done for AS to understand some of the broad issues faced by developing countries may come as a surprise. This Section has dealt in very general terms with the theoretical basis upon which policies to promote. Returning to the concept of market failure should help underline that strategies which rely on market solutions and which could work in the developed world, may fail in developing countries.

Quick check	
Use AD and AS analysis to assess the impact of HIV AIDs on Malawi.	

Thinking like an economist

Analyse the economic effects of not having a market from which small businesses can receive overdraft facilities.

Research task

Pick a developing country and see how far the analytical tools revisited in this Section might explain low levels of economic growth.

5.29 Domestically driven policies to promote development

Synoptic link

The section draws directly on all the work you have done so far in looking at:

■ application of micro and macro theory to development
■ development theory
■ problems of developing countries
■ regional variations in development.

Introduction

You should understand that development economics is very complex and it should follow that simple one-size-fits-all solutions to development issues are not likely to work and, as will be shown later in Section 5.31, have probably increased poverty and suffering. Those countries which have had the most sustained growth, such as China and South Korea, have adopted a range of measures which have involved both government and private sector development and activity. Both have developed comprehensive policies, which have included economic, social and political objectives to promote development. In the past, some countries have tended to focus, or be forced to focus, on strategies which target particular sectors of the economy. Developing countries have tended to adopt strategies which focus on one or more sectors of their economies:

■ agriculture
■ industry
■ tourism.

Agriculture

High levels of employment in the agricultural sector are associated with low levels of economic development. Thus in the world's poorest countries, the bulk of the population work on the land. If countries develop agricultural productivity usually rises, but the relative importance of agriculture tends to decline. Moreover, it has already been noted that the dependence on one or two primary products places developing countries in a very vulnerable position. For these reasons, some countries have ignored the importance of agriculture and concentrated on the development of the industrial sector.

This view was commonplace in the 30 years following the Second World War, and has been shown to be mistaken because:

■ for some countries, agricultural resources are their most valuable
■ an emphasis on industrialisation and neglect of rural areas has accelerated urbanisation creating a new set of negative externalities
■ ignoring agriculture can lead to a fall in domestic food production resulting in higher imports of foreign food using up limited foreign currency
■ those living in rural areas are often those in greatest need in terms of access to clean water, medical supplies and education.

On the other hand, agricultural development can make a positive contribution to the development process as:

■ growth in agricultural productivity can contribute to the creation of more wealth which can provide for locally-financed infrastructure improvements and an emerging market for agricultural capital and relatively low-technology consumer goods

- agricultural developments can provide the basis for industrial developments which give developing countries more opportunity to benefit from the value added of manufacturing. Clearly it would be in the interest of many countries not just to produce and sell coffee beans to the developed world but also to process those beans, selling on the final product.

In spite of the obvious advantages, there are a number of constraints which have to be overcome if agricultural productivity is to be increased.

- Cultural and social issues: in many countries, especially those with a history of slavery, working on the land has low status and even small increases in prosperity can fuel the desire to live in cities. Similarly the better-off people may prefer to consume imports of foreign produced food rather than rely on local consumption.
- As has been noted earlier, in some countries gross inequalities in income and wealth derive from very unequal land holdings. Redistributing land from the rich to the poor can be a prerequisite for agricultural development but this involves great social change and the potential of conflict as can be seen today in Zimbabwe.
- It is in the interest of developed countries to encourage the production and export of primary crops and to limit the ability of third world countries to use their own resources to manufacture goods for export to the developed countries.
- Even worse, the US and EU pay subsidies to their farmers to produce primary crops which can be grown in developing countries. The USA used to spend more on subsidies to its own cotton farmers than it did on aid to Africa, which forced down the world price of cotton below that which enabled African producers to survive.

In economic development, M.P. Todaro argues that improving productivity in the agricultural sector of developing countries has three necessary conditions.

1. Land Reform: as explained earlier, Latin America has too many large landlords, whereas patterns of ownership in South East Asia are much more fragmented. Collectivisation and co-operative developments offer potential for both increasing productivity and ensuring that the benefits are more widely distributed.
2. Supportive policies: Todaro argues that governments need to develop farmer-friendly rural institutions involving the availability of credit, seed and fertiliser supplies, effective communications and access to water. Many of these are low technology solutions.
3. Integrated development: finally it is argued that agricultural improvements must be accompanied by other developments to ensure that those living in rural areas have access to education, decent housing, and medical services.

Thinking like an economist

Use demand and supply analysis to show the problems of primary product dependency – is that the end of the problem?

Industrial development

The linear development theorists, and those focusing upon sectorial change, have all emphasised the importance of the development of a manufacturing sector to provide a possible way of:

- reducing the outflows of foreign exchange to pay for imported manufactured goods
- generating foreign exchange earnings to improve the balance of payments and provide funds for further investment
- providing employment opportunities to meeting the growing demand for jobs.

Interestingly, the first two bullet points provide the basis for two alternative strategies which have been used in developing countries since the Second World War.

Import substitution

Import substitution has developed especially in response to the non-availability of supplies from the developed world in times of war. Many developing countries invested heavily in developing their own capacity to produce relatively low-technology consumer goods. In order to do this they used tariffs to protect their infant industries from cheaper foreign imports. In theory the successful development of these industries would contribute to improved living standards, more employment opportunities and generate funds for investment in intermediate and capital goods. These strategies appear to have met with limited success as governments tended to be reluctant to reduce tariff barriers. This together with the creation of local monopolies has often meant that there were fewer incentives to make production more efficient. Consequently countries such as Brazil, Pakistan and Argentina, which tried this strategy, found that after some initial economic growth, progress slowed and they did not move on to the next stages of industrial development. Other factors contributing to this failure include:

- dependence on second-rate, hand-me-down technology from the developed world. For example, Lada cars were built using machinery previously used to produce an earlier outdated Fiat model.
- raised expectations and globalisation has meant that many people in developing countries demand globally-marketed products rather then domestically-produced substitutes which are often perceived to be inferior goods, for example, local coke compared with Coca Cola
- failure to address other issues contributing to poverty, and the lack of development such as disempowerment, access to clean water, medical supplies and education.

Export-led growth

Some countries in east Asia adopted a different strategy, modelled on the success of the Japanese in transforming their economy from a backward primary producer to a world leader in production of motor vehicles and a wide range of electronic goods. The Japanese protected domestic producers by using import controls but encouraged competition between producers in their domestic markets. Successful companies were rewarded with import licenses to import the most up-to-date and appropriate technologies from more developed countries. Although it is an oversimplification, it is said that the Japanese government helped identify those industries which were likely to grow fastest over the succeeding ten to twenty years. Economic planning was then undertaken to support the required technological developments. Thus, in the 1950s and 1960s, companies such as Honda and Suzuki targeted the perceived world market for small motorbikes and similar products. They invested heavily in modern technology and by producing for world rather than domestic markets they were able to exploit technical economies of scale. They were more efficient than competitors in the developed world and have become world leaders in this kind of production. This model has been applied to electronics manufacture and ICT with great success.

Other eastern Asian countries have developed variants upon this strategy, which appears to have been successful especially when linked to high domestic savings ratios identified in Section 5.27. This kind of approach coupled with undemocratic and autocratic governments has resulted in high levels of economic growth in countries such as Singapore and Taiwan and the most successful developing country of all, China.

Tourism

Growing incomes in developed countries, coupled with falling relative prices of air travel, have given another development strategy – tourism. The impact of this approach has been very mixed. On the positive side:
- tourism creates jobs
- tourist spending can provide markets for producers of artefacts and other support services.

However, there are a number of drawbacks to adopting the tourist approach to development:
- tourists bring foreign tastes and expectations and in many cases expect the food and service levels that they are used to. In the worst scenario, as in Antigua in the West Indies, it is estimated that 95 cents of every tourist dollar spent immediately leaves the local economy to pay for imported foodstuffs, energy supplies and as profit to the foreign owners of hotels
- tourists pose a threat to fragile ecosystems, such as coral reefs, and air transport is very damaging to the ozone layer

Research task

Choose a country which has adopted one of these strategies. What are the costs and the benefits of this development?

Hot potato

Tourists should pay an energy tax. Do you agree?

- tourists can represent a very visible demonstration of the inequalities between the developing and developed world, and this can lead to social unrest.

Nonetheless some countries such as Cuba and the Maldives consider that their beaches and cultures offer one of the few opportunities to earn foreign currency to help develop other sectors of their economies. Cuba has adopted a variant of the east Asia model by encouraging competition between differently managed state owned travel companies and uses import controls to try to ensure that tourist needs are sourced locally. There is also a high level of state intervention on the Maldives in which foreign investors are allowed to develop a local tourist infrastructure, which is very sensitive to the local ecology.

Summary

These three approaches to development offer different chances of success. Import substitution is now largely discredited. Tourism only contributes positively to development if it occurs within a highly-regulated framework. Export-led strategies appear most promising if accompanied by other strategies to tackle poverty and disempowerment. The success of these requires the co-operation of developed countries. This is not always forthcoming.

T he two main forms of external finance are as follows:

- investment by multinational companies (MNCs)
- foreign aid.

Consideration is also given to how countries and international institutions are responding to the slow and often negative progress made by most countries over the last two decades in reducing poverty and promoting development

Multinational investment

Some 500 companies control nearly 25 per cent of the total value of the world's economy, and provide an important source of inward investment to both developed and developing countries. Most investment goes to developed countries of which the major beneficiaries are illustrated in Table 1.

Table 1: Recipients of FDI: most favoured economies for future FDI by transnational corporations

Developing Asia	Latin America	Africa
China	Brazil	South Africa
Indonesia	Mexico	Egypt
Thailand	Argentina	Morocco

Source: UNCTAD 2001

The incentives for MNCs to invest in developing countries include access to:

- the extraction and export of raw materials and agricultural produce
- growing domestic markets, e.g. China today
- cheap, non-unionised labour especially in South East Asia.

The possible benefits to the developing country include:

- technology transfer, i.e. access to modern production techniques and new skills
- job creation
- investment in infrastructure.

The record of MNCs in promoting development is very mixed. They have been responsible for the mining and extraction of raw materials from poor countries which have received very little in return. They can be very powerful and capable of extracting very favourable terms for investment in particular countries, such as freedom from local taxation, and in some cases their activities can be very destabilising for the developing countries, for example oil exploration in Columbia and Ecuador. They use **transfer pricing** as a technique for understating the profits made from activities in particular countries.

One the other hand, external finance is required. The extraction of resources is often beyond the means of poorer countries and some MNCs are more ethically inclined than others. When governments are strong enough to negotiate wide ranging agreements with MNCs, they can help ensure that

Externally driven policies to promote development

Synoptic link

This section is devoted to exploring the costs and benefits to developing countries of different types of external finance. It links most closely with Sections 5.27 and 5.28, both of which identified the importance of finding ways of financing greater investment in order to stimulate developing economies and provide much need improvements in infrastructure, heath care and education.

Definition

Transfer pricing relates to internal trading within different parts of MNCs in which resources might be sold very cheaply from a developing to a developed country but thereafter they are traded internally at much higher prices.

they share more fairly in the profits of the particular activity, that local people are trained to take senior as well as lower level jobs, and that other ethical considerations are included.

Hot potato

Why is it so hard to judge the positive impact of MNCs on developing countries?

Foreign aid

Foreign Aid or, to give it its proper name, 'official development assistance or ODA', comes in two forms:
- bilateral assistance which is given from a developed country to a developing country
- multilateral assistance which comes from an agency such as the EU or World Bank.

Three characteristics apply to this form of assistance.
- It is undertaken by the official sector.
- Tackling development is the principle objective.
- It is given on 'concessional terms' which are meant to ensure that the interest rate and length of time for the repayment of loans is less demanding than would be the case with commercial loans.

Thus military aid should not be regarded as forming part of ODA flows. The effectiveness of aid is another major area of debate by development economists.

Bilateral aid

Todaro argues that there is no evidence to suggest that the bulk of aid is given with some notion of benefit to the donor country. The granting of aid is often linked directly to political considerations rather than any assessment of relative need in different countries. Thus in the days of the cold war between the USA and USSR, each would tend to give aid in return for political support. Today Arab countries friendly to the US are more likely to receive aid than those who are not.

Alternatively, there may be economic motives ranging from the notion that economic development will result in the growth of potential export markets to the narrow self-interest in which aid is tied to purchases of goods and services from donor countries. The effect of this is that most aid given by the US and UK is spent in the US and UK on American or British produced products or services.

These political and economic considerations mean that those countries in most need of aid, such as those in Sub-Saharan Africa, tend to receive less than some better-off countries.

Multilateral aid

Multinational aid, by which countries join together to provide aid and support to developing nations, can potentially be more helpful to developing countries. The main sources of multinational aid include:

- the UN
- the World Bank
- International Monetary Fund (IMF).

The UN

The UN is responsible for both emergency aid and assistance to promote long-term development. Its intervention has been very significant in supplying food to Ethiopia which appears to have presented a repetition of the mass starvation seen there in the mid-1980s. However, UN responses can be slow especially as it is necessary to obtain the agreement of most member states.

The IMF and the World Bank

The IMF was set up as a result of the Bretton Woods agreement after World War Two in an attempt to prevent a repeat of the financial crises that had marred international trade in the pre-war period. It is specifically designed to help countries through periods of balance of payment difficulties in order to avoid competitive devaluations. The leading economies each contributed to a fund to which each could draw upon if needed.

The World Bank was also created following Bretton Woods and the leading economic powers agreed to contribute to a fund which developing countries could draw upon to help fund growth and development. Both organisations have been effectively run and organised by the US and in the 1980s and 1990s followed right-wing economic policies associated with President Regan and PM Thatcher.

The activities of the World Bank and the IMF in the 1990s have brought enormous discredit to both these organisations. They are blamed by Nobel Prize Winning economist, Joseph Stiglitz, for exacerbating problems of poverty in Africa, Latin American and the former Soviet block by insisting on various forms of conditionality to aid packages and those designed to free developing countries from the crippling problem of debt. Aid and help with re-scheduling debt have been tied to the imposition of free market ideas, forcing countries to open capital markets to foreign competition, to privatise state owned organisations and to instigate internal austerity programmes as a means of combating inflation and balance of payments programmes. These policies given the generic title of '**structural adjustment**' have been applied on the presumption that market-based solutions work and that market failure is unlikely. Yet, as has already been demonstrated, markets in developing countries are much more likely to be imperfect or

Definition ""

Structural adjustment refers to neo-liberal economic policies to promote competition and reduce government intervention.

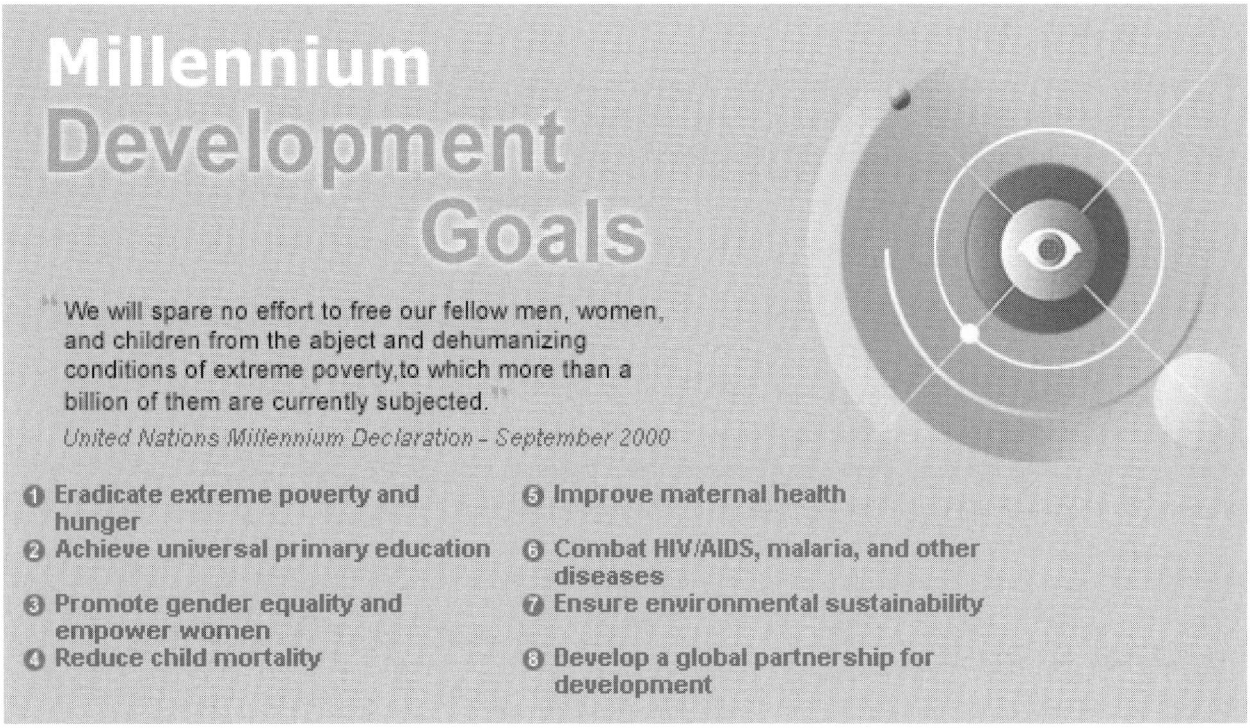

Millennium Development Goals

"We will spare no effort to free our fellow men, women, and children from the abject and dehumanizing conditions of extreme poverty, to which more than a billion of them are currently subjected."

United Nations Millennium Declaration – September 2000

1. **Eradicate extreme poverty and hunger**
2. **Achieve universal primary education**
3. **Promote gender equality and empower women**
4. **Reduce child mortality**
5. **Improve maternal health**
6. **Combat HIV/AIDS, malaria, and other diseases**
7. **Ensure environmental sustainability**
8. **Develop a global partnership for development**

Figure 1: An extract from the United Nation's Millennium Declaration.

Source: www.development.org

even missing. One of the results of reducing government intervention has been failures in capital markets resulting in the bankruptcy and closure of firms in Argentina. When the Russian government carried through privatisation programmes there was massive fraud by criminal elements. These examples of government failure have resulted in civil unrest in a number of countries, including Argentina and Indonesia, and have resulted in falling living standards in most of the ex-communist countries which have been forced to take rapid measures to liberalise their economies.

Those countries which have challenged the World Bank prescriptions for development have tended to do better than countries that accepted structural adjustment packages. Thus, South Korea and Malaysia appear to have recovered more quickly from the crash in eastern Asia of the late 1990s than those countries such as Thailand who were more compliant with the World Bank.

Economic development

Activity 1

(a) Explain what is meant by development.

(b) Do economic growth and development conflict?

Activity 2

(a) Identify five characteristics of developing economies.

(b) Research to what extent China might be regarded as a developing economy.

Activity 3

(a) Identify five obstacles to economic development faced by developing countries.

(b) Explain three ways a developing country may overcome these obstacles.

Activity 4

(a) How can the sectors in an economy be classified?

(b) Research how these sectors are changing in any two developing countries.

Activity 5

(a) Does trade promote economic growth?

(b) Does foreign aid always promote economic growth and development?

Activity 6

(a) What role does the World Bank play in economic development?

(b) What effect is globalisation having on developing countries?

The UK economy

Activity 1

(a) Define productivity

(b) Explain three causes of a rise in productivity.

Activity 2

(a) What determines the value of a country's exchange rate?

(b) What effect would a fall in the value of the pound have on the UK economy?

Activity 3

(a) What does the Laffer curve show?

(b) Should the UK government rely more on direct or indirect tax revenue?

Activity 4

(a) What does the Phillips curve indicate?

(b) Discuss how successful UK authorities have been in controlling inflation in recent years.

Activity 5

(a) What is meant by a budget deficit?

(b) Explain the link between a country's budget position and the economic cycle.

Activity 6

(a) What does a Lorenz curve show?

(b) How can the standard of living in the UK be assessed?

Q1 Answer the following question.

Improving living standards

Table 1: Measuring development

Country	HDI Rank	GDP per capita rank
Georgia	81	115
Iran	98	76
South Africa	107	51
Botswana	126	64
Tanzania	151	130

Source: Human Development Report 2002, UNDP, 2002

'The poor are different from us, they have less money. This simple fact explains why for many years the focus of economists and organisations, such as the World Bank, has stayed firmly on boosting GDP growth rates in the developing world. If 2.4 billion people in the world live on less than $2 a day, getting some more dollars into their pockets is a clear priority.

But is it a bit too simple? A World Bank report published yesterday painted a far more complex picture. Countries with the same growth rates can end up with very different numbers of people living in poverty and the same sorts of economic reforms can end up having very varied outcomes in different places.

It is also emphasised the fact that genuine economic progress requires more than money. Clean air and water, freedom from disease, access to education, and security from natural and financial disasters all matter to people as much as having the cash to buy food and goods. While these other aspects depend on GDP growth, growth alone is not enough.

Growth is correlated with improvements in other desirable indicators of quality of life. It reduces poverty and infant mortality, boosts literacy and life expectancy, and is linked with reduced deforestation and water pollution. But the causation is not all one way. Improvements in health, education and environmental standards can contribute to future growth. It can be argued that growth has to be high quality if it to be sustained.'

Source: 'There's more to becoming rich than GDP growth' by Diane Coyle, *The Independent*, 26/9/00, page 16.

1 (a) (i) What determines a country's HDI ranking? (2)

(ii) Using Table 1, comment on the differences in GDP per capita and HDI rankings of any of the two countries shown. (4)

(b) Apart from the items included in HDI, identify two other ways in which poor, developing countries differ from the UK. (2)

(c) (i) Explain how countries with the same growth rates can end up with very different numbers of people living in poverty. (2)

(ii) Explain the links between health and economic growth. (4)

(d) Discuss two ways developing countries could improve the 'quality of growth'. (6)

Select one of the following essay questions.

2 (a) Explain the contribution to economic development of the work of the IMF. (10)

(b) Discuss whether domestic or international institutions make a greater contribution to tackling the problems of development. (15)

3 (a) Explain why many developing countries rely heavily on primary production. (10)

(b) Discuss the problems experienced by developing countries when they attempt to diversify their economies. (15)

4 (a) Explain what is meant by Rostow's stages of growth. (10)

(b) Discuss how relevant Rostow's model is to the decisions faced by economic policy makers in developing countries. (15)

The UK economy

Q1 Answer the following essay question.

'Unemployment is edging upwards, and interest rates may be near the trough of the current cycle. The great consumer boom is almost spent. The uncomfortable question for the Chancellor of the Exchequer is, what happens next?

The Chancellor's hope is that investment and exports will rise to help public spending take up the slack, But with our main export markets in Europe scarcely growing at all, and the response of exporters to the recent devaluation of the pound negligible, the betting has to be that other types of expenditure will not pick up strongly enough to counteract the gradual but relentless slowdown in consumer spending now in prospect. In this case, the economy will grow well below potential for some time, leading to a series of familiar difficulties – not least a ballooning budget deficit as tax revenues decline, and associated pressures for spending cuts or tax rises.

There is a big gap in economic efficiency between the UK and its main competitors, much of which is connected with lack of investment, and it needs to be addressed if Britain's long-term economic performance is to improve. It may come as a shock to those who have taken at face value the claims of successive governments that they are living in the most successful and dynamic economy in Europe, but levels of efficiency are in fact substantially higher in France and Germany, as well as in America, than they are here.

In terms of the general level of prosperity (output per head of population), Britain has largely drawn level with France and Germany but this is because British people have been working longer hours while those on the Continent have been working less – longer hours have meant that output per person employed has been rising faster here than on the Continent.'

Source: 'Consumer boom cannot mask lagging productivity for ever' by Christopher Smallwood, *The Independent*, 4/8/03, Page 17

(a) (i) What is meant by a consumer boom? (2)

    (ii) State and explain two causes of a slowdown in consumer spending. (4)

(b) Explain why a devaluation may not increase export revenue. (4)

(c) Explain how an increase in investment could increase Britain's long-term economic performance. (6)

(d) Using the information in the extract, assess to what extent the UK's economic growth is sustainable. (4)

Answer one of the following essay questions.

2 (a) Explain what effect an increase in the marginal propensity to save is likely to have on the size of the national income multiplier. (10)

  (b) Discuss how changes in fiscal policy can influence the size of the multiplier. (15)

3 (a) Explain what may cause an increase in the money supply. (10)

  (b) Discuss what effect an increase in the money supply will have on economic performance. (15)

4 (a) Explain the effect of a rise in the value of the pound on the current account of the UK's balance of payments. (10)

  (b) Discuss how effective UK supply-side policies have been in increasing the UK's international competitiveness. (15)

Economic development

Data response question

1 (a) (i) A relatively straightforward introductory question. State the components of HDI, i.e. GDP per capita, life expectancy and education.
(ii) Georgia's HDI rank is higher than its GDP per capita rank. This indicates that the quality of life in the country is greater than the GDP figure suggests. In contrast Iran's GDP figure appears to overstate the quality of life in the country. When life expectancy and education are taken into account, the country has a lower ranking.

(b) State two other differences. You may select these from the passage, e.g. less access to clean water and less freedom from natural disasters. You may, alternatively, select from the knowledge you have gained from your studies, e.g. lower savings ratio and reliance on primary production.

(c) (i) There are three main reasons. One is that the initial level of real GDP of the countries may differ so that even with the same percentage changes in real GDP, some countries will still be much poorer than others. The other reasons are differences in the distribution of income and differences in population size.
(ii) Health and economic growth are positively related. Improvements in health will increase the productivity of workers and increase the productive potential of the economy. Increases in output will raise income and government tax revenue, enabling more to be spent on health care.

(d) You need to explain and evaluate two methods. The passage provides you with a number such as improved education and improved environmental standards. More state spending on education should raise productivity and should also enable people to enjoy life more. However, developing countries may not have additional resources to devote to education and more spending on education does not always result in improved educational standards.

Higher environmental standards may make the country a more attractive destination for tourists and multinational companies. It should also improve the health of the population and the quality of their lives. Again, though, it can be costly to achieve higher environmental standards and if the standards are unnecessarily high they may restrict economic growth.

Essay questions

2 (a) Here you need to identify how the IMF seeks to assist developing countries both in terms of restoring short-term stability and achieving longer-term structural reforms. Explain how its policies impact on developing countries' real GDP and living standards.

(b) A relatively demanding question. You should assess the contribution of domestic institutions, particularly governments and international organisations, such as the IMF, World Bank and the EU, and come to an overall conclusion. In your discussion you should assess domestic and international policies designed to overcome problems, such as a lack of investment and high levels of foreign debt. You should mention that the relative contributions vary between countries and over time.

3 (a) In your answer to this part you should refer to stages of development. Use comparative advantage theory and briefly refer to the trade restrictions imposed on developing countries by industrialised countries.

(b) Here you should pick up on the trade restrictions and discuss other problems including lack of investment, lack of skilled workers, lack of markets and resistance to change. You can make use of appropriate development theories including the Harrod–Domar and Lewis models. You should assess the extent of the problems, how easy they may be to overcome and recognise that the problems, and the extent of the problems, vary between developing countries.

4 (a) A straightforward question part. To gain high marks it is important that you show you can analyse each of the five stages, bringing out the key implications of the model.

(b) You need to assess the usefulness of Rostow's model. Discuss the extent to which savings and investment play a crucial role in development, whether countries have to pass through all the stages, the other factors that are important in achieving development, and the different challenges faced by developing economies in the twenty-first century.

The UK economy

Data response question

1 (a) (i) You should be able to work out a definition using the information provided in the passage. A consumer boom is a significant rise in consumer spending.
(ii) Identify two causes, such as a fall in confidence and a rise in direct taxation, and explain the link between these and consumer expenditure.

(b) Here you need to refer to the Marshall–Lerner condition. A devaluation will lower export prices and should increase demand for exports. The effect on export revenue will depend on the price elasticity of demand for exports. If demand is inelastic, a fall in price will reduce export revenue. You might also mention that while a devaluation should increase demand for UK products, export revenue will not rise if supply is inelastic.

(c) A good question. Explain how an increase in investment will not only raise aggregate demand, but will also increase aggregate supply.

Higher investment increases the productive potential of an economy, increasing its ability to achieve sustained economic growth. It would be useful to include an AD/AS diagram.

(d) You need to come to a conclusion, supported by evidence from the extract. The information contained in the article seems to suggest that, without changes, the UK's economic growth is not sustainable. The extract implies that the growth of aggregate demand is slowing down (consumer boom coming to an end, exports not growing and pressures for government spending cuts or tax rises). This will affect short-term, demand-led growth. The long-term, supply-led growth of the economy is threatened by a lack of investment. This could give rise to a supply constraint which you could illustrate with an AD/AS diagram. The last paragraph informs us that output in the UK has been rising due to longer working hours not increasing productivity – something that is not sustainable in the long run.

Essay questions

2 (a) Define the marginal propensity to save and give the full formula for the national income multiplier. Explain why an increase in a leakage (withdrawal) will reduce the size of the multiplier. It would be useful to include a numerical example.

(b) You need to recognise that changes in fiscal policy affect the size of the multiplier in a number of ways. An increase in government spending will raise national income. Higher national income usually increases the mps and mpm and so reduces the size of the multiplier. You should discuss, however, that the impact will depend in part on what the government spends more money on. For example, there may be an increase in government spending on the country's infrastructure. This may mean that little of the initial rise in spending goes on imports and less of the extra income generated may go on imported goods than expected if the improved infrastructure increases the UK's international competitiveness. Lower direct tax rates will obviously reduce mrt which will increase the size of the multiplier. However, the fall in mrt may be partially offset by a rise in mps and mpm if some of the extra disposable income is saved or spent on imports.

3 (a) Identify the causes of an increase in the money supply – credit creation, an increase in the monetary base and a net inflow of pounds sterling. Then explain how each one results in a rise in the money supply. For example, an increase in bank lending results in a rise in bank accounts and these count in the M4 measure of the money supply.

(b) To evaluate here you need to contrast the monetarist and Keynesian views of an increase in the money supply. In discussing these views, you can make use of the Quantity theory, transmission mechanisms and an AD/AS diagram. As monetarists think that an increase in the money supply greater than the increase in output will lead to inflation, you should assess the effects of inflation on an economy. Remember that Keynesians think the outcome will depend on how firms and households respond and on the state of the economy. For instance, you might mention that if an increase in the money supply lowers the rate of interest and this stimulates investment, UK economic performance may improve.

4 (a) Here you should explain what will happen to the price of UK exports and imports. In analysing the effect on export revenue and import expenditure, make use of the J-curve effect and the Marshall–Lerner condition.

(b) You need to show an awareness of the supply-side policies used by the UK government in recent years and to assess their impact on the quality and price of UK produced products and the ability of UK firms to respond to changes in world demand. In doing this you should consider the impact on productivity, investment and labour flexibility of such policies as privatisation, welfare to work and tax incentives. You should also recognise that the UK's international competitiveness has been affected by monetary policy (interest rates changes altering the value of the £ and influencing inflation) and by changes in other economies, for example changes in other countries' exchange rates, productivity levels, inflation rates.

PART 6/A2

Economics in the European context

Economics in the European context – an overview

Introduction

This module is designed to enable you to develop your skills as an economist. It accounts for twenty per cent of the total A level marks, the highest weighting of any A2 module.

The examination is a synoptic one – testing understanding of the connections between different elements of the subject. It is assessed by a $1\frac{3}{4}$ hour paper. The questions are based on a booklet of stimulus material which you will receive at least six weeks prior to the examination. The specification provides useful advice about how to approach the module. It stresses that:

> 'although candidates will require some additional knowledge of the appropriate context, the emphasis of the assessment of this module is on developing candidates' ability to think as economists and to make an effective use of the economists' 'tool kit' of concepts, theories and techniques which they have built up during their whole course of study.'

Europe

This topic is designed to provide a real world context in which you can apply the economist's tool kit referred to above. For example, arguments for and against protectionism and the aims of competition may be explored in an EU context.

You will investigate a range of aspects of the nature, organisation and future of Europe. Part 6 seeks to explore the key aspects identified in the specification including the single market, the arguments for and against UK participation in the single currency, transition economies, the likely impact of the entry of new members and the operation of the Common Agricultural Policy.

Maximising your grade

To achieve a high grade it is important to practise applying your knowledge and understanding of economic concepts, theories and techniques to EU issues, to develop your analytical and evaluative skills and to keep up-to-date with EU issues.

Particular emphasis is placed on assessing analytical and evaluative skills in the examination. Issues connected to the EU, especially whether the UK should join the single currency, can arouse strong feelings. Remember that as an economist you should assess arguments on the basis of relevant theory and evidence.

Developments are always taking place in terms of the performance of European economies, the policies pursued by the EU and the degree of integration. You should keep in touch with these developments by reading relevant articles in newspapers and economics magazines, watching the TV news and by visiting appropriate websites.

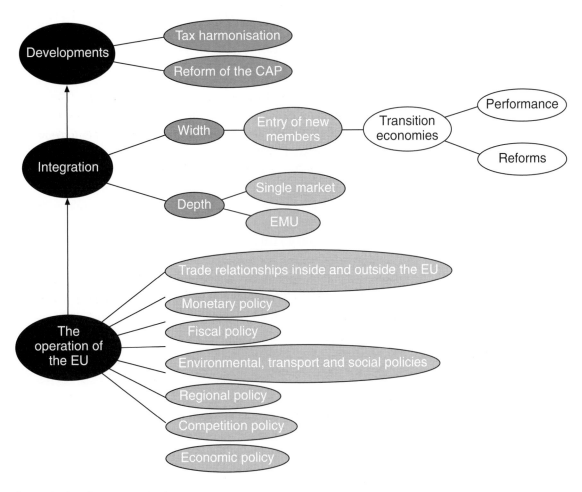

Economics in a European context

Trading blocs

Synoptic link

This section draws on the understanding of international trade you have gained at both AS and A2 levels. See AS Sections 3.23–3.26 and A2 Sections 5.12, 5.13 and 5.26.

Definitions

Common market: a group of countries with free movement of products, labour and capital.
Customs union: a group of countries with free trade between them and a common external tariff on imports from outside the area.
Trading bloc: a group of countries with preferential trading arrangements.

Thinking like an economist

Explain what factors influence where the UK imports from.

Introduction

The European Union (EU) has changed its name a number of times as its member countries have become more integrated. In the 1950s, six European countries – Belgium, France, Italy, Luxembourg, the Netherlands and West Germany – started to work together in the European Coal and Steel Community and the European Atomic Energy Community. In 1958, the same six countries formed the European Economic Community (EEC). In the beginning the area was a **customs union**. Now the EU has fifteen members, soon to be twenty-five, and is much more than a customs union.

A customs union

A customs union is a **trading bloc** that requires member countries to remove trade restrictions between each other. They also follow the same foreign trade policy by imposing the same tariffs on non-member countries. When on 1st January 1973, the UK joined the European Community (it had changed its name in 1967) it had to remove the taxes it imposed on imports coming from, for example, Germany while it had to impose the European Community's common external tariff on imports from, for example, New Zealand. This requirement to have a free trade approach with member countries while taxing products from outside the area has contributed to the change in the pattern of UK trade. Other EU countries are continuing to become more important as UK trading partners. In contrast, the importance of commonwealth countries as sources of UK imports and destination of UK exports continues to decline.

A common market

The EU moved from being a customs union towards being a **common market**. A common market is one in which not only is there free movement of products across national borders but also the free movement of labour and capital. In a common market it is not only tariffs on goods between member countries that are removed, but also non-tariff barriers (NTBs) including different product standards, restrictions on the movement of capital and differences in employment laws. One of the central aims of a common market is to increase actual and potential competition.

The development of the common market made it easier for firms to sell both goods and services to other EU countries without restrictions, and to set up production units elsewhere in the area. It also made it easier for people to live and work in other EU countries.

Economic and Monetary Union

Economic and Monetary Union (EMU) involves the harmonisation of economic policies to promote greater economic integration. Economic union concentrates on the creation of a single market through the removal of artificial trade barriers, a greater degree of co-ordination of economic policies and, in some cases, the development of common policies. Monetary union is concerned with greater co-ordination or centralisation of monetary policy.

The EU now operates a single currency, to which most members belong, a common agricultural policy (CAP) and competition, regional, social, transport and environmental policies which augment member governments' national policies. To date, there has been limited harmonisation of fiscal policy. Greater harmonisation of policies would move the EU more towards a single economy – referred to by some as 'the United States of Europe'.

Free trade area

A **free trade area** is one that does not involve much integration. It is a trade bloc where the member countries remove restrictions on the free movement of products between themselves. Apart from this there is no co-ordination of policies between the member countries.

The EU was always more than a free trade area. Some of its member countries, however, were originally members of the European Free Trade Area (EFTA) and the EU has important trading links with both EFTA and NAFTA (the North American Free Trade Area). EFTA was formed in 1960. Over the years, six of its members – Austria, Denmark, Finland, Portugal, Sweden and the UK – left to join the EU. EFTA currently consists of just four countries – Iceland, Liechtenstein, Norway and Switzerland. NAFTA came into being in 1992 and consists of the USA, Canada and Mexico.

The EU's relationship with NAFTA

The EU and NAFTA are the world's two largest trading blocs. While a considerable amount of trade flows between the two blocs, the relationship is somewhat fraught. Both frequently accuse the other of unfair competition. NAFTA complains particularly about the EU's use of export subsidies on agricultural products. These subsidies make EU agricultural products artificially cheap in foreign markets. In turn, the EU claims that the USA, in particular, distorts free trade by providing generous export credits to its farmers. These credits are short-term loans that are designed, in theory, to bridge the gap between the sale and payment of produce.

Trade disputes have broken out between the two trading blocs over a range of products including bananas, steel and beef. In 2003, the USA and the EU had been in dispute over genetically modified foods for more than four years. The USA was complaining about the EU's ban on GM food, imposed in 1999, which it claimed was costing US farmers more than $300m (£186m) a year.

Definitions

EMU: a group of countries that operate a single currency and co-ordinate economic policies.
Free trade area: a group of countries with free trade between them.

Research task

1 What are the benefits a country may gain from engaging in free trade?
2 Investigate how NAFTA compares in terms of economic size (real GDP) and population size with the EU.

Thinking like an economist

Analyse the effect of a trade war on economic welfare.

Quick check ✔

1 What effect has the UK's entry into the European Union had on its pattern of trade?

6.2 The new Europe

Synoptic link

This section builds on the previous one by examining the enlargement of the EU.

Introduction

During its history, more countries have joined the EU, thereby increasing its size. The largest single increase took place in 2004. To join the EU, countries have to meet a number of conditions. This is not an easy process for the accession countries since currently their economies exhibit significant differences from the current members.

The entry of the accession countries will have significant economic effects not only for the countries themselves but also for the current EU fifteen member countries.

Extension of the EU

In 1957, six countries – Belgium, France, Italy, Luxembourg, the Netherlands and West Germany – signed the Treaty of Rome to form the European Economic Community (EEC), which came into existence on 1 January 1958. This was a customs union. The name changed to the European Community (EC) in 1967. Nine countries joined later – Denmark, Ireland and the UK in 1973, Greece in 1981, Spain and Portugal in 1986 and Austria, Finland and Sweden in 1995. In addition in 1990, East Germany merged with West Germany to form Germany. The area's name was changed again in 1992 to the European Union to reflect the greater degree of integration that was occurring.

The accession countries

In December 2002 at the Copenhagen summit, the EU formally invited ten countries to join the EU. These ten accession countries joined on 1 May 2004. The countries are Cyprus, the Czech Republic, Estonia, Hungary, Latvia, Lithuania, Malta, Poland, Slovakia and Slovenia. All but two of these countries, Cyprus and Malta, are former command economies.

The accession countries' economies also differ from those of the current EU fifteen in a number of ways. Perhaps the two most striking are the size of their agricultural sectors and their income levels. All the accession countries have larger agricultural sectors than that of the current EU members. On average, 20 per cent of their labour force is employed in agriculture in comparison with an average of 4 per cent for the EU fifteen.

The accession countries, on average, also have smaller economies and lower income per head, some significantly lower income per head. Table 1 compares the income per head of the EU fifteen and that of the accession countries.

Table 1: A comparison of GDP per head in 2003

EU fifteen	GDP per head(€s)	Accession countries	GDP per head(€s)
1 Luxembourg	28,534	1 Cyprus	8,298
2 Denmark	20,081	2 Slovenia	6,016
3 Ireland	17,044	3 Malta	5,908
4 Sweden	16,244	4 Czech Republic	3,504
5 UK	16,026	5 Hungary	3,354
6 Netherlands	15,416	6 Poland	2,895
7 France	15,059	7 Slovakia	2,430
8 Finland	15,015	8 Estonia	2,423
9 Austria	14,910	9 Lithuania	2,041
10 Germany	14,793	10 Latvia	2,000
11 Belgium	14,200		
12 Italy	12,201		
13 Spain	9,509		
14 Greece	7,022		
15 Portugal	6,807		

Conditions for entry

The conditions that accession countries have to meet to join the EU were drawn up in 1993 and are known as the Copenhagen criteria. These include a functioning market economy, acceptance of EU legislation and a Western-style political system. These conditions mean that, for instance, a new member country has to be willing to permit the free movement of products, capital and labour, accept the requirements of economic, social, energy and environmental policies and be able, eventually, to join the European single currency.

To reach the required standard, the accession countries had to make relatively rapid progress. For example, Poland has had to take radical measures to reduce its levels of sulphur emissions and Hungary has had to spend more than fifteen million euros on improving its road and rail infrastructure.

The EU has given financial aid to the accession countries to help them meet the costs of complying to the EU's standards, rules and regulations. It has agreed that there will be a transition period of integration, in part to meet the concerns of the EU fifteen.

Trade creation: the increase in trade that arises due to member countries being able to buy products at lower prices due to the removal of tariff barriers between member countries.

Trade diversion: trade being diverted away from cheaper products outside the bloc towards higher cost products from inside the bloc.

Effects of membership on the accession countries

The accession countries, and a number of other countries, including Bulgaria, Romania and Turkey, want to join the EU because they believe they will experience a net gain. Those countries that do join will experience a number of effects, some of which may be advantageous and some potentially disadvantageous. The effects include:

- access to a very large and rich market: The accession countries will be able to sell to a market of more than 450 million people, many of whom enjoy high incomes.
- increased competition: The single market has resulted in a greater degree of competition between member countries. The accession countries' firms will have to modernise and increase their performance in terms of productivity, quality and price, i.e. raise efficiency.
- a change in the pattern of trade: The absence of barriers with the EU and a common external tariff (CET) on products from outside the EU will encourage the new entrants to trade more with fellow EU members. **Trade creation** and **trade diversion** will occur. The first happens when membership of a trading bloc increases the amount of specialisation and trade due to the elimination of trade barriers between members. Trade diversion involves changing the pattern of trade, with some trade being switched from non-members to members. The net effect on the accession countries' economies will depend on the extent to which they already trade with the EU and the relative efficiency of EU members.
- Increased investment from overseas: Firms from outside the EU, for example Japan and the USA, are attracted to set up branches and production units in the EU as it is a such a large, rich market. In addition, countries from the EU fifteen will be attracted to increase investment in the lower-cost accession countries. Higher foreign direct investment should create employment, bring with it knowledge and experience of advances in technology and developments in management technique and increase economic growth.
- Access to EU funds: The countries will be entitled to receive financial support from the CAP and from the EU's structural funds.
- Reduction in sovereignty of macroeconomic policy: National governments will have to give up some of the control of their economies to EU institutions. Most noticeably the accession countries will no longer be able to devalue their currencies or have their central banks alter their interest rates. There is a risk that the 'one size fits all' monetary policy may not be appropriate for countries at different stages of the economic cycle.

Thinking like an economist

Explain why entry into the EU may increase productive and allocative efficiency in a country.

Effects on the EU fifteen

The entry of new countries is already having an impact on the EU fifteen and will continue to do so for a number of years. Among the effects and possible effects are:

- reform of the EU's policies and procedures: The entry of countries with large agricultural sectors and relatively low GDP per head is forcing the EU to adapt the Common Agricultural Policy (CAP) and its expenditure programmes. A programme of EU budget reform was introduced under Agenda 2000, which restricted expenditure on enlargement and placed a limit on CAP expenditure.
- the poorer EU fifteen countries, Greece, Portugal and Spain, will receive less financial assistance from the EU.
- there may be large-scale movements of labour: With higher rates of unemployment and lower wages in the accession countries, the EU fifteen may experience significant levels of immigration. Of course, over time immigration may decline if the accession countries experience a rise in income and living standards. There may also be a reduction in illegal immigration.

Hot potato

Should Turkey be allowed to join the EU?

The process of joining

By April 2004, all 25 of the current and future member states had to ratify the Accession Treaty. Their integration into the EU will, to a degree, be a gradual process. Access to labour markets will be phased in. The countries will receive access to some aspects of the CAP straight away including export refunds, but direct payments for farmers will be phased in over ten years. Some aim to join the euro within four years but for most it will be some time before their economies converge sufficiently to be able to consider membership of the single currency.

The larger EU

The 2004 enlargement is unprecedented in terms of both the number of countries joining and their levels of GDP per head. The 25 member EU:

- will compose the largest trading bloc in the world
- will account for approximately 45 per cent of world exports
- will have more bargaining power in its negotiations with, for example, NAFTA and the WTO
- should create greater political stability in Europe
- will be more difficult to co-ordinate.

Whether the EU will prove to be more effective in raising the economic performance of its members and the living standards of its inhabitants will depend on whether the EU is still moving towards its optimum size or whether it has already passed it.

Thinking like an economist

Why is the existence of a functioning market economy necessary for membership of the EU?

6.3 Transition economies

Synoptic link

This section is linked to a range of AS sections, including Sections 1.1, 1.2, 2.2, 2.10–2.14 and 3.1.

Thinking like an economist

How are the three fundamental economic questions answered in a market economy?

Introduction

Transition economies are those economies that are moving away from operating planned economies towards developing market economies. This movement is motivated by the experience of the shortcomings of a planned economic system and the attraction of the advantages of a market system. Making the transition is, however, not an easy process and a number of the transition economies have experienced significant problems during the transition stage.

Planned economies

Planned economies, also known as centrally planned, command and collectivist economies, are ones in which the means of production are owned by the state and the state determines the answers to the three fundamental economic questions:

- what to produce
- how to produce
- for whom to produce.

The state determines what is produced and how it is to be produced by analysing the capabilities of the country's resources, its trade possibilities and what it perceives to be the needs and wants of its consumers. State planning bodies, such as Gosplan which was the central planning agency of the old Soviet Union, carry out input-output analysis, give instructions to state-owned enterprises as to what to produce and what resources to use, and co-ordinate the production process. They determine the distribution of income by setting and influencing wages and prices.

The European countries that are making the transition were, as planned economies, linked together through international trade. Each was a member of COMECON (the Council for Mutual Economic Assistance). This was a trade organisation that sought to encourage trade between members, to provide technical and financial assistance and to co-ordinate state planning across the area. The countries did not trade that much as they resorted to importing only when domestic production could not meet domestic demand. What trade did take place was predominantly with other members of COMECON.

Reasons for moving away from planned economies

Planned economies have a number of advantages. They usually have full employment of labour, the state should take into account social costs and benefits, provide public goods, avoid an inequitable distribution of income and ensure access to basic health services, education and housing for all.

The transition economies were motivated to move away from a planned economy because of the shortcomings of the system including high levels of bureaucracy, inefficiency, shortages, lack of choice and lack of consumer sovereignty.

A high number of resources were devoted to planning and managing the economy. The five-year plans, which most of the planned economies used, were expensive to draw up and were often based on inaccurate and inadequate information. It was also easier for the government to set targets in terms of quantity rather than in terms of both quantity and quality. Managers of state-owned enterprises often sacrificed quality to in order to achieve production targets.

The lack of competitive pressure and incentives provided by market forces meant that state-owned enterprises usually failed to achieve productive and allocative efficiency. The managers of the state-owned enterprises did not have the financial incentive to keep costs low and, in most cases, wage rates were not linked to individual productivity levels. It was difficult for the enterprises to achieve allocative efficiency as price levels, set and controlled by the state, did not move in line with changes in demand and supply. Governments did use a variety of methods, including questionnaires, consumer committees and analysis of sales levels, in a bid to gauge changes in consumer demand. However, the absence of price signals led to shortages and surpluses. Shortages were most significant in consumer goods. This reflected the fact that it was the government and not consumers who decided what was produced. Governments placed more emphasis on the production of capital goods, largely in a bid to increase economic growth and narrow the gap between themselves and western economies. Consumers also had little choice as the state-owned enterprises were usually run as monopolies producing standardised products. While there was full employment in the planned economies there was hidden unemployment with over-manning in a number of areas.

The process of transition

There are a number of measures that are taken to move an economy from a planned to a market system including:

- price liberalisation: the state ceases to set some prices and removes price limits on others. It allows most prices to be determined by market forces.
- privatisation: state-owned enterprises are sold off to the private sector and become subject to the competitive pressures and incentives provided by market forces.
- development of a private financial sector: this is important as private sector firms need to be able to raise finance via borrowing and the sale of shares and the government has to be able to sell government bonds and other government securities.
- removal of subsidies: the state removes subsidies so that, again, firms become responsive to market forces. Some subsidies, however, may be kept in the case of strategic and infant industries.

Thinking like an economist

Analyse the possible forms of market failure the transition economies may experience in the future.

- trade liberalisation: firms are to engage freely in international trade. This should enable resources to be allocated on the basis of comparative advantage, thereby raising output and economic welfare.
- reform of government institutions: government institutions, used to running a planned economy, have to adapt to running a market system. The role switches from virtual total control of the economy to overseeing the macroeconomy and seeking to correct market failure.
- development of appropriate entrepreneurial skills: the skills needed to run a private sector firm differ from those required to run a state-owned enterprise.

The speed of transition

There is debate about whether economies should move quickly or slowly towards a market economy. Shock therapy involves a quick movement with rapid privatisation, liberalisation of markets and the dismantling of old institutions. This is a demanding approach and problems can arise in trying to operate a market system before there is the necessary governmental, regulatory, social and financial infrastructure in place.

In contrast, the gradual approach takes place over a longer period so that there is time, for instance, for managers to learn new skills and appropriate institutions and markets to develop. This approach, though, runs the risk that people may not feel the pressure to change and some of the problems of both a planned and a market economy may occur.

Problems of transition

In this transitional stage, the economies are experiencing a number of problems. When many of the state-owned enterprises were privatised and state intervention in the economy was reduced, there was a major economic upheaval in economic activity. Some industries did expand but others, deprived of state subsidy and open to market forces, collapsed. Many workers, used to working for the same state concern throughout their working life, found it difficult change their jobs. Unemployment rose at a time when a welfare system to match the new economic system had not been adequately established. Output fell in many of the transition economies.

The removal of price controls led to a sudden increase in the price level. Inflation arose in some of the economies, including Georgia and Russia, to hyperinflation levels, due to the government increasing the money supply. Governments resorted to 'the printing press' largely because of the difficulty of raising finance to cover their spending in a situation where domestic financial markets were not fully developed and tax revenue was low.

Poverty and a marked increase in income inequality occurred. Under a planned economy there was low-priced or free housing, education and transport, often provided to workers and their families by the state-owned enterprises for which they worked. The removal of this provision before the development of adequate welfare systems led to problems of homelessness and a decline in the health standards of some. There was a rise in crime and an increase in the sale of demerit goods, including drugs and pornography. In the 1990s, such problems reduced the average life-span of the Russian population.

Different performance of transition economies

In Europe the transition economies are divided into groups.

- The Central and East European countries (CEE). This group includes former centrally-planned economies that previously had close links with the former Soviet Union. It consists of Albania, Bulgaria, Croatia, the Czech Republic, Estonia, Hungary, Latvia, Lithuania, Macedonia, Poland, Romania, the Slovak Republic and Slovenia.
- The Commonwealth of Independent States (CIS). This consists of the twelve countries that used to make up the former Soviet Union: Armenia, Azerbaijan, Belarus, Georgia, Kazakhstan, Moldova, Russia, Taijikstan, Turkmenistan, Ukraine and Uzbekistan.

To date, the performance of the CEE economies has been stronger than that of the CIS countries. They started to recover in the mid-1990s whereas in most of the CIS economics, recovery was delayed until the late 1990s. Their current economic growth rates are still higher than the CIS countries and, as noted in the previous section, eight are about to join the EU.

A number of factors may influence how successful economies are in making the transition. These include the economy's ability to attract FDI, the government's ability to control inflation, how rapidly investment and productivity grow and how rapidly appropriate markets and institutions can be developed.

Research task

Investigate the current relative economic performance of Russia and Poland.

Slovakia

As an example, Slovakia shows some of the problems that the transition economies are continuing to experience. It is attracting increasing amounts of FDI, productivity levels are rising and it is about to enter the EU. Its income levels, however, are still low. Its institutions are still not strong enough to fight corruption and there have been a number of scandals over share privatisation. There is also evidence of significant discrimination against the country's half a million-strong Roma minority, many of whom are unemployed and live in very poor housing.

Quick check

1 Identify the advantages and disadvantages of a planned economy.
2 Why may output fall and then rise during transition?
3 Distinguish between the shock therapy and gradual approaches to transition.
4 Discuss the problems economies have experienced in making the transition between planned and market economies.

The single market
6.4

Synoptic link

The previous section examined the increasing *width* of integration in the EU. This section discusses the increasing *depth* of integration.

Introduction

In England a firm based in Southampton, for example, can sell goods and services to consumers in York without having a tariff imposed on them, without having to pass through border controls, and without having to meet different quality standards. A dentist from Southampton can take up a job in York without obtaining a work permit and without having to possess different qualifications. A Southampton firm can also open a branch in York without any restriction on the amount of money it can move from Southampton to York. A consumer in Southampton can also easily compare the price of products produced by firms in Southampton and York as both use the same currency. This is because England is a single market.

A single market in the EU would be similar. To achieve such a situation the EU has been seeking to remove obstacles to free competition in the area. The process began with the formation of the EEC and is still on-going. Along the way there have been a number of key measures which have sought to create a competitive market in product, labour and capital markets.

The Treaty of Rome

The Treaty of Rome 1957, set out the basic aims of what was to become the EU. These included the elimination of tariffs and quotas on the import and export of goods between member countries, the establishment of a common external tariff, the abolition of obstacles to the free movement of people, services and capital between member states and the establishment of common policies for agriculture and transport.

These were ambitious aims. The EU achieved the removal of tariff and quota barriers on the free movement of goods relatively quickly as this is a condition of membership. However, in its first decades, a significant number of obstacles to the free movement of people, services and capital between member states, and thus competition on equal terms, remained.

The Single European Act

The Single European Act (SEA) was passed in February 1986 and came into force in July 1987. It main aim was to achieve the Treaty of Rome's objective of free trade within the EU by removing all remaining internal barriers and creating a fully integrated single market by the end of 1992. These barriers were not just on the movement of goods but also on services, capital and labour. The SEA had three guiding principles. These were:

- non-discrimination: national regulations should not discriminate between domestically-produced products and those produced elsewhere in the EU
- the burden of proof: members should accept imports from other member countries despite differences in product standards
- the burden of proof: any restrictions on imports from members on the grounds of health and safety have to based on sound scientific evidence.

The act outlined a series of measures designed to achieve competition on equal terms throughout the EU. These included the ending of customs controls at the frontiers of member states, the removal of non-tariff barriers such as restrictive public procurement policies by member governments, the reduction of subsidies by national member governments and the mutual recognition of other member states' qualifications. It also committed the EU to work towards a common policy on a range of areas including the environment, research and development and social and economic matters.

A series of directives came out of the SEA. For instance, one required major state contracts to be advertised at EU level with a reasonable time limit for bids to be received. Progress on the SEA's measures turned out to be relatively slow. Much of the progress that was made occurred on a case-by-case basis. This was, in part, because of the need to work out minimum quality standards on products and appropriate qualifications for different occupations.

The Maastricht Treaty

The Maastricht Treaty was signed in February 1992. It is also sometimes known as the Treaty on European Union. It sought to achieve some political objectives, most noticeably a common foreign and security policy. It also aimed to promote the single European market by encouraging the removal of remaining barriers to trade and increasing integration by replacing national currencies with a single European currency. It set out a timetable for EMU (economic and monetary union) to be achieved in three stages. Stage 1 was already in progress with the move towards a single market. The main features of stage 2 were to be increased co-ordination of national monetary policies and encouragement for governments to achieve greater similarity of economic performance (convergence). The third stage was to be the establishment of the European Central Bank (ECB) and the introduction of the single currency. The countries which belong the single currency are collectively known as the eurozone, the euro area or euroland.

Progress towards a single European market

Some noticeable progress has been made towards the creation of a single European market. For example, **exchange controls** have been removed in all the member countries and this has increased the geographical mobility of capital. The geographical mobility of labour has been encouraged by the mutual recognition of other member countries qualifications. However, the single market programme still has some way to go. For instance, differences in tax rates and tax bases between countries and state aid are still distorting competition between member states.

The effects of a single market

The EU is seeking to achieve a single market as it believes it will increase efficiency and economic welfare. The removal of barriers to competition

Definition

Exchange controls:
restrictions on the purchase of foreign currency and on the export of capital.

should enable countries to take full advantage of comparative advantage. Greater specialisation and trade should raise output, lower costs and prices, and raise quality. Enabling efficient firms to sell freely to a large market should enable them to take greater advantage of economies of scale. The greater competition created should promote not only allocative and productive efficiency but also dynamic efficiency.

The Cecchini Report of 1998 estimated that the completion of the single market programme may increase the real GDP of the EU by up to 6 per cent a year. As well as benefits, though, the movement towards the single market is bringing with it some threats to consumers, workers and firms. Overall, as already indicated, a single market should generate more income but it may be more unevenly distributed. Some firms will thrive in the more competitive environment, but others will be driven out of business – requiring workers to develop new skills and possibly to move from one area to another. There is also a risk that one or a few firms may can control over a market and abuse their market power.

Quick check

1   What were the aims of the Treaty of Rome?
2   Which barriers to free competition did the SEA concentrate on?
3   How does a single currency promote competition?
4   Why does the move towards a single market increase the need for regional policy?

Puzzler

To enable UK traders to compete on equal terms with French traders, should the UK government cut excise duty on cigarettes and alcohol?

Introduction

The timetable for Economic and Monetary Union (EMU) was set out in the Maastricht Treaty signed in 1992. Stage 1 was already in progress with the creation of the single market. The main features of stage 2 were to be increased co-ordination of national monetary policies and governments seeking to achieve greater similarity of economic performance (convergence). The third stage was to be focused on monetary union and was to involve the introduction of the single currency and the establishment of the European Central Bank (ECB). The ECB is based in Frankfurt. Its prime objective is to maintain price stability within the eurozone. It implements monetary policy and foreign exchange and reserve policies.

Economic and Monetary Union

Economic union is mainly concerned with the creation of a single market in Europe. As noted in the previous section, this involves the removal of barriers to free trade. It also includes the development of some common policies and the co-ordination of macroeconomic policies.

Monetary union in the EU context now involves not only the removal of barriers between national financial sectors and the free movement of capital within the bloc but also the adoption of a single monetary policy, with one interest rate, one exchange rate and one central bank overseeing control of the money supply.

The European single currency

The European single currency, the euro, is currently operated under a floating exchange rate system. However the European Central Bank (ECB) reserves the right to intervene if it considers it to be necessary. In addition, the changes to its interest rate, which it makes mainly to control inflation, have an impact on the value of the euro.

The single currency came into existence on 1 January 1999. So far, twelve out of the current fifteen members of the EU have joined. The three countries that have not joined are Denmark, Sweden and the UK.

Convergence criteria

To join the single currency (sometimes referred to as joining EMU) a country has to show that its economy is operating at a similar stage of the economic cycle as the rest of the members. The specific criteria are:
- the government budget must not exceed 3 per cent of GDP
- government debt should not be above 60 per cent of GDP
- the inflation rate should not exceed the average of the three members with the lowest inflation rates by more than 1.5 percentage points

Synoptic link

Before starting this section it would be useful to recap AS Sections 3.14 and 3.22, and A2 Sections 5.4, 5.15 and 5.16.

- long-term interest rates should not be more than 2 percentage points above the average of the three members with the lowest inflation rate
- a stable exchange rate.

Those members in the single currency have to continue to meet the limits on the fiscal deficits.

The UK government's criteria

Gordon Brown, the Chancellor of the Exchequer, has set down five conditions (or tests) that have to be met before the UK government will consider entry. These are:

- there must be sustainable convergence between the UK economy and the economies of the euro area countries
- there must be flexibility within the euro area for coping with economic change
- entry will be beneficial for promoting foreign direct investment in the UK
- entry will benefit UK financial services
- entry will be good for jobs and economic growth.

Research task

Investigate whether the UK currently meets the conditions necessary for entry into the single currency.

The effects of belonging to the single currency

Joining the single currency would have a number of effects for the UK, some potentially beneficial and some potentially harmful.

Benefits

These include:

- a reduction in transaction costs: UK firms and consumers would no longer have to spend money and time converting pounds into euros.
- elimination of exchange rate risk with the euro area: For example, UK firms would no longer be caught out by unexpected changes in the value of the pound against the euro. This would reduce firms' costs as they would no longer have to hedge against exchange rate risk and would create greater certainty.
- increased transparency: This is thought to be an important advantage. Having one currency makes it easier for firms and consumers to compare prices throughout the European Union. Consumers and firms will not have to spend time and effort converting prices into pounds before they decide which are the best offers. Competition should increase and price discrimination decrease. For example, the price difference in car radios in EU countries and in the UK should fall. In 1999, car radios were 36 per cent higher in price in London than in Rome.
- increased influence within the EU: Being part of the single currency would give the UK more say in the future direction of the EU. It would also make the EU a stronger economic power.
- lower interest rates: The EU, since its inception, has had a lower rate of interest than the UK. A lower interest rate may stimulate investment and economic growth in the UK.

- lower unemployment: The greater certainty created by a single currency and the lower rate of interest may increase economic growth and create more job opportunities.
- increased foreign direct investment: Some people claim that membership of the euro would attract more multinational companies to set up in the UK. It is argued that the UK would become a more attractive location because of the reduced transaction costs and reduced exchange rate uncertainty.

Costs

There would be transitional costs. These are the costs of changing over from using the pound to using the euro. For example, firms would have to convert their IT systems, show prices in both pounds and euros for a period of time, and train staff. However, transitional costs are one-off costs and are not a major consideration in deciding whether to join or not. More significant are the disadvantages which may be more long lasting including:

- reduction in independence of macroeconomic policy: The European Central Bank sets the rate of interest in the eurozone. In addition to no longer being able to operate its own interest rate, the UK government would lose the exchange rate as a policy tool and would have constraints imposed on its use of fiscal policy.
- asymmetric policy sensitivity: The UK economy differs from the rest of the EU in three main ways that may mean that it would be affected more significantly than other members by changes in policy. More UK consumer and corporate borrowing is undertaken on short-term, variable interest rate terms than in most EU countries. UK consumers also borrow more than consumers in most eurozone countries, in part to finance house purchases. The housing market in the UK is more important than in most of the eurozone as there are a greater proportion of owner-occupiers in the UK. So if the eurozone's interest rate were to rise this would affect UK consumers and firms more than those in other EU countries. However, there is an increasing tendency for loans to be taken out on fixed interest rate terms. Such a trend, if continued, will reduce the UK's sensitivity to interest rate changes.
- the UK trades more with the USA than other EU countries and so is affected more than the other countries by changes in the level of economic activity in the USA and changes in the value of the dollar. Its economic cycle, to date, has been more closely correlated with that in the USA than with that in the eurozone.
- the UK is also still a major exporter of oil so its economy is influenced more, and in a different way, to the other EU countries which are importers of oil, by changes in the world price of oil.
- lack of convergence: If there is not enough convergence between the UK and the eurozone or not enough flexibility to cope with economic change, then joining the euro would be likely to destabilise the UK economy.

Thinking like an economist

A country joins the single currency. Analyse the possible effect this may have on the efficiency of the country's firms.

Hot potato

Does membership of the single currency increase a country's economic performance?

Optimum currency area

In considering whether a country should join a single currency arrangement, some economists make use of the concept of an optimum currency area. Such an area is achieved when the arrangement provides net advantages to member countries. For this to happen it is important that prices and wages are flexible, and labour and capital are mobile. This is because if there is a country-specific shock, the rate of interest and the exchange will not adjust to offset the shock. What will have to happen is that wages and prices will have to change and workers and capital will have to move from one member country to another.

The effects of staying out

The UK government has not yet decided on entry. Staying out of an arrangement which most of the EU members has joined may have a number of effects on the UK economy including:

- a tendency for its exchange rate to be high because of its higher interest rate
- a risk of loss of foreign direct investment: The euro area has formed a large market which may prove more attractive to foreign direct investment (FDI) than the UK. This may particularly be the case if companies decide to locate close to each other to benefit from external economies of scale. Currently FDI is very important for the UK. Indeed the UK is the third largest recipient of FDI, after the USA and China.
- a risk that some of the UK's financial institutions may move to the euro area to be closer to the main financial dealings. Currently, though, the City of London remains Europe's leading financial centre due to its competitiveness, flexibility and adaptability.

Quick check

1 What is the main role of the ECB?
2 Why is it thought necessary for members of the single currency to limit any budget deficit?
3 Identify three of the criteria the government has set for UK entry into the single currency.
4 Explain how membership of the single currency reduces a country's economic sovereignty.

Introduction

Monetary policy for countries in the eurozone is operated by the European Central Bank (ECB) and for the countries outside, currently Denmark, Sweden and the UK, by their governments.

The first few years of the operation of the single currency have allowed economists to assess how effectively the ECB is carrying out its role. It has also provided information for the continuing debate on whether the UK should join the single currency.

The objectives of monetary policy in the eurozone

The objectives of monetary policy for the eurozone were set out in the Maastricht Treaty. The key objective is to maintain price stability. Subject to that objective, the EU wants monetary policy to foster sustainable economic growth and high employment.

The role of the ECB

The ECB has a number of functions including issuing banknotes, conducting foreign exchange operations and managing the official reserves of the member states. Its most well-known function, though, is to set interest rates. The ECB's Governing Council meets to consider a variety of economic indicators including, for instance, exchange rate movements, unemployment data, wage changes, retail sales, business and consumer confidence surveys.

Initially, the inflation target set for the ECB was a year on year increase in the harmonised index of consumer prices (HICP) for the eurozone of below 2 per cent. This target came in for two main criticisms. One was that it was too harsh. Measures of inflation, even the HICP, tend to overstate the rate of inflation. A target of less than 2 per cent is a very low target and concern was expressed that it risked pushing economies with an overvalued exchange rate into deflation. The target, between 0 per cent and 2 per cent was also essentially asymmetric. The assumption was that, in principle, the ECB wanted inflation to average 1.5 per cent. This meant that inflation could only go 0.5 per cent points above but 1.5 per cent points below.

In May 2003, the ECB announced it was softening its inflation target and redefining its monetary policy strategy. It stated that it would attach less importance to an analysis of the money supply in making its interest rate decisions. Its inflation target was changed to 'close to but below 2 per cent'. These changes make the target rather more asymmetric but not fully asymmetric and suggest that the ECB may set interest rates lower in the future.

Inflation targeting has a number of advantages. It allows the ECB's record to be assessed. Perhaps more importantly, firms, workers and households believe that the target indicates that the ECB is serious about controlling inflation. If so they will restrain their price rises, wage demands and spending and so not cause inflation to accelerate.

Record on interest rate changes

The ECB did not always achieve its initial inflation target. Between 2000 and 2003, inflation was above 2 per cent on a number of occasions but not significantly so. As measures of inflation tend to overstate the rate of inflation, the new target may prove to be a more realistic one.

One of the main criticisms of European monetary policy has not been that inflation has been too high but that the policy has tended to be too deflationary. It is thought that, on several occasions, the ECB has resisted cutting interest rates when there was no real risk of the inflation rate rising and when such a cut would have been beneficial for stimulating economic activity in a number of member states.

Another criticism made is based on the so-called 'one size fits all' nature of European monetary policy. The interest rate decided by the ECB applies to all the countries in the eurozone. There is a risk that an interest rate which may be appropriate for the area as a whole may be inappropriate for some individual member countries. Those member countries with overheating economies and high inflation will have low real rates of interest when they need high real interest rates, while economies with high levels of unemployment and low inflation will have high real interest rates. If all the economies are operating at a similar point in the economic cycle, having the same interest rate would not be a problem. In practice though, there are still significant differences in the eurozone economies. For instance, in 2003 unemployment in Spain was 11.8 per cent and only 3.7 per cent in the Netherlands. Inflation in Ireland was 3.3 per cent but 0.9 per cent in Germany, as measured by the HICP.

The euro's record

The euro was launched on 1 January 1999, and became a physical currency, used by households and firms, three years later on 1 January 2002. The value of the euro was initially rather weak, largely because of concern about the economic performance of the eurozone countries. In 2003, though, the value of the euro rose mainly due to the weakness of the dollar. This led to some pressure being put on the ECB to cut interest rates to avoid the value of the euro rising too high.

There is the problem that some countries joined the single currency at inappropriate exchange rates with, for example, Germany going in at too high a rate and Ireland at too low a rate. This has put deflationary pressure on Germany and inflationary pressure on Ireland.

There is evidence, though, that the euro has promoted international trade, investment and competition. A single currency removes a key source of

Thinking like an economist

1 Explain how a rise in interest rates could reduce inflation.
2 Why does a low rate of inflation usually result in a high real rate of interest?

uncertainty. The eurozone members no longer have to be worried about currency changes between them. This has made it easier for firms to plan ahead and to compare the costs of producing in different parts of the eurozone. These factors have encouraged them to undertake more investment. Foreign direct investment into the eurozone has also been attracted by both this greater certainty and by the ease of movement of capital. Trade within the area has grown with the trade that France and Germany do with the other eurozone countries having increased significantly.

There is some evidence that some suppliers took advantage of the changeover to the euro, when some consumers were uncertain about the internal purchasing power of the euro. However, the single currency, by making price differences more transparent, is now putting competitive pressure on the eurozone firms to keep their prices low.

The UK's position outside the eurozone

The UK economy has performed quite will outside the eurozone in the first few years of its existence. It has enjoyed low unemployment, low and stable inflation and an economic growth rate above that of the EU average. In contrast, unemployment in the eurozone has been relatively high and economic growth rates slow.

Some economists and politicians, though, argue that UK economic performance would be better if it joined the single currency. They point out that UK trade with other EU countries has grown more slowly than that of France and Germany. They also warn that while the UK remains the most popular destination for foreign direct investment in the EU, its share has fallen since 1999.

Will the UK join the single currency?

For the UK to join the single currency, it will have to meet not only the convergence criteria set down by the UK government (see Section 6.5). Gordon Brown, the Chancellor of the Exchequer, in October 1997 added that 'the key factor is whether economic benefits of joining for business are clear and unambiguous.'

For UK membership to stand any chance of reaping these benefits, it is important that the UK economy is converging with the eurozone. In early 2003, the National Institute of Economic and Social Research stated that the UK is now in a very similar position to the rest of Europe in terms of the symmetry of economic shocks. On 9 June 2003, Gordon Brown said that he did not think that four of his tests had been met yet – convergence with the eurozone economies, flexibility, investment and employment. He added that the latter two tests would be passed if the first two tests were achieved.

If the government thinks that the UK's economy is in line with the eurozone and all the necessary conditions have been met, it will put the decision on membership to the public in a national referendum.

Thinking like an economist

What determines the value of a currency?

Hot potato

Which presents the greater risk – a 'one size fits all' interest rate or exchange rate fluctuations?

Explain how inward foreign
direct investment affects long run
aggregate supply.

Those in favour argue that in addition to increased trade, investment and competitive pressure due to using the same currency, membership may bring less volatility of interest rates. If so this would make the UK housing market and so the economy more stable and would again promote investment. Those opposed point out that the eurozone lacks sufficient labour market flexibility and a large enough central budget to offset economic shocks. They are also concerned about giving up autonomy over monetary policy especially as the ECB has tended to operate a rather rigid monetary policy.

Quick check

1   In what circumstances is the ECB likely to raise the rate of interest?
2   In what ways was the ECB's inflation target changed in 2003?
3   In connection with European monetary policy, what is meant by 'one size fits all'?
4   In what circumstances would the UK join the euro?

Introduction

The success or otherwise of the EU as a trading bloc will depend in large part on the extent of convergence and integration. Convergence and integration are closely linked. Convergence is important for integration to succeed and integration promotes convergence.

The importance of convergence

The greater the degree of convergence, the more likely it is that the pursuit of common policies, including a single currency and interest rate, will benefit all economies. If all members have similar economies and react to external shocks in a similar way, it should be relatively easy to decide on, for example, one interest rate for the whole area.

If, however, the economies differ in a notable way, then different policy measures might be needed for each economy. Applying the same measure in such a situation is likely to result in some economies becoming deflated while others become overheated.

Types of convergence

There are two main types of convergence, both of which are important. One is cyclical convergence. This is achieved when member countries' economic cycles coincide. The other is structural convergence. This involves the economic structures of the member countries being similar. Structural convergence should mean that the economic cycles of the member countries continue to move in line for years to come.

Convergence and the UK economy

The importance of convergence has been recognised by Gordon Brown, the Chancellor of the Exchequer. It is his first and most important test for UK membership of the euro. He is taking steps to try to ensure greater convergence of the UK economy and the eurozone by making adjustments to the UK housing and labour markets.

Nature of integration

Barriers to a trading bloc acting as one economy come in a number of forms. These include not only tariffs, quotas, different currencies and interest rates, but also, for instance, differences in the tax base and tax rates and the policy approaches of member governments.

Due to the extent of these barriers, some of which are quite subtle, economic integration is not a quick or smooth process. Over time, for instance, a number of barriers to the free movement of labour between member states in the EU have been removed. The EU has, for example,

Convergence and integration

6.7

Synoptic link

This section builds on A2 Sections 6.2, 6.4, 6.5 and 6.6.

Thinking like an economist

Explain why the UK is more sensitive to interest rate changes than Italy.

**Thinking like
an economist**

Analyse why unemployment
remains high in some parts of the
EU while there are labour shortages
in other parts.

abolished work permits in the area, harmonised working conditions and has sought to provide more job information. Nevertheless barriers still exist to the geographical mobility of labour as evidenced by differing unemployment rates between member states.

The levels of integration

As economies in a trade bloc move towards economic and monetary union, the level of integration increases. This integration can be analysed in terms of what is being integrated.

1. Product market integration: This involves the removal of barriers to the free movement of goods and services between member countries.
2. Factor market integration: This is concerned with the removal of barriers to the free movement of labour and capital.
3. Policy integration: This is a higher level of integration and concerns greater co-ordination of economic policies between member states or the centralisation of policy making. In its approach to policy integration, the EU has adopted the principle of subsidiarity. This involves taking political decisions at the lowest possible level. The EU operates policies at a centralised level only when it considers that is more efficient due the externalities and/or economies of scale involved.

Integration can also be examined in terms of how it is being achieved. Economists distinguish between negative and positive integration. Negative integration covers the removal of barriers to integration (1 and 2 above). Positive integration, in contrast, is concerned with a move towards a greater integration of policy making (3 above).

The benefits and costs of integration

Integrating member countries' economies may result in a number of benefits and costs.

Benefits

- The larger market available to firms should enable them to take greater advantage of internal economies of scale. The ability of firms to locate near to other firms in the same industry, forming clusters, may also lead to greater external economies of scale.
- Output and welfare should rise as trade within the area should be based, to a greater extent, on comparative advantage.
- Firms, including domestic monopolies, will face more competition. This should make them more allocatively and productively efficient.
- Greater co-ordination or centralisation of policy-making may result in more appropriate policy measures being implemented. The ECB, for example, has a better track record in setting interest rates than some national governments.
- The very process of integration should help to promote economic convergence.

Costs

- Diseconomies of scale, both internal and external, may be experienced if firms and industries grow too large.
- Regional differences may widen. While the area as a whole may enjoy higher output and income, low productivity regions may experience a fall in output, income and employment levels.
- Over time markets may become more concentrated. Firms may merge to form monopolies and oligopolies on a European scale.
- EU authorities may follow inappropriate policies.
- There is always a risk that economies may convergence towards a lower level of economic performance than some individual members countries have been experiencing.

Quick check

1 Why is convergence important for the success of economic integration?
2 Distinguish between cyclical and structural convergence.
3 What does policy integration involve?
4 Is greater integration necessarily beneficial?

Fiscal policies

Synoptic link

This section is linked to AS
Section 3.14 and A2 Sections 5.5–5.7.

Thinking like
an economist

What effect is the move
towards trade liberalisation likely to
have on the sources of the
EU's revenue?

Introduction

The EU operates its own budget and influences member countries' budget positions and fiscal policies.

The EU's budget

The EU budget, like a national government's budget, is a record of its spending and revenue. However, unlike a national government's budget, it must always balance. This is because the sole aim of the EU's budget is to raise the funds needed to finance the EU's spending programmes. It is not used to influence the level of aggregate demand in the EU. The EU's budget, as a percentage of GDP, is much smaller than a national government's budget. It was 1 per cent of EU GDP in 2002. This smaller percentage is accounted for by the narrower coverage of EU expenditure.

The main items of EU spending are the Common Agricultural Policy (CAP) and the structural funds used for regional development and social policy. Minor items of spending include development aid, spending on energy programmes and administration.

The EU receives its revenue from four key sources:
1. customs duties
2. agricultural levies
3. VAT levy – set at 1 per cent of member countries' VAT revenue
4. GNP (national income) based resource. Member countries contribute a proportion of their national income. A ceiling has been placed on this at 1.27 per cent of GNP for the period 2000-2006.

Some countries, for example Ireland and Greece, are net beneficiaries of the EU budget. This means that they receive more from EU spending than they contribute to the EU budget. Other countries, including Austria and the UK, are net contributors. The UK was concerned about its initial relatively high net contribution and negotiated a significant rebate.

EU policy and member governments' budget positions

The EU influences member countries' budget positions in a number of ways. The fundamental way is that all member countries are expected to avoid 'excessive' budget deficits.

Those countries wanting to join the single currency have to meet specific convergence criteria. These contain two criteria that place a limit on fiscal deficits. These are that a government must not have a budget deficit in excess of 3 per cent of GDP and that its national debt should not be above 60 per cent of GDP. Once in they are expected to continue to meet these criteria.

The countries' governments have to submit convergence programmes to the European Commission and the ECOFIN (the Council of EU Finance Ministers) about how they are progressing towards the convergence criteria.

The Stability and Growth Pact

The Stability and Growth Pact states the medium-term objective for the budget positions of countries in the single currency should be close to balance or in surplus. Countries are allowed to react to normal cyclical fluctuations but are required to keep to the budget deficit limit of 3 per cent of GDP, except in exceptional circumstances.

The eurozone countries have to submit stability programmes and annual updates to the European Commission and ECOFIN. These have to explain how the government is moving towards the medium-term budgetary objective, what is expected to happen to national debt and how economic activity will influence its financial position. The ECOFIN assesses these stability programmes. If it is concerned that a country will not achieve the fiscal targets of the pact, it will make recommendations on how the government can take the necessary adjustment measures.

If a country exceeds the 3 per cent budget deficit limit, it will first receive a warning. If the deficit persists it may be fined up to 0.5 per cent of GDP.

Assessment of the 3 per cent budget deficit limit

The EU argues that a limit has to be placed on the budget deficits that governments can operate in a single currency to ensure price stability and economic growth. If a government, or group of governments, operate large budget deficits they will add to aggregate demand and possibly the money supply. This is likely to put downward pressure on the euro that may generate inflationary pressure and result in a higher rate of interest for all member countries.

Some, however, argue that the Stability and Growth Pact is too harsh and needs reform. A budget deficit over 3 per cent may not be significant if it results from capital spending or if it stimulates higher employment and incomes.

Some argue that Gordon Brown's golden fiscal rule is more appropriate. This allows governments to borrow for capital spending but not, over the medium term, for current spending. Gordon Brown's public sector rule that national debt should not exceed 40 per cent of GDP, however, is harsher than the EU's.

It is also claimed that fiscal flexibility is more important when governments cannot independently use monetary policy to influence the level of economic activity in their countries.

Thinking like an economist

1 Explain why a government is likely to experience a budget deficit during a slowdown in economic activity.
2 Explain how a government could reduce a budget deficit.

Hot potato

Why may a government be reluctant to reduce a budget deficit?

Tax harmonisation

As well as influencing member governments' budget and national debt positions, the EU is seeking to ensure that variations in the tax base and tax rates across member countries do not distort competition and so create inefficiency. Currently there are considerable variations in the **tax burden** across the EU with, for instance, Sweden being relatively highly taxed and Greece relatively lightly taxed.

The Treaty of Rome stated as an objective the harmonisation of indirect taxes. A move towards this was made with the requirement for member countries to adopt VAT as their main indirect tax. The SEA also stated the objective of harmonising rates of VAT and excise duty. Agreement was achieved that countries standard rate of VAT should not be below 15 per cent. Nevertheless there is still considerable variation in the coverage and rates of VAT and the rates of excise duties across the EU. There is also some evidence that this does distort competition with countries with lower tax rates, but not necessarily lower costs of production, attracting more custom. Concern has also been raised about how differences in corporation tax, taxes on savings and income tax are influencing direct and portfolio investment and the ease that firms experience in recruiting key workers.

Definition

Tax burden: the total amount of tax paid as a percentage of GDP.

> ### Quick check
>
> 1 How does the EU's budget differ from a national government's budget?
> 2 What limits does the Stability and Growth Pact impose on member governments?
> 3 How do the limits of the Stability and Growth Pact differ from Gordon Brown's fiscal rules?
> 4 Explain how variations in the tax base and tax rates can distort competition.

Introduction

Unemployment is a significant issue for the European Union as unemployment, particularly in the eurozone, is high. A major cause of this high unemployment is thought to be a lack of labour market flexibility.

Individual member countries seek to reduce unemployment although the measures which members of the eurozone can take are constrained by the membership of the single currency. The EU itself also seeks to reduce unemployment.

EU unemployment performance

Table 1: Unemployment rates %

	EU	Eurozone	UK	USA
2000	7.8	8.4	5.5	4.0
2001	7.4	8.0	5.1	4.8
2002	7.6	8.3	5.1	5.8
2003	7.9	8.7	5.2	5.7

Table 1 shows that unemployment is higher in the EU than the USA. It also shows that unemployment in the eurozone exceeds both that of the USA and the UK. The USA and the UK both have more flexible labour markets than those in the eurozone.

Lack of wage flexibility

One cause of EU unemployment is claimed to be a lack of wage flexibility. If wages do not adjust fully and quickly to changes in demand, unemployment is likely to result. Figure 1 shows aggregate demand for labour falling from ADL to ADL1. If the wage rate does not fall, unemployment of QX–Q will result.

In recent years there have been a number of occasions when the aggregate demand for labour has fallen in the EU. One was the early to mid-1990s, when the aspirants to membership of the single currency introduced deflationary fiscal and monetary policies in order to met the Maastricht criteria. Another was the demand shock caused by the 11 September 2001 terrorist attack in the USA.

Wages in the eurozone are inflexible for a number of reasons. A major reason is that wages in the area are determined on the basis of national, collective bargaining to a much greater extent than in the UK and the USA. This can prevent wages reflecting different demand pressures in different areas. If wages are the same in both depressed and in prosperous areas, there will be little incentive for workers to move to the prosperous regions and for capital to move to the depressed regions.

Synoptic link

This section builds on AS Sections 3.4 and 3.17, and links to A2 Section 4.13.

Research task

Using the Economist magazine or website, find out the current unemployment figures for the EU, euroland, the UK and the USA. Assess the relative performance of these areas/countries.

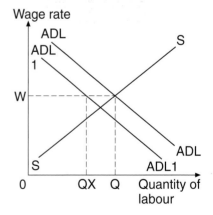

Figure 1: The effect of inflexible wages

It is thought that unions in a number of the eurozone countries have been pushing up wage rates above their equilibrium levels. Unions in Germany, where there is largely a centralised wage bargaining system, have been particularly militant in pursuit of wage rises. In France, whilst unions represent only a relatively small proportion of the labour force, they exert a considerable influence on the political determination of minimum wage and the length of the working week.

Rigidity of employment relationships

If employers believe that it would be difficult to sack workers should demand fall, they may be reluctant to take on many workers when demand is high. Employment protection legislation in many EU countries makes sacking workers a costly and lengthy process with employers having to consult with unions and local and national authorities. In contrast in the USA, where there is less government intervention in labour markets, a fall in demand tends to result initially in a greater rise in unemployment but then later a smaller rise.

Generous unemployment benefits and some state employment can reduce labour market flexibility. Unemployment benefits are higher in most EU countries than in the UK and eligibility rules are laxer. It may be claimed that this reduces the incentive for the unemployed to search for work and to be prepared to accept offers of employment at the going wage rate. The labour market can also be distorted by more generous pay and conditions in state employment than in private sector employment. In France, for instance, civil servants can claim a full pension after 37 years employment compared with 40 years for their private sector colleagues.

Rigidity of employment relationships can also create unemployment by reducing the pressure on workers to accept change. If there is resistance to change, what is sometimes called 'eurosclerosis', labour productivity will grow more slowly.

Government intervention and labour costs

Government intervention can cause unemployment by raising labour costs. In addition to the costs imposed by employment legislation, governments in the EU raise labour costs by imposing taxes on the employment of workers, such as National Insurance contributions and their equivalents, and imposing limits on working hours, health and safety standards and maternity and paternity rights.

If government intervention pushes wage costs above their equilibrium levels, unemployment can occur. Of course, it is possible that government intervention will not have an adverse effect on employment if it is correcting market failure. For instance, if a labour market is a **monopsony**, the wage rate and employment may be lower if there is no government intervention.

Policy approaches

Eurozone member countries' choice of government policy measures is constrained by their membership of the single currency. Monetary policy is in the hands of the European Central Bank. Member states can use expansionary fiscal policy to stimulate aggregate demand and raise employment. However, government's use of fiscal policy is restricted by the Stability and Growth Pact. When a government employs expansionary fiscal policy, its spending will rise relative to tax revenue. This may result in a budget deficit but the Stability and Growth Pact requires national governments to keep their budget deficits below 3 per cent. An economy that is experiencing high unemployment is likely to have low tax revenue and high spending on unemployment and other benefits. If though its budget deficit is close to 3 per cent, its ability to raise its spending and cut tax rates would be very limited.

EU governments both in and out of eurozone, though, can use supply-side policies and, in the long run, supply-side policies are likely to be more effective in reducing structural and frictional unemployment. Germany and Austria have relatively efficient vocational training and this is thought to keep down youth unemployment in the two countries. The Scandinavian members of the EU also make extensive use of training and help workers search for jobs. The UK's New Deal is a supply-side approach.

Thinking like an economist

Explain how expansionary fiscal policy may reduce unemployment.

The costs of a more flexible market

A more flexible labour market should result in lower unemployment but it is not without costs. Workers in a more flexible labour market will be likely to experience greater income inequality and greater fluctuations in pay. Any period of unemployment they experience should be shorter, but they will have a greater chance of being unemployed. Workers will also have to be prepared to be more adaptable and more mobile.

The Luxembourg Process

In November 1997 the Extraordinary European Council on Employment announced an unemployment initiative known as the Luxembourg Process. This initiative is based on four 'pillars'.

1. Improving employability by providing on-the-job training.
2. Encouraging the adaptability of firms and their workers through consultation between workers and employers' organisations. This is designed to increase both the adaptability and mobility of firms and workers.
3. Increasing equality of opportunity. Possible measures here include improving child-care facilities and encouraging firms to operate family-friendly employment policies. The main aims are to increase female participation rates, to narrow the gap between male and female wage rates and to reduce female unemployment.

4. Promoting entrepreneurship. Measures here concentrate on making it easier for new firms to get started and include deregulation.

Within each of the pillars there are detailed policy guidelines. Each member country is asked to submit National Action Plans, which explain what policies the government is implementing in the context of the Luxembourg Process. The Council monitors the progress of these policies and can make recommendations to individual member states.

The Luxembourg Process is based on the belief that Europe's high unemployment arises largely from structural problems. It combines both direct intervention and market-based measures. It does not, however, explicitly seek to encourage greater flexibility of wages or employment conditions.

Quick check

1 Explain how a lack of wage flexibility can cause unemployment.
2 Identify three ways in which government intervention can raise labour costs.
3 How does membership of the single currency restrict a government's choice of policy measures.
4 What are the key features of the Luxembourg Process?

Introduction

EU regional policy seeks to work with national governments to reduce regional imbalances in the member countries and to help those regions lagging behind. The EU sees regional differences as a significant issue, as they can contribute to economic inefficiency and can generate inequality and a lack of social cohesion. As a result the EU spends a considerable amount on regional policy.

Regional problems

Regional disparities generate a number of problems. Poor (depressed) regions usually have low real GDP per head, high unemployment and net outward migration. They tend to be dominated by a few traditional industries, have poor transport infrastructure, low educational attainment, low productivity and difficulty attracting investment. Some of the poor regions are also heavily dependent on agriculture.

These key features suggest that many poor regions are having difficulties adjusting industrial structure to changing economic circumstances. It is interesting to note that prosperous regions may also experience some problems. These include congestion, pressure on social capital and a shortage of workers.

The need for regional policy

Market theory would suggest that regional problems would soon be self-correcting. Unemployed workers would move from poor regions to prosperous regions where more jobs and higher wages would be on offer. Capital would move from the prosperous regions to the poor regions where factor prices would be cheaper and labour would be more available. In practice, though, due to a variety of forms of market failure including a lack of labour mobility, regional disparities are not self-correcting. Indeed the disparities may increase. Poor regions tend to become poorer and rich regions richer. Some of the best workers and some firms will move out of poor regions due to their relatively low incomes. This will further reduce demand in these poor regions and make them even less attractive sites for inward investment. In the rich regions success often breeds success with firms moving to them. As a result governments intervene in an attempt to reduce regional disparities.

With the greater geographical concentration of industry within the EU, limits imposed on national government fiscal policy measures and the one-size-fits-all EU monetary policy, the role of EU regional policy is increasing. Before it joined the single currency Greece, for instance, could have cut its interest rate and lowered the value of its exchange rate to stimulate demand across the country. There was also no limit on how much the government could spend on regional aid to its depressed regions.

Regional problems

6.10

Synoptic link

Regional policies were touched on in AS Section 3.16.

Thinking like an economist

1 Explain the link between low educational attainment, low productivity and difficulty attracting investment.

2 Explain why the unemployed may find it difficult to move from poor to prosperous regions.

The aims of EU regional policy

EU regional policy seeks to remove regional differences in order to achieve greater equity, social cohesion and efficiency. The EU is concerned about differences in economic prosperity both between member countries and between regions within the countries. The EU currently contains some rich regions including Ile de France and the South East of England, but also poor regions including most of Portugal, the south of Spain, and all of Greece.

The accession countries are poorer than the current members and the EU provided them with pre-accession regional assistance. It will continue to give them help to bring their economies up to the EU average and to reduce regional imbalances for some time after their membership.

The EU also uses regional policy to increase economic efficiency. If there are unemployed resources in some regions, potential output is lost and productive efficiency is not achieved. The existence of unemployed resources in some regions, including not only workers but also factories, hospitals and schools, while there is a shortage of resources in other areas, will mean that allocative efficiency is also not achieved.

Having regions with different levels of economic activity makes it difficult to implement EU wide policies. This is because policy measures will have a different impact on prosperous and poor regions. For instance, a decision by the ECB to raise its rate of interest may have little effect on a prosperous region but may raise unemployment still higher in a poor region.

EU regional policy objectives

Initially the EU identified six objectives for regional policy but, for the period 2000-2006, these objectives have been simplified into three categories.
1. To help the regions lagging behind in their development, i.e. those having a real GDP per head of less than 75 per cent of the EU average, and helping the Finnish and Swedish sub-arctic regions which would not be economically viable without assistance.
2. To help regions in industrial decline. The EU seeks to help these regions and their firms and labour force to adapt to change.
3. To support education, training and employment. Such measures should increase the employability of workers by raising their skills and adaptability. It is thought these measures are particularly significant in the case of youth and long-term unemployment.

Regional policy spending

EU regional policy spending is intended to complement national government regional policy assistance. It comes through the European Regional Development Fund and through other programmes including the

Research task

Using a PPF diagram, analyse the effect on the EU economy of a reduction in regional unemployment.

Thinking like an economist

Explain the links between the EU's three regional policy objectives.

Social Fund and the Cohesion Fund. Collectively, the EU funds used for regional assistance are referred to as the structural funds. This spending is largely in the form of non-repayable grants.

The EU devotes its funds to a range of projects and employment schemes. Objective 1 receives the greatest amount of funding, accounting for almost three-quarters of all EU structural fund spending. Structural funds account for approximately 35 per cent of the EU budget and are the second most important form of spending after the Common Agricultural Policy.

The significance of EU regional policy

EU regional policy can claim a number of successes. For instance, the rise in educational attainment in Ireland can be partly attributed to EU regional aid. The improved quality of Irish education has raised productivity, encouraged more foreign direct investment and contributed to higher economic growth.

There are, however, still considerable regional disparities and with the imminent entry of the accession countries, the disparities will widen. This suggests that EU regional policy will play an even more important role in the future.

Quick check

1 What are the characteristics of a poor region?
2 Why, in the absence of government intervention, are regional differences likely to continue?
3 What are the main disadvantages of regional differences?
4 Explain how educational and training projects can help poor regions.

The Common Agricultural Policy

Synoptic link

This section draws on the work you did on market equilibrium (AS Section 1.12) and government failure (AS Section 2.14).

Definition

The Common Agricultural Policy (CAP): the agricultural policy measures of the EU.

Thinking like an economist

What effect would the setting of a minimum price above equilibrium have on producer surplus?

Introduction

The **Common Agricultural Policy (CAP)** consists of a series of measures to regulate agriculture in the EU. Throughout the world there is considerable government intervention in agricultural markets. This arises in part because of the instability of agricultural prices in free markets and because agriculture is often regarded to be a strategic industry. Intervention though can create problems and the CAP has come in for considerable criticism. This criticism is one of the factors behind the recent reforms of the CAP.

The objectives of the CAP

The objectives of the CAP were set out in Article 39 of the Treaty of Rome:
1. to increase agricultural productivity
2. to ensure a fair standard of living for the agricultural community
3. to stabilise agricultural markets
4. to make the area self-sufficient in agricultural products
5. to ensure affordable prices for consumers.

While the CAP has been relatively effective in terms of the first, third and fourth objectives, it has been criticised for its performance on the second and fifth objectives. Farmers' incomes have not risen in line with other incomes and consumers are paying relatively high prices.

Price support

One of the best-known and most criticised features of the CAP is the policy of setting prices usually above the world equilibrium price. Figure 1 shows the effect of setting a minimum price of butter above the market price.

To maintain the price at this artificially high level, two main measures are used. The interventionist agency of the CAP buys up the surplus created and an import tax (tariff) is placed on produce from outside the EU. Some of the surplus is destroyed, some stored and some is exported at low, subsidised prices. The import tax is set so that the price of non-EU produce is above that of the minimum price.

This minimum price guarantee has a number of significant disadvantages, which reduce welfare inside and outside the EU. Consumer surplus is reduced as people have to pay higher prices and tax revenue has to be used not only to buy up the surplus but also to store it. The import tariff and export subsidy distort comparative advantage and make it difficult for developing countries to sell agricultural products to the EU and at home.

Other measures

As well as price support, the CAP includes a range of other measures designed to achieve its objectives. These include production subsidies, investment grants, direct income payments unrelated to production, conservation measures and health regulations. The CAP measures have resulted in the EU, along with Japan, being the world's most heavily subsidised agricultural producers.

Arguments in favour of the CAP

Some arguments can be advanced in support of the CAP. The CAP does seek to achieve a level playing field in agriculture by replacing different national policies with one EU-wide approach.

While it can be debated whether all farmers, particularly UK farmers, have benefited from the CAP in recent years, small farmers in Greece and Portugal, for instance, have enjoyed significant benefits. The help to some poor rural areas has been important and in some cases, for example by making hill farming viable, the CAP has protected the environment. It can also be argued that the security the CAP has provided for farmers has encouraged investment, which has raised productivity, and resulted in self-sufficiency and above in a number of agricultural products.

Criticisms of the CAP

The CAP has come in for severe criticism on a number of grounds, most of which emphasise the inefficiencies it causes.

- It is expensive to operate. It is the largest item of expenditure in the EU budget. In the mid-1970s, it accounted for 75 per cent of EU spending although it had fallen to just below 50 per cent by the start of the 2000s. Many argue much of this expenditure is not well spent, particularly expenditure on storing surpluses such as 'wine lakes' and 'butter mountains'.
- It reduces competitive pressure in the industry. Farmers have not faced the same pressures to keep their costs low and to be responsive to changes in consumer tastes as they would in a free market. The necessary restructuring which has been forced on other industries has been delayed. Farmers have not always acted in a commercial way, for instance not insuring against foot and mouth.
- It enables small and inefficient farmers to survive. Significant advantage can be taken of economies of scale in farming. In a free market environment many of the small farms in France, for example, would merge to form more efficient units.
- It discourages diversification. A significant number of farmers in the EU are over-reliant on one or two crops.
- It disadvantages consumers. As a result of the CAP measures, EU consumers pay higher prices and higher taxes.
- It creates unfair competition with developing countries. Tariffs imposed on developing countries' agricultural products makes it difficult for them to sell to the EU. The dumping of EU surpluses in their markets also makes it difficult for them to compete at home. The EU is the second largest exporter of agricultural products in the world but it does not have a comparative advantage in the vast majority of these products.

Thinking like an economist

Explain why agriculture may be regarded as a strategic industry.

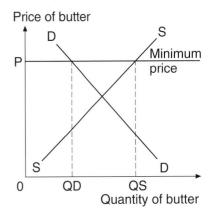

Figure 1: The effect of setting a minimum price above the equilibrium level

Thinking like
an economist

In what circumstances may a
subsidy to producers increase
economic efficiency?

- It causes a misallocation of resources both in the EU and the world. This reduces world output and world living standards.
- In some cases it causes environmental damage by, for example, encouraging land which is rich in wildlife but of poor agricultural value to be used for agriculture.

Pressure for reform

Internal criticism and consumer pressure are some of the driving forces behind the reform of the CAP. A number of other factors are also contributing to the pressure on the EU to find ways to make the policy more efficient and cost effective. One is concern that the cost might rise significantly with the entry of countries with large and low-productivity agricultural sectors. Another is pressure from the WTO which wants the EU to open up its markets and to compete on more equal terms with non-EU members. Farm trade has been the main stumbling bloc in the Doha round of trade negotiations, held under the auspices of the WTO. There is also environmental pressure from consumers concerned about the harmful effects that intensive farming and the use of pesticides are having.

Reforms

In 1992, reforms known as MacSharry reforms were proposed and finally approved in December 1995. These sought to bring CAP prices closer to world levels and to increase competitive pressures from outside by reducing the level of support prices on a range of products, including cereals. The emphasis on help for farmers was switched, in part, from price support to direct income payments. To qualify for these direct income payments, farmers (except small farmers) had to set aside at least 15 per cent of arable land. They were also given grants to turn land over to ecological, forestry or recreational use. These reforms did reduce surpluses and did improve the environment to a certain extent.

Then in 1999 the Fischler reforms introduced more cuts in minimum prices and further shifted help from price support to direct payments. Together, the MacSharry and Fischler reforms have moved the cost of the CAP away from consumers towards taxpayers. They also lead to a more efficient allocation of resources within the EU and the world by lowering agricultural prices and making EU agriculture more subject to market forces. They did, however, leave agriculture still relatively heavily subsidised.

A further set of reforms was introduced under the title Agenda 2000 motivated, in part, by the imminent enlargement of the EU. Yet again support prices were lowered and there was a further switch from price support to direct subsidies. More emphasis was placed on environmental objectives. It also placed a limit on CAP expenditure.

In June 2003 there was agreement on yet another set of reforms based on proposals by Franz Fischler, the EU farm commissioner. These further cut the link between subsidy and output in order to reduce the incentive for farmers to overproduce. Although, due to fierce lobbying led by France, production-linked subsidies were kept in most farm sectors, a greater proportion of assistance was 'decoupled' and more of CAP spending was channelled into programmes that do not distort trade, such as rural development. The reforms were largely welcomed, although there was criticism that they made the CAP even more complex, created some uncertainty and did not tackle the high barriers to imports still existing in the case of a range of agricultural products.

Some believe the reforms should go further. These people point to the example of New Zealand, which ended agricultural subsidies in the mid-1980s. As a result farmers became more efficient. They cut their costs and became more responsive to changes in consumer demand, diverting into new areas such as wine.

Comparison of some of the CAP measures

As mentioned earlier, the system of price support has been heavily criticised. Figure 2 shows that consumers lose out in a number of ways in comparison with a free market situation. They pay a higher price for the product (P1 rather than P) and consume a smaller quantity (QD rather than Q). They also enjoy less consumer surplus (P1AE in comparison with PAB) and have to pay taxes not only to fund the purchase of the surplus but also to store it.

Consumers do better under a system of production subsidies. As Figure 3 shows, a subsidy causes the supply curve to shift to the right. This results in consumers paying a lower price and enjoying higher consumer surplus (P1AH). Less tax has to be used because while the subsidy has to be funded, tax revenue does not have to be used to purchase unsold stock – the market clears.

A subsidy might be justified on the grounds that farming can generate positive externalities. If the positive externalities are estimated incorrectly, however, there can still be overproduction. Direct payments avoid the problem of overproduction but they have high costs of administration and the possibility of fraud. The payments are conditional on farmers carrying out certain activities, such as setting aside land for environmental purposes. This means that tax revenue is used not only to make the payments but also to check that farmers are meeting the requirements.

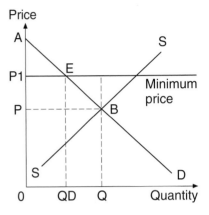

Figure 2: The effects of price support on price, quantity and consumer surplus

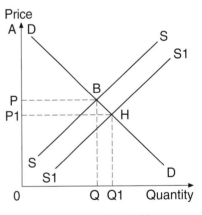

Figure 3: The effect of a subsidy

Environmental, transport and social policies

Synoptic link

This section builds on market failure and on both the transport and work and leisure modules.

Thinking like an economist

Explain two ways that the polluter pays principle could be enforced.

Research task

Investigate the EU's role at international environmental conferences.

Introduction

The EU seeks to promote greater co-ordination or a common policy in a range of areas. These include the environment, transport and social policies. To date, some progress has been made but a common approach has not been fully achieved in any of these areas. Differences exist in, for instance, the use of renewable energy resources, subsidies to public transport and the number of days holiday workers enjoy.

EU environmental policies

Over time, EU environmental policies have come to be based on three key principles:

- the polluter pays principle
- the precautionary principle, i.e. that action should be taken to protect the environment where there are significant risks even if scientific evidence is not conclusive
- the need to achieve sustainable development.

The Single European Act set out the EU's environmental aims as:

- to preserve, protect and improve the quality of the environment
- to contribute towards protecting human health
- to ensure a prudent and rational utilisation of natural resources.

The Maastricht Treaty emphasised the need to integrate environmental issues into all its policies and introduced the precautionary principle. In 1997 the Amsterdam Treaty made explicit reference to the need to achieve sustainable development.

EU environmental measures

Most of EU environmental policy makes use of regulations and taxes. For example, the EU sets targets for the recycling of waste, for CO_2 emissions and for the quality of sea bathing water. It has promoted the use of some taxes including the landfill tax (a tax on the amount of waste being buried in landfill sites) and the aggregates tax (a tax on extracted materials such as gravel and sand).

Fewer tradable permit systems are in use in the EU than in the USA, but this might be going to change with the development of the market in carbon trading. The EU now often makes use of its collective power and acts as a single negotiating body at international environmental conferences.

Transport policy

The Treaty of Rome set out the objective of the adoption of a common policy in the sphere of transport. Progress on this objective has been slow, in part because each member country has its own transport objectives. EU

transport policy seeks to achieve an efficient allocation of resources within the transport sector and between that sector and other sectors, meeting individual transport market requirements at least resource cost and an equitable distribution of benefits and costs from transport activities.

The EU has had some achievements in the transport market including the easing of frontier crossings, the removal of restrictions on road-haulage firms undertaking road-haulage business within other EU countries on their return journey, and has provided funding, through structural funds, for a number of infrastructure projects. The main impact on the transport market, though, comes from the European Commission's competition policy. This has, for instance, liberalised EU air passenger transport.

Social policy

The EU's social policy seeks to establish common social standards across the area. The aim is to achieve social cohesion, equity and a level playing field. The Treaty of Rome set out the objectives of improving living standards and working conditions, occupational health and safety, promoting employment and the free movement of labour and equal pay for men and women doing the same work.

Initially EU social policy tended to concentrate mainly on labour market policy and, in particular, measures to retrain unemployed workers. As it has developed, however, it has focused not only on labour market policy but also on the reduction of poverty and social exclusion.

Much of EU social policy is operated by means of directives. These set out the objectives the EU wants member countries to achieve but leaves it to member countries on how to achieve them. Many of the directives which have been issued are less restrictive than national regulations. For instance, The Working Time Directive, adapted by the EU in 1993 and adopted by the UK in 1998, set out a maximum working week of 48 hours. For all the EU member countries, except the UK and Denmark which had no limit, this was less stringent than their existing legislation.

The Social Chapter

The Social Chapter, which grew out of the Social Charter, seeks to harmonise social legislation and lists the 'fundamental rights' of EU workers. The Social Charter was adopted at the Strasbourg Council in 1989. It emphasised that in the development of a single market, social aspects should be given the same importance as economic aspects and that job creation should be given top priority. Some economists were concerned that the single market could lead to social dumping – the driving down of employment and social conditions to the lowest level. With greater mobility of capital, there is a risk that firms may move from countries where there are strong employment rights and high taxes to countries where there are few restrictions on firms. This would be likely to reduce working conditions and pay and make it more difficult for governments to fund social benefits.

The Social Charter formed the basis of the Social Chapter which was included as in the Maastricht Treaty. It lists what are seen as the basic rights of EU workers including the right of freedom of movement, the right to belong or not to belong to a trade union, the right to strike, the right of women and men to equal treatment, the right to receive vocational training and the right to have safe working conditions. In addition, it emphasises the need to promote vocational training, the protection of children, gender equality and consultation between firms and their workers.

The UK initially opted out of the Social Chapter. It was concerned that it would raise firms' costs and make the UK a less attractive destination for foreign direct investment. The new Labour government did, however, sign up to the Social Chapter. It has introduced a number of the Social Chapter's directives. As well as the Working Time Directive, it implemented the Works Council Directive in 1998 and the Parental Leave Directive in 1999. The former directive means that all UK-based firms with a labour force of 1000 or over and with 150 or more workers based in more than two EU countries, have to set up consultation committees which deal with transnational issues. The latter directive increased paid maternity leave from 14 to 18 weeks and gave both men and women the right to have three months' unpaid leave after the birth of a child.

Quick check

1 How may a landfill tax improve the environment?
2 Why is it difficult to achieve a common EU transport policy?
3 What are the aims of EU social policy?
4 Why did EU social policy become more significant with the development of the single European market?

Puzzler

Will globalisation increase or reduce the risk of social dumping?

Introduction

The EU's competition policy is administered by the Competition Department of the European Commission (EC). Its authority comes from articles laid out in the Treaty of Rome and subsequent legislation.

The policy aims to achieve a more efficient allocation of resources by increasing competitive pressure on firms throughout the EU. In pursuit of this aim, the policy applies to monopolies, mergers and what the EC perceives to be unfair competition in markets involving more than one member state. Such unfair competition includes the formation of cartels, price discrimination and government subsidies. EU competition policy acts alongside national competition policy.

The theory behind EU competition policy

EU competition policy is based on the belief that competitive pressure will raise economic efficiency. The advantages claimed for a competitive market include consumer choice, low prices, high quality and a quick response to changes in consumer demand.

A competitive market provides both a carrot and a stick to firms to be economically efficient. The incentive (carrot) is that if a firm can lower its costs and produce what consumers want, it will attract more consumers and so earn higher profits. The punishment (stick), though, is that if a firm does not keep its costs and prices low and does not respond to what consumers want, it will make a loss and may go out of business. This competitive pressure may come from the existence of a large number of firms in the industry (actual competition) or concern that failure to achieve economic efficiency will result in the entry of new firms (potential competition).

EU competition policy focuses less on the number of firms in any particular industry and more on the behaviour of the firms. A firm or group of firms may have significant market power but if it or they act in a way expected of a competitive market the EC is unlikely to intervene.

Restrictive practices

Restrictive practices between firms within a member state are left to national governments to deal with. The EU, though, bans agreements between firms which restrict competition and affect trade between member countries. The assumption behind the ban is that such restrictive practices are against the public interest. For example, the formation of a cartel is likely to result in higher prices and may also lead to less choice and lower quality.

In October 2002, the EC found that Nintendo (the Japanese video games manufacturer), John Menzies (the sole UK distributor of Nintendo products), and distributors in six other European countries guilty of operating a price fixing cartel which pushed up prices. Nintendo was fined £94m and John Menzies £5.5m.

Synoptic link

Before starting this section, check over AS Sections 2.12 and 2.13.

Thinking like an economist

1 Distinguish between a perfectly competitive market and a perfectly contestable market.
2 Explain why cartels are often short-lived.

Monopoly power

EU policy on firms with a dominant market position is based on the belief that the possession of such a position does not necessarily mean a firm will act in an anti-competitive way. The EU is not concerned about the mere existence of monopoly. What does concern it is abuse of monopoly power. The EC will take action if it finds that a firm is abusing its dominant position.

There are a range of ways in which a dominant firm can use its power to exploit consumers. The most obvious way is to restrict output and so raise price, reduce consumer surplus, increase producer surplus and profits. The firm may also engage in price discrimination, charging different prices to different groups of consumers for the same product, again in order to increase profits. It may also seek to reduce potential and actual competition. In the first case it may use limit pricing, i.e. setting price below the maximum profit level, in order to discourage the entry of new firms. In the second case the firm may be more aggressive, setting price low enough to drive out competitors. If a firm is suspected of abusing its market power, the EC will investigate. If found guilty the firm will be fined and will be ordered to stop the uncompetitive activity.

Mergers

Since 1990, the EC has had the authority to assess mergers and acquisitions over a given value and where less than two-thirds of the combined turnover comes from one member state. In such circumstances, the parties to the merger must notify the EC. The Commission then decides whether or not to carry out an investigation. If it does carry out an investigation it may allow it with conditions or may decide to stop it.

In practice the EC investigates very few mergers and prohibits even fewer. The EC has been criticised for what is seen as its too permissive approach. It is, however, not an easy task. This is because whilst a merger may not always be in the public interest, in some cases it may increase economic efficiency. A larger, combined firm may be able to take greater advantage of economies of scale, may have more confidence and funds to innovate and be able to compete more effectively in world markets.

Government aid

The EC prohibits government aid if it distorts or threatens to distort competition and affects trade between member states. There are a number of ways a government may assist its firms including subsidies, investment grants and public procurement (preferential purchasing). Exceptions may be allowed if the assistance serves some EU purpose.

What the EC is concerned about is that state aid can prevent a 'level playing field' being achieved, with domestic firms being able to charge lower prices and undercut rival countries' firms at home and abroad.

Research task

Using newspapers, magazines or websites, find a recent case where the EC has taken action against what it perceived to be an abuse of monopoly power. Decide whether you think the EC's action was justified.

Making connections

1 What conditions are necessary for price discrimination to occur?
2 What are the main motives behind mergers?

Thinking like an economist

The UK government provides financial assistance to the UK rail industry. On what grounds may it justify such assistance?

In recent years the EC has begun to scrutinise state aid much more closely as it is now seen as one of the main threats to competition in the EU. Between 1997 and 2001, state aid throughout the EU fell from €98bn to €86bn under pressure by the EC to reduce state assistance to unprofitable firms. As Table 1 shows, the UK spent less of its GDP on state aid to industry than any other EU country.

The EC is urging governments to redirect their state aid from propping up unprofitable firms towards environmental protection, the development of small and medium-sized businesses, job creation programmes and research and development.

The car market

In October 2002, the EC introduced measures to increase competition in the car market and reduce the wide differences in car prices in the EU. The measures will come into force in October 2005 and include allowing:
- dealers to advertise and open showrooms anywhere in the EU
- dealers to sell more than one brand in the same showroom
- dealers not having to offer repair services; if they do not, they will have to sub-contract to a suitable repairer
- supermarkets to become dealers if they meet manufacturers quality criteria.

Quick check

1 Explain how competition may benefit consumers.
2 Identify two possible disadvantages and two possible advantages of a monopoly.
3 In what circumstances will the EC prevent a merger going ahead?
4 Using a diagram, explain the effect of a government granting a subsidy to a firm.

Table 1: State aid in EU member states in 2001

Country	Total state aid (billion euros)	Total aid as % of GDP
Finland	2.1	1.58
Denmark	2.4	1.36
Belgium	3.3	1.34
Luxembourg	0.3	1.30
Ireland	1.3	1.20
Germany	23.3	1.14
Greece	1.3	1.04
Portugal	1.2	1.04
France	15.8	1.10
Italy	12.0	1.01
Austria	2.1	0.99
Netherlands	4.0	0.98
Spain	4.7	0.74
Sweden	1.9	0.71
UK	10.6	0.66
EU	86.3	0.99

Right from the start of your course you should get used to considering topics in a European context. Then when you start this module you should first gain some further background knowledge on Europe and continue to develop your economic knowledge and skills. On receipt of the stimulus material, pay particular attention to the introduction. This will give you a good overview of the focus of the material. Then use the extracts as the basis for discussion and research. Read the following extracts and then see if you would agree with the areas to follow up. You may find that you may wish to add other ones.

Extract 1

New ECB chief Trichet attacks French profligacy

'French banker Jean-Claude Trichet yesterday used the hearing that confirmed him as president of the European Central Bank to castigate his country for budget profligacy.

France is in breach of the rules which forbid eurozone countries to exceed a budget deficit of 3% of gross domestic product – rules that were unanimously agreed by all eurozone governments before the single currency's introduction in 1999, he noted.

"It seems to me that it is up to all partners to be up to their responsibility," he told the hearing. "Given the current deficits that some member states have, to say that we can just continue like that is not appropriate from an economic point of view."

Mr Trichet's criticisms of the French deficit came as the ECB warned France and Germany to get their finances in order.

"Recent fiscal developments in the euro area are of great concern. There is growing evidence that most countries will miss their budgetary targets for 2003 by a significant margin," the bank said in its monthly health check on the eurozone economies, pointing at Germany, France, Italy and Portugal as particular causes of concern.

The fresh round of criticism of Paris and Berlin comes as the debate about the EU's tattered stability and growth pact intensifies.

A European Commission idea to use a legal loophole to let the eurozone's two biggest budget transgressors, France and Germany, off the hook has caused widespread consternation. Senior Dutch government officials said yesterday they would sue the Commission if it went through with the plan.

MEP Theresa Villiers, one of the Tories who abstained in the vote, said the ECB head faced a difficult task. "Mr Trichet is clearly an able and intelligent banker. However, he had no solutions to offer to remedy the dismal economic performance of the eurozone. He will be taking on an impossible job – finding one interest rate to suit twelve different countries."

Source: 'New ECB chief Trichet attacks French profligacy by Andrew Osborn and Heather Stewart, *The Guardian*, 12/9/03, Page 20.

Extract 2

EU fines Nintendo £94m for rip-off

Nintendo, the Japanese video games manufacturer, was yesterday found guilty of ripping off its customers in continental Europe for most of the 1990s and fined £94m by the European Commission. Edinburgh-based John Menzies, the sole UK distributor of Nintendo products, was also punished for its role in the scam.

The Commission said Menzies had helped Nintendo operate the price-fixing cartel, along with distributors in six other European countries, and fined it £5.5m. Nintendo immediately said it would appeal against the size of the fine although it did not contest the Commission's findings.

The price-fixing concerned the Nintendo 64 games consoles and the pocket versions called Game Boy together with the accompanying games cartridges. The cartel existed, it added, from 1991 until 1998.

'Every year millions of European families spend large amounts of money on video games,' said Mario Monti, the EU competition commissioner. 'They have the right to buy games and consoles at the lowest price the market can possibly offer and we will not tolerate collusive behaviour intended to keep prices artificially high.'

The Commission found that the UK market was actually one of the cheapest in Europe but that Nintendo and Menzies colluded to ensure that cheap UK products were not re-exported to continental Europe where prices could be up to 66 per cent dearer.

Source: 'EU fines Nintendo £94m for rip-off' by Andrew Osborn, *The Guardian*, 31/10/02, page 28.

Exam guidance

Suggestions for further research and discussion

Extract 1

1. The causes of a budget deficit.
2. The consequences of a budget deficit.
3. The effect of some countries in a single currency arrangement running budget deficits on the money supply and the exchange rate of the area.
4. The Growth and Stability Pact – including advantages and disadvantages.
5. Is it possible to have an interest rate which would suit all the members of the single currency?
6. How are the eurozone economies performing relative to the UK and USA?

Extract 2

1. The abuse of market power.
2. Advantages and disadvantages of monopoly.
3. The operation of a cartel.
4. Competition policy.
5. Price discrimination.
6. Uncompetitive behaviour.

A2 further reading

Part 4

Sections **4.1** G.Hale, *Labour Markets*, Heinemann, 2001, Chapter 1

Sections **4.3, 4.4, 4.5** A.Griffiths, and S. Ison, *Business Economics*, Heinemann, 2001, Chapters 2, 3-7

Sections **4.2–4.5** I.Wilson, *The Economics of Leisure*, Heinemann, 2003, Chapters 1-4, 5 & 6

Sections **4.6–4.15** G.Hale, *Labour Markets*, Heinemann, 2001, Chapters 1, 2, 3, 4, 6, 7

Sections **4.16–4.18, 4.21, 4.22, 4.25, 4.27–4.32** C.Bamford, *Transport Economics*, 3rd edn., Heinemann, Chapters 1, 2, 3, 4, 5, 6, 7

Sections **4.19–27** A.Griffiths and S.Ison, *Business Economics*, Chapters 1, 3, 4, 5, 6, 9

Section **4.31** S.Munday, *Markets and Market Failure*, Chapter 6

Sections **4.16–4.18, 4.21, 4.22, 4.25, 4.27–4.32** C.Bamford, *Transport Economics*, 3rd edn., Heinemann, Chapters 1, 2, 3, 4, 5, 6, 7

Sections **4.19–27** A.Griffiths and S.Ison, *Business Economics*, Chapters 1, 3, 4, 5, 6, 9

Section **4.31** S.Munday, *Markets and Market Failure*, Heinemann, 2000, Chapter 6

Part 5

Sections **5.1, 5.2, 5.5–5.7, 5.9, 5.10, 5.12, 5.13, 5.15, 5.16, 5.17, 5.19–5.21** C.Bamford, and S.Grant, *The UK Economy in a Global Context*, Heinemann, 2000, Chapters 1, 2, 3, 4, 5, 6, 7, 8

Sections **5.1, 5.7, 5.8, 5.10, 5.15, 5.16, 5.19** D.Smith, *UK Current Economic Policy*, 3rd edition, Heinemann, 2003, Chapters 1, 3, 4, 5, 8

Section **5.4** C. Bamford, and S.Munday, *Markets*, Heinemann 2002, Chapter 6

Sections **5.10, 5.11, 5.14, 5.15** M.Russell, and D.Heathfield, *Inflation and UK Monetary Policy*, 3rd edition, Heinemann, 1999, Chapters 4, 5, 6, 7, 8, 9

Section 5.19 G.Hale, *Labour Markets*, Heinemann, 2001, Chapter 5

Section 5.18 C.Bamford and S.Grant, T*he UK Economy in a Global Context*, Heinemann, 2000, Chapter 6

Sections 5.22–5.27, 5.28–5.30 F.Nixson, *Development Economics*, 2nd edn., Heinemann, 2001, Chapters 1, 2, 3, 4, 5, 7, 8, 9, 10

Section 5.27 S.Grant, *Economic Growth and Business Cycles*, Heinemann, 1999, Chapter 4

Part 6

Sections 6.1–6.13 B.Hill, *The European Union*, 4th edition, Heinemann, 2001, Chapters 1, 3, 4, 5, 6, 8, 9, 10

Section 6.5 C.Bamford and S.Grant, *The UK Economy in a Global Context*, Heinemann, 2000, Chapter 5

Sections 6.5, 6.6 M.Russell and D.Heathfield, *Inflation and UK Monetary Policy*, 3rd edition, Heinemann, 1999, Chapter 10

Sections 6.5, 6.6, 6.10 D.Smith, *UK Current Economic Policy*, 3rd edition, Heinemann, 2003, Chapters 8, 9

Section 6.9 G.Hale, *Labour Markets*, Heinemann, 2001, Chapter 5

Glossary

Ability to pay principle	The rule that people with higher incomes should pay more in tax.
Absolute advantage	The ability to produce output using fewer resources than other regions or countries.
Accelerator theory	The view that net investment is determined by the rate of change in real GDP.
Aggregate demand	The total demand for a county's goods and services at a given price level.
Aggregate supply	The total amount a country's producers supply at a given price level.
Balance of payments	A record of money flows coming in and going out of a country.
Benefit principle	The rule that the amount people pay in tax should be related to the benefit they derive from public expenditure.
Bilateral monopoly	A market with a single buyer and seller.
Claimant count	A measure of unemployment which includes those receiving job seekers' allowance.
Common Agricultural Policy (CAP)	The agricultural policy measures of the EU.
Common market	A group of countries with free movement of products, labour and capital.
Comparative advantage	Relative efficiency – the ability to produce a product at a lower opportunity cost than other regions or countries.
Consumption	Household spending on goods and services.
Contestable market	A market in which there are no barriers to entry and exit.
Cost-push inflation	Increases in the price level caused by increases in the costs of production.
Credit creation	The ability of banks to create loans (money) by a multiple of any increase in cash deposits.
Customs union	A group of countries with free trade between them and a common external tariff on imports from outside the area.

Deflationary fiscal policy	Decreases in public expenditure and/or increases in taxation designed to decrease aggregate demand.
Demand-pull inflation	Increases in the price level caused by increases in aggregate demand.
Demand-side shocks	Unexpected changes in aggregate demand.
Depreciation	A fall in the value of the currency.
Derived demand	Demand for one item depending on the demand for another item.
Devaluation	A deliberate reduction in the value of a fixed exchange rate by the government.
Discrimination	Treating one group differently from other groups.
Disposable income	Income after direct taxation has been deducted and state benefits have been added.
Dumping	The sale of products at less than cost price.
Economic and Monetary Union (EMU)	A group of countries that operate a single currency and co-ordinate economic policies.
Economic growth rate	The percentage change in real GDP.
Economic rent	A surplus paid to a factor of production above what is needed to keep it in its current occupation.
Economically active	Those in employment plus those unemployed.
Economically inactive	People who are neither in employment nor unemployed.
Elasticity of demand for labour	The responsiveness of demand for labour to a change in the wage rate.
Elasticity of supply of labour	The responsiveness of the supply of labour to a change in the wage rate.
Exchange control	Restrictions on the purchase of foreign currency and on the export of capital.
Fiscal policy	Changes in government spending and taxation.

Fisher equation	An equation that shows the relationship between the money supply, the velocity of circulation, the price level and output (MV = PY).
Fixed exchange rate	An exchange rate fixed against other currencies that is maintained by the government.
Floating exchange rate	An exchange rate determined by market forces.
Free trade area	A group of countries with free trade between them.
Full employment	A situation where those wanting to work can gain employment at the going wage rate.
Geographical immobility	Barriers to the movement of workers between different areas.
Goodhart's law	The view that any measure of the money supply behaves differently when it is targeted.
Hard currencies	Currencies such as the dollar ($), pound (£) and euro (€), which are freely used for international trade. Many currencies of developing countries are acceptable as a means of payment for international trade.
Hot money flows	Short-term financial flows seeking to take advantage of differences in interest rates and exchange rates.
Human capital	Education, training and experience that a worker possesses.
Hypothecated tax	A tax raised for a specific purpose.
Hysteresis	The view that unemployment generates unemployment.
Income effect of a wage change	The effect on the supply of labour caused by the change in the ability to buy leisure time.
Infant industries	Newly established industries which have not yet grown large enough to take full advantage of economies of scale; also called sunrise industries.

Inflation	A sustained rise in the general price level.
Injections	Additions to the circular flow.
Investment	Spending on capital goods.
J-curve effect	The tendency for a fall in the exchange rate to make the trade position worse before it gets better.
Just-in-time	A business concept to minimise the costs of holding stocks, which describes the practise of ensuring the required supplies are received as close as possible to the time that they are needed for production or supply to the final consumer.
Labour Force Survey	A measure of unemployment based on a survey using the ILO definition of unemployment.
Labour Productivity	Output per worker hour
Law of diminishing marginal returns	Applies to short-run costs faced by a firm. The law states that if a firm seeks to increase production in the short run, its average costs of production will firstly fall, then bottom out, and then rise. This means that the short-run average cost curve is always drawn as being U-shaped.
Leakages	Withdrawals from the circular flow.
Liquidity preference theory	The view that the rate of interest is determined by the demand and supply of money.
Liquidity ratio	The proportion of liquid assets to bank deposits.
Liquidity trap	A situation where it is not possible to reduce the rate of interest below its current level.
Loanable funds theory	The view that the rate of interest is determined by the demand and supply of loanable funds.
Long-run Phillips curve	A curve that indicates there is no long-run trade off between unemployment and inflation.

Macroeconomic equilibrium	A situation where aggregate demand equals aggregate supply and real GDP is not changing.
Marginal cost	The change in cost brought about by changing production by one unit.
Marginal productivity theory	The view that demand for a factor of production depends on its marginal revenue product.
Marginal propensity to consume	The proportion of extra income consumed.
Marginal propensity to import (MPM)	The proportion of extra income spent on imports.
Marginal propensity to save (MPS)	The proportion of extra income saved.
Marginal rate of tax (MRT)	The proportion of extra income taken in tax.
Marginal revenue product of labour	The change in a firm's revenue resulting from employing one more worker.
Marginal revenue	The change in revenue brought about by changing sales by one unit.
Marginal tax rate	The proportion of extra income that is taken in tax.
Marshall-Lerner condition	The view that for a fall in the exchange rate to be successful in improving the balance of payments, the combined elasticities of demand for exports and imports must be greater than one.
Monetarists	A group of economists who believe that increases in the money supply in excess of increases in output will cause inflation.
Monetary Policy Committee	A committee of the Bank of England with the responsibility for meeting the government's inflation target.
Monetary policy	Government changes in the money supply, the rate of interest and the exchange rate.
Monopolistic competition	A market structure in which there are a large number of firms selling a similar product.

Monopoly	A single seller.
Monopsonist	A single buyer.
Multiplier	The process by which any change in a component of aggregate demand results in a greater final change in real GDP.
NAIRU (the non-accelerating inflation rate of unemployment)	The level of unemployment which exists when the labour market is in equilibrium.
Net exports	The value of exports minus the value of imports.
Normal profit	The level of profit needed to keep a firm in the market in the long run.
Occupational immobility	Barriers to workers changing occupations.
Oligopoly	A market structure which is dominated by a few sellers.
Oligopsonist	One of a few dominant buyers.
Opportunity cost	The best alternative forgone
Output gap	The gap between potential and actual output.
Parity	The price of one currency in terms of another currency or group of currencies.
Participation rate	Proportion of those of working age in the working population (labour or workforce).
Perfect competition	A market structure with many buyers and sellers, free entry and exit and an identical product.
Phillips curve	A graph showing the relationship between unemployment and inflation.
Protectionism	The restriction on the free movement of products between countries.
Public Sector Net Borrowing (PSNB)	Excess of public expenditure over revenue.
Quantity theory	The view that a change in the quantity of money causes a direct and proportionate change in the price level.
Quota	A limit on imports.

Reflationary fiscal policy	Increases in public expenditure and/or cuts in taxation designed to increase aggregate demand.
Replacement ratio	The relationship between unemployment benefit and income from employment.
RPI	The Retail Price Index – a weighted consumer price index.
Social benefits	Private benefits and positive externalities attributable to a particular use of economic resources.
Social cost	Both the private cost and negative externality attributed to a particular use of economic resources.
Substitution effect	The effect on the supply of labour influenced by a change in the opportunity cost of leisure.
Supernormal profit	Profit earned where average revenue exceeds average cost (which includes normal profit).
Supply-side policies	Policies designed to increase aggregate supply by improving the efficiency of markets.
Supply-side shocks	Unexpected changes in aggregate supply.
Sustainable economic growth	Economic growth that does not endanger future generations' ability to expand productive capacity.
Tariff	A tax on imports.
Tax burden	The total amount of tax paid as a percentage of GDP.
Terms of trade	The ratio of export to import prices.
Trade creation	The increase in trade that arises through member countries being able to buy products at lower prices due to the removal of tariff barriers between member countries.
Trade diversion	Trade being diverted away from cheaper products outside the bloc towards higher cost products from inside the bloc.
Trade union	An association of workers.

Trading bloc	A group of countries with preferential trading arrangements.
Transfer earnings	The amount a factor of production could earn in its next best-paid occupation.
Transfer payments	Money transferred from one person or group to another not in return for any good or service.
Transfer pricing	Internal trading within different parts of MNCs in which resources might be sold very cheaply from a developing to a developed country but thereafter they are traded internally at much higher prices.
Transmission mechanism	The process by which changes in the money supply influence the economy.
Unemployment	A situation where people are out of work but are willing and able to work.
Velocity of circulation	The number of times money changes hands in a given time period; also sometimes called the income velocity of circulation.
Wage differentials	Differences in wages.
Working population	Those who are economically active, i.e. in employment or unemployed.
World Trade Organisation (WTO)	An international organisation which promotes free international trade and rules on international trade disputes.

Index

abnormal profits *see* supernormal
    profits
accelerator effect 324–5
accession countries 414–17, 444
age 160, 166, 183, 194, 312,
    320–1
aggregate demand 92, 95, 112–13,
    116–19, 338, 352–3, 388
    increasing 125, 129, 131, 134,
        135, 323
    and inflation 132–3, 331
    for labour 179
    and monetary policy 126–7, 343
    and public spending 130, 313–14
aggregate supply 92, 95, 114–16,
    118–19, 352, 388
    increasing 128–9, 132–3, 134
    of labour 125, 183–4
agriculture 366, 390–2, 414
    see also CAP
aid 385, 396–8, 415
air transport 269, 273, 274, 277
airlines 220, 221, 245, 248, 250,
    264
allocative efficiency 59, 60, 176,
    236, 237, 346
Asia 373–6, 380, 391, 393, 398
average costs 40, 42–3, 226–9, 232

balance of payments 99, 108–9,
    130, 136–7, 169, 294, 343
    and exchange rates 127, 136,
        308, 339
Bank of England 294, 297, 306,
    317, 330, 341
    setting interest rate 133, 135,
        340, 342–3, 345
banks 17, 127, 303, 317, 329–30,
    341, 372
barriers to entry and exit *see*
    market structures
benefits 213, 215, 310, 314, 315
    unemployment 128, 217, 312,
        313, 315, 355, 440
borrowing 38–9, 109, 126, 303,
    329–31, 427
    government 135, 297, 312–13,
        317, 320
Brown, Gordon 426, 431, 433, 437

budget 124, 315–18, 436–7
buses 220, 221, 223–4, 264, 271
business cycles 135
business objectives 25, 33, 44–5,
    234–5

CAP (Common Agricultural Policy)
    348, 413, 416, 417, 436,
    446–9
capital 9, 36, 73, 134, 357, 369
capital goods 12–13, 112–13, 125,
    298–9, 324–5
cars 220, 221, 222, 224
cartels 177, 253
China 373, 374, 376, 382, 387,
    393, 428
circular flow 120–1, 388
collusion 177, 253–4, 256, 260
command economies 414, 418–19
Common Agricultural Policy *see*
    CAP
comparative advantage 144–5,
    319, 332–5, 344, 359, 381–2
competition 34, 46–7, 58–61, 145,
    173–8, 336, 423, 447
    policies 257–60, 451
    promoting 54, 82–3, 137, 261–4
    see also monopolies;
        monopolistic competition;
        oligopolies; perfect
        competition
Competition Commission 80–1,
    258–9
competitiveness 109, 127, 137,
    361–3, 371, 376
    UK 346, 360, 363
complements 18, 19, 23, 30–1, 34,
    166, 181, 335
congestion 170, 225, 269, 273,
    277–80, 314
consumer goods 12–13, 324–5
consumer surpluses 14, 15, 251
consumption 112, 120, 125, 126,
    303, 314
consumption goods 12–13, 324–5
contestable markets 175, 178, 254,
    256
convergence 423, 425–6, 427, 431,
    433, 434, 435, 436–7

corporation tax 124, 128, 137, 216, 310, 346, 438
cost benefit analysis 74–5, 273–6
costs 32, 34, 40–1, 67, 127, 226–9, 230–2
  average 40, 42–3, 226–9, 232
  of congestion 277–8
  external 62–3, 73
  of inflation 107
  marginal 40, 228–9
  social 63, 74, 273, 274, 275
  of unemployment 105
  wages 160, 163, 179, 181, 335, 440
credit creation multiplier 329–31
cross elasticity of demand 22–3
Cuba 369, 371–2, 385–6, 387, 394
current account 108–9, 137, 294, 297, 330

debt 135, 312, 341, 344, 369, 397
demand 18–19, 29–31, 33, 34–5, 315, 316, 324
  cross elasticity of 22–3
  derived 36–7, 179, 219–20
  income elasticity of 22, 31, 34, 172, 221
  for labour 179–81, 187–91
  price elasticity of 20–1, 181, 250–1, 339
  for transport 219–20, 225
  see also aggregate demand
demerit goods 61, 70, 76, 76–7
deregulation 129, 137, 263–4, 346, 363
derived demands 36–7, 179, 219–20
developing countries 301, 319, 358, 369, 384–9, 397, 397–8
development policies 390–4
  trade 148, 334, 381, 382, 446, 447
  see also Asia; Latin America; Sub-Saharan Africa
development 290, 292, 381–2
  Asia 373–6, 380, 393
  indicators 364–7
  Latin America 368–72, 380
  promoting 390–8

Sub-Saharan Africa 377–80
  theories 383–6
direct controls 54, 76–7, 267, 275, 319–21, 355
direct taxes 124, 125, 128, 212, 309, 310–11, 323
discrimination 161–2, 191, 193–4, 211, 421
  legislation 202, 213, 320–1
diseconomies of scale 42, 43, 231–2, 435
disposable income 18, 19, 125, 128, 130, 132, 310, 323
  and demand 21, 22, 165, 168
  proportion spent 112, 313, 314

ECB (European Central Bank) 423, 425, 429–30, 432, 441
  and interest rates 340, 345, 427, 430, 434
economic development see development
economic growth 99, 102–3, 141, 298, 338, 364, 387
  Latin America 369, 370
  promoting 134–5
  rate 294, 295
Economic and Monetary Union see EMU
economic performance 94, 294, 294–7, 330–1, 421, 435
  UK 143, 294–7
economies of scale 42–3, 64, 66, 231–2, 241, 393, 434, 447
education 134, 190–1, 204, 211, 298, 314, 335, 355
  improving productivity 128, 137, 148, 163, 201, 216, 346, 445
  and unemployment 355, 356, 444
efficiency 58–9, 144, 245, 335
  economic 359, 444, 453
  of markets 128, 176–8
elasticity 20
  see also demand; supply
employment 160–3, 168–9, 216, 440
EMU (Economic and Monetary Union) 412–13, 423, 425–8

enterprise 9, 36, 73, 83, 137, 208, 387–8, 420

entry and exit *see* market structures

environment 85, 169–70, 298, 393, 448, 449, 450

equilibrium 243–4
  output 92, 116–17
  prices 14, 28–9, 35

ERM (Exchange Rate Mechanism) 345

ethnic minorities 161–2, 188, 190, 191, 202, 205

EU (European Union) 197, 411, 414–17, 415, 416, 422–4
  budget 436–8
  competition policy 260, 451, 453–5
  environmental policies 450
  exchange rates 425, 426
  harmonisation 344, 412–13, 438
  inflation targets 429–30
  integration 433–5
  interest rates 340, 426
  labour market policy 451–2
  labour mobility 417, 423, 433–4
  protectionism 146–7, 381
  regional policy 443–5
  Social Chapter 203, 355, 451–2
  structural funds 416, 436, 444–5
  trade 319, 382, 413, 416
  transport policy 450–1
  and UK 344, 348, 349, 360, 412, 426–8, 436
  unemployment 439–42
  and USA 167, 319, 413
  and WTO 417, 448
  see also CAP; convergence; ECB; ERM; single currency; Stability and Growth Pact

euro *see* single currency

European Central Bank *see* ECB

Exchange Rate Mechanism *see* ERM

exchange rates 39, 126, 172, 306–8, 313, 376, 427
  changes 127, 140–1, 337–40, 371
  and competitiveness 136, 166, 362

EU 425, 426
  and trade 127, 136, 334, 338–9

exports 100, 109, 120, 141, 142, 145, 336
  and exchange rates 127, 136, 338–9
  net 113, 127, 132, 331

externalities 54, 60–1, 62–5, 74–5, 268, 299, 389
  see also negative externalities; positive externalities

factors of production 8–9, 36–7, 72–3, 179, 387–8

FDI (foreign direct investment) 294, 307, 357, 358, 360–1, 383, 395–6, 416
  UK 307, 360, 363, 427, 428, 431

fiscal policy 124–5, 134, 314, 315–16, 322–5, 427, 443
  deflationary 132, 136, 315
  reflationary 137, 172, 315
  UK 297, 344–6, 427

foreign exchange markets 39

foreign interference 371–2, 376, 379

full employment 98, 131, 294, 297, 316, 323, 331, 418

game theory 247–8

GDP (Gross Domestic Product) 92, 100, 364–5, 415
  see also real GDP

gender 160–1, 162, 166, 183, 188, 190, 190–1, 202

Gini coefficient 210, 299, 367, 370

globalisation 11, 27, 160, 220–1, 334, 357–9, 392

government aid 454–5

government borrowing 135, 297, 312–13, 317, 320, 341, 344

government failure 84–5, 267, 268, 347–9

government intervention 54–5, 56, 76–84, 92, 96, 128, 129, 347–9
  concentrated markets 258–60
  congestion 278–80

and externalities 64, 69, 75, 76–9
income and wealth 212–13
labour market 200–3, 204–6, 440
leisure 170–1, 178
prices 35
to reduce poverty 216–17
to reduce unemployment 255–6
reducing 397–8
South East Asia 375–6
wage rates 188, 190
government spending 113, 120, 124, 135, 136, 312–14, 315
on benefits 105, 124
increasing 125, 134, 316, 356
and multiplier 121, 323, 324
public sector wages 320
Gross Domestic Product *see* GDP

harmonisation 344, 348, 412–13
HDI (Human Development Index) 300, 314, 364, 366–7
hidden economy 101, 298, 310
HPI (Human Poverty Index) 301, 364
human capital 134, 201, 375–6, 379
Human Development Index *see* HDI
Human Poverty Index *see* HPI
hyper-inflation 369, 370, 420
hypothecated taxes 311

IMF (International Monetary Fund) 103, 359, 364, 372, 376, 379, 385, 397
imports 27, 34, 100, 120, 127, 130, 142
and balance of payments 99, 109, 136–7
and exchange rates 136, 141, 338–9
restrictions 136–7, 137, 145, 148–9, 319, 334, 336, 393
substitution 392, 394
income elasticity of demand 22, 31, 34, 172, 221

income tax 105, 124, 127, 212, 309, 310–11, 438
cuts 125, 172, 314, 323
cuts as incentives 128, 137, 216, 297, 315, 345, 356
rises 120, 132
and unemployment 355, 356
incomes 98, 99, 100, 112, 140, 207, 307
accession countries 414–15
circular flow 120–1, 388
and demand 19, 31, 222
distribution 101, 209–13, 311, 313–14, 370, 375, 418
inequalities 73, 209, 299, 370, 375, 387, 388–9
from tourism 168–9
and working hours 182, 185
see also disposable income
indirect taxes 105, 124, 212, 309, 310–11, 315, 438
inequalities 6, 207–13, 299, 367–8, 370, 387, 388–9
infant industries 137, 149, 392
inflation 98, 102, 106–7, 129, 140, 330–1, 343
effect of exchange rates 127, 338, 371
EU targets 429–30
hyper-inflation 369, 370, 420
monetarist model 326–7, 328
Phillips curves 350–3
policies to control 132–3
UK 135, 294, 295, 295–6, 297, 345, 346
information 200, 204, 238–9, 389
failure 70–1, 71, 84, 192, 320, 347
integration, EU 433–5
interest rates 38–9, 134, 136, 172, 303–5, 313, 331, 349
changes 126, 127, 130, 341, 343
to combat inflation 132, 307
EU 340, 426
and exchange rates 339–40
set by Bank of England 133, 135, 340, 342–3, 345
set by ECB 340, 345, 416, 425, 427, 430, 434
UK 349, 427, 428, 432

International Monetary Fund *see*
        IMF
international trade *see* trade
investment 112–13, 120, 137, 310,
        324, 325, 338
    and interest rates 126, 303, 304
    net 294, 297, 346
    in transport 269, 271–2
    see also FDI

Keynesian economic thought 115,
        117, 118, 119, 313, 323
    on government intervention 92,
        347
    on inflation 327–8, 331
    on unemployment 118, 200, 201,
        205, 217, 354, 356
knowledge *see* information

labour 8, 27, 135, 179, 181
    costs 137, 163, 179, 203
    demand 179–81, 187–91
    flexibility 355, 439–40, 441
    immobility 73, 193, 336
    mobility 37, 160, 186, 204–5,
        224, 320, 417, 423, 433–4
    supply 36, 125, 134, 182–91
    see also productivity
labour disputes 197, 200
labour market 160–3, 200–3,
        204–6, 353, 451–2
    failure 192–4, 204, 320
Latin America 368–72, 380, 391
leisure 159, 164–7, 172–8, 182–3
liquidity preference theory 303,
        304–5
living standards 98, 101, 103, 109,
        298–9, 314, 336, 378–9
loanable funds theory 303–4
Lorenz curves 210, 299
Luxembourg Process 441–2

Maastricht Treaty (1992) 423, 450,
        452
marginal costs 40, 228–9
marginal productivity theory
        180–1

marginal revenue product *see* MRP
market failure 54–7, 60–73, 76, 92,
        128, 129, 388–9, 397–8
    cost benefit analysis 74, 273
    labour market 192–4, 204, 320
    and sport 170–1
    transport market 265–8
    see also government
        intervention
market power 43, 47, 66–7, 174–5,
        231, 250
market structures 46–7, 173–8
    see also monopolies;
        monopolistic competition;
        oligopolies; perfect
        competition
markets 4, 17, 28–35, 379, 385
    concentration 220, 257–60, 435
    contestable 175, 178, 254, 256
    money markets 38–9
merit goods 61, 70, 71, 78–9, 193
MEW (measurable economic
        welfare) 300, 314
minimum wage 190, 201–2, 213,
        216, 319, 356
MNCs (multinational companies)
        27, 335, 357–8, 360–1, 372,
        395–6
mobility 37, 160, 186, 204–5, 224,
        320, 417, 423, 433–4
monetarism 261, 326–8, 330–1
monetary policy 126–7, 132, 133,
        134, 136, 137, 172
    EU 416, 429–32, 430, 443
    UK 341–3, 344–6, 431–2
Monetary Policy Committee *see*
        MPC
money 16–17, 36
money market 38–9
money supply 126, 127, 304–5,
        317–18, 329–31, 341, 348
    and inflation 326–8, 330–1, 371
monopolies 47, 61, 66–7, 174–5,
        177–8, 199, 246, 419
    abuses 81, 260, 262, 454
    government policies 258–9
    natural 82, 259, 262–3
    power 54, 82–3, 251–2, 256,
        389, 454
    price setting 67, 250, 454

regulation 80–1, 82
transport industry 231, 240–2,
    250–1, 259, 262–3
monopolistic competition 46, 47,
    174, 175, 176–7, 243–5
monopsonies 192, 198–9, 201, 440
MPC (Monetary Policy Committee)
    126, 133, 341, 342, 346
MRP (marginal revenue product)
    180–1, 190–1
multinational companies *see* MNCs
multiplier effect 120–1, 125,
    168–9, 322–5

NAIRU (non-accelerating inflation
    rate of unemployment) 352,
    354–6
negative externalities 62–3, 70,
    74–5, 76–7, 266–7, 273,
    274–5, 389
  pollution 54, 62, 76, 77, 299
new classical economic thought
    92, 116–17, 117, 118, 119,
    200, 323
  on competitiveness 363
  on development 385
  on government borrowing 313
  on government intervention 92,
    347, 348–9
  on unemployment 115, 118, 201,
    205, 206, 217, 354, 355, 356
New Deal 131, 205–6, 356, 441
new technologies 24–5, 27, 160,
    165, 224, 393
  IT 27, 223, 232, 319, 357, 358
  for production 32, 34, 113, 255,
    325, 353, 393
nominal GDP 100, 101
non-accelerating inflation rate of
    unemployment *see* NAIRU
normal profits 41, 173–4, 234, 235

oligopolies 46, 47, 66, 174, 175,
    246–9, 250, 435
  behaviour 177, 178, 246–7, 250,
    253–6, 260
oligopsonies 192, 198, 201

output 92, 101, 102, 103, 116–17,
    134, 136, 299

Pareto Optimal 59, 265
perfect competition 46, 47, 59,
    192, 241, 243, 246
  behaviour in 173–4, 176, 236–9
PFI (Private Funding Initiative)
    271–2
Phillips curves 350–3
planned economies 414, 418–19
PLCs (public limited companies)
    44, 255
pollution 85, 103, 169–70, 267,
    273, 298, 299
  as negative externality 62, 76
  taxes 275, 314
  tradable permits 77, 266, 275,
    450
positive externalities 54, 64–5, 70,
    74–5, 193, 274–5, 389
  government intervention 78–9,
    266, 320, 449
poverty 73, 103, 214–17, 290, 298,
    301, 420–1
  developing countries 370, 378–9,
    387, 392, 394, 397
price discrimination 67, 171, 250,
    251, 271
price elasticity of demand 20–1,
    181, 250–1, 339
price fixing 35
price levels 92, 116, 130, 326, 328,
    419
price mechanism 60–1, 72, 76, 78
price wars 248, 249, 255, 259
prices 18–19, 30–1, 67, 127,
    173–4, 177, 419
  equilibrium 14, 28–9, 35
  and supply 24, 26
Private Funding Initiative *see* PFI
private goods 68
private sector 9, 44, 137, 165, 317,
    380, 419, 440
  transport 220, 221
  wage rises 320
privatisation 129, 137, 363, 385,
    398
  railways 259, 261, 262–3

UK 82, 83, 200, 211, 261–3, 264, 346
producer surpluses 14–15, 252
production 9, 101
  costs of 32, 34, 40–1, 127, 226–9
  factors of 8–9, 36–7, 72–3, 179, 387–8
  possibilities 12–13, 388
productive efficiency 58–9, 60, 176, 236–7, 346
productivity 101, 148, 179, 180–1, 371, 376
  as economic indicator 294, 295, 296, 297
  increasing 128, 129, 137, 163, 203, 346
profits 24–5, 36, 41, 45, 72, 234
  normal 41, 173–4, 234, 235
  supernormal 41, 173–4, 175, 178, 234, 236–7, 244
property rights 266–7, 268
protectionism 93, 146–9
PSNB (Public Sector Net Borrowing) 316–18
public goods 61, 68, 69, 220
public sector 9, 44, 82–3, 165–6, 220, 221, 275, 380
  pay and conditions 200, 320, 440
Public Sector Net Borrowing (PSNB) 316–18

quality of life 101, 103, 299–302, 365–7
quantity theory 327, 330–1
quasi public goods 69, 171
quotas 136, 146, 319, 381, 422

railways 220, 221, 223, 240, 259, 269, 276, 277
  privatisation 261, 262–3, 270
real GDP 100–2, 103, 116, 125, 130, 310, 311, 314
  and investment 310, 324
  and living standards 298–9
redistribution 324, 386, 387
regional policy 200–1, 443–5

regulation 75, 76–7, 80–1, 129, 246, 275, 355, 450
  of privatised industries 26, 82, 262
resources 6, 8–9, 11, 103, 187, 368, 377–8, 389, 395
Retail Price Index (RPI) 106
revenue 40–1, 233–4
road pricing 279–80
road transport 222–3, 224–5, 264, 269, 270, 275
  see also congestion
RPI (Retail Price Index) 106
Russia 373, 374, 387, 398, 420

savings ratios 376, 383, 393
shocks 119, 295, 359, 372, 376, 398, 428, 431, 432, 439
single currency 344, 345, 417, 423, 425, 429–32, 441
Single European Act (1986) 422–3, 438, 450
single market 422–4
Smith, Adam (1723–1790) 7, 60–1, 309
social benefits 74, 273, 274–5
Social Chapter 203, 355, 451–2
social costs 63, 74, 273–4, 275
social efficiency 265–6
social policy, EU 451–2
Soviet Union 374, 383, 386, 396, 418, 421
specialisation 10–11, 16, 332–4
speculation 141, 304, 305, 307, 308, 376
sport 170–1
Stability and Growth Pact 318, 437, 441
state aid 454–5
structural funds 416, 436, 444–5
Sub-Saharan Africa 377–80, 396
subsidies 54, 75, 137, 165–6, 275, 419, 423
  agriculture 391, 446–7, 449
  transport 267, 271
substitutes 18, 19, 21, 23, 30, 34, 166, 181
supernormal profits 41, 173–4, 175, 178, 234, 236–7, 244

supply 24–5, 28–9, 32–5
  elasticity of 26–7, 28, 33, 34
  of labour 182–9, 204–5
  see also aggregate supply
supply-side policies 134, 137,
    216–17, 297, 345–6, 349
  labour 128–9, 131, 204–5, 441

tariffs 136–7, 146–9, 319, 323,
    381, 382, 392, 412
  EU 422, 446, 447
taxation 71, 78, 120, 121, 136,
    212, 313, 323
taxes 54, 124, 124–5, 200, 267,
    271, 309–11, 423
  cuts 130, 205, 211, 297, 316, 323
  direct 124, 125, 128, 212, 309,
    310–11, 323
  EU 344, 423, 438, 450
  indirect 105, 124, 212, 309,
    310–11, 315, 438
  pollution 275, 314
  revenue 103, 105, 124, 315,
    315–16
  road transport 269–70, 280
  see also corporation tax; income
    tax
technology *see* new technologies
tourism 168–70, 393–4
tradable permits 77, 266, 275, 450
trade 10–11, 16, 17, 97, 144–5,
    220, 332–6, 357–8
  barriers 336, 381, 382, 385, 393,
    412, 423
  and development 381–2
  disputes 381–2, 413
  effect of inflation on 107
  EU 416
  and exchange rates 338–9
  terms of 16, 141, 338–9
  transition economies 420
  UK 142, 412, 427
  see also balance of payments;
    protectionism
trade unions *see* unions
trading blocs 136, 381, 412–13,
    417, 433–5
training 135, 160, 185, 186, 188,
    193, 201, 204, 319–20

  and productivity 128, 137, 163,
    216
  subsidies 201, 213
  and unemployment 206, 355,
    356, 441, 444
  for women 190–1
transition economies 418–21
transmission mechanism 326–8,
    342
transport 159, 168, 218–20,
    267–72, 273–6, 450–1
  costs 334, 357, 358
  deregulation 263–4
  market structures 236–49, 259
  markets 261–4, 268, 273–6
  privatisation 261, 262–3
  UK 220–5, 269–72
  see also airlines; railways
Treaty of Rome (1957) 422, 438,
    446, 450, 453

UK (United Kingdom) 11, 183, 197,
    209, 293, 301, 335, 374
  balance of payments 108
  borrowing 427
  competitiveness 346, 360, 363
  direct controls 319–20, 320–1
  economic performance 99, 143,
    294–7
  and EU 344, 348, 349, 360, 412,
    426–8, 436
  exchange rate 306–7, 427, 428
  FDI 307, 360, 363, 427, 428, 431
  fiscal policy 297, 344–6, 427
  inequalities 211–12, 299, 367
  inflation 135, 294, 295, 295–6,
    297, 345, 346
  interest rates 349, 427, 428, 432
  labour market 160–3, 204
  leisure 165–7
  minimum wage 190, 202, 213,
    216, 356
  monetary policy 341–3, 344–6,
    431–2
  New Deal 131, 205, 356, 441
  poverty 214–17
  and single currency 426–8,
    431–2

and Social Chapter 203, 355,
452
trade 142, 412, 427
transport 220–5, 269–72
unemployment 104, 296, 297,
427
and USA 167, 348, 427
UN (United Nations) 103, 367, 397,
398
unemployment 104–5, 118, 136,
148–9, 149, 192, 312
ethnic minorities 161–2
EU 439–42
and exchange rates 141, 338
and labour supply 185, 186, 199
long-term 160, 192, 355, 444
and poverty 215, 216
reducing 99, 130–1, 213, 355–6
and taxes 125, 205, 345
UK 104, 296, 297, 427
see also benefits; full
employment; minimum wage;
NAIRU; New Deal; Phillips
curves; unions
unions 129, 188, 195–7, 223, 440
bargaining power 190, 191,
196–7, 202, 261, 353
reform 202–3, 261, 346
and unemployment 129, 192,
196–7, 206, 355
USA (United States of America) 85,
183, 359, 362, 391, 428, 450
aid from 385, 396
and China 374, 376
cold war 386, 396
economic performance 295–7
and EU 167, 413
interest rates 340, 349
and international organisations
103, 372
labour market 204, 440
and Latin America 371–2
trade 147, 358, 369, 382
trade disputes 319, 413
and UK 167, 348, 427
unemployment 296, 297
USSR *see* Soviet Union

VAT (value added tax) 105, 124,
212, 309, 310, 344, 438

wage costs 160, 163, 179, 181,
335, 440
wage differentials 162, 189–91,
193–4
wage rates 36, 148, 161, 187–91,
215, 335, 419, 439–40
government intervention 132,
200, 201–2, 320
and labour supply 182, 183, 184,
185, 186, 188–9, 205
and unions 195–6, 198–9
and working hours 182–3
wealth 8, 11, 17, 207–9, 211, 370,
387
distribution 209, 212–13, 375
women 160–1, 162, 164, 183, 188,
190, 190–1, 202
working hours 182–3, 184, 185,
203, 205, 211, 299, 310, 451–2
and leisure 164, 165, 168, 182–3
part-time 190, 191, 211, 356
World Bank 364, 365–6, 367, 372,
376, 379, 385, 397–8
WTO (World Trade Organization)
103, 137, 319, 357, 359, 382
and EU 417, 448